MW00932564

Colonials, Indians, and the Great Swamp Fight of 1637

Sheila M. Sabo

Copyright © 2012 Sheila M.Sabo

All rights reserved.

ISBN:1479161306
ISBN-13:9781479161300

CONTENTS

Chapter One

By Right of Conquest

"There was a nation of the Indians on the southern parts of New England, called Pequods, seated on a fair navigable river, twelve miles to the eastward of the mouth of the great and famous river of Connecticut, who (as was commonly reported about the time when New England was first planted by the English) being a more fierce, cruel, and warlike people than the rest of the Indians, came down out of the more inland parts of the continent, and by force seized upon one of the godliest places near the sea, and became a terror to all their neighbors, on whom they had exercised several acts of inhuman cruelty; insomuch that being flushed with victories over their fellow Indians, they began to thirst after the blood of any foreigners, English or Dutch, that accidently came amongst them, in a way of trade, or upon other accounts."

In 1637, the first war in the New England colonies was declared against the Pequot Indians. Although it was a short war of scarcely two months, it was the first war fought on land that would later become the United States. Following the first settlements in Connecticut, the Pequot had become enraged at the sale of lands between the colonists and the river tribes they had conquered. Consequently, the Pequot were determined to exterminate the settlers through continuous attacks. The first written accounts of hostilities against the settlers were the murders of a Captain Stone and his crew of twelve men, who were known River traders in the region. Next was John Oldham, the founder of Wethersfield, Connecticut, followed by an attack on Gardiner's Fort at Saybrook, Connecticut, in which Lieutenant Lionel Gardiner as well as two soldiers at Saybrook cornfield found with their bodies cut in half and hung on trees. It was after these incidences and

1

several other attacks that war was officially and reluctantly declared against the Pequot. The colonists retaliated by attacking Pequot forts on Block Island and Mystic, Connecticut, ending with the "Great Swamp Fight" in what is today Southport, Connecticut.

Twelve years after the settlement of Plymouth, Massachusetts, the colonists were continually adapting to the New England environment as well as adjusting to Dutch traders, local River Indians clans and the hostility of the Pequot. Between 1631 and 1637, the small population in Massachusetts was expanding and people became anxious to obtain new settlements. During this time period long standing tensions between various Indian groups in Connecticut, Massachusetts, and Rhode Island also increased. But the settlers continued to pursue their dreams and three settlements in Connecticut were established. The story of the newcomers and their steadfastness to endure the hardships in their new lands is expressed though the correspondences and journal entries inserted throughout these chapters. The circumstances leading up to the Pequot war, and the actions involving the battles of the war, are told through the writings of William Bradford, the second Governor of Plymouth, John Winthrop, Governor and Deputy Governor of Massachusetts, Roger Ludlow, Deputy Governor of Massachusetts, Roger Williams, the founding father of Rhode Island, and the soldiers who commanded the battles of that war. It is necessary to give insight into the settlers' lives before their arrival, their expedition to Connecticut, and the turbulence during these times, as a prelude to the declaration of war. As time progresses to the settlement of Fairfield (Southport) in 1639, and the land surrounding the area of the Great Swamp Fight, few written records remain. What remains are the archaeological artifacts which give possible links to the Pequot War and clues to the lifestyles of the early settlers. Secondary writings are included which gives insight into the traditions passed down by the first settlers of Southport.

Thomas Dudley, Deputy Governor, Massachusetts, 1630 -1631
Now concerning the English that are planted here, I find that about the year 1620, certain English, set out from Leyden, in Holland, intending their course for Hudson's river, the mouth whereof lieth south of the river of the Pecoates, but ariseth, as I am informed, northwards in about 43°, and so a good part of it within the compass of our patent. These, being much weather-beaten and wearied with seeking the river, after a most tedious

John Winthrop

voyage arrived at length in a small bay lying north-east from Cape Cod, where landing about the month of December, by the favor of a calm winter, such as was never seen here since, begun to build their dwellings in that place which now is called New Plymouth; where, after much sickness, famine, poverty, and great mortality, (through all which God by an unwonted providence carried them,) they are now grown up to a people healthful, wealthy, politic and religious; such things doth the Lord for those that wait for his mercies. These of Plymouth came with patents from King James, and have since obtained others from our sovereign, King Charles.

There was about the same time one Mr. Weston, an English merchant, who sent divers men to plant and trade, who sat down by the river of Wesaguscus. But these coming not for so good ends as those of Plymouth, sped not so well; for the most of them dying and languishing away, they who survived were rescued by those of Plymouth out of the hands of Chickatabott and his Indians, who oppressed these weak English, and intended to have destroyed them, and the Plymotheans also, as is set down in a tract written by Mr. Winslow, of Plymouth. Also, since, one Captain Wollaston, with some thirty with him, came near to the same place, and built on a hill which he named Mount Wollaston. But being not supplied with renewed provisions, they vanished away, as the former did. Also, divers merchants of Bristow, and some other places, have yearly for these eight years, or there abouts, sent ships hither at the fishing times to trade for beaver; where their factors dishonestly, for their gains, have furnished the Indians with guns, swords, powder and shot.

Arrived at Charlestown, Governor Winthrop, deputy-Governor Dudley, Sir Richard Saltonstall, Mr. Johnson, Ludlow, Nowell, Pynchon, and Bradstreet, with the Massachusetts Colony Charter, as also Mr. Wilson and Phillips ministers, with about fifteen hundred people, brought over in twelve ships from England. But many of our people being sick of fevers and the scurvy, we are thereby unable to carry up our ordnance and baggage so far, the governor and several patentees dwell in the great house last year built by Mr. Graves, and the rest of their servants; the multitude set up cottages, booths, and tents about the town-hill and their meeting place is abroad under a tree, where Mr. Wilson and Phillips preach.

But having had a long passage, some of the ships seventeen, some eighteen weeks a coming, many people arrive sick of the scurvy, which increases for want of houses, and by reason of wet lodging in their cottages having no fresh food to cherish them. And though the people are very pitiful and loving, yet the sickness with other distempers so prevails, that the well are not able to tend them. Upon which many die, and are buried about the Hill. It having been reported in England that there were now provisions enough here, divers ships came not so well supplied as otherwise they would, and there being miserable damage of our provisions at sea, and yet some imprudently selling much of the remainder to the Indians for beaver, we fall into great and threatening straits for want of food. Upon which the governor and other gentlemenshire and despatch away Mr. William Pierce with his ship the Lion of Bristol. The mortality increasing many died weekly, yea almost daily, among whom were Mrs. Pynchon, Mrs. Coddington, Mrs. Phillips and Mrs. Alcock, a sister of Mr. Hooker's; so that the ships being now on their return, some for England, some for Ireland, there was not much less than an hundred, some think many more, partly out of dislike of our government, which restrained and punished their excesses, and partly through fear of famine, not seeing other means than by their labour to feed themselves, returned back, and glad were we so to be rid of them. Others also afterwards hearing of men of their own disposition at Pascataway, went from us to them whereby though our numbers were lessened, yet we accounted ourselves nothing weakened by their removal.

Half our cows and almost all our mares and goats sent us out of England died at sea, and those intended to be sent us out of Ireland were not sent at all : all which, together with the loss of our six months building, occasioned by our intended removal to a town to be fortified, weaken our estates, especially the estates of the undertakers, who were three or four thousand pounds (sterling) engaged of about two hundred tons, for Ireland, to buy more, and come back with all speed; with whom goes Mr. Revil, one of the five undertakers here, Mr. Vassal, one of the assistants, with his family, and Mr. Bright the minister sent hither the year before. in the joint stock, which is now not above so many hundreds, yet many of us labor to bear it as comfortably as we could, remembering the end of our coming hither, and knowing the power of God, who can support and raise us again, and useth to bring his servants low that the meek may be made glorious by deliverance.

It goes harder with this poor people in their beginnings, because of the scarcity of all sorts of grain this year in England; every bushel of wheat meal standing them in fourteen shillings (sterling) and every bushel of peas ten shillings, and not easy to be procured neither. (And) coming into this country, we found some English at Salem and some few at Charlestown, who were very destitute; and planting time being past, shortly after, provision was not to be had for money. And the unsubdued wilderness yielding little food, many were in great straits for want of provision for themselves and their little ones. We quickly built boats, and some went a fishing. Bread was with many a very scarce thing, and flesh of all kinds as scarce: and oh the hunger that many suffered, and saw no hope in an eye of reason to be supplied, but with fish.

The sachim in New-England, whom I saw the last summer, upon the river of Naponset, near to the Mattachusetts fields, dwelleth Chickatabott, who hath between fifty and sixty subjects. This man least favoreth the English of any sagamore (for so are the kings with us called, as they are sachims southwards), we are acquainted with, by reason of the old quarrel between him and those of Plymouth, wherein he lost seven of his best men; yet he lodged one night the last winter at my house in friendly manner. About seventy or eighty miles westward from these are seated the Nipnett men, whose sagamore we know not, but we hear their numbers exceed any but the Pecoates and the Narragansets, and they are the only people we yet hear of in the inland country. Upon the river of Mistick is seated sagamore John, and upon the river of Saugus sagamore James, his brother, both so named by the English. The elder brother, John, is a handsome young man, conversant with us affecting English apparel and houses, and speaking well of our God. His brother James is of a far worse disposition yet repaireth often to us. Both these brothers command not above thirty or forty men, for aught I can learn. Near to Salem dwelleth two or three families subject to the sagamore of Agawam, whose name he told me, but I have forgotten it. This sagamore hath but few subjects, and them and himself tributary to sagamore James, having been before the last year (in James's minority) tributary to Chickatabott. Upon the river Merrimack is seated sagamore Passaconaway, having under his command four or five hundred men, being esteemed by his countrymen a false fellow, and by us a witch. For any more northerly, I know not, but leave it to after Relations.

John Winthrop, History of New England

1631

February

10.] The frost brake up; and after that, though we had many snows and sharp frost, yet they continued not, neither were the waters frozen up as before. It hath been observed, ever since this bay was planted by the Englishmen, viz., seven years, that at this day the frost hath broken up every year. The poorer sort of people (who lay long tents, etc.) were much afflicted with the scurvy, many died, especially at Boston and Charlestown; but when this ship came and brought stores of juice of lemons, many recovered speedily. It hath been always observed here, that such as fell into discontent, and lingered after their former conditions in England, fell into the scurvy and died.

Of the old planters, and such as came the year before, there were but two, (and those servants,) which had the scurvy in all the country. At Plymuth not any had it, no not of those, who came this year, whereof there were above sixty. Whereas, at their first planting there, near the half of their people died of it.

March

23.] Chickatabot came with his sannops and squaws, and presented the governor with a hogshead of Indian corn. After they had all dined, and each had a small cup of sack and beer, and the men tobacco, he sent away all his men and women, (though the governor would have stayed them, in regard of the rain and thunder). Himself and one squaw and one sannops stayed all night, and, being in English clothes, the governor set him at his own table, where he behaved himself as soberly, etc., as an Englishman. The next day after dinner he returned home, the governor giving him cheese and peas and a mug and some other small things.

26.] John Sagamore and James his brother, with divers sannops, came to the Governor to desire his recovery of twenty beaver skins, which one Watts in England had forced him of. The governor entertained them kindly, and gave him his letter with directions to Mr. Downing in England, etc.

April

The beginning of this month we had very much rain and warm weather. It is a general rule, that when the wind blows twelve hours in any part of the east, it brings rain and snow in great abundance.

4.] Wahginnacut, a sagamore upon the River Quonehtacut (Connecticut) which lies west of Naragancet, came to the governor at Boston, with John Sagamore, and Jack Straw, (an Indian, who had lived in England and had served Sir Walter Raleigh, and was now turned Indian again,) and divers of their sannops, and brought a letter to the governor from Mr. Endecott to this effect: That the said Wahginnacut was very desirous to have some Englishmen to come plant in his country, and offered to find them corn, and give them yearly eighty skins of beaver, and that the country was very fruitful, etc., and wished that there might be two men sent with him to see the country. The governor entertained them at dinner, but would send none with him. He discovered after, that the said sagamore is a very treacherous man, and at war with the Pekoath (a far greater sagamore). His country is not above five days journey from us by land.

13.] Chickatabot came to the governor, and desired to buy some English clothes for himself. The governor told him, that English sagamores did not use to truck; but he called his tailor and gave him order to make him a suit of clothes; whereupon he gave the governor two large skins of coat beaver, and, after he and his men had dined, they departed, and said he would come again three days after for his suit.

15.] Chickatabot came to the governor again, and he put him into a very good new suit from head to foot, and after he set meat before them; but he would not eat till the governor had given thanks, and after meat he desired him to do the like, and so departed.

16.] There was an alarm given to all our towns in the night, by occasion of a piece which was shot off, (but where could not be known,) and the Indians having sent us word the day before, that the Mohawks were coming down against them and us.

June

14.] At a court, John Sagamore and Chickatabot being told at last court of some injuries that their men did to our cattle, and giving consent to make satisfaction, and now one of their men was complained of for shooting a pig, and for which Chickatabot was ordered to pay a small skin of beaver, which he presently paid.

July

3.] Canonicus, son of the great sachem of Naraganset, came to the governor's house with John Sagamore. After they had dined, he gave the governor a skin, and the governor requited him with a fair pewter pot, which he took very thankfully, and stayed all night.

30.] Mr. Ludlow, in digging the foundation of his house in Dorchester, found two pieces of French money: one was coined in 1596. They were in several places, and above a foot within the firm ground.

August

8.] The Tarentines, to the number of one hundred, came in three canoes, and in the night assaulted the wigwam of the sagamore of Agawam, by Merrimack, and slew seven men, and wounded John Sagamore, and James, and some others.

17.] Mr. Shurd of Pemaquid, sent home James Sagamore's wife, who had been taken away at the surprise at Agawam, and writ that the Indians demanded fathoms of wampampeague and skins for her ransom.

1632

April

12.] The governor received letters from Plimouth, signifying, that there had been a broil between their men at Sowamset and the Naraganset Indians, who set upon the English house there to have taken Owsamequin, the sagamore of Packanocott, who was fled thither with all his people for refuge and that Capt. Standish, being gone thither to relieve the three English, which were in the house, had sent home in all haste for more men and other provisions, upon intelligence that Canonicus, with a great army, was coming against them. Withal they write to our governor for some powder to be sent with all possible speed, (for it seemed they were unfurnished.) Upon this the governor presently dispatched away the messenger with so much powder as he could carry, viz. twenty-seven pounds.

16.] The messenger returned, and brought a letter from the governor, signifying, that the Indians were retired from Sowams to fight with the Pequins, which was probable, because John Sagamore and Chickatabott were gone with all their men, viz. John Sagamore with thirty, and Chickatabott with twenty to Canonicus, who had sent for them.

August

14.] This summer was very wet and cold, (except now and then a hot day or two,) which caused great store of musketoes and rattlesnakes. The corn, in the dry, sandy grounds, was much better than other years, but in the fatter grounds much worse, and in Boston, etc., much shorn down close by the ground with worms.

Mr. Oldham had a small house near the wear at Watertown, made all of clapboards, burnt down by making fire in it when it had no chimney.

30.] Notice being given of ten sagamores and many Indians assembled at Muddy River, the governor sent Captain Underhill with twenty musketeers, to discover; but at Roxbury they heard they were broke up.

September

4.] One Hopkins of Watertown, was convict for selling a piece and pistol, with powder and shot to James Sagamore, for which he was sentenced to be whipped and branded in the cheek. It was discovered by an Indian, one of James's men, upon promise of concealing him, (for otherwise he was sure to be killed).

One Jenkins, late an inhabitant of Dorchester, and now removed to Cape Porpus, went with an Indian up into the country with stores of goods to truck, and, being asleep in a wigwam of one of Passaconamy's men, was killed in the night by an Indian, dwelling near the Mohawk's country, who fled away with his goods, but was fetched back by Passaconamy. There was much suspicion, that the Indians had some plot against the English, both for that many Narragansett men, etc. gathered together, who, with those of these parts, pretending to make war upon the Neipnett men, and divers insolent speeches were used by some of them, and they did not frequent our houses as they were wont, and one of their pawawes told us, that there was a conspiracy to cut us off to get our victuals and other substance. Upon this there was a camp pitched at Boston in the night, to exercise the soldiers against need might be; and Capt. Underhill (to try how they would behave themselves) caused an alarm to be given upon the quarters, which discovered the weakness of our people, who, like men amazed, knew not how to behave themselves, so as the officers could not draw them into any order. All the rest of the plantations took the alarm and answered it; but it caused much fear and distraction among the common sort, so as some, which knew of it before, yet through fear had forgotten, and believed the Indians had been upon us. We doubled our guards, and kept watch each day and night.

14.] The rumor still increasing, the three next sagamores were sent for, who came presently to the governor.

1633

January

1.] Edward Winslow chosen governor of Plimouth, Mr. Bradford having been governor about ten years, and now by importunity gat off.

June

2.] Capt. Stone arrived with a small ship with cows and some salt. The governor of Plimouth sent Capt. Standish to prosecute against him for piracy. The cause was, being at the Dutch plantation, where a pinnace of Plimouth coming, and Capt. Stone and the Dutch governor having been drinking together, Capt. Stone, upon pretence that those of Plimouth had reproached them of Virginia, from whence he came, seized upon their pinnace, (with the governor's consent,) and offered to carry her away, but the Dutchmen rescued her; and of the council of Plimouth to pass it by, yet, upon their earnest prosecution at court, we bound over Capt. Stone (with two sureties) to appear in the admiralty court in England, &c. But, after, those of Plimouth, being persuaded that it would turn to their reproach, and that it could be no piracy, with their consent, we withdrew the recognizance.

15.] Mr. Graves, in the ship Elizabeth Bonadventure, from Yarmouth, arrived with ninety-five passengers, and thirty-four Dutch sheep, and two mares. They came from Yarmouth in six weeks.

19.] A day of thanksgiving was kept in all the congregations, for our delivery from the plots of our enemies, and for the safe arrival of our friends.

July

2.] At a court it was agreed, that the governor, John Winthrop, should have, towards his charges this year, £150, and the money, which he had disbursed in public businesses, as officers wages, being between two and three hundred pounds, should be forthwith paid.

12.] Mr. Edward Winslow, Governor of Plimouth, and Mr. Bradford, came into the bay, and went away the 18th. They came partly to confer about joining in a trade to Connecticut, for beaver and hemp. There was a motion to set up a trading house there, to prevent the Dutch, who were about to build one but, in regard the place was not fit for plantation, there being three or four thousand warlike Indians, and the river not to be gone into but by small pinnaces, having a bar affording but six feet at high water, and for that no vessels can get in for seven months in the year, partly by reason of the ice, and then the violent stream, we thought not fit to meddle with it.

24.] Much sickness at Plimouth, and about twenty died of pestilent fevers.

John Deforest, History of the Indians of Connecticut

The Dutch settlements on the Hudson were at first conducted by the United Company of the New Netherlands; but this corporation was replaced in 1621 by another, far more extensive and powerful, the famous West India Company. In 1632, Hans Eencluys, a servant of the company, landed at the mouth of the Connecticut, purchased a point of land from the natives, and erected there the arms of the States General of the Netherlands. This spot he named Kievet's Hook, from the cry of a species of bird known to us as the *peweet,* but called by the Dutch, *kieveet.* His object was to secure to the company the trade of the river valley, a design which Van Twiller, Governor of the New Netherlands, prosecuted on a greater scale during the following year. He sent Jacob Van Curler and a party of men to the Connecticut valley, with orders to purchase a tract of land which had already been selected, and erect and fortify a trading post upon it. This spot was on the west bank of the river, and covered a portion of the ground now occupied by the city of Hartford. There were two parties to which he might apply for a purchase: the Pequots, who claimed the country by right of conquest; and Sequeen or Sequassen, the former sachem, who now, it seems, was an exile. Van Curler took the most natural course, and applied to Wapyquart, or Wopigwooit, the grand sachem of the Pequots, whom he styles in the treaty, chief of Sickenames (Mystic) River, and owner of the Connecticut. Wopigwooit was nothing loth to sell lands so far from his own fortresses, and which, perhaps, he held by an uncertain tenure; and, on the eighteenth of June, 1633, a treaty of sale and purchase was effected between the two parties. A tract of land one Dutch mile in length along the river, and extending one third of a mile into the country, was passed over, by the Pequots, into the possession of the Dutch. For this territory Wopigwooit received twenty seven ells of a kind of coarse cloth called duffals, six axes, six kettles, eighteen knives, one sword blade, one pair of shears, and some toys. At the request of an Indian named Altarbaenhoet, probably a sagamore of the river tribes, the Dutch obtained permission from Wopigwooit that Sequeen might return to his country and take up his residence at or near the trading house. It was declared in the deed that Sequassen accepted this offer with the knowledge of Magarittinne, chief of Sloop's Bay: this being the name which the Dutch gave to the western part of Narragansett Bay. These circumstances serve to identify Sequassen with the Sequeen here mentioned: for Sequassen, as we shall subsequently see, sold a vast tract around Hartford to the English, as chief sachem of the country; and Sequassen, too, will be mentioned as a relation and a close ally of the Narragansett chieftains.

The little territory thus purchased was made free for purposes of trade to all nations of Indians. It was to be a territory of peace. The hatchet was to be buried there. No warrior was to molest his enemy while within its bounds. Van Curler erected on it a small trading fort, armed it with two pieces of cannon, and named it the House of Good Hope. The Pequots soon broke through the above conditions, by killing some Indians, their enemies, who came to the house to trade. The Dutch were so incensed at this act of violence, that, to punish it, they, in some way or other, contrived to despatch Wopigwooit and several of his men. The old chieftain was succeeded by his son Sassacus, a renowned warrior and a noble and high-spirited man, but doomed to be the last grand sachem of his tribe. A desultory war ensued between the Dutch and Pequots, which lasted some months, if not a year or two, and, of course, interrupted the trade which had opened between the two parties. These events were, it would seem, of considerable importance in their bearing on the future history of the tribe. It seems at least possible that it was the death of Wopigwooit which led to the fatal massacre of Stone and his crew; and it is certain, that it was the loss of the Dutch trade which induced the Pequots to invite the English of Massachusetts Bay to settle in Connecticut.

The Puritans, or Pilgrims, had now been established thirteen years on the shores of this bay, and although their numbers did not much exceed two thousand, they already began to complain of being cramped for want of room. Their increasing strength commanded the respect of the surrounding natives; and the smaller tribes seem to have conceived the idea of obtaining, by their protection, freedom from the oppression of the larger ones. As early as April, 1631, a sagamore named Waghinacut, probably a Podunk, came to Massachusetts for the purpose of inducing the English to send a colony to his part of the country. Accompanied by John Sagamore, an inconsiderable sachem living between the Charles and Mystic Rivers, and by an Indian named Jack Straw, who had been in England and spoke English, he called on Governor Winthrop in Boston. He explained that he wanted some of the English to settle in his country on the great river Connecticut; offered, if they would do so, to provide them with corn, and give them eighty skins of beaver; boasted of the fertility of the land, and asked that, to verify his statements, two men might be sent to explore it. Winthrop entertained the sachem and his friends at dinner; but could not be persuaded to promise a settlement, or even to send people to examine the country. He afterwards found, as he says, that Waghinacut was a very treacherous man, and was at war with a far greater sachem named Pekoath.

At Plymouth, Waghinacut was equally unsuccessful, although the people of that colony were more disposed than the Bostonians to undertake the settlement. But a greater degree of enterprise was soon awakened among the English by the reports of the immense trade in furs which the Dutch were carrying on in the Connecticut valley. Winthrop sent a letter to Governor Van Twiller, protesting against his settlements on that river as interfering with the charter of New England. The colonists began to dispatch vessels to Connecticut to trade, and several were thus sent at least as early as 1633. During the same year, John Oldham, who was afterwards killed by the Block

Islanders, travelled across the country, with three companions, to the Connecticut River. Here one of the sachems of the land entertained them in hospitable style, and made them a present of some beaver skins. They carried back to Massachusetts a specimen of the wild hemp which grew in the country, and reported that it contained many desirable places of settlement capable of supporting many hundreds of inhabitants. In July, therefore, of 1633, Winslow and Bradford, of Plymouth, made a proposition to the government of Massachusetts, to establish a trading post on the Connecticut, for obtaining hemp and furs. Governor Winthrop refused, alledging the unfavorable reports which had been received from other quarters respecting the country. The river, he said, was held by warlike tribes of Indians who could raise three or four thousand warriors; there was a bar at its mouth so shallow that it could be crossed, even at high water, only by small pinnaces; and, for seven months in the year, no vessel could navigate the river at all on account of the ice and the violence of the stream. Undiscouraged by these representations the Plymouth people determined to effect the settlement alone; and in October, of the very same year, William Holmes was sent thither with a vessel, a small company of men, and the frame of a house. He sailed up the river, passed the Dutch Fort, at Hartford, in spite of the remonstrances and threats of the garrison, and erected his trading-house in the present township of Windsor, a little below the junction of the Farmington with the Connecticut. Holmes is said to have brought back, in his vessel, the original sachems of the country, who had been driven away by the Pequots; and to have made his purchase of the country from them. Thus, on the very first settlement of the English in Connecticut, they offered a distinct, though, perhaps, an unintentional, insult and injury, to the most powerful tribe in the country. The Pequots had conquered this portion of the Connecticut valley; and had obliged its original owners to submit to their authority. Their claim had been acknowledged by the Dutch. It was confirmed by immemorial Indian custom and it was at least as just as that by which some civilized and christianized nations hold large portions of the globe. It was highly praiseworthy, indeed, for the English to pay a suitable sum to the original owners of the soil; but they ought, in justice, as well as policy, to have bestowed some respect upon the well known claim of the Pequots. Two reasons probably operated to prevent them from doing this: one that they may have considered the Pequots robbers and intruders; the other that, by refusing to acknowledge the Pequot title, they could, with a better appearance of reason, deny the justice of that of the Dutch. The offended tribe, however, did not make this an immediate occasion of

hostility with the English; although we know not how much influence it may have had upon its policy towards them on another occasion and at a subsequent time. It was not until afterwards that the event occurred, which may be considered as the germ of that hostility, which eventually sprung up between the Pequots and the English.

William Bradford, Plymouth Plantation
1633

William Bradford

Having had formerly converse and familiarity with the Dutch, (as is before remembered,) they, seeing them seated here in a barren quarter, told them of a river called by them the Fresh River, but now is known by the name of Conightecute River, which they often commended unto them for a fine place both for plantation and trade, and wished them to make use of it. But their hands being full otherwise, they let it pass. But afterwards their coming a company of banished Indians into these parts, that were driven out from thence by the potency of the Pequents, which usurped upon them, and drove them from thence, they often solicited them to go thither, and they should have much trade, especially if they would keep a house there. And having now good store of commodities, and also need to look out where they could advantage themselves to help them out of their great engagements, they now began to send that way to discover the same, and trade with the natives. They found it to be a fine place, but had no great store of trade; but the Indians excused the same in regard of the season, and the fear the Indians were in of their enemies. So they tried diverse times, not without profit, but saw the most certainty would be by keeping a house there, to receive the trade when it came down out of the inland. These Indians, not seeing them very forward to build there, solicited them of the Massachusetts in like sort (for their end was to be restored to their country again); but they in the Bay being but lately come, were not fit for the same; but some of their chief made a motion to join with the partners here, to trade jointly with them in that river, the which they were willing to embrace, and so they should have built, and put in equal stock together. A time of meeting was appointed at the Massachusetts, and some of the chiefs here was appointed to treat with them, and went accordingly; but they cast many fears of danger and loss and the like, which was perceived to be the main obstacles, though they alleged they were not provided of trading goods. But those hear offered at present to put in sufficient for both, provided they would become engaged for the half, and prepare against the next year. They confessed more could not be offered, but thanked them, and told them they had no mind to it. They then answered; they hoped it would be no offence unto them, if themselves went on without them, if they saw it meet. They said there was no reason they should; and thus this treaty broke off, and those here took convenient time to make a beginning there; and were the first English that both discovered that place, and built in the same, though they were little better then thrust out of it afterward as may appeared.

But the Dutch began now to repent, and hearing of their purpose and preparation, endeavored to prevent them, and got in a little before them, and made a slight forte, and planted two pieces of ordnance, threatening to stop their passage. But they having made a small frame of a house ready, and having a great new bark, they stowed their frame in her hold, and boards to cover and finish it, having nails and all other provisions fitting for their use. This they did the rather that they might have a present defense against the Indians, who were much offended that they brought home and restored the right Sachem of the place (called Natawanute); so as they were to encounter with a double danger in this attempt, both the Dutch and the Indians. When they came up the river, the Dutch demanded what they intended, and whither they would go; they answered, up the river to trade (now their order was to go and seat above them). They bid them strike, and stay, or else they would shoot them; and stood by there ordnance ready fitted. They answered they had commission from the Governor of Plimoth to go up the river to such a place, and if they did shoot, they must obey their order and proceed; they would not molest them, but would go on. So they passed along, and though the Dutch threatened them hard, yet they shoot not. Coming to their place, they clapped up their house quickly, and landed their provisions, and left the company appointed, and sent the bark home; and afterwards palisadoed their house about and fortified themselves better.

The Dutch sent word home to the Monhatas (Manhattans) what was done; and in process of time, they sent a band of about seventy men, in warlike manner, with colors displayed, to assault them; but seeing them strengthened, and that it would cost blood, they came to parley, and returned in peace. And this was their entrance there, who deserved to have held it, and not by friends to have been thrust out, as in a sort they were, as will after appear. They did the Dutch no wrong, for they took not a foot of any land they bought, but went to the place above them, and bought that tract of land which belonged to these Indians which they carried with them, and their friends, with whom the Dutch had nothing to doe. But of these matters more in another place.

It pleased the Lord to visit them this year with an infectious fever of which many fell very sick, and upward of twenty persons

died, men and women, besides children, and sundry of them their ancient friends which had lived in Holland, and in the end (after he had much helped others) Samuel Fuller, who was their surgeon and physician, and had been a great help and comfort unto them; as in his faculty, so otherwise, being a man godly, and forward to do good, being much missed after his death; and he and the rest of their brethren much lamented by them, and caused much sadness and mourning amongst them; which caused them to humble themselves, and seek the Lord; and towards winter it pleased the Lord the sickness ceased. This disease also swept away many of the Indians from all ye places near adjoining; and ye spring before, especially all ye month of May, there was such a quantity of a great sort of flies, like (for bigness) to wasps, or bumble-bees, which came out of holes in ye ground, and replenished all ye woods, and eat ye green things, and made such a constant yelling noise, as made all ye woods ring of them, and ready to deaf ye hearers. They have not by ye English been heard or seen before or since. But ye Indeans told them sickness would follow, and so it did in June, July, August, and ye chief heat of summer.

John Winthrop, History of New England
1633
September
4.]   The Griffin, a ship of three hundred tons, arrived. This ship was brought in by John Gallop a new way by Lovell's Island, at low water, now called Griffin's Gap. She brought about two hundred passengers, having lost some four, (whereof one was drowned two days before, as he was casting forth a line to take mackerel). In this ship came Mr. Cotton, Mr. Hooker, and Mr. Stone.

About ten days before this time, a bark was set forth to Connecticut and those parts, to trade. John Oldham, and three with him, went over land to Connecticut, to trade. The sachem used them kindly, and gave them some beaver. They brought of the hemp, which grows there in great abundance, and is much better than the English. He accounted it to be about one hundred and sixty miles. He brought some black lead, whereof the Indians told him there was a whole rock. He lodged at Indian towns all the way.

12.] Capt. John Stone (of whom mention is made before) carried
himself very dissolutely in drawing company to drink, and being found upon
the bed in the night with one Bancroft's wife, he
was brought before the governor, and though it appeared he was in drink,
and no act to be proved, yet it was thought fit he should abide his trial, for
which end a warrant was sent out to stay his pinnace, which was ready to
set sail; whereupon he went to Mr. Ludlow, one of the assistants, and used
braving and threatening speeches against him, for which he raised some
company and apprehended him, and brought him to the governor, who put
him in irons, and kept a guard upon him till the court, (but his irons were
taken off the same day). At the court his indictment was framed for adultery, but
found *ignoramus* by the great jury; but, for his other misdemeanors, he was
fined £100, which yet was not levied of him; and ordered upon pain of
death to come here no more, without license of the court; and the woman
was bound to her good behavior.

October

2.] The bark Blessing, which was sent to the southward returned. She had
been at an island over against Connecticut, called Long Island, because it is
near fifty leagues long, the east part about ten leagues from the main, but
the west end not a mile. There they had store of the best wampampeak,
both white and blue. The Indians there are very treacherous people. They
have many canoes so great as one will carry eighty men. They were also in
the River of Connecticut, which barred at the entrance, so as they could not
find above one fathom of water. They were also at the Dutch plantation
upon Hudson's River (called New Netherlands), where they were very kindly
entertained, and had some beaver, and other things, for such commodities as
they put off. They shewd the governor (called Gwalter Van Twilly) their
commission, which was to signify to them, that the King of England had
granted the river and country of Connecticut to his own subjects; and
therefore desired them to forbear to build there. The Dutch governor wrote
back to our governor, (his letter very courteous and respectful, as it had
been to a very honorable person,) where he signified, that the Lords the
States had granted the same parts to the West India Company, and
therefore requested that we would forbear the same till the matter were
decided between the King of England and the said lords. The said bark did
pass and repass over the shoals of Cape Cod, about three or four leagues
from Nantucket Isle, where the breaches are very terrible, yet they had three
fathoms water all over.

The company of Plymouth sent a bark to Connecticut, at this time, to erect a trading house there. When they came, they found the Dutch had built there, and did forbid the Plymouth men to proceed; but they set up their house notwithstanding, about a mile above the Dutch. The river runs so far northward, that it comes within a day's journey of a part of Merrimack and runs thence N.W. so near the Great Lake, as allows the Indians to pass their canoes into it over land. From this lake, and the hideous swamps about it, come most of the beaver which is traded between Virginia and Canada, which runs forth of this lake; and Patomack River in Virginia comes likewise out of it, or very near, so as from this lake there comes yearly to the Dutch about ten thousand skins, which might easily be diverted by Merrimack, if a course of trade were settled above in that river.

November.] A great mortality among the Indians. Chickatabot, the sagamore of Naponsett, died, and many of his people. The disease was the small pox. Some of them were cured by such means as they had from us; many of their children escaped, and were kept by the English.

December

5.] John Sagamore died of the small pox, and almost all his people; (above thirty buried by Mr. Maverick on Winesemett in one day). The towns in the bay took away many of the children but most of them died soon after. James Sagamore of Sagus died also, and most of his folks. John Sagamore desired to be brought among the English, (so he was) and promised (if he recovered) to live with the English and serve their God. He left one son, which he disposed to Mr. Wilson, the pastor of Boston, to be brought up by him. He gave to the governor a good quantity of wampompeague, and to divers others of the English he gave gifts, and took order for the payment of his own debts and his men's he did in a persuasion that he should go to the Englishmen's God. Divers of them, in their sickness, confessed that the English men's God is a good God; and that, if they recovered, they would serve him. It wrought much with them, that when their own people forsook them, yet the English came daily and ministered to them and yet few, only two families, took any infection by it. Among others, Mr. Maverick of Winesemett is worthy of a perpetual remembrance. Himself, his wife, and their servants, went daily to them, ministered to their necessities, and buried their dead, and took home many of their children. So did other of their neighbors. This infectious disease spread to Pascataquack, where all the Indians (except one or two) died.

John Deforest, History of the Indians of Connecticut

During the summer of 1633, Captain Stone, a dissolute, intemperate man, came in a small vessel from Virginia to trade on the coast of New England. After remaining a short time at Massachusetts Bay, and causing the magistrates some trouble by his disorderly conduct, he sailed, with a Captain Norton and seven others on board, for the Connecticut River. Before long a report came back to Boston, that Stone and his whole company had been killed, his vessel burned, and the plunder taken from it divided between the Pequots and Nehantics. It was said that, on reaching the mouth of the river, Stone opened a trade with the natives and sent three of his crew on shore to hunt for wild fowl. The Indians appeared perfectly friendly, and were suffered to come on board and loiter about the little vessel at pleasure. Stone finally went to sleep in the cabin, in presence of the sachem; and the rest of the crew collected unsuspiciously and without any precautions in the galley. Meantime the three men on shore had been attacked by a party of Indians and put to death, either by surprise, or so far off that the noise of the conflict could not be heard. When the chief thought proper he knocked out the brains of the unconscious captain; and, on the instant, his followers seized the firearms about the vessel and presented them at the startled English. One of the latter, however, aimed a musket in his own defense; and, such was the fear of the natives for this weapon in the hands of a white man, that they all leaped overboard at once. But, in the rush and confusion, a quantity of powder ignited, and blew up the vessel, destroying the greater part, if not all, of the little crew. The Indians now climbed on board again, dispatched any who might have remained alive, and plundered the cargo. Such was one of the accounts of this transaction which circulated among the English colonists. The perpetrators in the tragedy were undoubtedly Pequots, although among them there may have been some of their tributaries, the Western Nehantics. The English made no immediate attempts to punish them; but it was not long before circumstances took place which gave them a favorable opportunity of demanding satisfaction.

The position of the Pequots was at this time by no means so favorable as it had been; and uninterrupted success and conquest no longer seemed to follow on their war paths. They could not press back the Narragansetts with so firm a hand as formerly, and they had even lost the sovereignty of Block Island, which appears to have passed lately under the domination of the Nehantics. If their authority had been thrown off by the Indians in the upper valley of the Connecticut, encouraged and incited, doubtless, to this act, by the presence and advice of the Dutch, if not of the English, traders. Besides this, Uncas, sagamore of Mohegan, had, since the death of Wopigwooit, broken out into open rebellion. Lastly, their war with the Dutch, while it cost them the lives of a number of their warriors, probably gave them still more annoyance by breaking up an intercourse which they had sufficient acuteness to perceive was not only a source of amusement but of profit and power. In the following year, as the war with the Dutch still continued, Sassacus resolved to make an effort to conciliate the English, and obtain for his people some portion of their trade. During the month of October, 1634, a Pequot messenger arrived at the Bay, bringing, according to the fashion of Indian ambassadors, a present from his sachem, which he presented to the deputy governor, Roger Ludlow. He also laid down two bundles of sticks, indicative of the number of beaver and other skins which the Pequots would give the English, and promised that they should be accompanied by a large amount of wampum. He then demanded a league between his people and the pale faces. Ludlow accepted the present which was made to himself, and gave, in return, a moose coat of equal value for the Pequot chieftain. But, as the messenger was a man of low rank, he told him that Sassacus must show his respect for the English by sending deputies of greater quality than he, and enough of them, before he could treat with the authorities of the colonies. This answer was highly proper, inasmuch as it was in accordance with the customs of the Indians, among whom embassies to states of importance were always committed to persons of rank and consideration.

The messenger departed, and a fortnight afterwards two Pequot sagamores arrived at the residence of Ludlow, bringing another present. The deputy governor received them with civility and conducted them to Boston, where negotiations were opened, although Dudley, the Governor, was still absent. The sagamores were told that the English were desirous of peace with their tribe, but would never consent to a treaty till the Pequots had surrendered the murderers of Stone, and made restitution for the plunder and destruction of his Vessel. The Indians did not deny that their nation was responsible for the murder, but asserted that Stone had provoked his fate by his violent and alarming conduct. They said that, on entering the Connecticut, he forcibly seized two Indians of that region, and kept them on board his vessel to make them pilot it up the river. After a while he and two of his men landed, taking with them the two captives, with their hands still closely bound behind them. Nine Indians watched the party, and at night, when the

English had gone to sleep on the shore, they killed them and liberated their countrymen. The vessel, with the remainder of the crew, was afterwards blown up; but of this they knew nothing, neither the manner, nor the cause. They stated in addition that the sachem whom they had when Stone was put to death, had been killed by the Dutch; and that all the Indians concerned in the murder had died of the small pox except two. These, they cautiously added, Sassacus would probably be willing to deliver to the English, provided the guilt could be proved upon them.

Such was the story of the Pequot ambassadors; and it was related with such an appearance of truth that the English, who had no good evidence to the contrary, were strongly inclined to believe it. The conditions of a treaty were agreed upon, and the paper being drawn up was signed by both parties. The English were to have as much land in the country of the Connecticut as they needed, provided they would make a settlement; and the Pequots were to give them all possible assistance in effecting their settlement. The Pequots were to surrender the two murderers, whenever they were demanded; and to pay the English forty beaver skins, thirty otter skins, and four hundred fathoms of wampum. They were likewise to give all their custom to the English, who, on the other hand, were to send them a vessel immediately, not to defend them, but to trade with them. Such was the substance of the treaty between the Pequots and the colony of Massachusetts Bay, made and signed in November, 1634.

The morning after the business was concluded, Boston was thrown into a hubbub by the report that two or three hundred Narragansetts were waiting at a place called Neponsett to kill the Pequot messengers on their way home. A few armed citizens were collected and marched away to Neponsett, with a message to the Narragansetts to come and have a talk with the governor. Then was seen the value of Indian reports; for no doubt this story was brought in by some of the Indians of the neighboring country. On reaching Neponsett the white men found only two sagamores, with about twenty warriors, who said that they were out on a hunting expedition, and had come hither simply to make their old friends at Neponsett a visit. Whether this story was true or not, they at all events showed themselves quite ready to oblige the English and allowed the two ambassadors to depart unmolested.

The authorities of the colony now undertook to negotiate a peace between the two hostile tribes. For this purpose they offered the

Narragansetts a part of the wampum which was to be paid by the Pequots. This was in accordance with the wish of the Pequot deputies, who had commissioned them to do so, and had promised so large a quantity as four hundred fathoms for no other purpose. The circumstance shows the pride of Sassacus, who was desirous to obtain peace, but unwilling to ask it directly of his ancient and hereditary enemies. The Narragansetts do not seem to have been more averse to peace than the Pequots; for it is clear that a treaty was concluded between the two tribes which continued till the fall of 1636.

Captain Roger Clap's Memoirs
    There was also one Capt. Stone, about the year 1633 or 1634, who carried himself very proudly, and spake contemptuously of our magistrates, and carried it lewdly in his conversation. For his misdemeanour, his ship was stayed; but he fled, and would not obey authority; and there came warrants to Dorchester to take him dead or alive. So all our soldiers were in arms, and sentinels were set in divers places; and at length he was found in a great cornfield, where we took him and carried him to Boston; but for want of one witness, when he came to his trial, he escaped with his life. He was said to be a man of great relation, and had great favor in England and he gave out threatening speeches. Though he escaped with his life, not being hanged for adultery, there being but one witness, yet for other crimes he was fined, and payed it; and being dismissed, he went towards Virginia. But by the way putting into the Pequot country, to trade with them, the Pequots cut off both him and his men, took his goods, and burnt his ship. Some of the Indians reported that they roasted him alive. Thus did God destroy him that so proudly threatened to ruin us, by complaining against us when he came to England. Thus God destroyed him, and delivered us at that time also. About that time, or not long after, God permitted Satan to stir up the Pequot Indians to kill divers Englishmen, as Mr. Oldham, Mr. Tilly, and others; and when the murderers were demanded, instead of delivering them, they proceeded to destroy more of our English about Connecticut; which put us upon sending out soldiers, once and again, whom God prospered in their enterprises until the Pequot people were destroyed.

William Bradford, Plimouth Plantation
1634
    This year (in the forepart of the same) they sent forth a barke to trade at the Dutch-Plantation; and they met there with on Captain Stone, that had

lived in Christopher's, one of the West-Ende Islands, and now had been some time in Virginia, and came from thence into these parts. He kept company with the Dutch Governor, and, I know not in what drunken fit, he got leave of the Governor to cease on their barke, when they were ready to come away, and had done their market, having the value of 500li. worth of goods aboard her; having no occasion at all, or any color of ground for such a thing, but having made the Governor drunk, so as he could scarce speak a right word; and when he urged him hear about, he answered him, "Als't u beleeft." (That is, if you please.) So he gat aboard, (the chief of their men and merchant being ashore,) and with some of his own men, made the rest of theirs weigh anchor, set sail, and carry her away towards Virginia. But diverse of the Dutch sea men, which had been often at Plimouth, and kindly entertained there, said one to another, "Shall we suffer our friends to be thus abused, and have their goods carried away, before our faces, whilst our Governor is drunk?" They vowed they would never suffer it; and so got a vessel of two and pursued him, and brought him in again, and delivered them their bark and goods again. Afterwards Stone came into the Massachusetts, and they sent and commenced suite against him for this fact; but by mediation of friends it was taken up, and the suite let fall. And in the company of some other gentlemen Stone came afterwards to Plimouth, and had friendly and civil entertainment amongst them, with the rest; but revenge boiled with his brest, (though concealed,) for some conceived he had a purpose (at one time) to have stabbed the Governor, and put his hand to his dagger for that end, but by Gods providence and the vigilance of some was prevented. He afterward returned to Virginia, in a pinass, with one Captain Norton & some others; and, I know not for what occasion, they would need go up Conigtecutt River; and how they carried themselves I know not, but the Indeans knocked him in the head, as he lay in his cabin, and had thrown the covering over his face (whether out of fear or desperation is uncertain); this was his end. They likewise killed all the rest, but Captain Norton defended him self a long time against them all in the cook-room, till by accident the gunpowder took fire, which (for readiness) he had set in an open thing before him, which did so burn, & scald him, & blind his eyes, as he could make no longer resistance, but was slain also by them, though they much commended his valor. And having killed the men, they made a pray of what they had, and chaffered away some of their things to the Dutch that lived there. But it was not long before a quarrel fell between the Dutch & them, and they would have cut off their bark; but they slue the chief sachem with the shot of a murderer.

John Winthrop. History of New England

1634

January

21.] News came from Plimouth, that Capt. Stone, who this last summer went out of the bay or lake, and so to Aquamenticus, where he took in Capt. Norton, putting in at the mouth of Connecticut, in his way to Virginia, where the Pequins inhabit, was there cut off by them, with all his company, being eight. The manner was thus: Three of his men, being gone ashore to kill fowl, were cut off. Then the sachem, with some of his men, came aboard, and staid with Capt. Stone in his cabin, till Capt. Stone (being alone with him) fell on sleep. Then he knocked him on the head, and all the rest of the English being in the cook's room, the Indians took-such pieces as they found there ready charged, and bent them at the English; whereupon one took a piece, and by accident gave fire to the powder, which blew up the deck; but most of the Indians, perceiving what they went about, shifted overboard, and after they returned, and killed such as remained, and burned the pinnace. We agreed to write to the governor of Virginia, (because Stone was one of that colony,) to move him to revenge it, and upon his answer to take further counsel.

20.] Hall and the two others, who went to Connecticut November 3, came now home, having lost them-selves and endured much misery. They informed us, that the small pox was gone as far as any Indian plantation was known to the west and much people dead of it, by reason whereof they could have no trade. At Narragansett, by the Indians' report, there died seven hundred; but, beyond Pascataquack, none to the eastward.

February

1.] Such of the Indians' children as were left were taken by the English, most whereof did die of the pox soon after, three only remaining, whereof one, which the governor kept, was called Know-God, (the Indians usual answer being, when they were put in mind of God, Me no-know God.)

May

15.] Those of Newtown complained of straightness for want of land, especially meadow, and desired leave of the court to look out either for enlargement or removal, which was granted; whereupon they sent men to see Agawam and Merrimack, and gave out they would remove.

July

Six of Newtown went in the Blessing, (being bound to the Dutch plantation,) to discover Connecticut River, intending to remove their town thither.

September

4.]   The general court began at Newtown, and continued a week, and then was adjourned fourteen days. The main business which spent the most time, and caused the adjourning of the court, was about the removal of Newtown. They had leave, the last general court, to look out some place for enlargement or removal, with promise of having it confirmed to them, if it were not prejudicial to any other plantation; and now they moved that they might have leave to remove to Connecticut. This matter was debated divers days, and many reasons alleged pro and con. The principal reasons for their removal were, 1.Their want of accommodation for their cattle, so as they were not able to maintain their ministers, nor could receive any more of their friends to help them; and here it was alleged by Mr. Hooker, as a fundamental error, that towns were set so near each to other.2. The fruitfulness and commodiousness of Connecticut, and the danger of having it possessed by others, Dutch or English. 3. The strong bent of their spirits to remove thither.

Against these it was said, 1. That, in point of conscience, they ought not to depart from us, being knit to us in one body, and bound by oath to seek the welfare of this commonwealth. 2. That, in point of state and civil policy, we ought not to give them leave to depart. 1. Being well were now weak and in danger to be assailed. 2. The departure of Mr. Hooker would not only draw many from us, but also divert other friends that would come to us. 3. We should expose them to evident peril, both from the Dutch (who made claim to the same river, and had already built a fort there) and from the Indians, and also from our own state at home, who would not endure they should sit down without a patent in any place which our king lays claim unto. 3. They might be accommodated at home by some enlargement which other towns offered. 4. They might remove to Merrimack, or any other place within our patent. 5. The removing of a candlestick is a great judgment, which is to be avoided.

Upon these and other arguments the court being divided, it was put to vote; and, of the deputies, fifteen were for their departure, and ten against it. The governour and two assistants were for it, and the deputy and all the rest of the assistants were against it, (except the secretary, who gave no vote), whereupon no record was entered, because there were not six assistants in the vote, as the patent requires. Upon this grew a great difference between the governour and assistants, and the deputies. They would not yield the assistants a negative voice, and the others (considering how dangerous it might be to the commonwealth, if they should not keep that strength to balance the greater number of the deputies) thought it safe to stand upon it. So, when they could proceed no further, the whole court agreed to keep a day of humiliation to seek the Lord, which accordingly was done, in all the congregations, the 18th day of this month; and the 24th the court met again. Before they began, Mr. Cotton preached, (being desired by all the court, upon Mr. Hooker's instant excuse of his unfitness for that occasion.) He took his text out of Hag. ii. 4, &c. out of which he laid down the nature or strength (as he termed it) of the magistracy, ministry and people, viz.—the strength of the magistracy to be their authority; of the people, their liberty; and of the ministry, their purity; and showed how all of these had a negative voice, &c. and that yet the ultimate resolution, &c. ought to be in the whole body of the people, &c. with answer to all objections, and a declaration of the people's duty and right to maintain their true liberties against any unjust violence, &c. which gave great satisfaction to the company. And it pleased the Lord so to assist him, and to bless his own ordinance, that the affairs of the court went on cheerfully; and although all were not satisfied about the negative voice to be left to the magistrates, yet no man moved aught about it, and the congregation of Newtown came and accepted of such enlargement as had formerly been offered them by Boston and Watertown; and so the fear of their removal to Connecticut was removed.

November

5.] The Rebecka came from Narragansett with five hundred bushels of corn given to Mr. John Oldham. The Indians had promised him one thousand bushels, but their store fell out less than they expected. They gave him also an island in the Narragansett Bay, called Chippacursett, containing about one thousand acres, six miles long, and two miles broad. This is a very fair bay, being above twelve leagues square, with diver's great islands in it, a deep channel close to the shore, being rocky. Mr. Peirce took the height there, and found it forty-one degrees, forty-one minutes, being not above half a degree to the southward of us. In his voyage to and fro, he went over the shoals, having, most part, five or six fathom, within half a mile and less of the shore from the north part of Cape Cod to Nantucket Island, which is about twenty leagues—and, in the shallowest place, two and an half fathom. The country on the west of the Bay of Narragansett is all champaign for many miles, but very stony, and full of Indians. He saw there above one thousand men, women and children, yet the men were many abroad on hunting. Nantucket is an island full of Indians, about ten leagues in length east and west.

6.] There came to the Deputy Governor, about fourteen days since, a messenger from the Pequod sachem, to desire our friendship. He brought two bundles of sticks, whereby he signified how many beaver and two otter skins he would give us for that end, and great store of wampampeague, (about two bushels, by his description.) He brought a small present with him, which the deputy received, and returned a moose coat of as good value, and withal told him, that he must send persons of greater quality, and then our governour would treat with them. And now there came two men, who brought another present of wampampeague. The deputy brought them to Boston, where most of the assistants were assembled, by occasion of the lecture, who, calling to them some of the ministers, grew to this treaty with them: That we were willing to have friendship, &c. but because they had killed some Englishmen, viz. Capt. Stone, &c. they must first deliver up those who were guilty of his death. They answered, that the sachem, who then lived, was slain by the Dutch, and all the men, who were guilty, were dead of the pox, except two, and that if they were worthy of death, they would move their sachem to have them delivered, (for they had no commission to do it) but they excused the fact, saying that Capt. Stone, coming into their river, took two of their men and bound them, and made them show him the way up the river, which when they had done, he, with two others and the two Indians, (their hands still bound,) went on Shore, and nine of their men watched them, and when they were asleep in the night, they killed them; then going towards the pinnace to have taken that, it suddenly blew up into the air. This was related with such confidence and gravity, as, having no means to contradict it, we inclined to believe it. But, the governour not being present, we concluded nothing; but some of us went with them the next day to the governor.

The reason why they desired so much our friendship was, because they were now in war with the Narragansett, whom, till this year, they had kept under, and likewise with the Dutch, who had killed their old sachem and some other of their men, for that the Pequods had killed some Indians, who came to trade with the Dutch at Connecticut; and, by these occasions, they could not trade safely any where. Therefore they desired us to send a pinnace with cloth, and we should have all their trade. They offered us also all their right at Connecticut, and to further us what they could, if we would settle a plantation there.

When they came to the governour, they agreed, according to the former treaty, viz. to deliver us the two men, who were guilty of Capt. Stone's death, when we would send for them ; to yield up Connecticut; to give us four hundred fathom of wampampeague, and forty beaver, and thirty otter skins; and that we should presently send a pinnace with cloth to trade with them, and so should be at peace with them, and as friends to trade with them, but not to defend them.

The next morning news came, that two or three hundred of the Narragansett were come to Cohann, viz. Naponsett, to kill the Pequod ambassadors. Presently we met at Roxbury, and raised some few men in arms, and sent to the Narragansett men to come to us. When they came there were no more but two of their sachems, and about twenty more, who had been on hunting thereabouts, and came to lodge with the Indians at Cohann, as their manner is. So we treated with them about the Pequods, and, at our request, they promised they should go and come to and from us in peace, and they were also content to enter further treaty of peace with them; and in all things showed themselves very ready to gratify us. So the Pequods returned home, and the Narragansett departed well satisfied; only they were told in private, that if they did make peace with the Pequods, we would give them part of that wampampeague, which they should give us; for the Pequods held it dishonorable to offer them any thing as of themselves, yet were willing we should give it them, and indeed did offer us
so much for that end. The agreement they made with us was put in writing, and the two ambassadors set to their marks—one a bow with an arrow in it, and the other a hand.
December
22.] By a letter from Plimouth it was certified, that the Dutch of Hudson's River had been at Connecticut, and came in warlike manner to put the Plimouth men out of their house there; but when they stood upon their defense, they departed, without offering any violence.

John Deforest, History of the Indians of Connecticut
The English soon began to found settlements in the country, as indeed they would have done had they formed no treaty to that effect with the Pequots. A few men came over, by land, through the forests, and settled in a rude manner at Wethersfield, some thirty miles up the Connecticut River. They suffered great hardships from cold and hunger during the first winter;

and some of them would, perhaps, have perished, had it not been for the friendly assistance of the Indians. During 1635 larger parties, with women and children, came; and from this time the colony of Connecticut must be considered as firmly established. The Indians received them joyfully, and their sachems, Sehat of Poquonnuc, Arramament of Podunk, and the more famous Sowheag and Sequassen, sold them land without stint or hesitation. Sequassen sold them Hartford and the whole region westward, including the territories of the Tunxis, as far as the country of the Mohawks. Nassecowen, of Windsor, a sagamore, or at least a landholder, was "so taken in love with the coming of the English," that, "for some small matter," he gave them all his possessions on the eastern side of the river.

The first Indian deeds of sale at Windsor, Hartford, and Wethersfield, were never preserved, or, at least, have never come to my knowledge. There is, however, in the Colonial Records, a brief notice that the settlers of Wethersfield made a satisfactory purchase of their territory from Sowheag, the sachem. The tract thus obtained measured six miles in width, north and south, and nine miles in length, of which six miles were on the west side of the river. In the records of Windsor we have also one deed remaining, of the date of April 25th, 1636, which conveys to the English a tract on the east side of the Connecticut, lying between the Podunk and Scantic Rivers, and extending a day's march into the country. The price given for this territory was twenty cloth coats and fifteen fathoms of sewan or wampum; part to be paid at the time, and part when the next English pinnace came up the river. The deed was signed by Arramament, sachem at Podunk; Sheat, sachem of Poquonnuc; Cogrenosset of Poquonnuc, and eight others, who claimed an interest in the lands.

It is worthy of observation, that three of the signers, Poxen, Wonochocke and Towtonemou, styled them-selves Mohegans; or, as it is once or twice expressed, Mohegoneak. This circumstance leads us to advert to the history of this portion of the Pequot nation. The treaty between the colonial government and the Pequots seems to have been imperfectly observed on both sides. Sassacus paid none of the wampum and other articles which he had promised, nor is there any proof that, for two years after the treaty, the colonists ever sent a vessel to the Pequot country to trade. The only article which the English fulfilled was that of planting colonies in Connecticut; and the only article which the Pequots fulfilled was that of allowing them to do so without opposition.

John Winthrop, History of New England

1635

May

6.] Watertown and Roxbury had leave to remove whither they pleased so as they continued under this government. The occasion of their desire to remove was, for that all towns in the bay began to be much straitened by their own nearness to one another, and their cattle being so much increased June 3. A bark of forty tons arrived, set forth with twenty servants, by Sir Richard Saltonstall, to go plant at Connecticut.

August

16.] The Dorchester men being set down in Connecticut, near the Plymouth trading house, the governor, Mr. Bradford, wrote to them, complaining of it as an injury, in regard of their possession and purchase of the Indians, whose right it was, and the Dutch sent home into Howland for commission to deal with our people in Connecticut.

September

1.] There came also John Winthrop, the younger, with Commission from the Lord Say, Lord Brook, and divers other great persons in England, to begin a plantation and to be

governour there. They sent also men and ammunition, and £2000 in money, to begin a fortification at the mouth of the river.

Agreement of the Seabrook Company with John Winthrop, Jr. Articles made (between the right honorable the Lord Viscoft, Say & Seale, Sir Arthur Hesilrige, Barronet, Sir Richard Saltonstall, Kt., Henry Laurence, Henry Darley and George Fenwick, Esquiers, on the one part, & John Winthrope the younger, Esquire, of the other part) the 7th of July, 1635.

First, that we in our own names, and the rest of ye company, do by these presents constitute and appoint John Winthrop, the younger, Governor of the river Connecticut in New England and of the harbors and places adjoining, for the space of one whole year from the time of his arrival there. And the said John Winthrop doth undertake & covenant for his part, that he will with all convenient speed repairs to those places, and there abide as aforesaid, for the best advancement of the companies service. Secondly, ye so soon as he comes to the Bay, he shall endeavor to provide able men, to the number of fifty at the least, for making of fortifications and building of houses at the river Connecticut and the harbor adjoining, first for their own present accommodation, and then such houses as may receive men of quality, which latter houses we would have to be built within ye fort. Thirdly, that

John Winthrop Jr.

he shall employ those men according to his best ability, for ye advancement of the companies service, especially in ye particulars above mentioned, during the time of his government, and shall also give a true and just account of all moneys and goods committed to his managing. Fourthly, that for such as shall plant there, now in the beginning, he shall take care that they plant themselves either at the harbor or near the mouth of the river, that these places may be the better strengthened for their own safety; and to that end, that they also sit down in such bodies together, as they may be most capable of an entrenchment, provided that there be reserved unto the fort for the maintenance of it, one thousand or fifteen hundred acres at the least, of good ground, as near adjoining thereunto as may be. Firstly, that forasmuch as this service will take him off from his own employments, the company do engage themselves to give him a just and due consideration for the same. In witness whereof we have hear unto interchangeably subscribed our names W. Say & Seale. Ric: Saltonstall. A. Hesilrige. Geo: Fenwick.
He: Laurence. Hen: Darley

John Winthrop, History of New England
1635
October
6.] Two shallops, going laden with goods to Connecticut, were taken in the night with an easterly storm, and cast away on Brown's Island, near the Gurnett's Nose and all the men drowned.
15.]　About sixty men, women, and little children, went by land toward Connecticut with their cows, horses, and swine, and after a tedious and difficult journey, arrived safe there.
November
3.] Mr. Winthrop, Jr., the governor appointed by the lords for Connecticut, sent a bark of thirty tons, and about twenty men, with all needful provisions, to take possession of the mouth of the Connecticut, and to begin some building.
9.]　About this time an open pinnace, returning from Connecticut, was cast away at Manamet Bay; but all the men (being six) were saved, and came to Plymouth, after they had wandered ten days in extreme cold and deep snow, not meeting with any Indian or other persons.

31

26.] There came twelve men from Connecticut. They had been ten days upon their journey, and had lost one of their company, drowned in the ice by the way; and had been all starved, but that, by God's providence, they lighted upon an Indian wigwam. Connecticut River was frozen up the 15th of this month.

28.] Here arrived a small Norsey bark, of twenty-five tons, sent by the Lords Say, etc. with one Gardiner an expert engineer or work base, and provisions of all sorts, to begin a fort at the mouth of Connecticut. She came through many great tempests; yet through the Lord's great providence, her passengers, twelve men, two women and goods, all safe. Mr. Winthrop had sent, four days before, a bark, with carpenters and other workmen, to take possession of the place, (for the Dutch intended to take it) and to raise buildings.

Lion Gardiner, Relation of the Pequot War

In the year 1635, I, Lion Gardener, Engineer and Master of works of Fortification in the legers of the Prince of Orange, in the Low Countries, through the persuasion of Mr. John Davenport, Mr. Hugh Peters with some other well-affected Englishmen of Rotterdam, I made an agreement with the forenamed Mr. Peters for £100 per annum, for four years, to serve the company of patentees, namely, the Lord Say, the Lord Brooks [Brook,] Sir Arthur Hazilrig, Sir Mathew Bonnington [Bonighton], Sir Richard Saltingstone [Saltonstall], Esquire Fenwick, and the rest of their company, [I say] I was to serve them only in the drawing, ordering and making of a city, towns or forts of defense. And so I came from Holland to London, and from thence to New-England, where I was appointed to attend such orders as Mr. John Winthrop, Esquire, the present Governor of Conectecott, was to appoint, whether at Pequit [Pequot] river, or Conectecott, and that we should choose a place both for the convenience of a good harbor, and also for capableness and fitness for fortification. But I landing at Boston the latter end of November, the aforesaid Mr. Winthrop had sent before one Lieut. Gibbons, Sergeant Willard, with some carpenters, to take possession of the River's mouth, where they began to build houses against the Spring; we expecting, according to promise, that there would have come from England to us 300 able men, whereof 200 should attend fortification, 50 to till the ground, and 50 to build houses. But our great expectation at the River's mouth, came only to two men, viz. Mr. Fenwick, and his man, who came with Mr. Hugh Peters, and Mr. Oldham and Thomas Stanton, bringing with them some Otterskin coats, and Beaver, and skeins of wampum, which the Pequits [Pequots] had sent for a present, because the English had required those Pequits [Pequots] that had killed a Virginean [Virginian], one Capt. Stone, with his Bark's crew, in Conectecott River, for they said they would have their lives and not their presents; then I answered, Seeing you will take Mr. Winthrop to the Bay to see his wife, newly brought to bed of her first child, and though you say he shall return, yet I know if you make war with these Pequits, he will not come hither again, for I know you will keep yourselves safe, as you think, in the Bay, but myself, with these few, you will leave at the stake to be roasted, or for hunger to be starved, for Indian corn is now 12s. per bushel, and we have but three acres planted, and if they will now make war for a Virginian and expose us to the Indians, whose mercies are cruelties, they, I say, they love the Virginians better than us: for, have they stayed these four or five years, and will they begin now, we being so few in the River, and have scarce holes to put our heads in? I pray ask the Magistrates in the Bay if they have forgot what I said to them when I returned from Salem?

For Mr. Winthrop, Mr. Haines, Mr. Dudley, Mr. Ludlow, Mr. Humfry, Mr. Belingam [Bellingham], Mr. Coddington, and Mr. Nowell;— these entreated me to go with Mr. Humfry and Mr. Peters to view the country, to see how fit it was for fortification. And I told them that Nature had done more than half the work already, and I thought no foreign potent enemy would do them any hurt, but one that was near. They asked me who that was, and I said it was Capt. Hunger that threatened them most, for, (said I,) War is like a three-footed Stool, want one foot and down comes all; and these three feet are men, victuals, and munitions, therefore seeing in peace you are like to be famished, what will or can be done if war? Therefore I think, said I, it will be best only to fight against Capt. Hunger, and let fortification alone awhile; and if need hereafter require it, I can come to do you any service: and they all liked my saying well. Entreat them to rest awhile, till we get more strength here about us, and that we hear where the seat of the war, will be, may approve of it, and provide for it, for I had but twenty-four in all, men, women, and boys and girls, and not food for them for two months, unless we saved our corn-field, which could not possibly be if they came to war, for it is two miles from our home. Mr. Winthrop, Mr. Fenwick, and Mr. Peters promised me that they would do their utmost endeavor to persuade the Bay-men to desist from war a year or two, till we could be better provided for it; and then the Pequit Sachem was sent for, and the present returned, but full sore against my will. So they three returned to Boston, and two or three days after came an Indian from Pequit, whose name was Cocommithus, who had lived at Plimoth, and could speak good English; he desired that Mr. Steven [Stephen] Winthrop would go to Pequit with an £100 worth of trucking cloth and all other trading ware, for they knew that we had a great cargo of goods of Mr. Pincheon's, and Mr. Steven Winthrop had the disposing of it. And he said that if he would come he might put off all his goods, and the Pequit Sachem would give him two horses that had been there a great while. So I sent the Shallop, with Mr. Steven Winthrop, Sergeant Tille [Tilly], (whom we called afterward Sergeant Kettle, because he put the kettle on his head,) and Thomas Hurlbut and three men more, charging them that they should ride in the middle of the river, and not go ashore until they had done all their trade, and that Mr. Steven Winthrop should stand in the hold of the boat, having their guns by them, and swords by their sides, the other four to be, two in the fore cuddie, and two in aft, being armed in like manner, that so they out of the loop-holes might clear the boat, if they were by the Pequits assaulted; and that they should let but one canoe come aboard at once, with no more but four Indians in her, and when she had traded then another, and that they should lie no longer there than one day, and at night to go out of the river; and if they brought the two horses, to take them in at a clear piece of land at the mouth of the River, two of them go ashore to help the horses in, and the rest stand ready with their guns in their hands, if need were, to defend them from the Pequits, for I durst not trust them. So they went and found but little trade, and they having forgotten what I charged them, Thomas Hurlbut and one more went ashore to boil the kettle, and Thomas Hurlbut stepping into the Sachem's wigwam, not far from the shore, enquiring for the horses, the Indians went out of the wigwam, and Wincumbone, his mother's sister, was then the great Pequit Sachem's wife, who made signs to him that he should be gone, for they would cut off his head; which, when he perceived, he drew his sword and ran to the others, and got aboard, and immediately came an abundance of Indians to the waterside and called them to come ashore, but they immediately set sail and came home, and this caused me to keep watch and ward, for I saw they plotted our destruction.

John Winthrop, History of New England
December
10.] The ship Rebecca, about sixty tons, came from Connecticut, and brought in her about seventy men and women, which came down to the river's mouth to meet the barks which should have brought their provisions; but, not meeting them, they went aboard the Rebecca, which, two days before,

34

was frozen twenty miles up the river, but a small rain falling set her free; but coming out, she ran on ground at the mouth of the river, and was forced to unlade. They came to Massachusetts in five days, which was a great mercy of God, for otherwise they had all perished with famine, as some did. While the Rebecca lay there, the Dutch sent a sloop to take possession of the mouth of the river; but our men gate two pieces on shore, and would not suffer them to land.

The second and third of this month fell a snow about knee deep, and much wind from the N. and N.E.

William Bradford, Plimouth Plantation

Some of their neighbors in the Bay, hearing of the fame of Conightecute River, had a hankering mind after it, (as was before noted,) and now understanding that the Indians were swept away with the late great mortality, the fear of whom was an obstacle unto them before, which being now taken away, they began now to prosecute it with great eagerness.

The greatest differences fell between those of Dorchester plantation and them here; for they set their mind on that place, which they had not only purchased of the Indians, but where they had built; intending only (if they could not remove them) that they should have but a small moiety left to the house, as to a single family; whose doings and proceedings were conceived to be very injurious, to attempt not only to intrude themselves into the rights and possessions of others, but in effect to thrust them out of all. Many were the letters and passages that went between them hear about, which would be too long here to relate the effects of which no place was free.

This year two shallops going to Conigtecutt with goods from ye Massachusetts of such as removed thither to plant, were in an easterly storm cast away in coming into this harbor in ye night; the boats men were lost, and ye goods were driven all along ye shore, and stowed up & down at high water mark. But ye Governor caused them to be gathered up, and drawn together, and appointed some to take an inventory of them, and others to wash & dry such things as had need thereof; by which means most of the goods were saved, and restored to ye owners. Afterwards another boat of theirs (going thither likewise) was cast away near unto Manoanscusett, and such goods as came a shore were preserved for them. Such crosses they met with in their beginnings; which some imputed as a correction from God for their intrusion (to the wrong of others) into the place. But I dare not be bold with Gods judgments in this kind.

From Plimouth House

Sir, The Massachusetts men are coming almost daily, some by water, and some by land, who are not yet determined where to settle, though some have a great mind to the place we are upon, and which was last bought. Many of them look at that which this river will not afford, except it be at this place which we have, namely, to be a great town, and have commodious dwellings for many together. So as what they will doe I cannot yet resolve you; for this place there is none of them say any thing to me, but what I hear from their servants (by whom I perceive their minds), I shall doe what I can to withstand them. I hope they will hear reason; as that we were here first, and entered with much difficulty and danger, both in regard of the Dutch and Indians, and bought the land, (to your great charge, already disbursed,) and have since held here a chargeable possession, and kept the Dutch from further encroaching, which would else long before this day have possessed all, and kept out all others, etc. I hope these and such like arguments will stop them. It was your will we should use their persons and messengers kindly, and so we have done, and do daily, to your great charge; for the first company had well nie starved had it not been for this house, for want of victuals; I being forced to supply twelve men for days together; and those which came last, I entertained the best we could, helping both them (and the other) with canoes, and guides. They got me to go with them to the Dutch, to see if I could procure some of them to have quiet settling near them; but they did peremptorily withstand them. But this later company did not once speak thereof, etc. Also I gave their goods house room according to their earnest request, and Mr. Pynchon's letter in their possible commercial value — hemp and black lead (which I thought good to send you, here enclosed). And what trouble and charge I shall be further at I know not; for they are coming daily, and I expect these back again from below, whither they are gone to view the country. All which trouble and charge we undergo for their occasion, may give us just cause (in the judgment of all wise and understanding men) to hold and keep that we are settled upon. Thus with my duty remembered, etc. I rest.

Yours to be commanded, Jonathan Brewster

William Bradford, Plimouth Plantation

I am now to relate some strange and remarkable passages. There was a company of people lived in the country, up above in the river of Conigtecut, a great way from their trading house there, and were enemies to those Indeans which lived about them, and of whom they stood in some fear (being a stout people). About a thousand of them had enclosed themselves in a fort, which they had strongly palisadoed. About three or four Dutch men went up in the beginning of winter to live with them, to get their trade, and prevent them for bringing it to the English, or to fall into amity with them; but at spring to bring all down to their place. But their enterprise failed, for it pleased God to visit these Indeans with a great sickness, and such mortality that of one thousand above nine hundred and a half of them died, and many of them did rot above ground for want of burial, and the Dutch men almost starved before they could get away, for ice and snow. But about February, they got with much difficulty to their trading house; whom they kindly relieved, being almost spent with hunger and cold. Being thus refreshed by them diverse days, they got to their own place, and the Dutch were very thankful for this kindness.

This spring, also, those Indeans that lived about their trading house there fell sick of the small pox, and died most miserably; for a sorer disease cannot befall them; they fear it more then the plague; for usually they that have this disease have them in abundance, and for want of bedding & lining and other helps, they fall into a lamentable condition, as they lie on their hard mats, the pox breaking and mattering, and running one into another, their skin cleaving (by reason thereof) to the mats they lie on; when they turn them, a whole side will flee of at once, (as it were,) and they will be all of a gore blood, most fearful to behold; and then being very sore, what with cold and other distempers, they die like rotten sheep. The condition of this people wait so lamentable, and they fell down so generally of this disease, as they were (in the end) not able to help one another; no, not to make a fire, nor to fetch a little water to drink, nor any to bury the dead; but would strivie as long as they could, and when they could procure no other means to make fire, they would burn the wooden trays and dishes they ate their meat in, and their very bows and arrows; and some would crawl out on all four to get a little water, and some times die by the way, and not be able to get in again. But those of the English house, (though at first they were afraid of the infection,) yet seeing their woeful and sad condition, and hearing their pitiful cries and lamentations, they had compassion of them, and daily fetched them wood & water, and made them fires, got them victuals whilst they lived, and buried them when they died. For very few of them escaped, notwithstanding they did what they could for them, to the hazard of themselves. The chief Sachem himself now died, and almost all his friends & kindred. But by the marvelous goodness and providence of God not one of the English was so much as sick, or in the least measure tainted with this disease, though they daily did these offices for them for many weeks together. And this mercy which they shewed them was kindly taken, and thankfully acknowledged of all the Indeans that knew or heard of the same; and their men here did much commend and reward them for the same.

Lion Gardener was sent over by Lords Say and Seal and Lord Brook to construct a fort at the mouth of Connecticut River, to command it. He was said to be a skilful engineer, and on that account was selected. He had seen some service in the Low Countries under Gen. Fairfax. He came into this Country about the year 1633 or 1634 and erected the fort at Saybrook in Connecticut, which was so named in honor of Lords Say and Seal and Lord Brook: but how long he continued to command the fort I do not recollect. He commanded it when Capt. John Mason conquered the Pequots, for Mason in his history, you recollect, says, This Lt. Gardiner, complimented or entertained him with many big guns, on his arrival at the fort after the conquest of the Pequots. He remained at Saybrook four years. A son was born to him 29 April 1636, which was the first white child born in Connecticut.

Lion Gardiner to John Winthrop, Jr.
To the Worshipfull Mr. John Winthrop Junior Esquire at
Bostowne in the bay these present.

Worshipfull Sir, — I have received your letter, wherein I do understand that you are not like to return, if and according to your order I have sent your servants Robert and Sara. I wonder that you did not write to me, but it is no wonder, seeing that since your and Mr. Phenix departure, there hath been no provision sent, but, on the contrary, people to eat up that small, now no store, that we had. Hear hath come many vessels with provision, to go up to the plantations, but none for us. It seems that we have neither masters nor owners, but are left like so many servants whose masters are willing to be quit of them; but now to late I wish that I had putt my thoughts in practice, that was to stay and take all such provisions out of the vessels, as was sufficient for a year; summer goods God's good providence hath not only brought, but also stayed, but if they could have gone, I did intend to have taken all the victuals out, and kept them for our necessity; and seeing that you, Mr. Peters, and Phenwicke knows that it was against my mind to send the Pequitts presents again, and I with these few men are, by your wills and likings, put into a warlike condition, there shall be no cause to complain of our fidelity and endeavors toward you, and if I see that there be not such care for us that our lives may be preserved, then must I be forced to shift as the Lord shall direct. I wish that it may be for God's glory and all your credits and profits. Hear is not 5 shillings of money and no beaver. The Dutch man will bring us some corn and rye, but we have no thing to pay him for it. Mr. Pincheon had a bill to receive all the wampompeage we had; we have not so much as will pay for the mending of our old boat. I have sent your cows up to the plantations with 2 oxen; 2 of them we have killed and eaten, with the goats: a ram goat was brought from the Manatos, but the enemy got him and all the great swine, 22, in one day, and had gotten all the sheep and cows likewise, had we not sallied out. It was on the Sabbath day, and there were four men with the cows with firelocks. For the sheep, I have kept them thus long, and when the pinckes comes down I hope they will bring hay for them, for I have not hay for them to eat by the way, if I should sent them to the bay; but now for our present condition; since Mr. Phenwicke is gone for England, I hope you will not be forgetful of us, and I think if you had not been gone away and he had not come, we had not as yet been at wars with the Indians upon such terms; they up the river when I sent to them how it stood with us, & in what need we wear, did jeer or mock us, but time and patience will show the effect of it. I hear that the Bachelor is to bring us provision, I pray you forget us not when she comes from the Bermudas with some potatoes, for hear hath been some Virginians that hath taught us to plant them after another way, and I have put it in practice, and found it good. I pray you when you pay or recken with the owners of the pincke which brought the guns heather, to shorten them for three weeks time and diet, for Sergeant Tilley for pilateinge (planting) the pincke up with the cows. I have, instead of your man Robert, hired Azarias for twenty shillings per month, or else I should not have let him come away. Hear is two men and their wives come from the Dutch plantation, a tailor and a ship write, and I sett them both to work, but I have neither money nor victuals to pay them. I do intend to set the Dutch man to work to make a Dutch smack sail, which shall carry thirty or forty ton of goods, and not draw three foot and a half of water, principally to transport goods and passengers up the river in safety. I pray let us not want money or victuals that some things may go forward. Mr. Peter said when he was hear that I should sell victuals to John Nott, Richard Graves, and them that came from the Dutch plantation, out of that little we had, and if all failed he would supply us with more, and fish like wise, to sell, but we have neither fish nor flesh to sell for others nor yet for ourselves. Your wisdom will understand the meaning of this writing.

Lion Gardiner to John Winthrop, Jr.

Saybrook, this 6 of November 1636

We have great cause of fear that William Quick with all the men & barke are taken by the Indians, coming down the river; the Hope & they came down together from Watertown, & came together 20 miles. William Quick stayed there behind, & we fear went ashore a fowling. The Hope came in yesterday at noon, the wind hath been very fair to have brought them down ever since, & yet they are not come. We sadly fear the event: Pray for us & consider, &c. &c. &c.

Nov 7, late at night.

Immediately after the writing this they came in dark night beyond expectation: but I think it would be good if no vessels may be suffered to come, but the men known & fitted with arms suitable, charged not to go ashore, for they venture not only their own Hues but wrong others also. The Indians are many hundreds of both sides the river, & shoot at our pinnaces as they go up & down, for they furnish the Indians with peeces, powder, & shot, & they come many times & shoot our own pieces at us, they have 3 from us already, 5 of Capt Stones, one of Charles his, Pardon our hast,

Your assured friend to command,

Lion Gardiner

Lion Gardiner to John Winthrop, Jr.

To the Worshipful Mr. John Winthrop at Boston, Ipswich, or elsewhere, these deliver.

Worshipfull Sir, — These are to certify you how the Lord hath been pleased to deal with us this winter: it hath pleased him, of his goodness and mercy, to give us rest from the Indians all this winter, but one the 22nd of the last month I, with ten men more with me, went about our neck of land to fire some small bushes and marshes, where we thought the enemy might have lien in ambush, and about half a mile from home we startled 3 Indians, and having possibility to have cut them short, we running to meet them, and to fire the marsh, but whilst our men was setting it one fire, there rushed out of the woods, 2 several ways, a great company of Indians, which though we gave fire upon them, yet they run one to the very muzzles of our pieces, and so they shot 3 men down in the place, and 3 more men shot that escaped, of which one died the same night; and if the Lord had not putt it into my mind to make the men draw their swords, they had taken us all alive, so that sometime shouting and sometime refraining, keeping them of with our

swords, we recovered a bare place of ground, which this winter I had cleared for the same use, and they durst not follow us any further, because it is under command of our great guns, of which I hope they have had some experience, as we hear by the relation of other Indians, and your friend Sacious and Nebott are the chief actors of the treachery & villainy against us. As concerning my sheep, which you writ to me of, I took order with Mr. Gibbins about them, but if he be not yet come home, I would entreat you that they may be kept with yours, until you hear from him. Thus hoping that you will be a means to stir up our friends in the bay, out of there dead sleep of security, to think that your condition may be as ours is, unless some speedy course be taken, which must not be done by a few, but by a great company, for all the Indians have their eyes fixed upon us, and this year they will all join with us against the Pequtt, and it is to be feared that the next year they will be against us. We have used 2 sheets of your lead, which was in square foot. I have writ to the governour to pay you so much again. I have sent you your bead steed, and would have made a better, but time would not permit, for we watch every other night, never putting of our clothes, for the Indians show themselves in troupes about us, every day, as this bearer can certify you more at large. Thus committing you, your wife, father, and mother, Mr. Peter, and the rest of our friends, to God, I rest
Your assured friend to command, Lion Gardiner

21 Feb. 1636
Mr. Ludlowe, Mr. Phelps,
Mr. Steele, Mr. Westwood,
Mr. Swaine;

Whereas it was ordered that Samuel Wakeman, George Hubbert, & Ancient Stoughton were to consider of the boundes of Dorchester toward the Falls and of Watertown towards the mouth of the River; The said Samuel Wakeman and George Hub-bard thinks meet that the plantation of Dorchester shall extend towards the Falls, on the same side the plantation stands, to a Brook called Kittle Brook and so over the great River upon the same line that Newtown & Dorchester doth between them. And so it is ordered by the Court.

It is ordered that the plantation now called Newtown shall be called and named by the name of Hartford Town; likewise the plantation now called Watertown shall be called and named Wethersfield.

Samuel Wakeman and Ancient Stoughton doe think meet that the boundes of Wethersfield shall be extended toward the Rivers mouth in the same side it stands in to a Tree six miles downward from the bounds between them & Hartford [marked with] N: F: and [to run in an east] and west line, [and over] the great River, the said Wethersfield to begin at the mouth of Pewter Pott Brook and there to run due east into the Country three miles and downward six miles in breadth, which is ordered accordingly

It is ordered that the plantation called Dorchester shall be called Windsor.

The boundes between Weathersfield & Hartford are agreed on the side wherein they stand to be at a Tree marked N: F: and to which the Pale of the said Hartford is fixed, to go into the Country due east and on the other side of the great River from Pewter Pott Brook at the lower side of Hocanno due east into the Country, which is now ordered accordingly.

The bounds between Hartford and Windsor is agreed to be at the upper end of the great meadow of the said Hartford toward Windsor at the Pale that is now there set up by the said Hartford which is abutting upon the great River upon a due east line and into the Country from the said Pale upon a due west line as parallel to the said east line as far as they have now paled *and.* afterward the boundes to go into the Country upon the same west line. But it is to be so much shorter towards Windsor as the place where the Girth that comes along at the end of the said meadow and falls into the said great River is shorter then their Pale & over the said great River the said Plantation of Windsor is to come to the Rivers mouth that falls into the saide great River of Conectecott and there the said Hartford is to run due east into the Country, which is ordered accordingly.

John Winthrop, History of New England
1636
February
24.] Mr. Winslow of Plimouth came to treat with those of Dorchester about their land at Connecticut, which they had taken from them. It being doubtful whether that place were within our patent or not, the Plimouth men, about three years since, had treaty with us about joining in erecting a plantation and trade there. We thought not fit to do any thing then, but gave them leave to go on. Whereupon they bought a portion of land of the Indians, and built a house there, and the Dorchester men (without their leave) were now setting down their town in the same place; but, after, they desired to agree with them; for which end Mr. Winslow came to treat with them, and demanded one sixteenth part of their lands, and £100, which those of Dorchester not consenting unto, they brake off, those of Plimouth expecting to have due recompense after, by course of justice, if they went

on. But divers resolved to quit the place, if they could not agree with those of Plimouth.

April 1.] Those of Dorchester, who had removed their cattle to Connecticut before winter, lost the greatest part of them this winter; yet some, which came late, and could not be put over the river, lived very well all the winter without any hay. The people also were put to great straits for want of provisions. They eat acorns, and malt, and grains. They lost near £2000 worth of cattle.

May 31.] Mr. Hooker, pastor of the church of Newtown and most of his congregation went to Connecticut. His wife was carried in a horse litter; and they drove one hundred and sixty cattle, and fed of their milk by the way.

Emigrants Going to Settle in Connecticut

Chapter Two

How Great a Matter a Little Fire Kindleth

"In the fore part of this year, the Pequents fell openly upon ye English at Conightecut, in ye lower parts of ye river, and slew sundry of them (as they were at work in ye fields), both men and women, to ye great terror of ye rest; and went away in great pride and triumph, with many high threats. They also assaulted a fort at ye River's mouth, though strong and well defended; and though they did not prevail, yet it struck them with much fear and astonishment to see their bold attempts in the face of danger; which made them in all places to stand upon their guard, and to prepare for resistance, and earnestly solicit their friends and confederates in ye Bay of Massachusetts."

John Deforest, History of the Indians of Connecticut

Thus matters went on, till an event took place which roused the colonists to think of the obligations of their allies if not of their own. John Oldham, of Dorchester, a man of energetic but turbulent disposition, was the commander of a pinnace which made trading voyages along the coast for corn and other Indian commodities. In the spring of 1636 he sailed, with a crew of two boys and two Narragansett Indians, to barter with the Pequots. This was done, as we are informed by Winthrop, in consequence of the treaty with them; but, as the treaty was made in 1634, the Pequots might justly have complained of the tardiness of the English in fulfilling its conditions. Oldham finished his dealings with them, however, in safety: but having, on his return, stopped at Manisses or Block Island, he was there murdered by the islanders. The crime was discovered and punished by another trader, John Gallop, who was voyaging from the Connecticut to the eastern part of Long Island. Passing near Manisses on his way, he saw Oldham's pinnace with sixteen Indians on board, and a canoe, manned by other Indians and loaded with goods, putting off for the shore. Gallop recognized the pinnace and, running close to, gave a hail in English, but received no answer. He now began to suspect what had occurred; and his suspicions were strengthened by observing that the Indians were armed with guns and other English weapons. Presently a sail was raised on board the pinnace; and the wind and tide being both off the island, it began to drive northward towards the Narragansett shore. Gallop hesitated no longer, but bore up ahead of the little craft, and commenced firing duck shot among the Indians with such effect that they all took refuge under the hatches. He then stood off some distance, and, turning round, run down upon the pinnace's quarter with such violence as almost to overset her. Six Indians, terrified by the shock, leaped overboard, and were drowned in swimming for the shore. Gallop gave the pinnace another blow with his heavier vessel, but as no more Indians would make their appearance, he commenced firing with his muskets through her thin sides. Startled by this, six others of the plunderers jumped overboard and sank; and the victors, who only consisted of three men and two boys, then boarded their prize. Two Indians came on deck, surrendered and were bound; but as Gallop feared they would untie each other, and could not easily keep them asunder, he coolly threw one of them into the sea. Two others, armed with swords, still remained under the hatches, posted so advantageously that they could neither be killed nor made prisoners. The body of John Oldham was found under an old sail, his head split open, his arms and legs gashed as if the Indians had been trying to cut them off, and the flesh still warm. Gallop and his crew put these melancholy remains into the sea, carried the sails and the remainder of the cargo on board their own vessel, and then attempted to tow the pinnace away, with the two Indians still in the hold. But some wind and a good deal of sea coming on towards night, he was obliged to loose her, and she drifted over to the Narragansett shore.

Not long after, three Narragansetts, sent by the sachems of the tribe, came into Boston, two of whom were those who had been with Oldham. They brought a letter from Roger Williams, a Baptist clergyman residing in their country, written on behalf of Canonicus the grand sachem. It expressed his great grief for what had occurred, and affirmed that Miantinomo, his nephew, had gone, with seventeen canoes and two hundred men, to punish the murderers. The magistrates examined the third

Indian so sharply that he made some confessions, which may have been true, and may have been extorted from him by terror. He said that a plot had been formed to murder Oldham because he traded with the Pequots; that all the Narragansett sachems were engaged in it except Canonicus and Miantinomo; and that his two companions were accomplices in the crime. The authorities finally sent the three men safely back to Canonicus; but made known to him the suspicions which they entertained both of them and himself. They demanded that he should surrender Oldham's two boys, and should inflict a suitable punishment upon the guilty islanders. The boys were soon sent to Boston; and Canonicus and Miantinomo afterwards succeeded in convincing the colonial magistrates that they were guiltless of any participation in the murder.

William Bradford, Plimouth Plantation

   After his second expulsion Oldham had some thoughts of returning to England. Bradford, in a letter to Cushman dated June 9, gave this warning: "We have rid ourselves of the company of many of those who have been so troublesome unto us, though I fear we are not yet rid of the troubles themselves. I hear Oldham comes himself into England, the which, if he do, beware of him, for he is very malicious, and much threatens you." He remained at Nantasket (Nantucket), and becoming reconciled to New Plymouth, was to take charge of Thomas Morton, of Mare Mount, when the latter was sent prisoner to England in the summer of 1628. Returning to New England late in 1629 or early in 1630, Oldham was admitted a freeman of Boston in 1631, and settling at Watertown, engaged in a trade with the Indians. He had returned with a grant obtained from John Gorges, brother of Robert Gorges, under which he and his associate, John Dorrell, claimed lands lying between Charles and Abousett rivers, embracing most of the territory now occupied by Charlestown, Cambridge and Somerville. This same territory was granted by the Council for New England to the Massachusetts Company, which regarded Oldham's grant as "void in Law, yet his Claim being to this, you may in your Discretion prevent him by causing some to take Possession of the chief Part thereof." The restlessness and speculative leanings of Oldham were shown in his negotiations with the Massachusetts Company, to whom he caused no little distraction and delay in business, "through the Variety of his vast Concepts of extraordinary Gain of three for one propounded to us, to be made and raised in three Years, if he might have the Managing of our Stock, preferring to bee contented for his own Employment, so he might have the over plus of the Gaines; with

47

whom, after long Time spent in sundry Treaties, finding him a Man altogether unfit for us to deal with, we have at last left him to his own Way: And as we are informed, he, with some others, are providing a Vessel, and is minded, as soon as he can dispatch, to come for New England, pretending to settle himself in Massachusetts Bay; claiming a Title and Right, by a Grant from Sir Ferdinand Gorges Sonne, which we are well satisfied, by good Council, is void in Law. He will, admit of no Terms of Agreement, unless we will leave him at liberty to trade for Beaver with the Natives, which wee deny to the best of our own Planters; nether is he satisfied to trade himself with his own Stock and Means, which we conceive is so small that it would not much hinder us, but he doth interest other men, who for ought we know are never likely to be beneficial to the planting of the country, their own Particular Profits (though to the overthrow of the general Plantation) being their chief Aim and Intent. . . . We fear, that as he hath been obstinate and violent in his Opinions here, so he will persist, and bee ready to draw each Party to himself there, to the great Hindrance of the common Quiet; wee have therefore thought fit to give you Notice of his Disposition, to the end, you may beware how you meddle with him, as also that you may use the best Means you can to settle an Agreement with the old Planters so as they may not harken to Mr. Oldham's dangerous though vain Propositions: Wee find him a Man so affected to his own Opinion as not to be removed from it, neither by Reason nor any Persuasion; and, unless he may bear sway, and have all Things carried to his good Liking, we have little Hope of Quiet or comfortable Subsistence where he shall make his Abode; and, therefore, if you shall see just Cause, wee hereby require you and the Council there, to exercise that Power we have, and our Privileges will bear us out in it, to suppress a Mischief before it take too great a Head, not that we would wrong him, or any Man that will live peaceably within the Limits of our Plantation. But, as the Preservation of our Privileges will chiefly depend (under God) upon the first Foundation of our Government, so if we suffer so great an Affront as we find is intended towards us, by the Proceedings of Mr. Oldham, and his Adherents, in our first Beginnings, we may be sure they will take Hart and be emboldened to do us a far greater injury hereafter.

John Winthrop, History of New England
1636
July 20.] John Gallop, with one man more, and two little boys, coming from Connecticut in a bark of twenty tons, intending to put in at Long Island to trade, and being at the mouth of the harbor, were forced, by a sudden

change of the wind, to bear up for Block Island or Fisher's Island, lying before Narragansett, where they espied a small pinnace, which, drawing near unto, they found to be Mr. Oldham's (an old planter, and a member of Watertown congregation, who had been long out a trading, having with him only two English boys, and two Indians of Narragansett). So they hailed him, but had no answer; and the deck was full of Indians, (fourteen in all,) and a canoe was gone from her full of Indians and goods. Whereupon they suspected they had killed John Oldham, and the rather, because the Indians let slip and set up sail, being two miles from shore, and the wind and tide being off the shore of the island, whereby they drove towards the main at Narragansett. Whereupon they went ahead of them, and having but two pieces and two pistols, and nothing but duck shot, they bear up near the Indians, (who stood ready armed with guns, pikes, and swords,) and let fly among them, and so galled them as they all gate under hatches. Then they stood off again, and returning with a good gale, they stemmed her upon the quarter and almost overset her, which so frightened the Indians, as six of them leaped over-board and were drowned. Yet they durst not board her, but stood off again, and fitted their anchor, so as, stemming her the second time, they bored her bow through with their anchor, and so sticking fast to her, they made divers shot through her, (being but inch board,) and so raked her fore and aft, as they must needs kill or hurt some of the Indians; but, seeing none of them come forth, they gate loose from her and stood off again. Then four or five more of the Indians leaped into the sea, and were likewise drowned. So there being now but four left in her, they boarded her; whereupon one Indian came up and yielded; him they bound and put into hold. Then another yielded, whom they bound. But John Gallop, being well acquainted with their skill to untie themselves, if two of them be together, and having no place to keep them asunder, he threw him bound into the sea; and, looking about, they found John Oldham under an old seine, stark naked, his head cleft to the brains, and his hand and legs cut as if they had been cutting them off, and yet warm. So they put him into the sea; but could not get to the other two Indians, who were in a little room underneath, with their swords. So they took the goods which were left, and the sails, etc., and towed the boat away; but night coming on, and the wind rising, they were forced to turn her off, and the wind carried her to the Narragansett shore.

26.] The two Indians, which were with Mr. Oldham, and one other, came from Canonicus, the chief sachem of Narragansett, with a letter from Mr. Williams to the governor, to certify him what had befallen Mr. Oldham, and how grievously they were afflicted, and that Miantunnomoh was gone, with seventeen canoes and two hundred men, to take revenge, etc. But, upon examination of the Indian who was brought prisoner to us, we found that all the sachems of the Narragansett, except Canonicus and Miantunnomoh, were the contrivers of Mr. Oldham's death; and the occasion was, because he went to make peace, and trade with the Pequods last year, as is before related. The prisoner said also, that Mr. Oldham's two Indians were acquainted with it; but, because they were sent as messengers from Canonicus, we would not imprison them. But the governor wrote back to Mr. Williams to let the Naragansetts know, that we expected they should send us the two boys, and take revenge upon the islanders; and withal gave Mr. Williams a caution to look to himself, if we should have occasion to make war upon the Naragansetts, for Block Island was under them. And the next day, he wrote to Canonicus by one of those two Indians, and that he had suspicion of him, etc., yet he had sent him back, because he was a messenger, but did expect that, if he should send for the said two Indians, he should send them to us to clear themselves.

30.] Mr. Oldham's two boys were sent home by one of Miantunnomoh 's men, with a letter from Mr. Williams, signifying that Miantunnomoh had caused the sachem of Niantic to send to Block Island for them; and that he had near one hundred fathom of wampum and other goods of Mr. Oldham's, which should be reserved for us; and that three of the seven, which were drowned, were sachems; and one of the two, which were hired by the sachem of Niantic, was dead also. So we wrote back to have the rest of those, which were accessory, to be sent to us, and the rest of the goods, and that he should tell Canonicus and Miantunnomoh, that we held them innocent; but that six other under-sachems were guilty, etc.

John Deforest, History of the Indians of Connecticut

The government of Massachusetts now turned its attention to the Pequots. They were said to have harbored some of the murderers of Oldham and, it was pretended, had thereby made themselves partakers in their guilt. A harsh and hasty measure, suggested by feelings of suspicion and exasperation, was adopted. It was resolved that an expedition should be fitted out to punish the Block Islanders, which should afterwards proceed to the country of the Pequots, and demand, or if necessary, extort, from them satisfaction. No thought of the policy of sending an armed force to threaten a high spirited and powerful nation of savages seems to have entered the minds of Governor Vane and his council. No idea seems to have occurred to them that it would be proper first to require the Pequots, in a peaceable manner, to do whatever they were bound as friends and allies to do. To this insult was added another insult and an injury. By the treaty of 1634 the Pequots had agreed to pay the colony four hundred fathoms of wampum: they could not be accused of having, since that time, committed any outrage upon Englishmen or English property: yet it was now resolved to demand of them six hundred additional fathoms of wampum and some of their children as hostages for its delivery.

Several small vessels were collected, ninety men were raised, and the whole force was placed under the command of John Endicott, a resident of Massachusetts. He was instructed to go first to Block Island, take possession of it in the name of the colony, spare the women and children, but put all the men to the sword. More than a dozen of the island warriors had been slain by Gallop and his little crew; but nothing short of their extermination, it seems, could sufficiently avenge the murder of a single white man. From Block Island Endicott was to proceed to the country of the Pequots, obtain the murderers of Stone and one thousand fathoms of wampum, demand some of their children as hostages, for the performance of these conditions, and if the children were refused to take them by force.

It was nearly dusk when the little fleet of Endicott reached the shore of Block Island. A strong wind was blowing, and the surf was dashing heavily on the rocks. The English could see only a single Indian, walking along the shore as if deserted; and some of them began to think that the rest of the inhabitants had fled to the main land. Others suspected, with more wisdom, that they should find them concealed behind a low mound which ran along the edge of the water. John Underhill, a brave soldier though a bad man, moved towards the shore in a shallop containing about a dozen soldiers. As he neared the landing place, fifty or sixty tall warriors rose from behind the earthen rampart, and, advancing a few steps towards the invaders, let fly among them a volley of arrows. One of these missiles penetrated into the neck of a young man, through a collar so stiff that Underhill likens it to an oaken board. The captain himself received one through his coat sleeve, while another rebounded from the helmet which, at parting, his wife had, with difficulty, persuaded him to wear. The heavy surf tossed the boat about in such a manner that the English did not dare to run it on the beach, nor, while in it, could they take any aim with their muskets. They sprang into the water, therefore, up to their waists, fired and hurried on to the shore. Endicott was landing at the same time, and the Indians, not daring to wait a close conflict with so many Englishmen, took to their heels, and were soon out of sight in the thicket.

As it was now late, the invaders encamped on shore, stationed sentinels, and passed the night in expectation of an attack. They were unmolested, however, and, when morning dawned, commenced ranging over the island in search of the inhabitants. It seemed to them about ten miles long by four broad; its surface rough and composed of small hills; containing no good timber but great quantities of dwarf oaks. Paths led here and there through the brushwood, so narrow that the English were obliged to march along them in single file. They found two villages, containing together about sixty wigwams, some of which were large and comfortably built, but all deserted except by a few dogs. The English burnt down the wigwams, staved the canoes, carried away some mats and baskets, shot some of the dogs, and laid waste about two hundred acres of corn. They spent two days in searching this small island; but its inhabitants had concealed themselves so closely in the swamps and thickets that very few of them could be found. A captain named Turner, stepping into a swamp, met several warriors, and fired a number of shots at them. In reply they discharged their arrows, one of which struck upon his corselet with a force as if it had been the push of a pike. Underhill says that some fourteen of the islanders were killed and others wounded; but the Narragansetts reported, as we learn from Hubbard, that the English only succeeded in killing one.

Having accomplished what they could at Block Island, Endicott and his men re-embarked and sailed to the little fort of the Connecticut settlers at Saybrook. Lieutenant Gardiner, who commanded the garrison, was greatly astonished at the appearance of such an armament; and on learning its object, argued vehemently against the enterprise and the manner in which it was to be conducted. "You have come to raise a nest of wasps about our ears," said he, "and then you will flee away." "But," he adds, in his history of the Pequot war, "as they came without our knowledge, so they went away against our will."

Finding, at last, that the expedition could not be prevented from proceeding, Gardiner determined to reinforce it with two shallops and twenty men. The fleet was detained four days at Saybrook by stress of weather, and then continued its voyage. As it glided along near the coast of the Western Nehantics, the natives, surprised at seeing so many vessels together, and totally unsuspicious, apparently, of the object of their visit, came running in numbers to the shore. "What cheer Englishmen?" they shouted. "What do you come for?" As the voyagers were unwilling to waste time, and still more to put the Indians on their guard, they made no answer to these questions, and kept steadily on their course. The natives continued to run along the shore abreast of the fleet until they came to the mouth of the Thames; and, seeing that the strangers persevered in refusing to communicate with them, they changed their questions and began to cry: "Are you angry, Englishmen? Will you kill us? Do you come to fight?" No answer was returned; the vessels silently entered the river, cast anchor at a distance from either shore and remained in quiet until morning.

During the whole night loud cries and doleful shouts reverberated from the forests which lined either bank: for the Pequots, apprehending that the white men had come to invade them, were continually calling to each other and sounding the alarm. Early in the morning an Indian was seen making his way out to the vessels in a canoe. On reaching them he appeared to be a man advanced in years, of a tall and large form, and dignified in his appearance and carriage. When he came to speak, his expressions were grave and majestic; and he soon showed himself to be of a keen and ingenious mind. He demanded the object of the strangers in coming to the country of the Pequots. Captain Endicott replied that the Pequots or their allies had destroyed an English vessel, and killed ten Englishmen, on the Connecticut River; that their sachem had agreed to surrender the murderers, but had never yet fulfilled his agreement; that the English had now come for them, and, if the Pequots were wise, they would immediately give them up; that they must also pay one thousand fathoms of wampum for their destruction of English property and their faithlessness in observing the treaty; and that, if they could not pay so large a sum down, they must surrender twenty children of their principal men as hostages.

The ambassador must have listened with astonishment and indignation to these last demands; but he replied with courtesy, and ingeniously endeavored to justify the conduct of his tribe. "We know not," said he, "that our people have slain any of the English. True it is that we have killed such a number of men, and in such a place, as you mention; and this was our reason for doing it. Not long before the coming of these men into the river, there was a certain vessel came to us in way of trade. We used the people of it well, and traded with them, and believed them to be such as would not wrong us in the least matter. But wishing to destroy our sachem, they laid a plot for that purpose; and thus did they accomplish their desire. They suffered none but him to come into their vessel, and then having seized him, they called to us as we stood on the shore and demanded a bushel of wampum for his life. This rung terribly in our ears, when we so little expected it; but, seeing there was no remedy, we collected this great quantity of wampum and put it into their hands. Then did they in truth send our sachem ashore, as they had promised; but not until they had slain him. This thing greatly exasperated our spirits and made us vow revenge. Shortly after came the other white men into the great river, and pretended to trade as the first had done. We did not undeceive them, but seized the opportunity and went quietly on board their vessel. The son of our murdered sachem staid in the cabin with Captain Stone, until the captain, having drank more strong water than was good for him, fell asleep. Our sachem then took a little hatchet from under his robe and knocked him in the head. The rest of our people attacked the other white men; but when one of them took up a firebrand to set fire to the powder they leaped overboard into the river. In this manner they saved themselves, while the strangers were all blown up and destroyed. Could ye blame us for revenging the murder of our sachem? For we distinguished not between the Dutch and English, but supposed them to be all one people; and therefore we do not conceive that we have done you any wrong, having only endeavored to revenge the death of our sachem."

Such was the tale which this Pequot told in justification of the murder of Captain Stone and his companions. It referred unquestionably to the massacre of their grand chief, Wopigwooit; and such, perhaps, was in reality the manner in which the Dutch effected his death. The account differed greatly, it will be seen, from the story told by the Pequot messengers to Governor Dudley; yet of the two I am inclined to think that it was the most correct: more especially as it agreed, in several important particulars, with the version common among the colonists. But, true or not, Endicott refused to admit it as a justification. "You know well enough," said he, "the difference between the English and the Dutch; for you have had sufficient dealings with both; and therefore, seeing you have slain the king of England's subjects, we demand an account of their blood, for we our-selves are liable to account for them." "We do not know the difference between the Dutch and English," persisted the Pequot; "they are both strangers to us, and we took them to be all one; wherefore we boldly ask pardon, for we have not willfully wronged the English."

Capt. John Mason, Some Grounds of the War Against the Pequot

About the Year 1632 one Capt. Stone arrived in the Massachusetts in a Ship from Virginia; who shortly after was bound for Virginia in a small Bark with one Capt. Norton; who sailing into Connecticut River about two Leagues from the Entrance cast Anchor; there coming to them several Indians belonging to that Place whom the Pequots Tyrannized over, being a potent and warlike People, it being their Custom so to deal with their neighbor Indians; Capt. Stone having some occasion with the Dutch who lived at a trading House near twenty Leagues up the River, procured some of those Indians to go as Pilots with two of his Men to the Dutch: But being benighted before they could come to their desired Port, put the skiff in which they went, ashore, where the two Englishmen falling asleep, were both Murdered by their Indian Guides: There remaining with the Bark about twelve of the aforesaid Indians; who had in all probability formerly plotted their bloody Design; and waiting an opportunity when some of the English were on Shore and Capt. Stone asleep in his Cabin, set upon them and cruelly murdered every one of them, plundered what they pleased and sunk the Bark. These Indians were not native Pequots, but had frequent recourse unto them, to whom they tendered some of those Goods, which were accepted by the Chief Sachem of the Pequots: Other of the said Goods were tendered to Nynigrett Sachem of Nayanticke, who also received them.

The Council of the Massachusetts being informed of their proceedings, sent to speak with the Pequots, and had some Treaties with them: But being unsatisfied therewith, sent forth Captain John Endicott Commander in Chief, with Captain Underhill, Captain Turner, and with them one hundred and twenty Men: who were firstly designed on a Service against a People living on Block Island, who were subject to the Narragansett Sachem; they having taken a Bark of one Mr. John Oldham, Murdering him and all his Company: They were also to call the Pequots to an Account about the Murder of Capt. Stone; who are arriving at Pequot had some Conference with them; but little effected; only one Indian slain and some Wigwams burnt. After which, the Pequots grew enraged against the English who inhabited Connecticut, being but a small Number, about two hundred and fifty, who were there newly arrived; as also about twenty Men at Saybrook, under the Command of Lieutenant Lyon Gardner, who was there settled by several Lords and Gentlemen in England. The Pequots falling violently upon them, slew divers Men at Saybrook; keeping almost a constant Siege upon the Place; so that the English were constrained to keep within their pallizado Fort; being so hard

Beset and sometimes Assaulted, that Capt. John Mason was sent by Connecticut Colony with twenty Men out of their small Numbers to secure the Place: But after his coming, there did not one Pequot appear in view for one Month Space, which was the time he there remained. In the Interim certain Pequots about One Hundred going to a Place called Weathersfield on Connecticut; having formerly confederated with the Indians of that Place (as it was generally thought) lay in Ambush for the English; divers of them going into a large Field adjoyning to the town to their harbor, were there set upon by the Indians: nine of the English were killed outright, with some Horses, and two young Women taken Captives.

At their Return from Weathersfield, they came down the River of Connecticut (Capt. Mason being then at Saybrook Fort) in three Canoes with about one hundred Men, which River of necessity they must pass: We espying them, concluded they had been acting some Mischief against us, made a Shot at them with a Piece of Ordnance, which beat off the Beak Head of one of their Canoes, wherein our two Captives were: it was at a very great distance: They then hastened, drew their Canoes over a narrow Beach with all speed and so got away.

Upon which the English were somewhat dejected: But immediately upon this, a Court was called and met in Hartford the First of May, 1637, who seriously considering their condition, which did look very sad, for those Pequots were a great People, being strongly fortified, cruel, warlike, munitioned, and the English but a handful in comparison: But their outrageous violence against the English, having murdered about thirty of them, their great pride and insolency, constant pursuit in their malicious courses, with their engaging other Indians in their quarrel against the English, who had never offered them the least wrong; who had in all likelihood espoused all the Indians in the country in their quarrel, had not God by more than an ordinary Providence prevented: These things being duly considered, with the eminent Hazard and great peril they were in; it pleased God so to stir up the hearts of all men in general, and the Court in special, that they concluded some forces should forthwith be sent out against the Pequots; their grounds being just, and necessity enforcing them to engage in an offensive and defensive War; the management of which War we are nextly to relate. Gardiner, the diplomat, as remarkable in solving the problems of pioneers and savages as the rare Winthrop, who mediated successfully with kings, would have postponed war with the Pequots until the whites were stronger, by accepting their presents of wampum and skin-coats, for killing Captain

Stone, a Virginian, on the Connecticut, but the blundering shortsightedness of the rulers at "The Bay" had "raised the wind" by sending Endicott with troops thither. Unhappily, his Indian interpreter, Kitchimakin, forwarded boastfully a Pequot scalp to Canonicus, the Narragansett Chief, who passed the trophy derisively from Sachem to Sachem, enraging the Pequots to frenzy.

Lion Gardiner, Relation of the Pequot War

And suddenly after came Capt. Endecott, Capt. Turner, and Capt. Underhill with a company of soldiers, well fitted, to Seabrook, and made that place their rendezvous or seat of war, and that to my great grief, for, said I, you come hither to raise these wasps about my ears, and then you will take wing and flee away; but when I had seen their commission I wondered, and made many allegations against the manner of it, but go they did to Pequit, and as they came without acquainting any of us in the River with it, so they went against our will, for I knew that I should lose our corn-field; then I entreated them to hear what I would say to them, which was this: Sirs, Seeing you will go, I pray you, if you don't load your Barks with Pequits, load them with corn, for that is now gathered with them, and dry, ready to put into their barns, and both you and we have need of it, and I will send my shallop and hire this Dutchman's boat, there present, to go with you, and if you cannot attain your end of the Pequits, yet you may load your barks with corn, which will be welcome to Boston and to me: But they said they had no bags to load them with, then said I, here is three dozen of new bags, you shall have thirty of them, and my shallop to carry them, and six of them my men shall use themselves, for I will with the Dutchmen send twelve men well provided; and I desired them to divide the men into three parts, two parts to stand without the corn, and to defend the other one third part, that carried the corn to the water side, till they have loaded what they can. And the men there in arms, when the rest are aboard, shall in order go aboard, the rest that are aboard shall with their arms clear the shore, if the Pequits do assault them in the rear, and then, when the General shall display his colours, all to set sail together. To this motion they all agreed, and I put the three dozen of bags aboard my shallop, and away they went, and demanded the Pequit Sachem to come into parley. But it was returned for answer, that he was from home, but within three hours he would come; and so from three to six, and thence to nine, there came none. But the Indians came without arms to our men, in great numbers, and they talked with my men, whom they knew; but in the end, at a word given, they all on a sudden ran away from our men, as they stood in rank and file, and not an Indian more was to be seen: and all this while before they carried all their stuff away, and thus was that great parley ended. Then they displayed their colours, and beat their drums, burnt some wigwams and some heaps of corn, and my men carried as much aboard as they could, but the army went aboard, leaving my men ashore, which ought to have marched aboard first. But they all set sail and my men were pursued by the Indians, and they hurt some of the Indians, and two of them came home wounded. The Bay-men killed not a man, save that one Kichomiquim [Cutshamequin], an Indian Sachem of the Bay, killed a Pequit; and thus began the war between the Indians and us in these parts. So my men being come home, and having brought a pretty quantity of corn with them, they informed me (both Dutch and English) of all passages. I was glad of the corn. After this I immediately took men and went to our corn-field, to gather our corn, appointing others to come about with the shallop and fetch it, and left five lusty men in the strong-house, with long guns, which house I had built for the defense of the corn. Now these men not regarding the charge I had given them, three of them went a mile from the house a fowling; and having loaded themselves with fowl they returned. But the Pequits let them pass first, till they had loaded themselves, but at their return they arose out of their ambush, and shot them all three; one of them escaped through the corn, shot through the leg, the other two they tormented. Then the next day I sent the shallop to fetch the five men, and the rest of the corn that was broken down, and they found but three, as is above said, and when they had gotten that they left the rest; and as soon as they were gone a little way from shore, they saw the house on fire. Now so soon as the boat came home, and brought us this bad news, old Mr. Michell was very urgent with me to lend him the boat to fetch hay home from the Six-mile Island, but I told him they were too few men, for his four men could but carry the hay aboard, and one must stand in the boat to defend them, and they must have two more at the foot of the Rock, with their guns, to keep the Indians from running down upon them. And in the first place, before they carry any of the kocks of hay, to scour the meadow with their three dogs,—to march all abreast from the lower end up to the Kock, and if they found the meadow clear, then to load their hay; but this was also neglected, for they all went ashore and fell to carrying off their hay, and the Indians presently rose out of the long grass, and killed three, and took the brother of Mr. Michell, who is the minister of Cambridge, and roasted him alive; and so they served a shallop of his, coming down the river in the Spring, having two men, one whereof they killed at Six-mile Island, the other came down drowned to us ashore at our doors, with an arrow shot into his eye through his head.

In the 22nd of February, I went out with ten men, and three dogs, half a mile from the house, to burn the weeds, leaves and reeds, upon the neck of land, because we had felled twenty timber-trees, which we were to roll to the water-side to bring home, every man carrying a length of match with brimstone matches with him to kindle the fire withal. But when we came to the small of the Neck, the weeds burning, I having before this set two sentinels on the small of the Neck, I called to the men that were burning the reeds to come away, but they would not until they had burnt up the rest of their matches. Presently there starts up four Indians out of the fiery reeds, but ran away, I calling to the rest of our men to come away out of the marsh. Then Robert Chapman and Thomas Hurlbut, being sentinels, called to me, saying there came a number of Indians out of the other side of the marsh. Then I went to stop them, that they should not get the wood-land; but Thomas Hurlbut cried out to me that some of the men did not follow me, for Thomas Rumble and Arthur Branch, threw down their two guns and ran away; then the Indians shot two of them that were in the reeds, and sought to get between us and home, but durst not come before us, but kept us in a half-moon, we retreating and exchanging many a shot, so that Thomas Hurlbut was shot almost through the thigh, John Spencer in the back, into his kidneys, myself into the thigh, two more were shot dead. But in our retreat I kept Hurlbut and Spencer still before us, we defending ourselves with our naked swords, or else they had taken us all alive, so that the two sore wounded men, by our slow retreat, got home with their guns, when our two sound men ran away and left their guns behind them. But when I saw the cowards that left us, I resolved to let them draw lots which of them should be hanged, for the articles did hang up in the hall for them to read, and they knew they had been published long before. But at the intercession of old Mr. Michell, Mr. Higgisson [Higginson], and Mr. Pell, I did forbear. Within a few days after, when I had cured myself of my wound, I went out with eight men to get some fowl for our relief, and found the guns that were thrown away, and the body of one man shot through, the arrow going in at the right side, the head sticking fast, half through a rib on the left side, which I took out and cleansed it, and presumed to send to the Bay, because they had said that the arrows of the Indians were of no force.

Anthony Dike, master of a bark, having his bark at Rhode Island in the winter, was sent by Mr. Vane, then Governor. Anthony came to Rhode-

Island by land, and from thence he came with his bark to me with a letter, wherein was desired that I should consider and prescribe the best way I could to quell these Pequits, which I also did, and with my letter sent the man's rib as a token. A few days after, came Thomas Stanton down the River, and staying for a wind, while he was there came a troop of Indians within musket shot, laying themselves and their arms down behind a little rising hill and two great trees; which I perceiving, called the carpenter whom I had shewed how to charge and level a gun, and that he should put two cartridges of musket bullets into two sakers guns that lay about; and we levelled them against the place, and I told him that he must look towards me, and when he saw me wave my hat above my head he should give fire to both the guns; then presently came three Indians, creeping out and calling to us to speak with us: and I was glad that Thomas Stanton was there, and I sent six men down by the Garden Pales to look that none should come under the hill behind us; and having placed the rest in places convenient closely, Thomas and I with my sword, pistol and carbine, went ten or twelve pole without the gate to parley with them. And when the six men came to the Garden Pales, at the corner, they found a great number of Indians creeping behind the fort, or betwixt us and home, but they ran away. Now I had said to Thomas Stanton, "Whatsoever they say to you, tell me first, for we will not answer them directly to any thing, for I know not the mind of the rest of the English." So they came forth, calling us nearer to them, and we them nearer to us. But I would not let Thomas go any further than the great stump of a tree, and I stood by him; then they asked who we were, and he answered, Thomas and Lieutenant. But they said he lied, for he was shot with many arrows; and so I was, but my buff coat preserved me, only one hurt me. But when I spake to them they knew my voice, for one of them had dwelt three months with us, but ran away when the Bay-men came first.   Then they asked us if we would fight with Niantecut Indians, for they were our friends and came to trade with us. We said we knew not the Indians one from another, and therefore would trade with none. Then they said, "Have you fought enough"? We said we knew not yet. Then they asked if we did use to kill women and children? We said they should see that hereafter. So they were silent a small space, and then they said, We are Pequits, and have killed Englishmen, and can kill them as mosquetoes, and we will go to Conectecott and kill men, women, and children, and we will take away the horses, cows and hogs. When Thomas Stanton had told me this, he prayed me to shoot that rogue, for, said he, he hath an Englishman's coat on, and saith that he hath killed three, and these other four have their cloathes on their backs. I said, No, it is not the manner of a parley, but have patience and I shall fit them ere they go. Nay, now or never, said he; so when he could get no other answer but this last, I bid him tell them that they should not go to Conectecott, for if they did kill all the men, and take all the rest as they said, it would do them no good, but hurt, for English women are lazy, and can't do their work; horses and cows will spoil your corn-fields, and the hogs their clam-banks, and so undo them: then I pointed to our great house, and bid him tell them there lay twenty pieces of trucking cloth, of Mr. Pincheon's, with hoes, hatchets, and all manner of trade, they were better fight still with us, and so get all that, and then go up the river after they had killed all us. Having heard this, they were mad as dogs, and ran away; then when they came to the place from whence they came, I waved my hat about my head, and the two great guns went off, so that there was a great hubbub amongst them. Then two days after, came down Capt. Mason, and Sergeant Seely, with five men more, to see how it was with us; and whilst they were there, came down a Dutch boat, telling us the Indians had killed fourteen English, for by that boat I had sent up letters to Conectecott, what I heard, and what I thought, and how to prevent that threatened danger, and received back again rather a scoff, than any thanks, for my care and pains. But as I wrote, so it fell out to my great grief and theirs, for the next, or second day after, (as Major Mason well knows,) came down a great many canoes, going down the creek beyond the marsh, before the fort, many of them having white shirts; then I commanded the carpenter whom I had shewed to level great guns, to put in two round shot into the two Backers, and we levelled them at a certain place, and I stood to bid him give fire, when I thought the canoe would meet the bullet, and one of them took off the nose of a great canoe wherein the two maids were, that were taken by the Indians, whom I redeemed and clothed, for the Dutchmen, whom I sent to fetch them, brought them away almost naked from Pequit, they putting on their own linen jackets to cover their nakedness; and though the redemption cost me ten pounds, I am yet to have thanks for my care and charge about them: these things are known to Major Mason.

Then came from the Bay Mr. Tille, with a permit to go up to Harford [Hartford], and coming ashore he saw a paper nailed up over the gate, whereon was written, that no boat or bark should pass the fort, but that they come to an anchor first, that I might see whether they were armed and manned sufficiently, and they were not to land any where after they passed the fort till they came to Wethersfield; and this I did because Mr. Mitchel had lost a shallop before coming down from Wethersfield, with three men well armed. This Mr. Tille gave me ill language for my presumption, (as he called it), with other expressions too long here to write. When he had done, I bid him go to his warehouse, which he had built before I come, to fetch his goods from thence, for I would watch no longer over it. So he, knowing nothing, went and found his house burnt, and one of Mr. Plum's with others, and he told me to my face that I had caused it to be done; but Mr. Higgisson, Mr. Pell, Thomas Hurlbut, and John Green can witness that the same day that our house was burnt at Cornfield-point I went with Mr. Higgisson, Mr. Pell, and four men more, broke open a door and took a note of all that was in the house and gave it to Mr. Higgisson to keep, and so brought all the goods to our house, and delivered it all to them again when they came for it, without any penny of charge. Now the very next day after I had taken the goods out, before the sun was quite down, and we all together in the great hall, all them houses were on fire in one instant. The Indians ran away, but I would not follow them. Now when Mr. Tille had received all his goods I said unto him, I thought I had deserved for my honest care both for their bodies and goods of those that passed by here, at the least better language, and am resolved to order such malapert persons as you are; therefore I wish you and also charge you to observe that which you have read at the gate, 'tis my duty to God, my masters, and my love I bear to you all which is the ground of this, had you but eyes to see it; but you will not till you feel it. So he went up the river, and when he came down again to his place, which I called Tille's folly, now called Tille's point, in our sight in despite, having a fair wind he came to an anchor, and with one man more went ashore, discharged his gun, and the Indians fell upon him, and killed the other, and carried him alive over the river in our sight, before my shallop could come to them; for immediately I sent seven men to fetch the Pink down, or else it had been taken and three men more. So they brought her down, and I sent Mr. Higgisson and Mr. Pell aboard to take an invoice of all that was in the vessel, that nothing might be lost. Two days after came to me, as I had written to Sir Henry Vane, then Governor of the Bay, I say came to me Capt. Undrill [Underhill], with twenty lusty men, well armed, to stay with me two months, or 'till something should be done about the Pequits. He came at the charge of my masters. Soon after came down from Harford Maj. Mason, Lieut. Seely, accompanied with Mr. Stone and eighty Englishmen, and eighty Indians, with a commission from Mr. Ludlow and Mr. Steel, and some others; these came to go fight with the Pequits. But when Capt. Undrill [Underhill] and I had seen their commission, we both said they were not fitted for such a design, and we said to Maj. Mason we wondered he would venture himself, being no better fitted; and he said the Magistrates could not or would not send better; then we said that none of our men should go with them, neither should they go unless we, that were bred soldiers from our youth, could see some likelihood to do better than the Bay-men with their strong commission last year. Then I asked them how they durst trust the Mohegin [Mohegan] Indians, who had but that year come from the Pequits. They said they would trust them, for they could not well go without them for want of guides. Yea, said I, but I will try them before a man of ours shall go with you or them; and I called for Uncas and said unto him, You say you will help Maj. Mason, but I will first see it, therefore send you now twenty men to the Bass river, for there went yesternight six Indians in a canoe thither; fetch them now dead or alive, and then you shall go with Maj. Mason, else not. So he sent his men who killed four, brought one a traitor to us alive, whose name was Kiswas, and one ran away. And I gave him fifteen yards of trading cloth on my own charge, to give unto his men according to their desert. And having staid there five or six days before we could agree, at last we old soldiers agreed about the way and act, and took twenty insufficient men from the eighty that came from Harford [Hartford] and sent them up again in a shallop, and Capt. Undrill [Underhill] with twenty of the lustiest of our men went in their room, and I furnished them with such things as they wanted, and sent Mr. Pell, the sergeon, with them; and the Lord God blessed their design and way, so that they returned with victory to the glory of God, and honour of our nation, having slain three hundred, burnt their fort, and taken many prisoners. Then came to me an Indian called Wequash, and I by Mr. Higgisson inquired of him, how many of the Pequits were yet alive that had helped to kill Englishmen; and he declared them to Mr. Higgisson, and he writ them down, as may appear by his own hand here enclosed, and I did as therein is written. Then three days after the fight came Waiandance, next brother to the old Sachem of Long Island, and having been recommended to me by Maj. Gibbons, he came to know if we were angry with all Indians. I answered No, but only with such as had killed Englishmen. He asked me whether they that lived upon Long Island might come to trade with us. I said No, nor we with them, for if I should send my boat to trade for corn, and you have Pequits with you, and if my boat should come into some creek by reason of bad weather, they might kill my men, and I shall think that you of Long Island have done it, and so we may kill all you for the Pequits; but if you will kill all the Pequits that come to you, and send me their heads, then I will give to you as to Weakwash [Wequash], and you shall have trade with us. Then, said he, I will go to my brother, for he is the great Sachem of all Long Island, and if we may have peace and trade with you, we will give you tribute, as we did the Pequits. Then I said, if you have any Indians that have killed English, you must bring their heads also. He answered, not any one, and said that Gibbons, my brother, would have told you if it had been so; so he went away and did as I had said, and sent me five heads, three, and four heads for which I paid them that brought them as I had promised.

John Winthrop, History of New England
1636
August
8.] Lieutenant Edward Gibbons, and John Higginson, with Cutshamakin, the sagamore of Massachusetts, were sent to Canonicus to treat with him about the murder of John Oldham. They returned, being very well accepted and good success in their business. They observed in the sachem much state, great command over his men, and marvelous wisdom in his answers and the carriage of the whole treaty, clearing himself and his neighbors of the murder, and offering assistance for revenge of it, yet upon very safe and wary conditions.

25.] The governor and council, having lately assembled the rest of the magistrates and ministers, to advise with them about doing justice upon the Indians for the death of Mr. Oldham, and all agreeing that it should be attempted with expedition, did this day send forth ninety men, distributed to four commanders,—Capt. John Underhill, Capt. Nathaniel Turner, Ensign Jenyson, and Ensign Davenport; and over them all, as general, John Endecott, Esq., one of the assistants, was sent. They were embarked in three pinnaces, and carried two shallops and two Indians with them. They had commission to put to death the men of Block Island, but to spare the women and children, and to bring them away, and to take possession of the island; and from thence to go to the Pequods to demand the murderers of Capt. Stone and other English, and one thousand fathom of wampum for damages, etc., and some of their children as hostages, which if they should refuse, they were to obtain it by force. No man was impressed for this service, but all went voluntaries.

26.] Miantunnomoh, sachem of Narragansett, sent a messenger to us, with a letter from Mr. Williams, to signify to us, that they had taken one of the Indians, who had broken prison and was escaped away, and had him safe for us, when we would send for him, (we had before sent to him to that end;) and the other (being also of Block Island) he had sent away, (not knowing, as it seemed, that he had been our prisoner,) according to their promise, that they would not entertain any of that island, which should come to them. But we conceived it was rather in love to him; for he had been his servant formerly. We sent for the two Indians. One was sent us; the other was dead before the messengers came.

In August, 1636, Governor Vane sent one hundred men with Capt. Endecott to Block Island. His orders were to put to death all men, but spare the women and children. This enraged the Pequot. Before a month went by the Pequots were killing every settler who stirred outside his dooryard. Those who were taken were roasted alive, some hung up on trees, where their friends could see them, yet so mangled as hardly to be recognized when found. The Pequot lurked in ambush around Saybrook Fort and one day surprised a party while at work outside. Four were killed before they could get back to the fort. In order to show what an arrow shot could do, the captain of the fort sent Governor Vane a man's rib-bone with the arrow that had killed him still sticking in it so firmly that it could not be pulled out. A few days later, three hundred Pequot openly beset the fort. They dared the English to come out and fight while mocking them by imitating the cries of the people they had tortured. The Pequot continued with the killing of people, shooting cattle, destroying crops, burning houses. During the winter the Pequot tried to bring the Narragansett into a league with them against the English.

August

24.) John Endecott, Esq., and four captains under him, with twenty men a piece, set sail. They arrived at Block Island the last of the same. The wind blowing hard at N. E. there went so great a surf, as they had much to do to land; and about forty Indians were ready upon the shore to entertain them with their arrows, which they shot oft at our men; but, being armed with corselets, they had no hurt, only one was lightly hurt upon his neck, and another near his foot. So soon as one man leaped on shore, they all fled. The island is about ten miles long, and narrow paths. There were two plantations, three miles in sunder, and about sixty wigwams,—some very large and fair,— and above two hundred acres of corn, some gathered and laid on heaps, and the rest standing. When they had spent two days in searching the island, and could not find the Indians, they burnt their wigwams, and all their mats, and some corn, and staved seven canoes, and departed. They could not tell what men they killed, but some were wounded and carried away by their fellows.

Thence they went to the mouth of the Connecticut, where they lay wind-bound four days, and taking thence twenty men and two shallops, they sailed to the Pequot harbor, where an Indian came to them in a canoe, and demanded what they were, and what they would have. The general told him, he came from the governor of Massachusetts to speak with their sachems. He told him, Sassacus was gone to Long Island. Then he bade him go tell the other sachem, etc. So he departed; and in the mean time our men landed, but with much danger, if the Indians had made use of their advantage, for all the shore was high, rugged rocks, etc. Then the messenger returned, and the Indians began to gather about our men till there were about three hundred of them; and some four hours past while the messenger went to and fro, bringing still excuses for the sachem's not coming. At last the general told the messenger, and the rest of the Indians near, the particulars of his commission, and sent him to tell the sachem, that if he would not come to him, nor yield to those demands, he would fight with them. The messenger told him, that the sachem would meet him, if our men would lay down their arms, as his men should do their bows, etc. When the general saw they did but dally, to gain time, he bade them be gone, and shift for themselves; for they had dared the English to come fight with them, and now they were come for that purpose. Thereupon they all withdrew. Some of our men would have made a shot at them, but the general would not suffer them; but when they were gone out of musket shot, he marched after them, supposing they would have stood to it awhile, as they did to the Dutch. But they all fled, and shot at our men from the thickets and rocks, but did us no harm. Two of them our men killed, and hurt others. So they marched up to their town, and burnt all their wigwams and mats, but their corn being standing, they could not spoil it. At night they returned to their vessels, and the next day they went ashore on the west side of the river, and burnt all their wigwams, and spoiled their canoes; and so set sail, and came to the Narragansett, where they landed their men, and, the 14th of October, they came all safe to Boston, which was a marvelous providence of God, that not a hair fell from the head of any of them, nor any sick or feeble person among them. As they came by Narragansett, Cutshamakin, an Indian, who went with them for an interpreter, who, being armed with a corselet and a piece, had crept into a swamp and killed a Pequot, and having flayed off the skin of his head, he sent it to Canonicus, who presently sent it to all the sachems about him, and returned many thanks to the English, and sent four fathom of wampum to Cutshamakin. The soldiers who went were all voluntaries, and had only their victuals provided, but demanded no pay. The whole charge of the voyage came to about £200. The seamen had all wages. The Narragansett men told us after, that thirteen of the Pequods were killed, and forty wounded; and but one of Block Island killed.

At the last general court, order was taken to restrain the trade with the Indians, and the governor and council appointed to let it to farm, for a rent to be paid to the treasury.

Canonicus sent word of some English, whom the Pequods had killed at Saybrook; and Mr. Williams wrote that the Pequods and Naragansetts were at truce, and that Miantunnomoh told him, that the Pequods had labored to persuade them, that the English were minded to destroy all Indians.

Whereupon we sent for Miantunnomoh to come to us.

Instructions From The Massachusetts To John Winthrop Esq. First Governour of Connecticut to Treat with the Pequots.

To John Winthrop Jr. Esq., the First Governor of Connecticut;

Whereas it so falls out by the good Providence of God, that the place of your present residence is neare adjoyning unto certaine of the Natives who are called the Pequots, concerning whom we have divers things to enquire and satisfy ourselves in; our request to you therefore is, and by these presents we do give you full power, authority, and commission to treate and conferre with the sayd Pequots, in our names according to the instructions to these annexed, as if wee ourselves were present: and to make report backe agayne unto us of the issue and success of the whole before the next Generall Court (which, God willing is intended in the beginning of the 7th month). Thus recommending you, and your affayres to the blessing of Allmighty God, wee rest.

Your loving friends,

Henry Vane, Governor, John Winthrop, Deputy

Worshipful John Winthrop
Governor of the Fort in Connecticut River
Worshipful Sir, — Your last kindness with them formerly doth much oblige me to you to requite you according to my poor ability. In the mean time, I rest myself humbly thankful unto you for the same; being sorry I was not home when as your men came to my house. Sir, as yet, I have no intelligence from Plymouth concerning the business you spoke to me of,

expecting daily; which, as soon as I hear, I will certify you of their minds. Further, sir, I think it convenient to certify you concerning the Pequots, who continue still in their bloody minds towards the English. For, this week, having occasion to send my man to Mausick, the sachem thereof sent me word, that, upon the 23d of May last, they purposed to cut off our bark after she had done trading with them; who, for that end, appointed eighty men in canoes suddenly in the night to surprise her: but, by God's overruling power, at the very instant, our men had a fair wind, and so, unknown to them, escaped the danger. And, further, there is reported there, that shortly they intend an invasion both of English and natives in this river. Therefore, sir, it is, as I take it, necessary that you give notice to boats as they pass up and down, not to be too secure: for I will assure you, if you please but to examine some boats, they have not a gun in their boat; and, if there be any, you shall find them unserviceable. As also, that which I have complained of, many people goeth over land unarmed, to the hearting [heartening] of the enemy. As though we were so strong ourselves, or the enemy so weak, as that it is cowardice to fear any thing; whereas, in wisdom, all things considered, neither is true. Thus much for present to your worship, lest I should be tedious; and, with remembrance of my duty to yourself, I take my leave, and rest,

Yours to be commanded,

Jonathan Brewster.

From Plimouth House, this 18th June, 1636

Massachusetts, the 4th day

July, 1636.

The instructions which are recommended to John Winthrop Junr. Esq. 1636 Month: 5th 4 in his negotiation with the Pequots.

1. To give notice to the principall Sachem that you have received a commission from us to demand a solemne meeting for conference with them in a friendly manner about matters of importance.

2. In case they slight such a message and refuse to give you a meeting (at such place as yourself shall apoynt) then you are in our names to returne backe their present, (which you shall receive from us) and to acquaint them with all, that we hold ourselves free from any peace or league with them as a people guilty of English blood.

3. If they consent, and give you a meeting as afore sayd, that then you lay downe unto them how unworthily they have requited our friendship with them; for as much as that they have broken the very condition of the peace betwixt us, by the not rendering into our hands the murderers of Capt

Stone, (which we desire you once agayne solemnly to require of them), as also in that they so trifled with us in their present which they made proffer of to us, as that they did send but part of it, and put it off with this, as to say the old men did never consent to the giving of it; which dealings savor so much of dishonour and neglect, as that no people that desire friendship should put them in practice.

4. To let them know first what credible relation hath beene given us, that some of the chief of them were actors in the murder of Mr. Hamond and the other upon Long Hand; and since of another Englishman there: and of their late determination to have seized upon a Plimouth Barke lying in their harbour for trade; as by the more large descriptions of these things, which we also send unto you, will more distinctly appear. Of all these things we desire you to take the relation from their owne mouths and to informe us particularly of their severall answers: giving them to understand that it is not the manner of the English to take revenge of injury until the partys that are guilty have beene called to answer fairely for themselves.

5. To let them know that if they shall cleare themselves of these matters, we shall not refuse to hearken to any reasonable proposition from them for confirmation of the peace betwixt us. But if they shall not give you satisfaction according to these our instructions, or shall bee found guilty of any of the sayd murderers, and will not deliver the actors in them into our hands, that then (as before you are directed) you returne them the present, and declare to them that we hold ourselves free from any league or peace with them, and shall revenge the blood of our countrymen as occasion shall serve.

H. Vane, Governor

John Winthrop, Deputy Governor

It was evident that the Pequods were preparing for a general war of extermination against the whites, and that they were attempting to form an alliance with the Narragansetts was certain. The New England colonies were alarmed at the prospect and were especially desirous of preventing, if possible, the suggested alliance between these two tribes. There was no one among the colonists who was so highly regarded by the Narragansetts as Roger Williams, and no one whose advice they would be so likely to accept. A request therefore came to him from the Bay, that he would employ his good offices in the endeavor to induce the Narragansetts to turn aside the overtures of the Pequods for an offensive alliance against the whites. Williams did not hesitate, but at once set out for the wigwam of Canonicus.

It was a hazardous undertaking, made doubly so by the presence of the Pequod envoys, whom he found in consultation with the sachems of the Narragansetts. At the peril of his life he remained for several days, surrounded by Indians, sleeping among them at night, having no protection save the influence of the friendly disposition which he had maintained toward the natives, since his first coming among them. He had so far won their affections that he had received from the sachems as an earnest of their good-will, the gift of a large tract of land, at the head waters of the Narragansett Bay. That which he now asked of them was, perhaps, the greatest possible test of their friendly disposition; and there can be no higher evidence of his winning manner and sweet spirit,—of his "many precious parts,"—than the record of his success in this perilous undertaking.

William Bradford, Plimouth Plantation
1636

In the year 1634, the Pequents (a stout and warlike people,) who had made wars with sundry of their neighbors, and puft up with many victories, grew now at variance with the Narragansett, a great people bordering upon them. These Narragansett held correspondence and terms of friendship with the English of the Massachusetts. Now the Pequents, being conscious of the guilt of Captain Stones death, whom they knew to be an English man, as also those that were with him, and being fallen out with the Dutch, least they should have over many enemies at once, sought to make friendship with the English of the Massachusetts; and for that end sent both messengers and gifts unto them, as appears by some letters sent from the Governor hither:

Dear and Worthy Sir: etc. To let you know some what of our affairs, you may understand that the Pequents have sent some of theirs to us, to desire our friendship, and offered much wampum and beaver, etc. The first messengers were dismissed without answer; with the next we had diverse days conference, and taking the advice of some of our ministers, and seeking the Lord in it, we concluded a peace and friendship with them, upon these conditions: that they should deliver up to us those men who were guilty of Stones death, and if we desired to plant in Conightecute, they should give up their right to us, and so we would send to trade with them as our friends (which was the chief thing we aimed at, being now in war with the Dutch and the rest of their neighbors). To this they readily agreed; and that we should mediate a peace between them and the Narragansett; for which end they were content we should give the Narragansett part of that

Roger Williams

present, they would bestow on us (for they stood so much on their honor, as they would not be seen to give any thing of themselves). As for Captain Stone, they told us there were but two left of those who had any hand in his death; and that they killed him in a just quarrel, for (say they) he surprised two of our men, and bound them, to make them by force to show him the way up the river; and he with two other coming on shore, nine Indians watched him, and when they were asleep in the night, they killed them, to deliver their own men; and some of them going afterwards to the pinass, it was suddenly blown up. We are now preparing to send a pinass unto them, etc. Our pinass is lately returned from the Pequents; they put off but little commodity, and found them a very false people, so as they mean to have no more to doe with them. I have diverse other things to write unto you, etc.

Yours ever assured,

John Winthrop

After these things, and, as I take, this year, John Oldham, (of whom much is spoken before,) being now an inhabitant of the Massachusetts, went with a small vessel, and slenderly manned, a trading into these south parts, and upon a quarrel between him and the Indians was cut off by them (as hath been before noted at an island called by the Indians Munisses but since by the English Block Island. This, with the former about the death of Stone, and the baffoylling of the Pequents with the English of the Massachusetts, moved them to set out some to take revenge, and require satisfaction for these wrongs; but it was done so superficially, and without their acquainting of those of Conightecute and other neighbors with the same, as they did little good. But their neighbors had more hurt done, for some of the murderers of Oldham fled to the Pequents, and though the English went to the Pequents, and had some parley with them, yet they did but delude them, and the English returned without doing any thing to purpose, being frustrate of their opportunities by the others deceit. After the English were returned, the Pequents took their time and opportunities to cut off some of the English as they passed in boats, and went on fowling, and assaulted them the next spring at their habitations, as will appear in its place. I doe but touch these things, because I make no question they will be more fully and distinctly handled by them selves, who had more exact knowledge of them, and whom they did more properly concern.

John Winthrop, Boston, 12, Of the 1 month, 1634-35

The Rev'd. Roger Williams the subject of the following record was an Englishman of high standing, not only in his native country, but in the wilds of America. In 1631 disliking the formalities of the Church of England, he seceded from it and joined himself to the dissenters and fled to this country, to avoid the persecutions that then raged violently in England, civil and religious liberty were then strangers in New England, and Mr. Williams advocated them with an intrepidity that awakened the attention of the more rigid of the opposition and of many of his friends, on his arrival in this country, he first located himself at Boston, but at the time of his trial resided at Salem, where he had the charge of a large church and congregation, who esteemed him for his strong powers of mind, highly cultivated; his purity of character as a christian teacher, for his liberal and enlarged views on the subject of civil and religious liberty, with his accustomed pious frankness, he did not hesitate to advance his sentiments unreservedly, and denied the right of the civil magistrates to govern or legislate on ecclesiastical affairs. Which soon caused him to be arraigned upon the charges hereto annexed, and for which he was in October 1635, tried and sentenced to banishment from the colony. But the Court who had so unjustly banished him, still possessing too much of the milk of human kindness to drive Mr. Williams at that season of the year with his family, into the wilderness at the mercy of the savages, gave him liberty to remain in the colony until the next spring, upon condition that he should not disseminate his doctrines and opinions to their citizens—which favor he gladly accepted, and remained there until the January following, when he was informed, that his accusers were about to send him back to his persecuters in England, he therefore forth with made his escape from Salem, in the midst of winter, and fled to the Indians in Rhode Island, where he was kindly and favorably received, by the chief Sachem at Mount Hope, who made him a grant of a valuable tract of land at Seccunk, but even on this favored lot of his refuge, he was not long suffered to remain but was ordered by the colonist to cross the river, they claiming the lands upon which he was then located as belonging to the colony of Massachusetts. He accordingly in the spring (with his servant) crossed the river where he once more planted himself, and laid the foundation of the now city of Providence, where he resided many years, an instrument in the hands of the Lord, to protect the lives, liberty, and property of his persecutors in the colony from which he was banished; from the scalping knife and tomahawk of the ruthless savage, over whom he had gained an influence and control by his kindness to them, he alone was enabled to conciliate the angry passions and revengeful dispositions of the Indians about him, and save the bloodshed of the Massachusetts colonists. Mr. Williams soon after he formed his colony at Providence, became Law giver and Minister to his infant colony, and formed his constitution upon the broadest principles of civil and religious liberty, and equal rights, and was the first Governor in North America, "who held liberty of conscience to be the birthright of man."

Massachusetts Records, 1635.

"Whereas Mr. Roger Williams, one of the elders of the church of Salem, hath broached and divulged divers new and dangerous opinions, against the authority of magistrates, as also written letters of defamation both of magistrates and churches here, and that before any conviction, and yet maintaineth the same without retraction: It is therefore ordered, that the said Mr. Williams shall depart out of this jurisdiction within six weeks now next ensuing, which, if he neglects to perform, it shall be lawful for the Govr. and two of the magistrates, to send him to some place out of this jurisdiction, not to return any more, without licence from the court."

William Bradford, Plimouth Plantation
1633

Mr. Roger Williams (a man godly & zealous, having many precious parts, but very unsettled in judgmente) came over first to ye Massachusets, but upon some discontente left ye place, and came hither, (where he was friedly entertained, according to their poore abilitie,) and exercised his gifts amongst them, & after some time was admitted a member of ye church; and his teaching well approved, for ye benefite wherof I still blese God, and am thankfull to him, even for his sharpest admonitions & reproufs, so farr as they agreed with truth. He this year begane to fall into some Strang oppions, and from opinion to practise; which caused some controversie betweene ye church & him, and in ye end some discontente on his parte, by occasion wherof he left them some thing abruptly. Yet after wards sued for his dismission to ye church of Salem, which was granted, with some caution to them concerning him, and what care they ought to have of him. But he soone fell into more things ther, both to their and ye goverments troble & disturbance. I shall not need to name perticulers, they are too well knowen now to all, though for a time ye church here wente under some hard censure by his occasion, from some that afterwards smarted them selves. But he is to be pitied, and prayed for, and so I shall leave ye matter, and desire ye Lord to shew him his errors, and reduse him into ye way of truth, and give him a setled judgment and constancie in ye same; for I hope he belongs to ye Lord, and yt he will shew him mercie.

Roger Williams to the General Court of Massachusetts Bay

I remember that upon the express advice of your ever honored Mr. Winthrop, deceased, I first adventured to begin a plantation among the thickest of these barbarians. That in the Pequot war it pleased your honored government to employ me in the hazardous and weighty service of negotiating a league between yourselves and the Narragansetts when the Pequot messengers, who sought the Narragansetts league against the English, had almost ended that my work and life together.

That at the subscribing of that solemn league, which by the mercy of the Lord, I had procured with the Narragansetts, your government was pleased to send unto me the copy of it, subscribed by all hands there, which yet I keep as a monument and a testimony of peace and faithfulness between you both.

Letter from Roger Williams to John Mason

First, when I was unkindly and unchristianly, as I believe, driven from my house and land and wife and children (in the midst of New England winter, now about 35 years past) at Salem, that ever honoured Governour Mr. Winthrop privately wrote to me to steer my course to the Nahigonset-Bay and Indians for many high and heavenly and publike ends, incouraging me from the freenes of the place from any English claims or pattents. I took his prudent motion as a hint and voice from God and waving all other thoughts and motions, I steered my course from Salem (though in winter snow which I feel yet) unto these parts, wherein I may say Peniel, and that is, I have seene the face of God.

2. I first pitch't and begun to build and plant at Secunk, now Rehoboth, but I received a letter from my antient friend Mr. Winslow, then Governour of Plymmouth, professing his owne and others love and respect to me, yet lovingly advising me, since I was fallen into the edge of their bounds and

they were loth to displease the Bay, to remove but to the other side of the water, and then he said I had the country free before me, and might be as free as themselves, and wee should be loving neighbour's together. These were the joynt understandings of these two eminently wise and christian Governours and others, in their day, together with their councell and advice as to the freedome and vacancie of this place, which in this respect and many other Providences of the most holy and only wise, I called Providence.

3. Sometime after Plymmouth great Sachim (Ousamaquin) upon occasion affirming that Providence was his land and therefore Plymmouth's land, and some resenting it, the then prudent and godly Governour Mr. Bradford and others of his godly councell answered, that if after due examination it should be found true what the barbarian said, yet having, to my loss of a harvest that yeare, been now (though by their gentle advice) as good as banished from Plymmouth as from the Massachusetts; and I had quietly and patiently departed from them, at their motion, to the place where now I was, I should not be molested and tost up and down againe, while they had breath in their bodies; and surely betweene those my friends of the Bay and Plymouth, I was sorely tested for fourteen weekes, in a bitter winter season, not knowing what bread or bed did meane; beside the yearly losse of no small matter in my trading with English and natives, being debarred from Boston, the chiefe mart and port of New England. God knows that many thousand pounds cannot repay the very temporary losses I have sustained. It lies upon the Massachusetts and me, yea and other colonies joining with them to examine, with feare and trembling before the eyes of flaming fire, the true cause of all my sorrows and sufferings. It pleased the Father of spirits to touch many hearts, dear to him, with some relentings; amongst which that great and pious soule Mr. Winslow melted, and kindly visited me at Providence, and put a piece of gold into the hands of my wife for our supply.

4. When the next yeare after my banishment, the Lord drew the bow of the Pequot warr against the country, in which, Sir, the Lord made yourselfe, with others, a blessed instrument of peace to all New England, I had my share of service to the whole land in that Pequot business, inferiour to very few that acted, for,

1. Upon letters received from the Governour and Councill at Boston, requesting me to use my utmost and speediest endeavours to breake and hinder the league laboured for by the Pequots against Monhegans and Pequots against the English (excusing the not sending of companie and supplies by the haste of the business) the Lord helped me immediately to

put my life into my hand, and, scarce acquainting my wife, to ship myself all alone in a poore canow, and to cut through a stormie wind with great seas, every minute in hazard of life, to the Sachem's house.

2. Three dayes and nights my business forced me to lodge and mix with the bloudie Pequot ambassadours, whose hands and arms, me thought, reaked with the bloud of my countrimen, murther'd and massacred by them on Connecticut river, and from whome I could not but nightly looke for their bloudie knives at my owne throate allso.

3. When God wondrously preserved me, and help't me to break to pieces the Pequot's negociation and designe and to make and promote and finish, by many travels and charges, the English league with the Nahiggonsiks and Monhiggins against the Pequots, and that the English forces march't up to the Nahiggonsik countrey, against the Pequots, I gladly entertained at my house in Providence, the general Stoughton and his officers, and used my utmost care that all his officers and soldiers should be well accommodated with us.

4. I marched up with them to the Nahiggonsik Sachems, and brought my countrimen and the barbarians, sachems and captains, to a mutuall confidence and complacence each in other.

5. Though I was ready to have march't further, yet upon agreement that I should keep at Providence as an agent betweene the Bay and the armie, I returned and was interpreter and intelligencer, constantly receiving and sending letters to the Govemour and Councell at Boston, in which work I judge it no impertinent digression to recite (out of the many scores of letters at times from Mr. Winthrop) this one pious and heavenly prophesie touching all New England of that gallant man, viz. "If the Lord turne away his face from our sins, and blesse our endeavours and yours at this turn against our bloudie enemies."

The Pequods, though disappointed in their attempts to secure the alliance of the Narragansets, resolved to maintain the conflict single handed. They probably thought, that it was better policy to make one desperate effort to overpower the English, though aided by the Narragansets, than to wait for the gradual approach of that ruin, which they had the forecast to apprehend from the multiplication of the colonists. It was a bold though a hopeless effort. The Indians having abundance of these forts of Foule upon their waters, take great pains to kill any of them with their Bow and Arrowes; and are marvellous desirous of our English guns, powder, and mot (though they are wisely and generally denied by the English yet with those which they get from the French, and some others (Dutch and English) they kill abundance of Fowle, being naturally excellent marks-men; and also more hardened to endure the weather, and wading, lying, and creeping on the ground. I once saw an exercise of training of the English, when all the English had mist the mark 91 feet up to shoot at, an Indian with his owne Peece (desiring leave to shoot) onely hit it.

John Winthrop, History of New England
1636
September
26.] The Governor and Council of Massachusetts declared war against the Indians on Manisses (Block Island) and sent Capt. John Endecott there with a force to subdue them. The Pequots were angered instead of subdued.
October
8.] After Mr. Endecott and our men were departed from the Pequod, the twenty men of Saybrook lay wind-bound there, and went to fetch some of the Indians corn; and having fetched every man one sackful to their boat, they returned for more, and having loaded themselves, the Indians set upon them. So they laid down their corn and gave fire upon them, and the Indians shot arrows at them. The place was open for the distance of musket shot, and the Indians kept the covert, save when they came forth, about ten at a time, and discharged their arrows. The English put themselves into a single file, and some ten only (who had pieces which could reach them) shot; the others stood ready to keep them from breaking in upon our men. So they continued the most part of the afternoon. Our men killed some of them, as they supposed, and hurt others; and they shot only one of ours, and he was armed, all the rest being without arms. He was shot through the leg. Their arrows were all shot compass, so as our men, standing single, could easily see and avoid them; and one was employed to gather up their arrows. At last they emptied their sacks, and retired safe to their boat.

About two days after, five men of Saybrook went up the river about four miles, to fetch hay in a meadow on Pequot side. The grass was so high as some Pequots, being hid in it, set upon our men, and one, that had hay on his back, they took; the others fled to their boat, one of them having five arrows in him, (but yet recovered). He who was taken was a godly young man, called Butterfield; (whereupon the meadow was named Butterfield Meadow).

About fourteen days after, six of Saybrook, being sent to keep the house in their corn-field, about two miles from the fort, three of them went forth on fowling, (which the lieutenant had strictly forbidden them). Two had pieces and the third only a sword. Suddenly about one hundred Indians came out of the covert, and set upon them. He who had the sword brake through them, (and received only two shot, not dangerous,) and escaped to the house, which was not a bow-shot off, and persuaded the other two to follow him; but they stood still till the Indians came and took them, and carried them away with their pieces. Soon after they burnt down the said house, and some outhouses and haystacks within a bow-shot of the fort, and killed a cow, and shot divers others; but they all came home with the arrows in them.

October

21.] Miantunnomu the sachem of the Narragansett (being sent for by the Governour) came to Boston with two of Canonicus sons and another sachem and near twenty sanaps. Cutshamakin gave us notice the day before. The governour sent twenty musketeers to meet him at Roxbury. He came to Boston about noon. The governour had called together most of the magistrates and ministers to give countenance to our proceedings and to advise with them about the terms of peace. It was dinner time and the sachems and their council dined by themselves in the same room where the governour dined, and their sanaps were sent to the inn. After dinner Miantunnomo declared what he had to say to us in propositions which were to this effect: That they had always loved the English and desired firm peace with us; that they would continue in war with the Pequods and their confederates, till they were subdued; and desired we should do so: They would deliver our enemies to us or kill them. That if any of theirs should kill our cattle, that we would not kill them, but cause them to make satisfaction: That they would now make a firm peace and two months hence they would send us a present. The governour told them they should have answer the next morning.

In the morning we met again and concluded the peace upon the articles underwritten, which the governour subscribed and they also subscribed with their marks and Cutshamakin also. But because we could not well make them understand the articles perfectly we agreed to send a copy of them to Mr. Williams who could best interpret them to them. So after dinner they took leave and were conveyed out of town by some musketeers and dismissed with a volley of shot. The magistrates of Massachusetts solicited his mediation with the Narragansetts, and he immediately accepted the hazardous commission, and succeeded in defeating the endeavors of the Pequods to win over the Narragansetts to a coalition.

THE ARTICLES.

1. A firm peace between us and our friends of other plantations, (if they consent) and their confederates, (if they will observe the articles &c.) and our posterities.
2. Neither party to make peace with the Pequods without the other's consent.
3. Not to harbor, &c., the Pequods, &c.
4. To put to death or deliver over murderers, &c.
5. To return our fugitive servants, &c.
6. We to give them notice when we go against the Pequods and they to send us some guides.
7. Free trade between us.
8. None of them to come near our plantations during the wars with the Pequods, without some Englishman or known Indian.
9. To continue to the posterity of both parties.

The Pequods, chagrined at their lack of success in turning the Narragansett against their white friends, prophesied to them that they would yet find the English to be treacherous and not their friends. Not long after, a circumstance occurred which at first seemed to give a color to this opinion. Four young men of the Bay, from the serving class, left the settlement with the intent of going to the Dutch plantation at Manhattoes. Midway between the Boston and the Narragansett country, they sat down to rest and to smoke. While thus engaged, a Narragansett Indian passed by, whom they called and invited to stop and smoke with them. The Indian incautiously accepted the invitation. The party of whites, seeing that their visitor, who was a trader, had with him a large quantity of wampum, besides cloth and beads, murderously attacked him and, after robbing him, left him for dead. The Indian, who was mortally wounded, revived sufficiently to drag himself home, where he died of his hurts. His friends lying in wait for the murderers captured three of them and delivered them to the authorities at Aquineck, where they were formally accused of robbery and murder.

The governor of Plymouth wrote to the deputy, that we had occasioned a war, etc., by provoking the Pequods, and no more, and about the peace with the Naragansetts, etc. The deputy took it ill, (as there was reason,) and returned answer accordingly, and made it appear: 1. That there was as much done as could be expected, considering they fled from us, and we could not follow them in our armour, neither had any to guide us in their country. 2. We went not to make war upon them, but to do justice, etc., and having killed thirteen of them for four or five, which they had murdered of ours, and destroyed sixty wigwams, etc., we were not much behind with them. 3. They had no cause to glory over us, when they saw that they could not save themselves nor their houses and corn from so few of ours. 4. If we had left but one hundred of them living, those might have done us as much hurt as they have or are likely to do. 5. It was very likely they would have taken notice of our advantage against them, and would have sitten still, or have sought peace, if God had not deprived them of common reason.

About the middle of this month, John Tilley, master of a bark, coming down Connecticut River, went on shore in a canoe, three miles above the fort, to kill fowl; and having shot off his piece, many Indians arose out of the covert and took him, and killed one other, who was in the canoe. This Tilley was a very stout man, and of great understanding. They cut off his hands, and sent them before, and after cut off his feet. He lived three days after his hands were cut off; and themselves confessed, that he was a stout man, because he cried not in his torture.

William Bradford, Plimouth Plantation

The Indians sent for Mr. Williams & made a grievous complaint; his friends and kindred were ready to rise in arms and provoke the rest thereunto, some conceiving they should now find ye Pequents words true: that ye English would fall upon them. But Mr. Williams pacified them, & told them they should see justice done upon ye offenders; & went to ye man & took Mr. James a physician with him. The man told him who did it and in what manner it was done; but ye physician found his wounds mortal, and that he could not live, (as he after testified upon oath, before ye jury in open court) and so he died shortly after, as both Mr. Williams, Mr. James & some Indians testified in court. The Govrt in ye Bay were acquainted with it, but referred it hither, because it was done in this jurisdiction; but pressed by all means yet justice might be done in it, or else ye country must rise and see justice done, otherwise it would raise a war. Yet some of ye rude & ignorant sort murmured that any English should be put to death for ye Indians. So at last they of ye island brought them hither, and being often examined, and ye evidence produced, they all in the end freely confessed in effect all yet the Indian accused them of, & that they had done it in ye manner aforesaid; and so, upon ye aforementioned evidence, were, cast by ye jury, & condemned, & executed for the same. And some of ye Narragansett Indians & of ye parties friends, were present when it was done, which gave them & all ye country good satisfaction.

To his much honored friend John Winthrop Esquire his house at Boston, from Thomas Hooker

Much Honored In Our Blessed Savior, — When I first heard of those heavy distractions which have risen so unexpectedly, I did rejoice from the root of my heart, that the Lord did, & hath graciously kept you from any taint of those new-coined conceits. The Lord strengthen & establish you in every holy word & work. In a good cause He hath given you gracious abilities to do Him much service, & I am persuaded He will bless you in such endeavors. You know my plainness: you can not keep your comfort, nor an honorable respect in Christ in the hearts of His, more then in keeping close to the truth. You shall have what interest I have in heaven to help you in that work. How the Pequents have made an inroad, by a sudden surprise, upon some of our brethren of Watertown (Wethersfield) slaying women & children, who were sent out carelessly, without watch & guard, this bearer will tell you.

Though we feel neither the time nor our strength fit for such a service, yet the Indians here, our friends, were so importunate with us to make war presently, that unless we had attempted some thing, we had delivered our persons unto contempt of base fear & cowardice, & caused them to turn enemies against us. Against our minds, being constrained by necessity, we have sent out a company, taking some Indians for guides with us. What is done, you will better hear it by report, and then I shall relate it by pen, for our men went down as these pinnaces came to us. Only we hear there is six of the Pequot slain by our Indians, not far from the fort. I hope you see a necessity to hasten execution, & not to do this work of the Lords revenge slackly. I shall commend the cause to your love & wisdom, & yourself to the rich mercy of our God in Christ, & in all thankfulness for all your love.

Capt. John Underhill, News From America
The cause of our war against the Block Islanders, was for taking away the life of one Master John Oldham, who made it his common course to trade amongst the Indians. He coming to Block Island to drive trade with them, the islanders came into his boat, and having got a full view of commodities which gave them good content, consulted how they might destroy him and his company, to the end they might clothe their bloody flesh with his lawful garments. The Indians having laid the plot, into the boat they came to trade, as they pretended; watching their opportunities, knocked him in the head, and martyred him most barbarously, to the great grief of his poor distressed

servants, which by the providence of God were saved. This island lying in the road way to Lord Say and the Lord Brooke's plantation, a certain seaman called to John Gallop, master of the small navigation standing along to the Mathethusis Bay, and seeing a boat under sail close aboard the island, and perceiving the sails to be unskillfully managed, bred in him a jealousy, whether that the island Indians had not bloodily taken the life of our countrymen, and made themselves master of their goods. Suspecting this, he bore up to them, and approaching near them was confirmed that his jealousy was just. Seeing Indians in the boat, and knowing her to be the vessel of Master Oldham, and not seeing him there, gave fire upon them and slew some; others leaped overboard, besides two of the number which he preserved alive and brought to the Bay. The blood of the innocent called for vengeance. God stirred up the heart of the honored Governor, Master Henry Vane, and the rest of the worthy Magistrates, to send forth a hundred well appointed soldiers, under the conduct of Captain John Endicott, and in company with him that had command, Captain John Underhill, Captain Nathan Turner, Captain William Jenningson, besides other inferior officers. I would not have the world wonder at the great number of commanders to so few men, but know that the Indians' fight far differs from the Christian practice; for they most commonly divide themselves into small bodies, so that we are forced to neglect our usual way, and to subdivide our divisions to answer theirs, and not thinking it any disparagement to any captain to go forth against an enemy with a squadron of men, taking the ground from the old and ancient practice, when they chose captains of hundreds and captains of thousands, captains of fifties and captains of tens. We conceive a captain signifieth the chief in way of command of any body committed to his charge for the time being, whether of more or less, it makes no matter in power, though in honor it does. Coming to an anchor before the island, we espied an Indian walking by the shore in a desolate manner, as though he had received intelligence of our coming. Which Indian gave just ground to some to conclude that the body of the people had deserted the island. But some knowing them for the generality to be a warlike nation, a people that spend most of their time in the study of warlike policy, were not persuaded that they would upon so slender terms forsake the island, but rather suspected they might lie behind a bank, much like the form of a barricade Myself with others rode with a shallop, made towards the shore, having in the boat a dozen armed soldiers. Drawing near to the place of landing, the number that rose from behind the barricade were between fifty or sixty able fighting men, men as straight as

82

arrows, very tall, and of active bodies, having their arrows notched. They drew near to the water side, and let fly at the soldiers, as though they had meant to have made an end of us all in a moment. They shot a young gentleman in the neck through a collar, for stiffness as if it had been an oaken board, and entered his flesh a good depth. Myself received an arrow through my coat sleeve, a second against my helmet on the forehead; so as if God in his providence had not moved the heart of my wife to persuade me to carry it along with me, (which I was unwilling to do), I had been slain. Give me leave to observe two things from hence; first, when the hour of death is not yet come, you see God useth weak means to keep his purpose unviolated; secondly, let no man despise advice and counsel of his wife, though she be a woman. It were strange to nature to think a man should be bound to fulfill the humor of a woman, what arms he should carry; but you see God will have it so, that a woman should overcome a man. What with Delilah's flattery, and with her mournful tears, they must and will have their desire, when the hand of God goes along in the matter; and this is to accomplish his own will. Therefore let the clamor be quenched I daily hear in my ears, that New England men usurp over their wives, and keep them in servile subjection. The country is wronged in this matter, as in many things else. Let this precedent satisfy the doubtful, for that comes from the example of a rude soldier. If they be so courteous to their wives, as to take their advice in warlike matters, how much more kind is the tender, affectionate husband to honor his wife as the weaker vessel? Yet mistake not. I say not that they are bound to call their wives in council, though they are bound to take their private advice (so far as they see it make for their advantage and their good); instance Abraham. But to the matter; The arrows flying thick about us, we made haste to the shore; but the surf of the sea being great, hindered us, so as we could scarce discharge a musket, but were forced to make haste to land. Drawing near the shore through the strength of wind, and the hollowness of the sea, we durst not adventure to run ashore, but were forced to wade up to the middle; but once having got up off our legs, we gave fire upon them. They finding our bullets to outreach their arrows, they fled before us. In the meanwhile Colonel Endecott made to the shore, and some of this number also repulsed him at his landing, but hurt none. We thought they would stand it out with us, but they perceiving we were in earnest, fled; and left their wigwams, or houses, and provision to the use of our soldiers. Having set forth our sentinels, and laid out our pardues, we betook ourselves to the guard, expecting hourly they would fall upon us; but they observed the old rule, 'Tis good sleeping in a whole skin, and left us free from an alarm.

The next day we set upon our march, the Indians being retired into swamps, so as we could not find them. We burnt and spoiled both houses and corn in great abundance; but they kept themselves in obscurity. Captain Turner stepping aside to a swamp, met with some few Indians, and charged upon them, changing some few bullets for arrows. Himself received a shot upon the breast of his corselet, as if it had been pushed with a pike, and if he had not had it on, he had lost his life.

A pretty passage worthy of observation, We had an Indian with us that was an interpreter; being in English clothes, and a gun in his hand, was spied by the islanders, which called out to him, what are you, an Indian or an Englishman? Come hither, saith he, and I will tell you. He pulls up his kock and let fly at one of them, and without question was the death of him. Having spent that day in burning and spoiling the island, we took up the quarter for that night. About midnight myself went out with ten men about two miles from our quarter, and discovered the most eminent plantation they had in the island, where was much corn, many wigwams, and great heaps of mats; but fearing less we should make an alarm by setting fire on them, we left them as we found them, and peaceably departed to our quarter; and the next morning with forty men marched up to the same plantation, burnt their houses, cut down their corn, destroyed some of their dogs instead of men, which they left in their wigwams.

Passing on toward the water side to embark our soldiers, we met with several famous wigwams, with great heaps of pleasant corn ready shelled; but not able to bring it away, we did throw their mats upon it, and set fire and burnt it. Many well-wrought mats our soldiers brought from thence, and several delightful baskets. We being divided into two parts, the rest of the body met with no less, I suppose, than ourselves did. The Indians playing least in sight, we spent our time, and could no more advantage ourselves than we had already done, and having slain some fourteen, and maimed others, we embarked ourselves, and set sail for Seabrook fort, where we lay through distress of weather four days; then we departed..

The Pequits having slain one Captain Norton, and Captain Stone, with seven more of their company, order was given us to visit them, sailing along the Nahanticot shore with five vessels. The Indians spying of us came running in multitudes along the water side, crying, "What cheer, Englishmen, what cheer, what do you come for?" They not thinking we intended war, went on cheerfully until they come to Pequit River. We thinking it the best way, did forbear to answer them; first, that we might the better be able to run through the work; secondly, that by delaying of them, we might drive them in security, to the end we might have the more advantage of them. But they seeing we would make no answer, kept on their course, and cried, "What, Englishmen, what cheer, what cheer, are you hoggery, will you cram us?" "That is, are you angry, will you kill us, and do you come to fight?" That night the Nahanticot Indians, and the Pequents, made fire on both sides of the river, fearing we would land in the night. They made most doleful and woeful cries all the night, (so that we could scarce rest) hallooing one to another, and giving the word from place to place, to gather their forces together, fearing the English were come to war against them.

The next morning they sent early aboard an ambassador, a grave senior, a man of good understanding, portly carriage, grave, and majestical in his expressions. He demanded of us what the end of our coming was. To which we answered, that the governors of the Bay sent us to demand the heads of those persons that had slain Captain Norton and Captain Stone, and the rest of their company, and that it was not the custom of the English to suffer murderers to live; and therefore, if they desired their own peace and welfare, they will peaceably answer our expectation, and give us the heads of the murderers.

They being a witty and ingenious nation, their ambassador labored to excuse the matter, and answered, we know not that any of ours have slain any English. True it is, saith he, we have slain such a number of men; but consider the ground of it. Not long before the coming of these English into the river, there was a certain vessel that came to us in way of trade. We used them well, and traded with them, and took them to be such as would not wrong us in the least matter. But our sachem or prince coming aboard, they laid a plot how they might destroy him; which plot discovereth itself by the event, as followeth. They keeping their boat aboard, and not desirous of our company, gave us leave to stand hallooing ashore, that they might work their mischievous plot. But as we stood they called to us, and demanded of us a bushel of wampampeke, which is their money. This they demanded for his ransom. This peal did ring terribly in our ears, to demand so much for the life of our prince, whom we thought was in the hands of honest men, and we had never wronged them. But we saw there was no remedy; their expectation must be granted, or else they would not send him ashore, which they promised they would do, if we would answer their desires. We sent them so much aboard, according to demand, and they, according to their promise, sent him ashore, but first slew him. This much exasperated our spirits, and made us vow a revenge. Suddenly after came these captains with a vessel into the river, and pretended to trade with us, as the former did. We did not discountenance them for the present, but took our opportunity and came aboard. The sachem's son succeeding his father, was the man that came into the cabin of Captain Stone, and Captain Stone having drunk more than did him good, fell backwards on the bed asleep. The sagamore took his opportunity, and having a little hatchet under his garment, therewith knocked him in the head. Some being upon the deck and others under, suspected some such thing; for the rest of the Indians that were aboard had order to proceed against the rest at one time; but the English spying treachery, run immediately into the cook-room, and, with a fire-brand, had thought to have blown up the Indians by setting fire to the powder. These devil's instruments spying this plot of the English, leaped overboard as the powder was a firing, and saved themselves; but all the English were blown up. This was the manner of their bloody action. Saith the ambassador to us, Could ye blame us for revenging so cruel a murder? for we distinguish not between the Dutch and English, but took them to be one nation, and therefore we do not conceive that we wronged you, for they slew our king; and thinking these captains to be of the same nation and people as those that slew him, made us set upon this course of revenge.

Our answer was, they were able to distinguish between Dutch and English, having had sufficient experience of both nations; and therefore, seeing you have slain the king of England's subjects, we come to demand an account of their blood, for we ourselves are liable to account for them. The answer of the ambassador was, we know no difference between the Dutch and the English; they are both strangers to us, we took them to be all one; therefore we crave pardon; we have not willfully wronged the English.—this excuse will not serve our turns, for we have sufficient testimony that you know the English from the Dutch. We must have the heads of those persons that have slain ours, or else we will fight with you. He answered, Understanding the ground of your coming, I will entreat you to give me liberty to go ashore, and I shall inform the body of the people what your intent and resolution is; and if you will stay aboard, I will bring you a sudden answer.

We did grant him liberty to get ashore, and our selves followed suddenly after before the war was proclaimed. He seeing us land our forces, came with a message to entreat us to come no nearer, but stand in a valley, which- had between us and them an ascent, that took our sight from them; but they might see us to hurt us, to our prejudice. Thus from the first beginning to the end of the action, they carried themselves very subtlety; but we, not willing to be at their direction, marched up to the ascent, having set our men in battalion. He came and told us he had inquired for the sachem, that we might come to a parley; but neither of both of the princes were at home; they were gone to Long Island.

Our reply was, we must not be put off thus, we know the sachem is in the plantation, and therefore bring him to us, that we may speak with him, or else we will beat up the drum, and march through the country, and spoil your corn. His answer, if you will but stay a little while, I will step to the plantation and seek for them. We gave them leave to take their own course, and used as much patience as ever men might, considering the gross abuse they offered us, holding us above an hour in vain hopes. They sent an Indian to tell us that Mommenoteck was found, and would appear before us suddenly. This brought us to a new stand the space of an hour more. There came a third Indian persuading us to have a little further patience, and he would not tarry, for he had assembled the body of the Pequents together, to know who the parties were that had slain these Englishmen. But seeing that they did in this interim convey away their wives and children, and bury their chiefest goods, we perceived at length they would fly from us; but we were patient and bore with them, in expectation to have the greater blow upon them. The last messenger brought us this intelligence from the sachem, that if we would but lay down our arms, and approach about thirty paces from them, and meet the heathen prince, he would cause his men to do the like, and then we shall come to a parley.

But we seeing their drift was to get our arms, we rather chose to beat up the drum and bid them battle. Marching into a champaign field we displayed our colors; but none would come near us, but standing remotely off did laugh at us for our patience. We suddenly set upon our march, and gave fire to as many as we could come near, firing their wigwams, spoiling their corn, and many other necessaries that they had buried in the ground we raked up, which the soldiers had for booty. Thus we spent the day burning and spoiling the country. Towards night embarked ourselves. The next morning, landing on the Nahanticot shore, where we were served in like nature, no Indians would come near us, but run from us, as the deer from the dogs. But having burnt and spoiled' what we could light on, we embarked our men, and set sail for the Bay. Having ended this exploit, came off, having one man wounded in the leg; but certain numbers of their slain, and many wounded. This was the substance of the first year's service. Now follow-eth the service performed in the second year.

This insolent nation, seeing we had used much lenity towards them, and themselves not able to make good use of our patience, set upon a course of greater insolence than before, and slew all they found in their way. They came near Seabrook fort, and made many proud challenges, and dared them out to fight.

The lieutenant went out with ten armed men, and starting three Indians they changed some few shot for arrows. Pursuing them, a hundred more started out of the ambushments, and almost surrounded him and his company; and some they slew, others they maimed, and forced them to retreat to their fort, so that it was a special providence of God that they were not all slain. Some of their arms they got from them, others put on the English clothes, and came to the fort jeering of them, and calling, Come and fetch your Englishmen's clothes again; come out and fight, if you dare; you dare not fight; you are all one like women. We have one amongst us that if he could kill but one of you more, he would be equal with God, and as the Englishman's God is, so would he be. This blasphemous speech troubled the hearts of the soldiers, but they knew not how to remedy it, in respect of their weakness.

The Conectecott plantation, understanding the insolence of the enemy to be so great, sent down a certain number of soldiers under the conduct of Captain John Mason, for to strengthen the fort. The enemy lying hovering about the fort, continually took notice of the supplies that were come, and forbore drawing near it as before; and letters were immediately sent to the Bay, to that right worshipful gentleman, Master Henry Vane, for a speedy supply to strengthen the fort. For assuredly without supply suddenly came, in reason all would be lost, and fall into the hands of the enemy. This was the trouble and perplexity that lay upon the spirits of the poor garrison. Upon serious consideration, the governor and council sent forth myself, with twenty armed soldiers, to supply the necessity of those distressed persons, and to take the government of that place for the space of three months. Relief being come, Captain John Mason, with the rest of his company, returned to the plantation again. We sometimes fell out, with a matter of twenty soldiers, to see whether we could discover the enemy or not. They seeing us (lying in ambush) gave us leave to pass by them, considering we were too hot for them to meddle with us. Our men being completely armed, with corselets, muskets, bandoleers, rests, and swords, (as they themselves related afterward), did much daunt them. Thus we spent a matter of six weeks before we could have anything to do with them, persuading ourselves that all things had been well. But they seeing there was no advantage more to be had against the fort, they enterprised a new action, and fell upon Water-towne, now called Wethersfield, with two hundred Indians. Before they came to attempt the place, they put into a certain river, an obscure small river running into the main, where they encamped, and refreshed themselves, and fitted themselves for their service, and by break of day attempted their enterprise, and slew nine men, women, and children. Having finished their action, they suddenly returned again, bringing with them two maids captives, having put poles in their canoes, as we put masts in our boats, and upon them hung our English men's and women's shirts and smocks, instead of sails, and in way of bravado came along in sight of us as we stood upon Saybrook fort. And seeing them pass along in such a triumphant manner, we much fearing they had enterprised some desperate action upon the English, we gave fire with a piece of ordnance, and shot among their canoes. And though they were a mile from us, yet the bullet grazed not above twenty yards over the canoe, where the poor maids were. It was a special providence of God it did not hit them, for then should we have been deprived of the sweet observation of God's providence in their deliverance. We were not able to make out after them, being destitute of means, boats, and the like. Before we proceed any farther to a full relation of the insolent proceeding of this barbarous nation, give me leave to touch upon the several accommodations that belong to this Saybrook fort.

This fort lies upon a river called Conectecott, at the mouth of it, a place of a very good soil, good meadow, diver's sorts of good wood, timber, variety of fish of several kinds, fowl in abundance, geese, ducks, seals, deer, roebuck, squirrels, which are as good as our English rabbits. Pity it is so famous a place should be so little regarded. It lies to the northwest of that famous place called Quinnipiac, which rather exceeds the former in goodness. It hath a fair river, fit for harboring of ships, and abounds with rich and goodly meadows. This lies thirty miles from the upper plantations, which are planted on the river Conectecott. Twelve miles above this plantation is situated a place called Agawam, no way inferior to the forenamed places. This country and those parts do generally yield a fertile soil, and good meadow all the rivers along. The river Conectecott is navigable for pinnaces sixty miles; it hath a strong fresh stream that descends out of the hills. The tide flows not about half way up the river. The strength of the freshet that comes down the river is so strong, that it stoppeth the force of the tide.

I told you before, that when the Pequents heard and saw Seabrook fort was supplied, they forbore to visit us. But the old serpent, according to his first malice, stirred them up against the church of Christ, and in such a furious manner, as our people were so far disturbed and affrighted with their boldness that they scarce durst rest in their beds; threatening persons and cattle to take them, as indeed they did. So insolent were these wicked imps grown, that like the devil, their commander, they run up and down as roaring lions, compassing all corners of the country for a prey, seeking whom they might devour. It being death to them for to rest without some wicked employment or other, they still plotted how they might wickedly attempt some bloody enterprise upon our poor native countrymen.

One Master Tilly, master of a vessel, being brought to an anchor in Conectecott river, went ashore, not suspecting the bloody-mindedness of those persons, who fell upon him and a man with him, whom they wickedly and barbarously slew; and, by relation, brought him home, tied him to a stake, flayed his skin off, put hot embers between the flesh and the skin, cut off his fingers and toes, and made hatbands of them; thus barbarous was their cruelty! Would not this have moved the hearts of men to hazard blood, and life, and all they had, to overcome such a wicked, insolent nation? But letters coming into the Bay, that this attempt was made upon Wethersfield in Conectecott River, and that they had slain nine men, women and children, and taken two maids captives, the council gave order to send supply. In the mean while the Conectecott plantations sent down one hundred armed soldiers, under the conduct of Captain John Mason, and Lieutenant Seely, with other inferior officers, who by commission were bound for to come to rendezvous at Seabrook fort, and there to consult with those that had command there, to enterprise some stratagem upon these bloody Indians. The Conectecott Company having with them threescore Mohiggeners, whom the Pequents had drove out of their lawful possessions, these Indians were earnest to join with the English, or at least to be under their conduct, that they might revenge themselves of those bloody enemies of theirs. The English, perceiving their earnest desire that way, gave them liberty to follow the company, but not to join in confederation with them; the Indians promising to be faithful, and to do them what service lay in their power. But having embarked their men, and coming down the river, there arose great jealousy in the hearts of those that had chief oversight of the company, fearing that the Indians in time of greatest trial might revolt, and turn their backs against those they professed to be their friends, and join with the Pequents. This perplexed the hearts of many very much, because they had had no experience of their fidelity. But Captain Mason having sent down a shallop to Saybrook fort, and sent the Indians over land to meet and rendezvous at Seabrook fort, themselves came down in a great massy vessel, which was slow in coming, and very long detained by cross winds. The Indians coming to Seabrook, were desirous to fall out on the Lord's day, to see whether they could find any Pequents near the fort; persuading themselves that the place was not destitute of some of their enemies. But it being the Lord's Day, order was given to the contrary, and wished them to forbear until the next day. Giving them liberty, they fell out early in the morning, and brought home five Pequents' heads, one prisoner, and mortally wounded the seventh. This mightily enouraged the hearts of all, and we took this as a pledge of their further fidelity. Myself taking boat, rowed up to meet the rest of the forces. Lying aboard the vessel with my boat, the minister, one Master Stone, that was sent to instruct the company, was then in prayer solemnly before God, in the midst of the soldiers; and this passage worthy observation I set down, because the providence of God might be taken notice of, and his name glorified, that is so ready for to honor his own ordinance. The hearts of all in general being much perplexed, fearing the infidelity of these Indians, having not heard what an exploit they had wrought, it pleased God to put into the heart of Master Stone this passage in prayer, while myself lay under the vessel and heard it, himself not knowing that God had sent him a messenger to tell him his prayer was granted. O Lord God, if it be thy blessed will, vouchsafe so much favor to thy poor distressed servants, as to manifest one pledge of thy love, that may confirm us of the fidelity of these Indians towards us, that now pretend friendship and service to us, that our hearts may be encouraged the more in this work of thine. Immediately myself stepping up, told him that God had answered his desire, and that I had brought him this news, that those Indians had brought in five Pequents' heads, one prisoner, and wounded one mortally; which did much encourage the hearts of all, and replenished them exceedingly, and gave them all occasion to rejoice and be thankful to God. A little before we set forth, came a certain ship from the Dutch plantation. Casting an anchor under the command of our ordnance, we desired the master to come ashore. The master and merchant, willing to answer our expectation, came forth, and sitting with us awhile unexpectedly revealed their intent, that they were bound for Pequit River to trade. Ourselves knowing the custom of war, that it was not the practice, in a case of this nature, to suffer others to go and trade with them our enemies, with such commodities as might be prejudicial unto us, and advantageous to them, as kettles, or the like, which make them arrow-heads, we gave command to them not to stir, alleging that our forces were intended daily to fall upon them. This being unkindly taken, it bred some agitations between their several commanders; but God was pleased, out of his love, to carry things in such a sweet, moderate way, as all turned to his glory, and his people's good.

These men, seeing they could not have liberty to go upon their design, gave us a note under their hands, that if we would give them liberty to depart, they would endeavor, to the utmost of their ability, to release those two captive maids, and this should be the chief scope and drift of their design. Having these promises, depending upon their faithfulness, we gave them liberty. They set sail and went to Pequit River, and sent to shore the master of the vessel to Sassacus, their prince, for to crave liberty to trade; and what would they trade for but the English maids? Which he much disliked. Suddenly withdrawing him-self he returned back to the vessel, and by way of policy allured seven Indians into the bark, some of them being their prime men. Having them aboard, acquainted them with their intent, and told them without they might have the two captives delivered safely aboard, they must keep them as prisoners and pledges, and therefore must resolve not to go ashore, until such time they had treated with the sagamore. One of the Dutch called to them on the shore, and told them they must bring the two captive maids, if they would have the seven Indians; and therefore, briefly, if you will bring them, tell us; if not, we set sail, and will turn all your Indians overboard in the main ocean, so soon as ever we come out. They taking this to be a jest, slighted what was said unto them. They weighing anchor set sail, and drew near the mouth of the river. The Pequents then discerned they were in earnest, and earnestly desired them to return and come to an anchor, and they would answer their expectation. So they brought the two maids, and delivered them safely aboard, and they returned to them the seven Indians. Then they set sail and came to Seabrook fort. Bringing them to Seabrook fort, request was made to have them ashore. But in regard of the Dutch governor's desire, who had heard that there was two English maids taken captives of the Pequents, and thinking his own vessel to be there a trading with them, he had managed out a pinnace purposely, to give strict order and command to the former vessel to get these captives, what charge soever they were at, nay, though they did hazard their peace with them, and to gratify him with the first sight of them after their deliverance. So they earnestly entreated us that they might not be brought ashore so as to stay there, or to be sent home until they had followed the governor's order; which willingly was granted to them, though it were thirty leagues from us; yet were they safely returned again, and brought home to their friends. Now for the examination of the two maids after they arrived at Seabrook fort. The eldest of them was about sixteen years of age. Demanding of her how they had used her, she told us that they did solicit her to uncleanness; but her heart being much broken, and afflicted under that bondage she was cast in, had brought to her consideration these thoughts—How shall I commit this great evil and sin against my God? Their hearts were much taken up with the consideration of God's just displeasure to them, that had lived under so prudent means of grace as they did, and had been so ungrateful toward God, and slighted that means, so that God's hand was justly upon them for their remissness in all their ways. Thus was their hearts taken up with these thoughts. The Indians carried them from place to place, and showed them their forts and curious wigwams and houses, and encouraged them to be merry. But the poor souls, as Israel, could not frame themselves to any delight or mirth under so strange a king. They hanging their harps upon the willow trees, gave their minds to sorrow; hope was their chiefest food, and tears their constant drink. Behind the rocks, and under the trees, the eldest spent her breath in supplication to her God; and though the eldest was but young, yet must I confess the sweet affection to God for his great kindness and fatherly love she daily received from the Lord, which sweetened all her sorrows, and gave her constant hope that God would not nor could not forget her poor distressed soul and body; because, saith she, his loving kindness appeareth to me in an unspeakable manner. And though sometimes, saith she, I cried out, David-like, I shall one day perish by the hands of Saul, I shall one day die by the hands of these barbarous Indians; and specially if our people should come forth to war against them.

Then is there no hope of deliverance. Then must I perish. Then will they cut me off in malice. But suddenly the poor soul was ready to quarrel with itself. "Why should I distrust God? Do not I daily see the love of God unspeakably to my poor distressed soul? And he hath said he will never leave me nor forsake me. Therefore I will not fear what man can do unto me, knowing God to be above man, and man can do nothing without God's permission. These were the words that fell from her mouth when she was examined in Seabrook fort. I having command of Seabrook fort, she spake these things upon examination, in my hearing.

Roger Williams to John Winthrop
May, 1637
Sir,-I have nothing certain to acquaint you with at present: there have been reports these ten days, that the Pequots are entered league by the hire of three or four bushels of beads, (black and white) with the Mauquawogs or Mohawks which signifies men-eaters in their language; these cannibals have been all the talk these ten days, and the Narragansetts are much troubled at them.

Two days since came tidings that these Mohawks and Pequots have slain many. Both English and the natives, at Connecticut Plantations. As yet I believe it not, and hope in the Lord's mercy it is false, yet since you please to make such good use of (poison) bad and lying news, (which for that end to awaken people I confess) I sent the last: I would not conceal this: I hope to send better in like manner after this; yet I sadly fear if the Lord please to let loose these mad dogs, their practice will render the Pequots cannibals too, and secondly (at the least) cut off all hopes of safe residence at Connecticut, and yet they are one hundred miles to the westward of Connecticut plantations.

I hope it will please the Most High to put his hook into their nose, as also to give wisdom in the managing of the war, that if it be possible a league may rather be firmly struck with them: they are most savage, their weapons more dangerous and their cruelty dreadful, roasting alive.

For his much honored, Mr. John Winthrop, Deputy Governor these.
Much Honored Sir, - The Pequots hear of your preparations, and comfort themselves in this, that a witch amongst them will link the pinnaces, by diving under water and making holes, &c., as alto that they mall now enrich themselves with store of guns, but I hope their dreams (through the mercy of the Lord) mall vain, and the devil and his lying sorcerers shall be confounded.

You may please, Sir, to take notice that it is of main consequence to take some course with the Wunnamowatuckoogs and Wusquowhananawkits, who are the furthermost

Neponset men, for the Pequots driven from the sea coast with ease, yet there secure and strengthen themselves, and are then brought down so much the nearer to you. Thus with my best respects to your loving self and Mrs. Winthrop, I rest,
Your Worships unfeigned, praying to meet you in this vale of tears or hills of mercy above,
Roger Williams.

John Winthrop, History of New England
1637
February 22.] The lieutenant of Saybrook, at the mouth of Connecticut, going out with nine men, armed with swords and pieces, they startled three Indians, whom they pursued till they were brought into an ambush of fifty, who came upon them, and slew four of their men, and had they not drawn their swords and retired, they had been all slain. The Indians were so hardy, as they came close up to them, not withstanding their pieces.
March 21.] Miantunnomoh sent twenty-six, with forty fathom of wampum and a Pequods hand. We gave four of the chief each a coat of fourteen shillings price, and deferred to return our present till after, according to their manner.
April 1.] Those of Connecticut returned answer to our public letters, wherein they showed themselves unsatisfied about our former expedition against the Pequods, and their expectations of a further prosecution of the war, to which they offer to send men, and signify their unpreparedness to declare themselves in the matter of government, in regard of their engagement to attend the answer of the gentle-men of Say brook about the same matter.
10.] Capt. Underhill was sent to Saybrook, with twenty men, to keep the fort, both in respect of the Indians, and especially of the Dutch, who, by their speeches and supplies out of Holland, gave cause of suspicion that they had some design upon it. The men were sent at the charge of the gentlemen of Saybrook, and lent by order of the council here, for fear any advantage should be taken by the adverse party, through the weakness of the place.

William Bradford, Plimouth Plantation
That which turned out most to their profit, in time, was an entrance into the trade of Wampompeake; for they now bought about fifty lire worth of it of them, and they told them how vendible it was for their fort Orania, (Now

Albany) and did persuade they would find it so in Kennebec; and so it came to pass in time, though at first it stuck, and it was two years before they could put of this small quantity, till ye inland people knew of it; and afterwards they could scarcely get enough for them, and for many years together. And strange it was to see the great alteration it made in a few years among ye Indians themselves; for all the Indians of these parts, and ye Massachusetts, had none or very little of it; but ye sachems and some special persons that wore a little of it for ornaments. Only it was made and kept among ye Narragansetts and Pequents, which grew rich and potent by it, and these people were poor and beggarly, and had no use of it. Neither did the English of this plantation, or any other in ye land till now that they had knowledge of it from ye Dutch, so much as know what it was, much less yet it was a commodity of that worth and value. But after it grew thus to be a commodity in these parts, these Indians fell into it also, and to learn how to make it; for ye Narragansetts do gather ye shells of which they make it from their shores. And it hath now continues a current commodity about this twenty years, and it may prove a drug in time. In ye meantime it makes ye Indians of these parts rich and powerful, and also proud thereby; and fills them with peeces, powder, and shots, which no laws can restrain.

In ye fore parte of this year, the Pequents fell openly upon ye English at Conightecute, in ye lower parts of ye river, and slew sundry of them, (as they were at work in ye fields,) both men & women, to ye great terrour of ye rest; and wente away in great pride & triumph, with many high threats. They allso assaulted a fort at ye rivers mouth, though strong and well defended; and though they did not their prevaile, yet it struk them with much fear and astonishmente to see their bould attempts in the face of danger; which made them in all places to stand upon their gard, and to prepare for resistance, and ernestly to solissite their friends and confederates in ye Bay of Massachusetts to send them speedy aide, for they looked for more forcible assaults. Mr. Vane, being then Govr, write from their Generall Courte to them hear, to joyne with them in this warr; to which they were cordially willing, but tooke opportunitie to write to them aboute some former things, as well as presente, considerable hereaboute. That which will best appear in ye Govr answer which he returned to ye same, which I shall here inserte.

John Winthrop to Roger Williams
1637
Sir: The Lord having so disposed, as that your letters to our late Govr is

fallen to my lott to make answer unto, I could have wished I might have been at more freedome of time & thoughts also, that I might have done it more to your & my owne satisfaction. But what shall be wanting now may be supplyed hereafter. For ye matters which from your selfe & counsell were propounded & objected to us, we thought not fitte to make them so publicke as ye cognizance of our Generall Courte. But as they have been considered by those of our counsell, this answer we thinke fitt to returne unto you. (1.) Whereas you signifie your willingnes to joyne with us in this warr against ye Pequents, though you cannot ingage your selves without the consente of your Generall Courte, we acknowledge your good affection towards us, (which we never had cause to doubt of,) and are willing to attend your full resolution, when it may most seasonably be ripened. Whereas you make this warr to be our peoples, and not to conceirne your selves, otherwise then by consequence, we do in parte consente to you therin; yet we suppose, that, in case of perill, you will not stand upon such terms, as we hope we should not doe towards you; and withall we conceive that you looke at ye Pequents, and all other Indeans, as a comone enimie, who, though he may take occasion of ye begining of his rage, from some one parte of ye English, yet if he prevaile, will surly pursue his advantage, to ye rooting out of ye whole nation. Therefore when we desired your help, we did it not without respecte to your owne saftie, as ours. (2) Whereas you desire we should be ingaged to aide you, upon all like occasions; we are perswaded you doe not doubte of it; yet as we now deale with you as a free people, and at libertie, so as we cannot draw you into this warr with us, otherwise then as reason may guide & provock you; so we desire we may be at ye like freedome, when any occasion may call for help from us. And whereas it is objected to us, that we refused to aide you against ye French; we conceive ye case was not alike; yet we cannot wholy excuse our failing in that matter. (4) Whereas you objecte that we began ye warr without your privitie, & managed it contrary to your advise; the truth is, that our first intentions being only against Block Hand, and ye interprice seeming of small difficultie, we did not so much as consider of taking advice, or looking out for aide abroad. And when we had resolved upon ye Pequents, we sent presently, or not long after, to you aboute it; but ye answer received, it was not seasonable for us to change our counsells, excepte we had seen and waighed your grounds, which might have out wayed our owne.

For our peoples trading at Kenebeck, we assure you (to our knowledge) it hath not been by any allowance from us; and what we have provided in this and like cases, at our last Courte, Mr. E. W. can certifie you.

And Sir; wheras you objecte to us yet we should hold trade & correspondancie with ye French, your enemise; we answer, you are misinformed, for, besids some letters which hath passed betweene our late Govr and them, to which we were privie, we have neither sente nor incouraged ours to trade with them; only one vessell or tow, for ye better conveace of our letters, had licens from our Govr to sayle thither.

Diverce other things have been privatly objected to us, by our worthy freind, wherunto he received some answer; but most of them concerning ye apprehention of perticuler discurteseis, or injueries from some perticuler persons amongst us. It concernes us not to give any other answer to them then this; that, if ye offenders shall be brought forth in a right way, we shall be ready to doe justice as ye case shall require. In the meane time, we desire you to rest assured, that such things are without our privity, and not a litle greeveous unto us.

Now for ye joyning with us in this warr, which indeed concerns us no other wise then it may your selves, viz.: the releeving of our freinds & Christian breethren, who are now first in ye danger; though you may thinke us able to make it good without you, (as, if ye Lord please to be with us, we may,) yet 3 things we offer to your consideration, which (we conceive) may have some waight with you. (First) If we should sinck under this burden, your opportunitie of seasonable help would be lost in 3. respects. 1. You cannot recover us, or secure your selves ther, with 3 times ye charge & hazard which now ye may. 2ly. The sorrowes which we should lye under (if through your neglect) would much abate of ye acceptablenes of your help afterwards. 3rd Those of yours, who are now full of courage and forwardnes, would be much damped, and so less able to undergoe so great a burden. The 2nd thing is this, that it concernes us much to hasten this warr to an end. before ye end of this somer, otherwise ye newes of it will discourage both your & our freinds from coining to us next year; with what further hazard & losse it may expose us unto, your selves may judge. The 3rd thing is this, that if ye Lord shall please to blesse our endeaours, so as we end ye warr, or put it in a hopefull way without you, it may breed such ill thoughts in our people towards yours, as will be hard to entertaine such opinione of your good will towards us, as were fitt to be nurished among such neigbours & brethren as we are. And what ill consequences may follow, on both sids, wise men may fear, & would rather prevente then hope to redress. So with my harty salutations to you selfe, and all your counsell, and other our good freinds with you, I rest, Yours most assured in ye Lord, Jo: Winthrop. Boston, ye 20. of ye 3. month," 1637. May 20th, 1637.

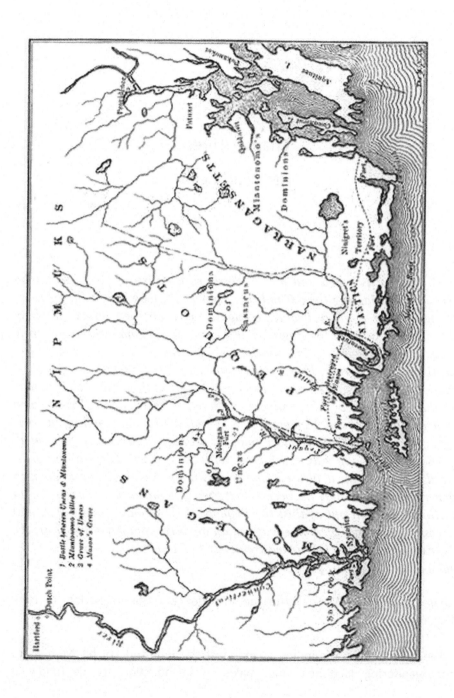

99

Chapter Three

The War Begins

"A Court was called and met in Hartford the First of May, 1637, who seriously considering their Condition, which did look very Sad, for those Pequots were a great People, being strongly fortified, cruel, warlike, munitioned, &c. and the English but an handful in comparison: But their outrageous Violence against the English, having Murdered about Thirty of them, their great Pride and Insolence, constant pursuit in their malicious Courses, with their engaging other Indians in their Quarrel against the English, who had never offered them the least Wrong; who had in all likelihood Espoused all the Indians in the Country in their Quarrel, had not God by more than an ordinary Providence prevented: These Things being duly considered, with the eminent Hazard and great Peril they were in; it pleased God so to stir up the Hearts of all Men in general, and the Court in special, that they concluded some Forces should forthwith be sent out against the Pequots; their Grounds being Just, and necessity enforcing them to engage in an offensive and defensive War; the Management of which War we are nextly to relate."
John Mason

Edward Johnson, Wonder-Working Providence of Sions Savior, in New England
1637
The great Jehovah, minding to manifest the multitude of his Mercies to the wandering Jacobites, and make an introduction to his following

wonders, causeth the darke clouds of calamities to gather about them, presaging some terrible tempest to follow, With eyes full of anguish, they face to the right, upon the damnable Doctrines, as so many dreadfull Engines set by Satan to intrap their poore soules; Then casting forth a left hand looke, the labour and want accompaning a Desert, and terrible Wildernesse affright them. Their memories minding them of their former plenty, it much aggravated the present misery, When with thoughts of retreating, they turne their backs about, the experienced incumbrances and deepe distresses of a dangerous Ocean hinders their thoughts of flight, besides the sterne looke of the Lordly Prelates, which would give them a welcome home in a famishing prison.) Then purposing to put on more stronger resolution, facing to the Front, behold a Messenger with sorrowfull tidings from their fellow brethren, that inhabited the bankes of the River Canectico, who having audience, informes them of the great insolency, and cruell murthers committed by a barbarous and bloudy people called Peaquods, upon the bodies of their indeared friends, these savage Indians lying to the South-west of the Mattacusets, were more warlike then their Neighbouring Nations, the Narrowganzet or Niantick Indians, although they exceeded them in number; also Mawhiggins (who were the best friends of the English, and a chiefe instrumentall meanes of their sitting down there) stood much in feare of these Peaquods, which were big, swollen with pride at this time, facing the English Fort built on the mouth of the River in their large Cannowes, with their Bowes and long Shafts, The English being then but weake in number and provision, were unable to manage the war against so numerous a company, being above thirty to one, yet their desires being beyond their meanes, they made some shot at them, forcing them to hast away faster then they willingly would. These Indians trusting in their great Troopes, having feasted their corps in a ravening manner, and leaving their fragments for their Sqawes, they sound an alarum with a full mouth, and lumbring voyce, and soone gather together without presse or pay, (their quarrell being as antient as Adams time, propagated from that old enmity betweene the Seede of the Woman, and the Seed of the Serpent, who was the grand signor of this war in hand and would very gladly have given them a large Commission, had not his own power been limited, neither could he animate them so much as to take off the gastly looke of that King of terror, yet however at his command they arme themselves: casting their quiver at their backs with Bowes ready bent, they troope up some of them, being extra-ordinarily armed with Guns, which they purchast from the Dutch (who had assuredly paid deare for this their courteous humour, not long since, had not some English Volunteers rescued them from the Indians hands). The most of them were armed also with a small Hatchets on a long handle. They had a small number of Mawhawkes, Hammers, which are made of stone, having a long pike on the one side, and a hole in the handle, which they tie about their wrists, They neede not provisions follow their Camp; because they are continually at home. But for their mats to shelter them from Raine or Snow, the Woods are as welcome to them as their Wigwams, fire they can make in all places by chafing two sticks together. Their food is ready drest at all times, parching Indian Corne in their fire they pound it to meale, and with foure or five spoonfull of it cast into their mouths, and a sup or two of water, which they take up with a leafe of a tree, this is their common repast, and indeed their chiefe viaticum. Thus furnisht for the war they troope away without any goodly equipage, to effect, as they suppose, some great designe, but within some few Miles of the Towne of Hartford, they were discovered by one of the English, who having with him a good Horse, hastens away to give intelligence of their approach, and by the way meeting with foure or five persons, hee advises them to haste away with all speed, for the Peaquods were at hand. The weaker Sex among them, being at this time not so credulous as they should have been, began to dispute the case with him, demanding what Peaquods they were, and questioning how they should come there; The horseman deeming it now no time for words, when the battell followed him so hard at the heeles, rod on his way, and soone after the sudden approach of the Indians forced them with feare to Seale to the truth of this evill tidings, and some of them with their dearest bloud; three Woemenkinde they caught, and carried away, but one of them being more fearfull of their cruell usage afterward then of the losse of her life at present, being borne away to the thickest of the company, resisted so stoutly with scratching and biting, that the Indian, exasperated therewith, cast her downe on the Earth, and beate out her braines with his Hatchet, the other two maids they led away and returned, their Commission reaching no farther at present, having taken these two prisoners they did not offer to abuse their persons, as was verily deemed they would, questioned them with such broken English, as some of them could speak, to know whether they could make Gunpowder. Which when they understood they could not doe, their prize proved nothing so pretious a Pearle in their eyes as before; for seeing they exceeded not their own Squawes in Art, their owne thoughts informed them they would fall abundantly short in industry, and as for beauty they esteeme black beyond any colour. Wherefore their Sqawes use that sinfull art of painting their Faces in the hollow of their Eyes and Nose, with a shining black, out of which their tip of their Nose appeares very deformed, and their cheeke bone, being of a lighter swart black, on which they have a blew crosse dyed very deepe.

This is the beauty esteemed by them, but yet their pride was much increased by this hostile Act of theirs, and the English were more and more condemned of them, notwithstanding the Dutch, who traded with these Indians, procured the Maides liberty againe. The Pequods became more decidedly hostile. They killed several white persons, and made strenuous efforts to induce the powerful Narraganset tribe to forget their mutual animosity, and join with them in a war of extermination against the English. "There had been," says Hutchinson, a fixed, inveterate enmity, between the two tribes; but on this occasion the Pequods were willing to smother it, their enmity against the English being the strongest of the two; and although they had never heard the story of Polypheme and Ulysses, yet they artfully urged, that the English were come to dispossess them of their country, and that all the Narragansets could hope for from their friendship, was the favor of being the last devoured: whereas, if the Indians would unite, they might easily destroy the English.

William Bradford, Plimouth Plantation

In the mean time, the Pequents, espetially in the winter before, sought to make peace with the Narigansets, and used very pernicious arguments to move them thereunto; as that the English were strangers and begane to overspred their countrie, and would deprive them thereof in time, if they were suffered to grow and increase; and if the Narigansets did assist the English to subdue them, they did but make way for their owne overthrow, for if they were rooted out, the English would soon take occasion to subjugate them; and if they would harken to them, they should not neede to fear the strength of the English; for they would not come to open battle with them, but fire their houses, kill their katle, and lye in ambush for them as they went abroad upon their occasions; and all this they might easily doe without any or little danger to them selves. The which course being held, they well saw the English could not long subsiste, but they would either be starved with hunger, or be forced to forsake the countrie; with many the like things; insomuch that the Narigansets were once wavering, and were halfe minded to have made peace with them, and joined against the English. But againe when they considered, how much wrong they received from the Pequents, and what an oppertunitie they now had by the help of the English to right them selves, revenge was so sweete unto them, as it prevailed above all the rest; so as they resolved to joyne with the English against them and did. The Court here agreed forthwith to send fifty men at their own charge; and with as much speed as possiblie they could, got them armed, and had made them ready under suffciente leaders, and provided a barke to carrie them provisions and tend them upon them for all occasions; but when they were ready to march (with a supply from the Bay) they had word to stay, for the enimy was as good as vanquished, and their would be no neede.

I shall not take upon me exactly to describe their proceedings in these things, because I expecte it will be fully done by them selves, who best know the carrage and circumstances of things; I shall therefore but touch them in generall. From Connightecute (who were most sencible of ye hurt sustained, & ye present danger), they sett out a partie of men, and an other partie met them from ye Bay, at ye Narigansets, who were to joyne with them. Ye Narigansets were Ernest to be gone before ye English were well rested and refreshed, espetially some of them which came last. It should seemed their desire was to come upon ye enemie suddenly, & undiscovered.

Ther was a barke of this place, newly put in ther, which was come from Conightecute, who did incouraged them to lie hold of ye Indeans forwardnes, and to shew as great forwardnes as they, for it would incouraged them, and expedition might prove to their great advantage. So they went on, and so ordered their march, as the Indeans brought them to a forte of ye enimies (in which most of their cheefe same with great silence, and surrounded it both with English & Indeans, that they might not breake out; and so assualted them with great courage, shooting amongst them, and entered ye forte with all speed; and those at first entered found sharp resistance from the enimie, who both shott at & grappled with them; others range into their hawses, & brought out fire, and sett them on fire, which soone tooke in their matts, &, standing close togeather, with ye wind, all was quickly on a flame, and thereby more were burnet to death then was otherwise slain; it burnet their bowstrings, & made them unserviceable. Those scaped ye fire were slaine with ye sword; some hewed to peeces, others rune throw with their rapiers, so as they were quickly dispatchte, and very few escaped. It was conceived they thus destroyed about 400 at this time. It was a fearfull sight to see them thus frying in ye fyer, and ye streams of blood quenching ye same, and horrible was ye stinck & sente ther of; but ye victory seemed a sweete sacrifice, and they gave the prays therof to God, who had wrought so wonderfuly for them, thus to inclose their enimise in their hands, and give them so speedy a victory over so proud & insulting an enimie. The Narigansett Indeans, all this while, stood round aboute, but aloofe from all danger, and left ye whole execution to ye English, except it were ye stoping of any yt broke away, insulting over their enimies in this their ruine & miserie, when they saw them dancing in ye flames, calling them by a word in their owne language, signifing, O brave Pequents! Which they used familierly among them selves in their own prayes, in songs of triumph after their victories. After this servis was thus happily accomplished, they marcht to the water side, wher they mett with some of their vesells, by which they had refreishing with victualls & other necessaries. But in their march ye rest of ye Pequents drew into a body, and acoasted them, thinking to have some advantage against them by reason of a neck of land; but when they saw the English prepare for them, they kept a loofe, so as they neither did hurt, nor could receive any. After their refreishing & repair to geather for further counsell & directions, they resolved to pursue their victory, and follow ye warr against ye rest, but ye Narigansett Indeans most of them forsooke them, and such of them as they had with them for guids, or, otherwise, they found them very could and backward in ye bussines, ether out of envie, or yt they saw ye English would make more profite of ye victorie then they were willing they should, or els deprive them of such advantage as them selves desired by having them become tributaries unto them, or ye like.

Increase Mather, Early History of New England
Winter, 1637, Only two Miles up the River two Men going in a Canoo to shoot Geese, the Indians hearing the Report of their Guns, came upon them. Those two English sought to save their Lives by padling, but the Indians pursued them with another Canoo shot at them and wounded one in his Head, who fell overboard, the other shot stoutly at the Indians, but at last being wounded and wearied, the Indians overtook him, he with his Paddle cleft one of the Indians Heads, but the rest took him, and tortured him to Death.

Feb. 22, 1637, The Lieut., with nine Souldiers well armed, went out of the fortFort to burn the Woods thereabouts, being gone Half a Mile from Home they were besett with about seventy Indians, who let fly their Arrows very fiercely; the English retreated, one Man presently was shot in the Neck, and then did they lay Hands on him, he drew his Sword, but that was taken from him; Then would he (as the Indians afterwards testified) have killed himself, with his own Knife, but that also did the Indians deprive him of, and cut off his Nose and Hands, and put him to a cruel Death; they shot down another Englishman with three Arrows, and a third had one of his Ribs cleft with an Arrow, so that he died immediately. A fourth was mortally wounded, and though he got Home alive, he died within fourteen hours, a fifth was sorely wounded, but afterwards recovered, and lived (the next Year) to behead that very Indian who had shot an Arrow into him. Yea, the Leiut. himself was wounded in this Skirmish. After this the Indians kept Leaguer before Saybrook Fort.

March 9, 1637, A Body of Indians, consisting (as was conjectured) of two or three hundred come within Musket shot of the Fort, challenging the English to come out and fight, mocking and upbraiding them with such Words as the English used when by them tortured to Death, and bragged that throughout, and afterwards hung them up by the Neck on a Tree by the River side, that the English might see them as they passed by; the Shallop they drew a Shore and set on Fire.

April 23, 1637, The Indians coming upon the English at Wethersfield, killed nine Persons, and took two young Women alive, and carried them away Captives, Means were used to effect their Deliverance, but at first, in vain.

May 15, 1637, Some of Uncas his Men being then at Saybrook, in order to assisting the English against the Pequots espyed seven Indians, and slyly encompassing them, slew five of them, and took one Prisoner, and brought him to the English Fort, which was great Satisfaction and Encouragement to the English, who before that Exploit had many Fears touching the Fidelity of the Moheag Indians. He whom they took Prisoner was a persideous Villain, one that could speak English well, having in Times past lived in the Fort, and knowing all the English there, had been at the slaughtering of all the English that were slaughtered thereabouts; he was a continual Spy about the Fort, informing Sasacus of what he saw or could learn. When this bloody Traitor was executed, his Limbs were by Violence pulled from one another, and burned. Some of the Indian Executioners barbarously taking his Flesh, they gave it to one another, and did eat it, withal singing about the Fire.

On May 8, a Dutch Sloop came by Saybrook Fort, having on board an Indian Captive, who said she was Momonottocks Squaw. The English there desired the Dutchmen to let them have the Squaw in order to redeeming the English Captives, offering to give them to the Value of two hundred Pound, provided that those Captives might be set at Liberty. The Dutchmen hoping to gain much by such an Indian were some of them loth to part with her. In Conclusion Capt. Underhill (who then commanded the Fort) having obtained the Consent of the Master of the Vessel, did take the Squaw out of the Sloop. Afterwards when the Moheags came to Saybrook that Squaw appeared to be one belonging to them, whom the Pequots had captivated, and (he made the Dutch believe she was Momonottucks Squaw, hoping that thereby she should obtain the more courteous Usage amongst those into whose Hands she was fallen, so that the Contest between the English and Dutch about her was needless. In the Interim the Dutch Governour sent another Sloop, with Order to redeem the English Captives if possible, and those Dutch did in Conclusion wilily accomplish their Design. For being arrived in the Pequot Country, certain Indians coming aboard to trade with them after they had been Trafficking they were clapt under Hatches, and told they should not be set at Liberty, except they would deliver the English Maids that were captivated, and presently hoysted Sayle, as if they would be gone. The Pequots on Shore called to them, declaring that if they would come to an Anchor, the English Captives should be brought to them, which was done, and the Men whom the Dutchmen had secured in their Sloop given in Exchange for the English Captives, who were also brought safe to Saybrook, May 16.

Phillip Vincent, A True Relation of the Late Battell Fought in New England

In February last they killed some English at Seabrook, a southerly plantation beyond Cape Cod, at the mouth of the river of Connecticut. Since that the lieutenant of the fort there, with ten men armed, went out to fire the meadows, and to fit them for mowing. Arriving there, he startled three Indians, which he pursued a little way, thinking to cut them off. But presently they perceived themselves encompassed with hundreds of them, who let fly their arrows furiously, and came desperately upon the muzzles of their muskets, though the English discharged upon them with all the speed they could. Three Englishmen were there slain, others wounded. The eight that remained made their way through the salvages with their swords, and so got under the command of the cannon of the fort, (otherwise they had been all slain or taken prisoners), one of the wounded falling down dead at the fort gate. The Indians thus fleshed and encouraged, besieged the fort as near as they durst approach. The besieged presently dispatched a messenger to the Governor at the Bay, to acquaint him with these sad tidings, who with all speed lent unto their aid Captain Underhill, with twenty soldiers. Not long after these salvages went to Water Towne, now called Wethersfield, and there fell upon some that were sawing, and slew nine more, whereof one was a woman, the other a child, and took two young maids prisoners, killing some of their cattle, and driving some away. Man's nature insulteth in victory and prosperity, and by good success is animated even in the worst of wicked actions. These barbarians triumphed and proceeded, drawing into their confederacy other Indians, as the Niantecut, and part of the Mohigans, of whom about fifty chose rather to join with the English, and sat down at New-Towne, at Connecticut (now called Hereford, as the other town that went from Dorchester thither is called Windsor). Fame increaseth by flying. The former sad news was augmented by the report of sixty men slain at Master Pincheon's plantation, and which proved false. The Narragansetts, neighbors to the Pequits, sent word to the English, that the Pequits had solicited them to join their forces with them. Hereupon the Council ordered that none should go to work, nor travel, no, not so much as to church, without arms. A corps of guard of fourteen or fifteen soldiers was appointed to watch every night, and sentinels were set in convenient places about the plantations, the drum beating when they went to the watch, and every man commanded to be in readiness upon an alarm, upon pain of five pound. A day of fast and prayers was also kept. Forty more were sent to strengthen the former twenty that went to the fort, and fifty under the command of Captain Mason, which being conjoined were about one hundred. Two hundred more were to be sent after them with all expedition.

The fifty Mohigans that joined with the English, scouting about, espied seven Pequits, killed five of them outright, wounded the sixth mortally, took the seventh prisoner, and brought him to the fort. He braved the English, as though they durst not kill a Pequit. Some will have their courage to be thought invincible, when all is desperate. But it availed this salvage nothing. They tied one of his legs to a post, and twenty men, with a rope tied to the other, pulled him in pieces, Captain Underhill shooting a pistol through him, to dispatch him. The two maids which were taken prisoners were redeemed by the Dutch. Those fifty sent from the three plantations of Connecticut with Captain Mason, being joined with Captain Underhill and his twenty men, (for the other forty were not yet arrived with them), immediately went upon an expedition against the Pequits, after they had searched for them. The manner was this. The English with some Mohigans went to the Naragansetts, who were discontented that they came no sooner, saying they could arm and set forth two or three hundred at six hours warning, (which they did accordingly, for the assistance of the English); only they desired the advice of the sagamore, Mydutonno, what way they should go to work, and how they should fall on the Pequits; whose judgment in all things agreed with the English, as though they had consulted together. Then went they to the Nayanticke, and he set forth two hundred more; but before they went, he swore them after his manner upon their knees. As they marched, they deliberated which fort of the Pequits they should assault, resolving upon the great fort, and to be there that night. Being on the way, and having a mile to march through swamps, the Nayanticke hearts failed, for fear of the Pequits, and so they ran away, as also did some of the Narragansetts. Of five or six hundred Indians, not above half were left; and they had followed the rest, had not Captain Underhill upbraided

them with cowardice, and promised them they should not fight or come within shot of the fort, but only surround it afar off. At break of day, the seventy English gave the fort a volley of shot, whereat the salvages within made a hideous and pitiful cry; the shot, without all question, flying through the palisadoes (which stood not very close) and killing or wounding some of them. Pity had hindered further hostile proceedings, had not the remembrance of the bloodshed, the captive maids, and cruel insolency of those Pequits, hardened the hearts of the English, and stopped their ears unto their cries. Mercy mars all sometimes; severe justice must now and then take place.

John Winthrop. History of New England
1637
May
2.] Mr. Haynes, one of our Magistrates, removed with his family to Connecticut.
12] We received a letter from him and others, being then at Saybrook, that the Pequots had been up river at Wethersfield, and had killed six men, being at their work, and twenty cows and a mare, and killed three   women, and carried away two maids.
   Mr. Winslow was sent from the governor and council of Plymouth to treat with us about joining against the Pequods. He declared first their willingness to aid is; but that they could not do anything till their general court, which was not till the first Tuesday in the fourth month. Then he made some objections: as, 1. our refusal to aid them against the French. 2. Our people's trading at Kennebec. 3. The Injury offered them at Connecticut by those of Windsor, in taking away their land there. 4. Their poverty, and our ability, which needed not any help from them.

To this answer was made by our governor and deputy: that, 1. We did not desire them to afford aid unto us, but to join against the common enemy, who, if he were not subdued, would prove as dangerous to them as to us, and, he prevailing, would cause all the Indians in the country to join to root out all the English. 2. For our refusal to aid them against the French, the case was not alike, for it was their private quarrel, and they were supposed to have commission from the King of France, and we though it no wisdom for us to engage ourselves in a war with the King of France; yet we acknowledged some failing in it. For our people trading at Kennebec, we answered, that we gave no allowance to it, nor had we heard of more than a boat or two that had been there. For the injury done them in Connecticut, we had dealt with them to give satisfaction, but it was not in our power to do them justice in it. He alleged also, that this war did not concern them, seeing the Pequods had not killed any of theirs. We answered, that Capt. Stone, etc., for whom this war was begun, were none of ours neither. He alleged further, that, in our first under-taking, they were not acquainted with it till two or three days before our forces were to go forth. We answered, we intended at the first to send only to Block Island, and for that we thought it not needful to trouble them, and our sending them thence to the Pequods was with hope to draw them to parley, and so to some quiet end. We concluded to write further to them from our next court. And whereas they propounded to have us promise to aid them in all their occasions, etc., we answered that, seeing, when we now treated with them about joining with us, they were at liberty and might withhold, except they saw reason to move them; so we desired to be left free, that we might judge of the reason of any such occasion as might fall out. According hereunto we writ to them on the 20th of May, 1673, and gave them some considerations, why they should join with us: as, 1. Because, if we should be overcome, it would cost them more to help us, and be less acceptable; 2. If we should prevail without them, it would occasion ill thoughts in our people towards theirs, etc. So we left it to them. Having received intelligence from Miantunnomoh, that the Pequods had sent their women and children to an island for their safety, we presently sent away forty men by land to the Narragansetts, and there to take in Miantunnomoh, (and he offered to send sixteen men with ours,) and so, in the night, to set upon them.

We also provided to send one hundred and sixty more after them to prosecute the war; and Mr. Stoughton, one of the magistrates, was sent with them, and Mr. Wilson, the pastor of Boston. These two were chosen thus in the open court.

Miantunnomoh sent us word, that Capt. Mason , with a company of the English upon the river, had surprised and slain eight Pequods, and taken seven squaws, and with some of them had redeemed the two English maids. 24.] By letters from Mr. Williams we were certified, (which the next day was confirmed by some who came from Saybrook,) that Capt. Mason was come to Saybrook with eighty English and one hundred Indians; and that the Indians had gone out there, and met with seven Pequods; five they killed; one they took alive, whom the English put to torture; and set all their heads upon their fort. The reason was, because they had tortured such of our men as they took alive.

The Dutch governor sent a sloop to Pequod to redeem the two English maids by what means soever, though it were with breach of their peace with the Pequods. The sloop offered largely for their ransom; but nothing would be accepted. So the Dutch, having many Pequods aboard, stayed six of them, (the rest leaped overboard,) and with them redeemed the two maids, who had been well used by the Pequods, and no violence offered them.

The Massachusetts and Plymouth colonies agreed to aid Connecticut and on April 18th, 1637, in a special session of the General Court and ordered a levy of one hundred and sixty men and granted six hundred dollars in all.

The First Day of May, 1637, Generall Corte at Harteford.
Mr. Ludlowe, Mr. Wells, Mr. Swaine, Mr. Steele, Mr. Phelps, Mr. Warde. *Committees.—* Mr. Whytinge, Mr. Webster, Mr. Williams, Mr. Hull, Mr. Chaplin, Mr. Talcott, Mr. Hosford, Mr. Mychell, Mr. Sherman.

It is ordered that there shall be an offensive war against the Pequoitt, and that there shall be ninety men levied out of the three Plantations, Harteford, Wethersfield and Windsor out of Hartford forty, Windsor thirty, Wethersfield eighteen: under the Command of Captain John Mason and in case of death or sickness under the Command of Robert Seely and the eldest Sergeant or military officer surviving, if both these miscarry.

On May 10, 1637 the Connecticut army of ninety whites and seventy Indians began their expedition down river landing at Fort Saybrook the next morning. Captain John Underhill with fourteen soldiers joined Captain Mason's army. Twenty men were sent back to guard the river settlements and the vessels. Every soldier received six dollars per day, six days a week, sergeants twenty dollars per day, lieutenants, twenty shillings per week; the

Captains forty shillings per week. Below is a list of soldiers from the towns of Hartford, Windsor, and Wethersfield;
From Hartford; Thomas Bull, Wm. Blumfield, John Brunson, Thomas Bunce, Thomas Barnes, Peter Blanceford, Benjamin Burr, John Clarke, Nicholas Clarke, Sergt. Philip Davis, Nicholas Desborough, Thomas Hales, Samuel Hales, William Haydn, John Hills, John Hallaway, Thomas Hollybut (Hurlburt), Jona. Ince, Benjamin Munn, Nicholas Jennings, Nicholas Olmstead, Richard Olmstead, John Purkas, William Pratt, William Phillips, Thomas Root, Thomas Spencer, Arthur Smith, Thomas Stanton, Rev. Samuel Stone, George Steele, Samuel Whitehead, John Warner, Stephen Hart, Zachary Field, William Cornwell, Thomas Munson.

From Windsor: Serj. Benedict Alvord, Thomas Buckland, Thomas Barber, John Dyer, **Richard Osborn**, Thomas Styles, Serj. Stares, Thomas Parsons, Thomas Gridley, William Trall, Nathan Gillett, James Egleston, George Chappell, Capt. John Mason. From Wethersfield: John Johnson, Jeremy Jagger, Lieut. Robert Seeley, Richard Westcoat, ____Merriman, Thomas Standish, Thomas Tibbals, Henry Smith, John Nott.

From Saybrook: Capt. John Underhill, Edward Pattison, James Rogers, Edward Lay, John Gallop, John Woods.

John Mason, An Epitome or Brief History of the Pequot War
    In the Beginning of May 1637 there were sent out by Connecticut Colony Ninety Men under the Command of Capt. John Mason against the Pequots, with Onkos an Indian Sachem living at Mohegan, who was newly revolted from the Pequots; being Shipped in one Pink, one Pinnace, and one Shallop; who sailing down the River of Connecticut fell several times a ground, the Water being very low: The Indians not being wonted to such Things with their small Canoes, and also being impatient of Delays, desired they might be set on Shore, promising that they would meet us at Saybrook; which we granted: They hastening to their Quarters, fell upon Thirty or forty of the Enemy near Saybrook Fort, and killed seven of them outright ;if having only one of theirs wounded, who was sent back to Connecticut in a Skiff: Capt. John Underhill also coming with him, who informed us what was performed by Onkos and his Men; which we looked at as a special Providence; for before we were somewhat doubtful of his Fidelity: Capt. Underhill then offered his Service with nineteen Men to go with us, if Lieutenant Gardner would allow of it, who was Chief Commander at Saybrook Fort; which was readily approved of by Lieutenant Gardner and accepted by us; In lieu of them we sent back twenty of our Soldiers to Connecticut.

Upon a Wednesday we arrived at Saybrook, where we lay wind bound until Friday; often consulting how and in what manner we should proceed in our enterprise, being altogether ignorant of the Country. At length we concluded, God assisting us, for Narragansett, and so to March through their Country, which Bordered upon the Enemy; where lived a great People, it being about fifteen Leagues beyond Pequot; The Grounds and Reasons of our so acting you shall presently understand:

First, The Pequots our Enemies, kept a continual Guard upon the River Night and Day.

Secondly, their Numbers far exceeded ours; having sixteen Guns with Powder and Shot, as we were informed by the two Captives aforementioned (where we declared the Grounds of this War) who were taken by the Dutch and restored to us at Saybrook; which indeed was a very friendly Office and not to be forgotten.

Thirdly, They were on Land, and being swift on Foot, might much impede our Landing, and possibly dishearten our Men; we being expected only by Land, 'there being no other Place to go on Shore but in that River, nearer than Narragansett.

Fourthly, By Narragansett we should come upon their Backs, and possibly might surprise them unawares, at worst we should be on firm Land as well as they. All which proved very successful as the Sequel may evidently demonstrate.

But yet for all this our Counsel, all of them except the Captain, were at a stand, and could not judge it meet to sail to Narragansett: And indeed there was a very strong Ground for it; our Commission limiting us to land our Men in Pequot River; we had also the same Order by a Letter of Instruction sent us to Saybrook.

But Capt. Mason apprehending an exceeding great Hazard in so doing, for the Reasons aforementioned, as also some other which I shall forbear to trouble you with, did therefore earnestly desire Mr. Stone that he would commend our Condition to the Lord, that Night, to direct how and in what manner we should demean ourselves in that Respect: He being our Chaplain and lying aboard our Pink, the Captain on Shore. In the Morning very early Mr. Stone came ashore to the Captain's Chamber, and told him, he had done as he had desired, and was fully satisfied to sail for Narragansett. Our Council was then called, and the several Reasons alleged: In fine we all agreed with one accord to sail for Narragansett, which the next Morning we put in Execution.

On Friday Morning we set Sail for Narragansett Bay, and on Saturday towards Evening we arrived at our desired Port, there we kept the Sabbath. On the Monday the Wind blew so hard at North West that we could not go on Shore; as also on the Tuesday until Sun set; at which time Capt. Mason landed and Marched up to the Place of the Chief Sachem's Residence; who told the Sachem, That we had not an opportunity to acquaint him with our coming Armed in his Country sooner; yet not doubting but it would be well accepted by him, there being Love betwixt himself and us; well knowing also that the Pequots and themselves were Enemies, and that he could not be unacquainted with those intolerable Wrongs and Injuries these Pequots had lately done unto the English; and that we were now come, God assisting, to Avenge our selves upon them; and that we did only desire free Passage through his Country. Who returned us this Answer, That he did accept of our coining, and did also approve of our Design; only he thought our Numbers were too weak to deal with the Enemy, who were (as he said) very great Captains and Men skilful in War. Thus, he spake somewhat slighting of us. On the Wednesday Morning, we Marched from thence to a Place called Niantic, it being about eighteen or twenty miles distant, where another of those Narragansett Sachems lived in a Fort; it being a Frontier to the Pequots. They carried very proudly towards us; not permtting any of us to come into their Fort. We beholding their Carriage and the Falsehood of Indians, and fearing least they might discover us to the Enemy, especially they having many times some of their near Relations among their greatest Foes; we therefore caused a strong Guard to be set about their Fort, giving Charge that no Indian should be suffered to pass in or out: We also informed the Indians, that none of them should stir out of the Fort upon peril of their Lives: so as they would not suffer any of us to come into their Fort, so we would not suffer any of them to go out of the Fort. There we quartered that Night, the Indians not offering to stir out all the while.

In the Morning there came to us several of Miantomo his Men, who told us, they were come to assist us in our Expedition, which encouraged divers Indians of that Place to Engage also; who suddenly gathering into a Ring, one by one, making solemn Protestations how gallantly they would demean themselves, and how many Men they would Kill. On the Thursday about eight of the Clock in the Morning, we Marched thence towards Pequot, with about five hundred Indians: But through the Heat of the Weather and want of Provisions some of our Men fainted: And having Marched about twelve Miles, we came to Pawcatuck River, at a Ford where our Indians told us the Pequots did usually Fish; there making an Alta, we stayed some small time: The Narragansett Indians manifesting great Fear, in so much that many of them returned, although they had frequently despised us, saying, That we durst not look upon a Pequot, but themselves would perform great Things though we had often told them that we came on purpose and were resolved, God assisting, to see the Pequots, and to fight with them, before we returned, though we perished. I then enquired of Onkos, what he thought the Indians would do? Who said, The Narragansetts would all leave us, but as for Himself; He would never leave us: and so it proved: For which Expressions and some other Speeches of his, I shall never forget him. Indeed he was a great Friend, and did great Service.

And after we had refreshed our selves with our mean Commons, we Marched about three Miles, and came to a Field which had lately been planted with Indian Corn: There we made another Alt, and called our Council, supposing we drew near to the Enemy: and being informed by the Indians that the Enemy had two Forts almost impregnable; but we were not at all Discouraged, but rather Animated, in so much that we were resolved to Assault both their Forts at once. But understanding that one of them was so remote that we could not come up with it before Midnight, though we Marched hard; whereat we were much grieved, chiefly because the greatest and bloodiest Sachem there resided, whose name was Sassacus: We were then constrained, being exceedingly spent in our March with extreme Heat and want of Necessaries, to accept of the nearest.

We then Marching on in a silent Manner, the Indians that remained fell all into the Rear, who formerly kept the Van; (being possessed with great Fear) we continued our March till about one Hour in the Night: and coming to a little Swamp between two Hills, there we pitched our little Camp; much wearied with hard Travel, keeping great Silence, supposing we were very near the Fort; as our Indians informed us; which proved otherwise: The Rocks were our Pillows; yet Rest was pleasant: The Night proved Comfortable, being clear and Moon Light: We appointed our Guards and placed our Sentinels at some distance; who heard the Enemy Singing at the Fort, who continued that Strain until Midnight, with great Insulting and Rejoicing, as we were afterwards informed: They seeing our Pinnaces sail by them some Days before, concluded we were afraid of them and durst not come near them; the Burthen of their Song tending to that purpose.

In the Morning, we awaking and seeing it very light, supposing it had been day, and so we might have lost our Opportunity, having purposed to make our Assault before Day; roused the Men with all expedition, and briefly commended ourselves and Design to God, thinking immediately to go to the Assault; the Indians showing us a Path, told us that it led directly to the Fort. We held on our March about two Miles, wondering that we came not to the Fort, and fearing we might be deluded: But seeing Corn newly planted at the Foot of a great Hill, supposing the Fort was not far off, a Champion Country being round about us; then making a stand, gave the Word for some of the Indians to come up: At length Onkos and one Wequash appeared; We demanded of them, Where was the Fort? They answered On the Top of that Hill: Then we demanded where were the Rest of the Indians? They answered, Behind, exceedingly afraid: We wished them to tell the rest of their Fellows, That they should by no means Fly, but stand at what distance they pleased, and see whether English Men would now Fight or not. Then Capt. Underhill came up, who Marched in the Rear; and commending ourselves to God, divided our Men: There being two Entrances into the Fort, intending to enter both at once: Captain Mason leading up to that on the North East Side; who approaching within one Rod, heard a Dog bark and an Indian crying Owanux! Owanux! Englishmen! Englishmen! We called up our Forces with all expedition, gave Fire upon them through the Pallizado; the Indians being in a dead indeed their last Sleep: Then we wheeling off fell upon the main Entrance, which was blocked up with Bushes about Breast high, over which the Captain passed, intending to make good the Entrance, encouraging the rest to follow. Lieutenant Seeley endeavored to enter; but being somewhat cumbered, stepped back and pulled out the Bushes and so entered, and with him about sixteen Men: We had formerly concluded to destroy them by the Sword and save the Plunder.

Whereupon Captain Mason seeing no Indians, entered a Wigwam; where he was beset with many Indians, waiting all opportunities to lay Hands on him, but could not prevail. At length William Heydon espying the Breach in the Wigwam, supposing some English might be there, entered; but in his Entrance fell over a dead Indian; but speedily recovering himself, the Indians some fled, others crept under their Beds: The Captain going out of the Wigwam saw many Indians in the Lane or Street; he making towards them, they fled, were pursued to the End of the Lane, where they were met by Edward Pattison, Thomas Barber, with some others; where seven of them were Slain, as they said. The Captain facing about, Marched a slow Pace up the Lane he came down, perceiving himself very much out of Breath; and coming to the other End near the Place where he first entered, saw two Soldiers standing close to the Pallizado with their Swords pointed to the Ground: The Captain told them that We should never kill them after that manner: The Captain also said, We must Burn them; and immediately stepping into the Wigwam where he had been before, brought out a Firebrand, and putting it into the Mats with which they were covered, set the Wigwams on Fire. Lieutenant Thomas Bull and Nicholas Olmsted beholding, came up; and when it was thoroughly kindled, the Indians ran as Men most dreadfully amazed.

And indeed such a dreadful Terror did the Almighty let fall upon their Spirits, that they would fly from us and run into the very Flames, where many of them perished. And when the Fort was thoroughly Fired, Command was given, that all should fall off and surround the Fort; which was readily attended by all; only one Arthur Smith being so wounded that he could not move out of the Place, who was happily espied by Lieutenant Bull, and by him rescued.

The Fire was kindled on the North East Side to windward; which did swiftly over-run the Fort, to the extreme Amazement of the Enemy, and great Rejoicing of our selves. Some of them climbing to the Top of the Pallizado; others of them running into the very Flames; many of them gathering to windward, lay pelting at us with their Arrows; and we repaid them with our small Shot: Others of the Stoutest issued forth, as we did guess, to the Number of Forty, who perished by the Sword.
What I have formerly said, is according to my own Knowledge, there being sufficient living Testimony to every Particular.

But in reference to Captain Underhill and his Parties acting in this Assault, I can only intimate as we were informed by some of themselves immediately after the Fight, Thus they Marching up to the Entrance on the South West Side, there made some Pause; a valiant, resolute Gentleman, one Mr. Hedge, stepping to-wards the Gate, saying, If we may not Enter, where-fore came we here; and immediately endeavored to Enter; but was opposed by a sturdy Indian which did impede his Entrance; but the Indian being slain by himself and Sergeant Davis, Mr. Hedge Enter the Fort with some others; but the Fort being on Fire, the Smoke and Flames were so violent that they were constrained to desert the Fort.
Thus were they now at their Wits End, who not many Hours before exalted

themselves in their great Pride, threatening and resolving the utter
Ruin and Destruction of all the English, Exulting and Rejoicing with Songs and Dances: But God was above them, who laughed his Enemies and the Enemies of his People to Scorn, making them as a fiery Oven: Thus were the Stout Hearted spoiled, having slept their last Sleep, and none of their Men could find their Hands: Thus did the Lord judge among the Heathen, filling the Place with dead Bodies! And here we may see the just Judgment of God, in sending even the very Night before this Assault, One hundred and fifty Men from their other Fort, to join with them of that Place, who were designed as some of themselves reported to go forth against the English, at that very Instant when this heavy Smoke came upon them where they perished with their Fellows. So that the Mischief they intended to us, came upon their own Pate: They were taken in their own snare, and we through Mercy escaped. And thus in little more than one Hour's space was their impregnable Fort with themselves utterly destroyed, to the Number of six or seven Hundred, as some of themselves confessed. There were only seven taken captive, and about seven escaped.

Of the English, there were two Slain outright, and about twenty Wounded: Some Fainted by reason of the sharpness of the Weather, it being a cool Morning, and the want of such Comforts and Necessaries as were needful in such a Case; especially our surgeon was much wanting, whom we left with our Barks in Narragansett Bay, who had Order there to remain until the Night before our intended Assault. And thereupon grew many Difficulties: Our Provision and Munitions near spent; we in the enemies Country, who did far exceed us in Number, being much enraged: all our Indians, except Onkos, deserting us; our Pinnaces at a great distance from us, and when they would come we were uncertain. But as we were consulting what Course to take, it pleased God to discover our Vessels to us before a fair Gale of Wind, sailing into Pequot Harbour, to our great Rejoicing.

We had no sooner discovered our Vessels, but immediately came up the Enemy from the other Fort; Three Hundred or more as we conceived. The Captain lead out a file or two of Men to Skirmish with them, chiefly to try what temper they were of, who put them to a stand: we being much encouraged there at, presently prepared to March towards our Vessels: Four or Five of our Men were so wounded that they must be carried with the Arms of twenty more. We also being faint, were constrained to put four to one Man, with the Arms of the rest that were wounded to others; so that we had not above forty Men free: at length we hired several Indians, who eased us of that Burthen, in carrying of our wounded Men. And Marching about one quarter of a Mile; the Enemy coming up to the Place where the Fort was, and beholding what was done, stamped and tore the Hair from their Heads: And after a little space, came mounting down the Hill upon us, in a full career, as if they would over run us; But when they came within Shot, the Rear faced about, giving Fire upon them: Some of them being Shot, made the rest more wary: Yet they held on running to and fro, and shooting their Arrows at Random. There was at the Foot of the Hill a small Brook, where we rested and refreshed our selves, having by that time taught them a little more Manners than to disturb us.

We then Marched on towards Pequot Harbour; and falling upon several Wigwams, burnt them: The Enemy still following us in the Rear, which was to windward, though to little purpose; yet some of them lay in Ambush behind Rocks and Trees, often shooting at us, yet through Mercy touched not one of us; And as we came to any Swamp or Thicket, we made some Shot to clear the Passage. Some of them fell with our Shot; and probably more might, but for want of Munitions: But when any of them fell, our Indians would give a great Shout, and then would they take so much Courage as to fetch their Heads. And thus we continued, until we came within two Miles of Pequot Harbour; where the Enemy gathered together and left us; we Marching on to the Top of an Hill adjoining to the Harbour, with our Colours flying; having left our Drum at the Place of our Rendezvous the Night before: We seeing our Vessels there Riding at Anchor, to our great Rejoicing, and came to the Water-Side, we there sat down in Quiet.

Captain Patrick being Arrived there with our Vessels, who as we were informed was sent with Forty Men by the Massachusetts Colony, upon some Service against the Block Islanders; Who coming to the Shore in our Shallop with all his Company, as he said to Rescue us, supposing we were pursued, though there did not appear any the least sign of such a Thing. But we could not prevail with Him by any Means to put his Men ashore, that so we might carry our Wounded Men a Board; although it was our own Boat in which he was: We were very much troubled; but knew not how to help our selves. At length we were fetched a Board to the great Rejoicing of our Friends.

Shortly after our coming a Board, there fell out a great Contest between Captain Underhill and Capt. Patrick: Captain Underhill claiming an Interest in the Bark where Captain Patrick was, which indeed was Underhill's Right; The

Contest grew to a great Height. At length we propounded, that if Patrick would Ride there with that Bark in Contention, and secure the Narragansett Indians, it being also the Place of Rendezvous to those Vessels that were expected from Massachusetts, until we Transported our Wounded Men to Saybrook five Leagues distant; then we would immediately return our Pink to convey the Narragansetts home: That which Captain Patrick seemed very readily to accept.

Capt. Underhill soon after set sail in one of our Barks for Saybrook: But before he was out of Sight; Captain Patrick signified by Writing, that he could not attend that Service, but he must wait for the Bay Vessels at Saybrook, wishing us, having the Honor of that Service to complete it, by securing the Narragansett Indians; which at first seemed very Difficult, if not Impossible: For our Pink could not receive them, and to march by Land was very Dangerous; it being near twenty Miles in the Enemies Country, our Numbers being much weakened, we were then about twenty Men; the rest we had sent home for fear of the Pequots Invasion. But absolutely necessitated to March by Land, we hasted ashore, with our Indians and small Numbers. Captain Patrick seeing what we intended, came ashore also with his Men; although in truth we did not desire or delight in his Company, and so we plainly told him: However he would and did march along with us.

About the midway between that and Saybrook, we fell upon a People called Nayanticks, belonging to the Pequots, who fled to a Swamp for Refuge: They hearing or espying of us, fled: we pursued them a while by the Track as long as they kept together: But being much spent with former Travel, and the Sabbath drawing on, it being about Two or Three of the Clock on the Saturday in the Afternoon; we leaving our Pursuit, hasted towards Saybrook, about Sun set we Arrived at Connecticut River Side; being nobly Entertained by Lieutenant Gardner with many great Guns: But were forced there to Quarter that Night: On the Morrow we were all fetched over to Saybrook, receiving many Courtesies from Lieut. Gardner.

And when we had taken Order for the safe Conduct of the Narragansett Indians, we repaired to the Place of our Abode: where we were Entertained with great Triumph and Rejoicing and Praising God for his Goodness to us, in succeeding our weak Endeavors, in Crowning us with Success, and restoring of us with so little Loss. Thus was God seen in the Mount, Crushing his proud Enemies and the Enemies of his People: They who were ere while a Terror to all that were round about them, who resolved to Destroy all the English and to Root their very Name out of this Country, should by such weak Means, even Seventy seven (there being no more at the Fort) bring the Mischief they plotted, and the Violence they offered and exercised, upon their own Heads in a Moment: burning them up in the fire of his Wrath, and dunging the Ground with their Flesh: It was the Lord's Doings, and it is marvelous in our Eyes! It is He that hath made his Work wonderful, and therefore ought to be remembered.

Immediately the whole Body of Pequots repaired to that Fort where Sassacus the Chief Sachem did reside; charging him that he was the only Cause of all the Troubles that had befallen them; and therefore they would Destroy both him and his: But by the Entreaty of their Counselors they spared his Life; and consulting what Course to take, concluded there was no abiding any longer in their Country, and so resolved to fly into several Parts. The greatest Body of them went towards Manhattan: And passing over Connecticut, they met with three English Men in a Shallop going for Saybrook, whom they slew: The English Fought very stoutly, as themselves confessed, wounding many of the Enemy.

To Governor Winthrop of the Massachusetts Colony

Being newly risen from court I was requested by our governor, who cannot at present write, to dispatch a messenger to you just to informe you that we have this day by solemn act of court ingaged ourselves to take part with you and our brethren of Connecticut in the war against the Pecoats, purposing to send fourth thirty men, for the land service besides the managing of the vessels which we provide will not be less than forty now we fear it will be longer than we willingly would for want of boats or vessels which are very scarce with us, unless you can furnish us for which we would willingly pay, as also some other necessaries hereunto belonging, tomorrow we shall know who are the men to go with them, but hereof our governor will write at large so soon as our court is ended and opportunity is offered. Another main end of our sending is in regard we have heard no more till since we rose this evening of the last expedition of our brethren of Connecticut and Capt. Underhill, and that is by Burning of the Pequod Fort, Capt. Standish his Indian who was sent this morning to Namasket and faith the defeat of the fort is true and that only three English were slaine in the taking of it. As also that the foresaid English and Capt. Patrick are still at Narragansett and have been some days which makes us jealous and shall be till we hear from you, and the rather because we heard nothing from any of them by letter when John Jenny came away. I pray you therefore let us hear, and let not this discourage the sending of your 160 men, but take such revenge as may be a service to after times for any barbarians to rise against us. If any letters be come from England I pray you to send them by the bearer, or such news as is worth the sending. I am sorry for the carriages of your people, God sanctify his hand and fit us for such trials as he hath appointed. Thus with my love to you and prayers for you and yours desiring you to salute my christian friends with you take leave remaining yours till death.

Plimouth the 5thof the 4th Month 1636, (June 5th, 1636) Edward Winslow

June 2, 1637. A Generall Corte at Harteford.

It is ordered there shall be sent forth thirty men out of the severall plantations in this River of Conectecott to sett downe in the Pequoitt Country and River in place convenient to maintain or right God by Conquest hath given to us, and Lieutenant Seely shall have the Command of them. The men are to be raised fourteen out of Harteford, ten out of Windsor, 6 out of Wethersfield. (The total population of the Pequot at this time was estimated at about three thousand, while a total of two hundred and fifty men lived in the three Connecticut colonies).

The court met again on June 6, 1637: It is ordered that ten more men shall be levied out of the plantations aforesaid to go to the design against the Pequots as an addition to the former thirty, five out of Hartford, Windsor three, and Wethersfield two. It is ordered Mr. Haine and Mr. Ludlowe shall go t the mouth of the River to treat and conclude with our friends of the Bay to join with their forces in persecuting or design against our enemies or if they can see cause by advise to enterprise any action according to the force we have, and to parley with the Bay about our setting down in the Pequot Country.

William Bradford, Plimouth Plantation

From Connecticut (who were most sensible of ye hurt sustained, and ye present danger), they set out a party of men, and another party met them from ye Bay, at ye Narragansetts, who were to join with them. Ye Narragansetts were ernst to be gone before ye English were well rested and refreshed, especially some of them which came last. It should seem their desire was to come upon the enemy suddenly, and undiscovered, there was a barke of this place, newly put in there, which was come from Connecticut, who did encourage them, and expedition might prove to their great advantage. So they went on, and so ordered their march, as the Indeans brought them to a forte of ye enemies (Mystic fort) in which most of their chief men were before day. They approached ye same with great silence, and surrounded it both with English and Indeans, that they night not break out; and so assaulted them with great courage, shooting amongst them, and entered ye forte with all speed; and those ye first entered found sharp resistance from the enemy, who both shot at and grappled with them; others ran into their houses and brought out fire and set them on fire, which soon took to their matts, and standing close together, with ye wind, all was quickly on a flame, and thereby more were burnt to death then was otherwise slain; it burnt their bowstrings, and made them unserviceable. Those yet escaped ye fire were slain with ye sword; some hewed to pieces, other rune throw their rapiers, so as they were quickly dispatched, and very few escaped.

It was conceived they thus destroyed about four hundred at this time. It was a fearful sight to see them thus frying in ye fire, and ye streams of blood quenching ye same, and horrible was ye stink and sent there of. The Narragansett Indians, all this while, stood round about, but aloof from all danger, and left ye whole execution to ye English, except it were stopping of any that broke away, insulting over their enemies in this their ruine and miserie, when they saw them dancing in the flames, calling them by a word in their owne language, signifying, O brave Pequents! Which they used familiarly among them selves in their own prayers, in songs of triumph after their victories. After this service was thus happily accomplished, they marcht to the water side, where they mett with some of their vessels, by which they had refreshing with victuals and other necessaries. But in their march the rest of the Pequents drew into a body, and acoasted them, thinking to have some advantage against them be by reason of a neck of land; but when they saw the English prepare for them, they kept aloofe, so as they neither did hurt, nor could receive any. After their refreshing and repair to gather for further counsell and directions, they resolved to pursue their victory and follow the war against the rest, but the Narriganssett Indeans most of them forsook them, and, and such of them as they had with them for guides, or other wise, they found them very could and backward in the business, either out of envy or that they saw the English would make more profit of the victory then they were willing they should, or els deprive them of such advantage as themselves desired by having them become tributaries unto them, or the like.

Roger Williams To John Winthrop. For his much honored Mr. Governor, and Mr. Winthrop, Deputy Governor of the Massachusetts, these.
New Providence, May, 1637
Sir,—the latter end of the last week I gave notice to our neighbor princes of your intentions and preparations against the common enemy, the Pequods. At my first coming to them Canonicus *(morofus aque ac barbarex fenex)* was very sour, and accused the English and myself for sending the plague amongst them, and threatening to kill him especially. Such tidings (it seems) were lately brought to his ears by some of his flatterers and our ill-willers.

I discerned cause of bestirring myself, and staid the longer, and at last (through the mercy of the most High) I not only sweetened his spirit, but possessed him, that the plague and other sicknesses were alone in the hand of the one God, who made him and us, who being displeased with the English for lying, stealing, idleness and uncleanness, (the natives' epidemical sins,) smote many thousands of ourselves with general and late mortalities.

Miantunnomu kept his barbarous court lately at my house, and with him I have far better dealing. He takes some pleasure to visit me, and sent me word of his coming over again some eight days hence. They pass not a week without some skirmishings, though hitherto little loss on either side. They were glad of your preparations, and in much conference with themselves and others, (waiting for instructions from them,) I gathered these observations, which you may please (as cause may be) to confider and take notice of: 1.They conceive that to do execution to purpose on the Pequods, will require not two or three days and away, but a riding by it and following of the work to and again the space of three weeks or a month, that there be a falling off and Roger Williams with Canonicus a retreat, as if you were departed, and a falling on again within three or four days, when they are returned again to their houses securely from their flight.
2. That if any pinnaces come in ken, they presently prepare for flight, women and old men and children, to a swamp some three or four miles on the back of them, a marvelous great and secure swamp, which they called Ohomowauke, which signifies owl's nest, and by another name, Cuppocommock, which signifies a refuge or hiding place, as I conceive.
3. That therefore Nayantaquit, (which is Miantunnomue's place of rendezvous,) to be thought on for the riding and retiring to of vessel or

vessels, which place is faithful to the Narragansetts and at present enmity with the Pequods.

4. They also conceive it easy for the English, that the provisions and munitions first arrive at Aquedneck, called by us Rhode Island, at the Narragansett's mouth, and then a messenger may be dispatched hither, and so to the bay, for the soldiers to march up by land to the vessels, who otherwise might spend long time about the cape and fill more vessels than needs.

5. That the assault would be in the night, when they are commonly more secure and at home, by which advantage the English, being armed, may enter the houses and do what execution they please.

6. That before the assault be given, an ambush be laid behind them, between them and the swamp, to prevent their flight, &c.

7. That to that purpose such guides as shall be best liked of to be taken along to direct, especially two Pequots, viz.: Wequash and Wuttackquickommin, valiant men, especially the latter, who have lived these three or four years with the Narragansetts, and know every pass and passage amongst them, who desire armor to enter their houses.

8. That it would be pleasing to all natives, that women and children be spared, &c.

9. That if there be any more land travel to Connecticut, some course would also be taken with the Wunhowatuckoogs, who are confederates with and a refuge to the Pequods.

Sir, if any thing be sent to the princes, I find that Canonicus would gladly accept of a box of eight or ten pounds of sugar, and indeed he told me he would thank Mr. Governor for a box full.

Sir, you may please to take notice of a rude view, how the Pequods lie:

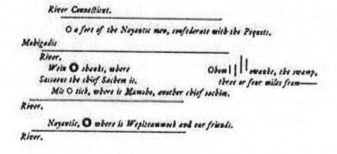

Thus, with my best salutes to your worthy selves and loving friends with you, and daily cries to the Father of mercies for a merciful issue to all these enterprises, I rest
Your worship's unfeigned respective
Roger Williams.

Not only did the persuasions of Williams induce the Narragansett to refrain from forming an alliance with the Pequods, but he succeeded also, as we have already learned, in committing the former to a friendship with the Bay people, and a continued hostility to their old enemies, the Pequods. In the summer of 1637 a party of Narragansett succeeded in overpowering a company of Pequods and killed three. Following their barbarous habit a hand of each was cut off and the three hideous trophies were sent to Boston. One of those who fell was the leader of the party of Pequods who murdered Stone and Norton, four years before.

John Winthrop, History of New England
1637
May
25.] Our English from Connecticut, with their Indians, and many of the Narragansetts, marched in the night to a fort of the Pequods at Mistick, and, besetting the same about break of the day, after two hours' fight they took it, (by firing it) and slew therein two chief sachems, and one hundred and fifty fighting men, and about one hundred and fifty old men, women, and children, with the loss of two English, whereof but one was killed by the enemy. Divers of the Indian friends were hurt by the English, because they had not some mark to distinguish them from the Pequods, as some of them had.
Presently upon this came news from the Narragansetts that all the English, and two hundred of the Indians, were cut off in their retreat, for want of powder and victuals. Three days after, this was confirmed by a post from Plymouth, with such probable circumstances, as it was generally believed. But three days after, Mr. Williams, having gone to the Narragansetts to discover the truth, found them mourning, as being confident of it; but that night some came from the army, and assured them all was well, and that the Pequods were fled, and had forsaken their forts. The general defeat of the Pequods at Mistick happened the day after our general fast.
June

3.] Upon the news from Mr. Williams, that the Pequods were dispersed, and some come in and submitted to the Narragansetts, (who would not receive them before he had sent to know our mind), the governor and the council thought it needless to send so many men, and therefore sent out warrants only for one half of the two hundred; but some people liked not of it, and came to the governor to have all sent. He took it ill; and though three of the ministers came with them to debate the matter, he told them, that if anyone, discerning an error in the proceedings of the council, had come, and a private manner, to acquaint and therewith, it had been well done; but to come, so many of them, and a public and popular way, was not well, and would bring authority into contempt. This they took well at his hands, and excused their intentions. So it was thought fit to send about forty men more, which was yielded rather to satisfy the people, and for any need that appeared. Upon our governor's letter to Plymouth, our friends there agree to send a pinnace, with forty men, to assist in the war against the Pequods; but they could not be ready to meet us at the first.

15.] There was a day of thanksgiving kept in all the churches for the victory obtained against the Pequods, and for other mercies.

New Providence, this last of the week, [May, 1637.]

Sir, I am much desired by Yotaash (the bearer hereof, Miantunnomue's brother) to interpret his message to you, viz.: that Miantunnomu requests you to bestow a Pequot squaw upon him.

I object, he had his mare sent him, he answers that Canonicus received but a few women and keeps them: and yet he saith his brother hath more right: for, himself and his brother's men first laid hold upon that company.

I object that all are disposed of, he answers, if so, he desires to buy one or two of some Englishman.

I object that here are many run away, which I have desired himself might convey home to you: he replies, they have been this fortnight busy (that is keeping of a kind of Christmas): and secondly, at present Miantunnomue's father-in-law lies a dying: as also that some of the runaways perished in the woods; three are at the Narragansett, and three within ten miles of this place; which I think may best be fetched by two or three Massachusetts Indians who may here get some one or two more to accompany and help.

Sir, you were pleased some while since to intimate some breach of league in Miantunnomu. I would not dishearten this man (from coming by my speech any way: but I could wish you would please to intimate your mind fully to him, as also that if there be any just exception which they cannot well answer, that use be made of it, (if it may be with the safety of the common peace,) to get the bits into their mouths, especially if their be good assurance from the Mohawks. So with my best salutes and earnest sighs to heaven, I rest your worship's unworthy, Roger Williams.

May, 1637

For his much honored, Mr. Governor of the Massachusetts.

Much Honored Sir, — I was bold to present you with two letters by Thomas Holyway, some weeks since. I am occasioned again at present to write a word by this bearer Wequash: whom (being a Pequot himself,) I commended for a guide in the Pequot expedition.

I presume he may say something to yourself, or to such other of my loving friends as may report unto your worship, what befell him at Cowefet.

He hath been five or six days now at my house, in which time I have had much opportunity to search into particulars, and am able to present you with naked truth. He came from Monahiganick to Cowefet within night and lodged with his friend called Pananawokshin. At Cowesit, an old man (Weeokamin,) hath made great lamentation for the death of two sons in the Pequot wars. This Weeokamun with divers of his consorts in the night time laid hold upon Wequash, intending to bind him, charging him with the death of his two sons. Much bickering there was between them, but no hurt done, only Weeokamun struggling with one of Wequash his company was fore bitten on the hand, and also bit the young man's fingers which are well again. So that their host kept peace in Canonicus his name, and brought them safe to me the next day: yet in the fray they loft a coat and other small things, which (coming forth before day) they left behind them.

I sent up a messenger to the Sachems to demand a reason of such usage and their goods. Canonicus sent his son, and Miantunnomu his brother (Yotaash) who went to Cowefet and demanded the reason of such usage, and the goods, and so came to my house, causing the goods to be restored, professing the Sachem's ignorance and sorrow for such passages, and given charge to all natives for their safe travel Having those messengers and Wequash at my house, I caused them solemnly to parley of what I knew was grievance betwixt them, and what else I could any way pick out from either of them, concerning ourselves the English, or the Pequots, or themselves. All which I carefully writ down the particulars, and shall readily, at your worship's pleasure, acquaint you with them: either concerning some squaws which Wequash acknowledged he parted with (and justly) to Canonicus and Miantunnomu, or other brablings which I thought not fit to trouble your worship with, without commission. For his much honored Mr. Governor [Henry Vane or Mr. Deputy Governor, John Winthrop these with Speed.

This last of the present week in the morning, May 13, 1637

Sir, Miantunnomu with a great train arrived the same day that Anthony Dike departed hence with his sad tidings, and confirmeth with the most the report of Anthony. The Narragansetts are at present doubtful of reality in all our promises: I have alleged the best arguments I have heard or could invent, to persuade reality of purpose and speedy performance, as also reasons of delay. Miantunnomu and his best Council here with him, have requested me earnestly to make this proffer to you. The Pequots are scarce of provision, and therefore (as usually so now especially) they are in some numbers come down to the seaside (and two Islands, by name Munnawtawkit and Manittuwond especially) to take sturgeon and other fish, as also to make new fields of corn, in case the English should destroy their fields at home.

Miantunnomu desires to go himself with one Wequash here at present with him, in this pinnace here left by Anthony, or any other that shall take him in at the Narragansett. He will put in forty or fifty or more as the vessel will stow. He will put in victuals himself for his men. He will direct the pinnace to the places, and in the night land his men, despoil them of their canoes, cut off the men he finds, (the greatest number being women and children, which for the most of them he would cut off,) as also spoil their fields: and this he proffers to do without landing an Englishman, with whom he will remain on board in English clothes which he desires for himself. John, a seaman aboard, calls the Island, Plum Island, and is very willing to go on the design, and thinks, as also Miantunnomu doth, that if within two or three days they went forth, they would be here again within four or five or less.

Sir, for myself I dare not advise: but if my thoughts be asked I shall (with all due submission) say this: — It will at present wedge them in from any starting aside until your forces shall follow. If they speed it will weaken the enemy and distress them, being put by their hopes: as also much enrage the Pequots for ever against them, a thing much desirable. Beside, the charge or danger of the English will be none, unless Miantunnomue's coarse clothes and a large coat for Wequash, the Pequot guide, a man of great use. The Most Holy and only Wise be pleased to smile upon the face of the English that be his: (we have all, if ever, cause to examine ourselves, our errands and work) in the face of Jesus Christ.

While I write, a Messenger is come to Miantunnomu from Neepemut, reporting a far greater slaughter then that Anthony brought word of, and since the former a great number at the Plantations, and some persons are mentioned, but I will not name either, but hope and long to hear it countermanded.

In case that Anthony or other seamen cannot be gotten suddenly, here is one with us willing to make up a third man, (to the other two left with the pinnace,) to carry the vessel, though I judge Anthony himself the fittest. Sir, Miantunnomu desired me to give you a hint that the six fathom of beads which he gave for the slaying of Audfah (the chief murtherers of Oldham) be repaid him, and lent now if it may be; his wars keep him bare.

Your worship's unfeigned respective
Roger Williams.

For any gratuities or tokens Canonicus desires sugar; Miantunnomu powder. My humble respects to all my loving friends. Sir, Miantunnomu is close in this his project, and therefore I think the messenger is sent only for the beads: it is very convenient that Miantunnomue's clothes and Wequash his coat be sent by him.

Johnson's Wonder-Working Providence of Sions

Of the gracious goodnesse of the Lord Christ, in saving his New England people, from the hand of the barbarous Indians. Lastly, for the frontispiece of their present distresse, namely the Indian war, they with much meeknesse and great deliberation, wisely contrived how they might best helpe their fellow brethren; hereupon they resolved to send a solemne Embassage to old Canonicus, chiefe Sachem of the narrow Ganset Indians, who be being then well stricken in yeares had caused his nephew Miantinemo to take the Government upon him, who was a very sterne man, and of a great stature, of a cruell nature, causing all his Nobility and such as were his attendance to tremble at his speech. The people under his Government were very numerous, besides the Niantick Indians, whose Prince was of neare alliance unto him; They were able to set forth, as was then supposed, 30,000 fighting men. The English sought by all meanes to keep these at least from confederating with the Pequods, and understanding by intelligence, that the Pequots would send to them for that end, endeavored to prevent them. Fit and able men being chosen by the English, they hast them to Canonicus Court, which was about fourscore miles from Boston.

The embassy to Canonicus is related so minutely and so vividly as to make it reasonable to conclude that Johnson was of the party, though Winthrop names only Edward Gibbons and John Higginson, with Cutshamakin, sagamore of Massachusetts. The Narragansetts dwelt in what is now southern Rhode Island. Their number of fighting men was probably some 1,500 or 2,000. If they had combined with the Pequots against the colonists, the latter might have been exterminated. That they were persuaded not to make this dangerous combination was due largely to the intercession of Roger Williams, whom they much regarded. The Indian King hearing of their coming, gathered together his chiefe Counsellors, and a great number of his Subjects to give them entertainment, resolving as then that the young King should receive their message, yet in his hearing. They arriving, were entertained royally, with respect to the Indian manner. Boiled Chestnuts is their White-bread, which are very sweet, as if they were mixt with Sugar; and because they would be extraordinary in their feasting, they strive for variety after the English manner, boyling Puddings made of beaten corne, putting therein great store of black berryes, somewhat like Currants. They having thus nobly feasted them, afterward give them Audience, in a State-house, round, about fifty foot wide, made of long poles stuck in the ground, like your Summer-houses in England, and covered round about, and on the top with Mats, save a small place in the middle of the Roofe, to give light, and let out the smoke.

In this place sate their Sachim, with very great attendance; the English coming to deliver their Message, to manifest the greater state, the Indian Sachim lay along upon the ground, on a Mat, and his Nobility sate on the ground, with their legs doubled up, their knees touching their chin; with much sober gravity they attend the Interpreters speech. It was matter of much wonderment to the English, to see how solidly and wisely these savage people did consider of the weighty undertaking of a War; especially old Canonicus, who was very discreet in his answers. The young Sachem was indeed of a more lofty spirit, which wrought his mine, as you may heare, after the decease of the old King. But at this time his answer was, that he did willingly embrace peace with the English, considering right well, that although their number was but small in comparison of his people, and that they were but strangers to the Woods, Swamps, and advantagious places of this Wildernesse, yet withall he knew the English were advantaged by their weapons of War, and especially their Guns, which were of great terror to his people, and also he had heard they came of a more populous Nation by far than all the Indians were, could they be joyn'd together. Also on the other hand, with mature deliberation, he was well advised of the Peaquods cruell disposition and aptnesse to make War, as also their neere neighbourhood to his people, who though they were more numerous, yet were they withall more effeminate, and lesse able to defend themselves from the sudden incursions of the Peaquods, should they fall out with them. Hereupon hee demes it most conducing to his owne and his peoples safety to direct his course in a middle way, holding amity with both. The English returne home, having gained the old Kings favour so farre, as rather to favour them then the Pequods, who perceiving their Neighbouring English I had sent forth aid to the Mattacusets government, thought it high time to seeke the winning all the Indians they could on their side, and among others they make their addresse to old Canonicus, who, instead of taking part with them, labours all he can to hush the War in hand, laying before them the sad effects of War; sometimes proving sad and mournfull to the very Victors themselves, but alwayes to the vanquished, and withall tells them what potent enemies they had to contend with, whose very weapons and Armor were matter of terror, setting their persons a side; as also that English man was no much hoggery yet, and therefore they might soone appease them, by delivering into their hands those persons that had beene the death of any of them, which were much better than that the whole Nation should perish for the present the Pequods seemed to be inclinable to the old Sachims counsell, but being returned home againe among their rude multitude (the chief place of cowardly boasting) they soon change their minde; yet the old Sachim sends the English word he had wrought with them, and in very deed, the English had rather make choice of Peace then Warre, provided it may stand with Truth and Righteousnesse: and therefore send forth a band of Soldiers, who arriving in the Pequod Country, address themselves to have a Treaty with them about delivering up the murtherers; they making shew of willingness so to doe bade them abide awhile and they would bring them, and in the mean time they were conversant among the Soldiers, and pointed to divers places where they could hit them with their Arrowes for all their Corslets. But their greatest number lying the while at the other side of a great hill, and anon appearing on the top of the hill, in sight of the English, those Indians that were among the English withdrawing toward them, no sooner were they come to their Companions, but all of a suddaine they gave a great shout, and shewed the English a fair pair of heeles, who seeing it would not availe any thing to follow them (they being farre swifter of foot than the English) made their returne home againe.

This bootlesse voyage incouraged the Indians very much, who insulted over them at the fort, boasting of this their deluding them, and withall, they blasphemed the Lord, saying Englishman's God was all one Flye, and that English man was all one Sqawe, and themselves all one Moorhawks. Thus by their horrible pride they fitted themselves for destruction. The English hearing this report, were now full assured that the Lord would deliver them into their hands to execute his righteous judgement upon these blasphemous murtherers; and therefore raised fresh Soldiers for the war, to the number of fourscore, or thereabout, out of the severall towns in the Matachusets, and although they were but in their beginnings, yet the Lord, who fore-intended their work, provided for all their wants, and indeed it was much that they had any bisket to carry with them in these times of scarcity, or any vessels to transport their men and ammunition: yet all was provided by the gracious hand of the most high; and the Soldiers, many of them, not onely armed with outward weapons, and armour of defence, but filled with a spirit of courage and magnanimity to resist, not onely men, but Devils; for surely he was more than ordinarily present with this Indian army, as the sequell will shew: as also for their further incouragement, the reverend and zealously affected servant of Christ, Mr. John Wilson, went with the army, who had treasured up heaps of the experimentall goodnesse of God towards his people. Having formerly passed through perils by Sea, perils by Land, perils among false brethren, etc. he followed the war purposely to sound an alarum before the Lord with his silver trumpet, that his people might be remembered before him: the Soldiers arriving in safety at the towne of Hartford, where they were encouraged by the reverend Ministers there, with some such speech as followes.

Fellow Soldiers, Country-men, and Companions in this Wildernesse worke, who are gathered together this day by the inevitable providence of the great Jehovah, not in a tumultuous manner hurried on by the floating fancy of every high hot headed braine, whose actions prove abortive, or if any fruit brought forth, it hath beene rape, theft, and murther, things inconsisting with natures light, then much lesse with a Soldiers valour; but you, my deare hearts, purposely pickt out by the godly grave Fathers of this government, that your prowesse may carry on the work, where there Justice in her righteous course is obstructed, you need not question your authority to execute those whom God, the righteous Judge of all the world, hath condemned for blaspheming his sacred Majesty, and murthering his Servants: every common Soldier among you is now installed a Magistrate;

then shew your selves men of courage. I would *not* draw low the height of your enemies hatred against you, and so debase your valour. This you may expect, their swelling pride hath laid the foundation of large conceptions against you and all the people of Christ in this wildernesse, even as wide as Babel's bottome. But, my brave Soldiers, it hath mounted already to the clouds, and therefore it is ripe for confusion; also their crueltie is famously knowne, yet all true-bred Soldiers reserve this as a common maxime, cruelty and cowardice are unseparable companions; and in briefe, there is nothing wanting on your enemies part, that may deprive you of a compleat victory, onely their nimbleness of foot, and the unaccessible swamps and nut-tree woods, forth of which your small numbers may intice, and industry compell them. And now to you I put the question, who would not fight in such a cause with an agile spirit, and undaunted boldnesse? yet if you look for further encouragement, I have it for you; riches and honour are the next to a good cause eyed by every Soldier, to maintain your owne, and spoile your enemies of theirs; although gold and silver be wanting to either of you, yet have you that to maintaine which is farre more precious, the lives, libertyes, and new pur-chased freedomes, priviledges, and immunities of the indeared servants of our Lord Christ Jesus, and of your second selves, even your affectionated bosome-mates, together with the chiefe pledges of your love, the comforting contents of harmlesse pratling and smiling babes; and in a word, all the riches of that goodnesse and mercy that attends the people of God in the injoyment of Christ, in his Ordinances, even in this life; and as for honour, David was not to be blamed for enquiring after it, as a due recompence of that true valour the Lord hath bestowed on him: and now the Lord hath prepared this honour for you, oh you couragious Soldiers of his, to execute vengeance upon the heathen, and correction among the people, to binde their Kings in chaines, and Nobles in fetters of Iron, that they may execute upon them the judgements that are written! this honour shall be to all his Saints. But some of you may suppose deaths stroke may cut you short of this: let every faithfull Soldier of Christ Jesus know, that the cause why some of his indeared Servants are taken away by death in a just war (as this assuredly is) it is not because they should fall short of the honours accompanying such noble designes, but rather because earths honours are too scant for them, and therefore the everlasting Crown must be set upon their heads forthwith. Then march on with a cheerfull Christian courage in the strength of the Lord and the power of his might, who will forthwith inclose your enemies in your hands, make their multitudes fall under your warlike weapons, and your feet shall soon be set on their proud necks.

After the Ministers of Christ had, through the grace that was given them, exhorted and encouraged these Soldiers appointed for the work, they being provided with certaine Indian guides, who with the close of the day brought them to a small river, where they could perceive many persons had been dressing of fish; upon the sight thereof, the Indian guides concluded they were now a feasting it at their fort, which was hard at hand. The English calling a Councill of war, being directed by the speciallest providence of the most high God, they concluded to storm the fort a little before break of day; at which time they supposed the Indians being up late in their jolly feasting, would bee in their deepest sleepe; and surely so it was, for they now slept their last: the English keeping themselves as covertly as they could, approached the fort at the time appointed, which was builded of whole Trees set in the ground fast, and standing up an end about twelve foot high, very large, having pitcht their Wigwams within it, the entrance being on two sides, with intricate Meanders to enter. The chiefe Leaders of the English made some little stand before they offered to enter, but yet boldly they rushed on, and found the passages guarded at each place with an Indian Bow-man, ready on the string, they soone let fly, and wounded the formost of the English in the shoulder, yet having dispatch'd the Porters, they found the winding way in without a Guide, where they soone placed themselves round the Wigwams, and according to direction they made their first shot with the muzzle of their Muskets downe to the ground, knowing the Indian manner is to lie on the ground to sleep, from which they being in this terrible manner awakened, unlesse it were such as were slaine with the shot. After this some of the English entered the Wigwams, where they received some shot with their Arrowes, yet catching up the fire-brands, they began to fire them, and others of the English Soldiers with powder, did the same: the day now began to break; the Lord intending to have these murtherers know he would looke out of the cloudy pillar upon them and now these women and children set up a terrible out-cry; the men were smitten down, and slaine, as they came forth with a great slaughter, the Sqawes crying out, oh much winn it! English-man, who moved with pitty toward them, saved their lives: and hereupon some young youth cryed, I squaw, I squaw, thinking to finde the like mercy. There were some of these Indians, as is reported, whose bodyes were not to be pierced by their sharp rapiers or swords of [for] a long time, which made some of the Soldiers think the Devil was in them, for there were some Powwowes among them, which work strange things with the help of Satan. But this was very remarkable, one of them being wounded to death, and thrust thorow the neck with a halbert; yet after all, lying groaning upon the ground, he caught the halberts speare in his hand, and wound it quite round. After the English were thus possessed of this first victory, they sent their prisoners to the pinnaces, and prosecute the Warre in hand, to the next Battalia of the Indians, which lay on a hill about two miles distant, and indeed their stoutest Soldiers were at this place, and not yet come to the fort; the English being weary with their night worke, and wanting such refreshing as the present worke required, began to grow faint, yet having obtained one victory, they were very desirous of another: and further, they knew right-well, till this cursed crew were utterly rooted out, they should never be at peace; therefore they marched on toward them. Now assuredly, had the Indians knowne how much weakned our Soldiers were at present, they might have born them downe with their multitude, they being very strong and agile of body, had they come to handygripes; but the Lord (who would have his people know their work was his, and he onely must order their Counsels, and war-like work for them) did bring them timely supply from the vessels, and also gave them a second victory, wherein they slew many more of their enemies, the residue flying into a very thick swamp, being unaccessible, by reason of the boggy holes of water, and thick bushes; the English drawing up their company beleagered the swamp, and the Indians in the mean time skulking up and down, and as they saw opportunity they made shot with their Arrowes at the English, and then suddainly they would fall flat along in the water to defend themselves from the retalliation of the Soldiers Muskets. This lasted not long, for our English being but a small number, had parted themselves far asunder, but by the providence of the most high God, some of them spyed an Indian with a kettle at his back going more inwardly into the swamp, by which they perceived there was some place of firm land in the midst thereof, which caused them to make way for the passage of their Soldiers, which brought this Warre to a period: For although many got away, yet were they no such considerable number as ever to raise Warre any more; the slaine or wounded of the English were (through the mercy of Christ) but a few: One of them being shot through the body, neere about the breast, regarding it not till of a long time after, which caused the bloud to dry and thicken on either end of the arrow so that it could not be drawne forth his body without great difficulty and much paine, yet did he scape his life, and the wound healed. Thus the Lord was pleased to assist his people in this Warre, and deliver them out of the Indians hands, who were very lusty proper men of their hands, most of them, as may appear by one passage which I shall here relate: thus it came to passe, As the Soldiers were uppon their march, close by a great thicket, where no eye could penetrate farre, as it often falls out in such wearisom wayes, where neither men nor beast have beaten out a path; some Soldiers lingering behinde their fellowes, two Indians watching their opportunity, much like a hungry hauke, when they supposed the last man was come up, who kept a double distance in his march, they sudden and swiftly snatched him up in their tallens, hoising him upon their shoulders, ran into the swamp with him; the Soldier unwilling to be made a Pope by being borne on mens shoulders, strove with them all he could to free himselfe from their hands; but, like a carefull Commander, one Captaine Davenport, then Lieutenant of this company, being diligent in his place to bring up the reare, coming up with them, followed with speed into the swamp after him, having a very severe cutlace tyed to his wrist, and being well able to make it bite sore when he set it on, resolving to make it fall foul on the Indians bones, he soone overtook them, but was prevented by the buckler they held up from hitting them, which was the man they had taken: It was matter of much wonder to see with what dexterity they hurled the poore Soldier about, as if they had been handling a Lacedaemonian shield, so that the nimble Captaine Davenport could not, of a long time, fasten one stroke upon them; yet, at last, dying their tawny skin into a crimson colour, they cast downe their prey, and hasted thorow the thickets for their lives. The Soldier thus redeemed, had no such hard usage, but that he is alive, as I suppose, at this very day: The Lord in mercy toward his poore Churches having thus destroyed these bloudy barbarous Indians, he returnes his people in safety to their vessels, where they take account of their prisoners: the Squawes and some young youths they brought home with them, and finding the men to be deeply guilty of the crimes they undertooke the Warre for, they brought away onely their heads as a token of their victory. By this means the Lord strook a trembling terror into all the Indians round about, even to this very day.

To His Much Honored Governor John Winthrop
New Providence, this 6th of the present week, towards midnight. [June 2, 1637.]

Sir,— By John Throckmorton I was bold to advertise of the late merciful success it hath pleased the Father of Mercies to vouchsafe to the first attempts of our countrymen against these barbarians.

After his departure toward you, I went over to the Narragansett, partly for intelligence and partly to encourage the Narragansetts in case the sad news of all their men and yours defeated were true.

I found the first news of the cutting off the whole Fort of the Pequots at Mystic to be certain and unquestionably true, as I sent, with little or no variation, of which hereafter.

The news of the cutting off three hundred Narragansetts and all the English held still for current and confirmed that they were oppressed with multitudes, their provision being spent and the English wanting powder and shot and the Narragansetts arrows. I gave the best reasons I could to persuade that they were all either gone together to Connecticut for provision, or upon some second assault upon the other of the Pequot Forts. As also I was bold to promise (in Mr. Governor's name) that although all these or more were cut off, yet there should be fresh supplies of the English who would never sheathe their swords, &c.

This fifth day part toward night I have received tidings (blessed for ever be the Lord of Hosts,) that the Narragansetts are all came safe home yesternight, (at noon I came from thence,) and brought word that the English were all safe, but the three first slain at the Fort with two of their own.

As also that indeed they fought thrice that day of their first victory with no loss of their side, and with the loss of two Pequots more. That themselves and the English prepared next day after for their other Forts, found all fled made themselves lords of one, in which both English and Narragansetts now keep. That Maumanadtuck one of their biggest, with great troops, (as before he gave out he could) is gone to Wunnashowatuckqut
(the further Neepmucks.) That Sassacus said he would go to Long Island, and thither is gone or hid in the swamps, but not a Pequot is to be found.

That Miantunnomu is come from Pequot to Nayantaquit, and was resolved homeward to send out to Wunnashowatuckqut where the enemy shelters and have Forts.

Now Sir, considering the work is effected (through the mercy of the Most High) in these parts, and that the Connecticut English, together with Capt. Patrick and his, are sufficient to maintain what they have gotten, and pursue Sassacus in all his motions thereabouts: I conceived (with submission) that it might save the country no small charge, and hazard, and loss, timely to advertise and give intelligence. The Wunnamowatuckoogs and Pequots with them are about the distance from you that we are: on them I conceive and understand the Narragansetts next fall.

If you see cause and grounds to make a stop for a day or two, if the Lord please, the second day or third of the next week I hope to acquaint you with Miantunnomue's and Canonicus their advice and desire, which it may be well to meet his companions at the hither Nipmucks and none to come this way, or some the one way and some the other. This morning, I go over (if the Lord please) to consult with them, hoping to be at home (if possible) tomorrow evening, and so to dispatch some messenger the second in the morning.

Sir, your late message to the Nipmucks (through the Lord's mercy) have wrought this effect, that whereas they staggered as neuters, they brought this present week divers baskets of their nokehick and chestnuts to Canonicus towards his wars.

Sir, I understand that the cause why the English hurt so many of the Narragansetts, was want of signs or marks. You may please therefore to provide some yellow or red for their heads: The Connecticut English had yellow but not enough.

Thus beseeching the God of Peace to be at peace with us, that all the fruit may be the taking away of our sin, (which if not removed will unstop worse vials) to guide your consultations and prosper your expeditions to the praise of His own most holy name, I rest

Your worship's faithful and affectionate in all civil bonds,

Roger Williams.

Honourable Sir,

It hath pleased God further to crowne our poore endeavours with success graciously as you sail largely and punctually under land by Capt. Patrick, to whome I leave the relation wholly, seeing a lively voyce will do it: and therefore I entreat your favour for this omission; especially because it is late in the night and a faire wind attends us. Surely there have been so many singular providences as are worthy of due observance and eternal praise. And allbeit we have not the whole of our desires, yet oh that we could extoll him for what we have and waite for more. Much is done, but not all, and if ought be well done I desire we may not be weary thereof but proceed as God shall minister new occasions. Capt. Patrick can informe you of our intentions for the future: both for Block Island, Long Island, Indians beyond. Allso if it shall appear usefull, and pleasing to you we will some of us come march through Neepenet: I earnestly desire the worke may be thoroughly done, and see we and our friends will suffer much by scattered wretches, if they be not closely followed. But I shall write more fully suddenly, and do desire to understand your pleasures: For we will prefer your minds before ours: But 'tis clear some must reside here or hereabouts. It is beyond my abilities for the present to resolve you which is best in all things, or particularly about planting Pequot. For though the place be subsistable, and an excellent harbour, and abundance of corne, and the same ground ready for English grayne forthwith, which is a great help to planters, yet the providence of God guided us to so excellent a country at Quinnipiac river and so all along the coast as we travelled, as I am confident we have not the like in English possession as yet, and probable 'tis the Dutch will seize it if the English do not. It is conceived generally far more worthy than Pequod notwithstanding the former considerations. It is too good for any but friends, Capt. Patrick can informe you the full. I heartily thanke you for your loving care of us about necessaries and do acknowledge your kind acceptance of our poore imperfect indeavours, craving your prayers for more grace that we may so increase in faithfullness and fruitfullness, such as may be God's honor and the fullfilling of your and our joy through Jesus Christ our Lord, and so, with my due respect to your self with the councell and magistrates I take leave,

Yours as in duty I am bound,

Israel Stoughton. Possession House in Pequod, the 4th day of the 5th weeke of our warrfare about midnight.

The Court of Plymouth Colony passed the following order June 7th, 1637:

Before William Bradford, Captain Miles Standish, gent, Governor, Timothy Hatherley, and Edward Winslow, John Jenney, gentlemen, Thomas Prince, justice of the peace of or sovereign lord the king, and Assistants in the government.

It is concluded and enacted by the Court that the colony of New Plymouth shall send forth aid to assist them of Massachusetts Bay and Conectecott in their wars against the Pequins Indians, in revenge of the innocent blood of the English which the said Pequins have barbarously shed, and refuse to give satisfaction for.

It is also enacted by the Court, that there shall be thirty persons sent for land service, and as many others as shall be sufficient to manage the barque.

Lieutenant William Holmes is elected to goe leader of the said company.

Mr. Thomas Prince is also elected by lot to be for the counsel of war, and to goe forth wth them. The names of the Soldiers that willingly offer themselves to goe upon the said Service, with Mr. Prince & the Lieutenant.

Voluntaries; Thomas Clarke, Richard Church, Constance Southerne, John Barnes, Mr. Nathaniel Thomas & his Mr. Gorton, man George Soule, Samuel Jenney, Thomas

Redding, Mr. Brewster, or Joseph Robinson, his man Edward Holman, John Cooke, if his family can William Paddy, Mr. Stephen Hopkins, John Heyward, Thomas Williams, Nicholas Presland, Thomas Pope, Phillip Delanoy, Francis Billington, Henry Willis, Perregrine White, Caleb Hopkins, Samuel Nash, Robert Mendall, John Hearker, Richard Clough, Henry Ewell, Joseph Biddle, William Tubbs George Kennerick, Thomas Halloway, John Irish, John Jenkins, Jacob Cooke, Giles Hopkins, John Phillips, Thomas Gorton. Henry Sampson,

Such as will go if they be present. Mr. Thomas Hill, James Coale, Thomas Boardman.

It is also enacted by the Court, that Mr. Hopkins and John Winslow for the town of Plymouth, Mr. Howland and Jonathan Brewster for the towne of Ducksborrow, and Mr. Gilson and Edward Forster for the towne of Scituate, shall be added to the Governor and Assistants to assess men towards the charges of the soldiers that are to be sent forth for the aid of the Massachusetts Bay and Conectecott.

June 21, 1637. A Generall Corte at Harteford. It is ordered there shall be sent forth thirty men out of the severall plantations in this River of Conectecott to sett downe in the Pequoitt Country & River in place convenient to maintain the right of God by Conquest hath given to us, and Lieutenant Seely shall have the Command of them. The men are to beraised fourteen out of Harteford, ten out out of Windsor, six out of Wethersfield.

26 June 1637, Harteford Generall Corte.

It is ordered that ten men more shall be levied out of the plantations aforesaide to goe to the designe agt the Pequoitts as an addition to the former thirty, five out of Harteford, Windsor three, and Wethersfield two.

It is ordered ye Mr. Haine and Mr. Ludlowe shall goe to the mouth of the River to treate and conclude with or friends of the Bay either to joine with their forces in persecuting or designe against our enemies or if they can see cause by advise to enterprise any action according to the force we have. And to Parley with the Bay aboute or setting downe in the Pequoitt Country.

This Court being assembled for the special occasion of persecuting the war against the Pequots, it was agreed & ordered, that the wars, having been undertaken upon just ground, should bee seriously persecuted, and for this end there shall be one hundred and sixty men provided to bee chosen out of the severall towns according to the portion under-written, out of the men to be named by the severall towns, and presented to the counsel, within one week, who shall give a call unto such of them as they may think fit, (and may impress such as are not freemen, at their discretion,) to the number of one hundred and twenty at the least; (these who were lately sent to Saybrook to bee accounted of said number of one hundred and sixty) and they shall provide among these men some fit to bee chosen officers, and such as shall be enrolled for this service shall have, every common soldier, twenty shillings per month, every sergeant, thirty shillings per month, besides their diets, and that the counsel shall take order herein for all other things concerning the said expedition, so as all may be in readiness (so far as is possible) be the end of the next Generall Court, and for training and preparing the soldiers, before they bee sent.

And for the furtherance of this expedition there shall bee six hundred levied forthwith, according to the last levy of three hundred. The counsel are also to treat wth our neighbors of Plimoth about such aide as they will send with us, and also with our friends upon Conecktecot, and shall have power to proceed wth them in the said treaty as occasion shall require.

Southport Swamp

Chapter Four

It Ended in Southport

"Driven to desperation, the colonists attacked their foes, destroyed their fort at Groton, and when they fled, pursued, overtook, and defeated them again, near where the Pequot Library building now stands. Over its portal, cut in imperishable granite, are these figures. How many as they go in and out, note their deep signification?"
Johnson, Annals of an old Parish Church

"The brief skirmish at the beginning admonished the English that they were now facing a brave and desperate foe, no loner entirely at their mercy. There was a rumor also, brought back by the two captive girls at Wethersfield, that the Pequots had some sixteen muskets, which they might craftily discharge upon their assailants unexpectedly. So they decided to hold a parley with the foe. Thomas Stanton was sent to speak with them, readily understanding their language, and offering to go upon this service. He soon returned with about two hundred ld men, women and children, including the local tribe. Then the warriors sent the challenge from the swamp that they would fight it out with the English to the end, and Stanton, going once more to them, to urge terms of their surrender, was met with a fierce volley of arrows, so as to scarcely escape with his life."
George Bodge, History of Indian Wars

Forest Morgan, Connecticut as a Colony and a State
Sassacus was not present at the swamp fight; for, learning of the spy's attempt, and deserted by his people, who accused him of being the author of all their misfortunes, he fled westward to the country of the Mohawks,

accompanied by a small number of his warriors. That tribe hated the Pequots as heartily as did the English, as was usually the case with any two Indian tribes, and were glad to see them annihilated; and in the following August, to conciliate such formidable warriors as the English, and please themselves besides, beheaded Sassacus, his brother, and five Sachems, sending their scalps to Connecticut.

Sassacus was perhaps fortunate in dying thus; to live like Uncas, degraded into a squalid and drunken dependent of the whites, was no fortune to covet. He had gained a great Indian position as a fearless and dogged fighter, and he never declined from that height. He needs no pity, and may have the respect due to courage and constancy, which are the bases of all human advance, and are not dependent on race.

After the contest in the swamp, Uncas and Miantonomo, head chief of the Narragansetts, met the Connecticut magistrates at Hartford, to divide their spoils. Two hundred captives were divided among the Indians, one hundred being allotted to the Mohegans, eighty to the Narragansetts, and twenty to the Nehantics; those remaining, together with other avails, were distributed between Massachusetts and Connecticut. A treaty between the English and the Mohegans and Narragansetts established perpetual peace between the two tribe of Indians and the English; the latter were to act as arbitrators should a member of one tribe be wronged by those of the other, and the Indian Sachems released all claims to the lands of the Pequots, which were to be considered as the absolute property of Connecticut. A large number of these captives secured by the colonies were shipped to the West Indies by their slave merchants; those given to their Indian allies were tortured and slain, and their heads and hands gleefully exhibited at the English settlements.

John Mason, Brief History of the Pequot War
About a Fortnight after our Return home, which was about one Month after the Fight at Mistick, there Arrived in Pequot River several Vessels from the Massachusetts, Captain Israel Stoughton being Commander in Chief; and with him about One hundred and twenty Men; being sent by that Colony to pursue the War against the Pequots: The Enemy being all fled before they came, except some few Stragglers, who were surprised by the Moheags and others of the Indians, and by them delivered to the Massachusetts Soldiers. Connecticut Colony being informed hereof, sent forthwith forty Men Captain Mason being Chief Commander; with some other Gent, (as the honored John Haines and Roger Ludlowe) to meet those

145

of the Massachusetts, to consider what was necessary to be attended respecting the future: Who meeting with them of the Massachusetts in Pequot Harbour; after some time of consultation, concluded to pursue those Pequots that were fled towards Manhattan, and so forthwith Marched after them, discovering several Places where they Rendezvoused and lodged not far distant from their several Removes; making but little haste, by reason of their Children, and want of Provision; being forced to dig for Clams, and to procure such other things as the Wilderness afforded: Our Vessels sailing along by the Shore. In about the space of three Days we all Arrived at New Haven Harbour, then called Quinnipiac. And seeing a great Smoke in the Woods not far distant, we supposing some of the Pequots our Enemies might be there; we hastened ashore, but quickly discovered them to be Connecticut Indians. Then we returned aboard our Vessels, where we stayed some short time, having sent a Pequot Captive upon discovery, we named him Luz; who brought us Tidings of the Enemy, which proved true: so faithful was he to us, though against his own Nation. Such was the Terror of the English upon them; that a Moheags Indian named Jack Eatow going ashore at that time, met with three Pequots, took two of them and brought them aboard.

We then hastened our march towards the Place where the Enemy was: And coming into a Corn Field, several of the English espied some Indians, who fled from them: They pursued them; and coming to the Top of an Hill, saw several Wigwams just opposite, only a Swamp intervening, which was almost divided in two Parts. Sergeant Palmer hastening with about twelve Men who were under his Command to surround the smaller Part of the Swamp, that so He might prevent the Indians flying; Ensign Davenport, Sergeant Jeffries &c, entering the Swamp, intended to have gone to the Wigwams, were there set upon by several Indians, who in all probability were deterred by Sergeant Palmer. In this Skirmish the English slew but few; two or three of themselves were wounded: The rest of the English coming up, the Swamp was surrounded.

Our Council being called, and the Question propounded, How we should proceed, Captain Patrick advised that we should cut down the Swamp; there being many Indian Hatchets taken, Captain Trask concurring with him; but was opposed by others: Then we must pallizado the Swamp; which was also opposed: Then they would have a Hedge made like those of Gotham; all which was judged by some almost impossible, and to no purpose, and that for several Reasons, and therefore strongly opposed. But some others advised to force the Swamp, having time enough, it being about three of the Clock in the Afternoon: But that being opposed, it was then propounded to draw up our Men close to the Swamp, which would much have lessened the Circumference; and with all to fill up the open Passages with Bushes, that so we might secure them until the Morning, and then we might consider further about it. But neither of these would pass; so different were our Apprehensions; which was very grievous to some of us, who concluded the Indians would make an Escape in the Night, as easily they might and did: We keeping at a great distance, what better could be expected?

Yet Captain Mason took Order that the Narrow in the Swamp should be cut through; which did much shorten our Leaguer. It was resolutely performed by Sergeant Davis. We being loath to destroy Women and Children, as also the Indians belonging to that Place; whereupon Mr. Thomas Stanton a Man well acquainted with Indian Language and Manners, offered his Service to go into the Swamp and treat with them: To which we were somewhat backward, by reason of some Hazard and Danger he might be exposed unto: But his importunity prevailed: Who going to them, did in a short time return to us, with near Two Hundred old Men, Women and Children; who delivered them-selves, to the Mercy of the English. And so Night drawing on, we beleaguered them as strongly as we could.

About half an Hour before Day, the Indians that were in the Swamp attempted to break through Captain Patrick's Quarters; but were beaten back several times; they making a great Noise, as their Manner is at such Times, it sounded round about our Leaguer: Whereupon Captain Mason sent Sergeant Stares to inquire into the Cause, and also to assist if need required; Capt. Trask coming also in to their Assistance: But the Tumult growing's to a very great Height, we raised our Siege; and Marching up to the Place, at a Turning of the Swamp the Indians were forcing out upon us; but we sent them back by our small Shot.

We waiting a little for a second Attempt; the Indians in the mean time facing about, pressed violently upon Captain Patrick, breaking through his Quarters, and so escaped. They were about sixty or seventy as we were informed. We afterwards searched the Swamp, and found but few Slain. The Captives we took were about One Hundred and Eighty; whom we divided, intending to keep them as Servants, but they could not endure that Yoke; few of them continuing any considerable time with their masters. Thus did the Lord scatter his Enemies with his strong Arm! The Pequots now became a Prey to all Indians. Happy were they that could bring in their Heads to the English: Of which there came almost daily to Winsor, or Hartford. But the Pequots growing weary hereof, sent some of the Chief that survived to mediate with the English; offering that If they might but enjoy their Lives, they would become the English Vassals, to dispose of them as they pleased, which was granted them. Whereupon Onkos and Miantunnomo were sent for; who with the Pequots met at Hartford. The Pequots being demanded, how many of them were then living? Answered, about One Hundred and Eighty, or two Hundred. There were then given to Onkos, Sachem of Moheags, Eighty; to Miantunnomo, Sachem of Narragansett, Eighty; and to Nynigrett, Twenty, when he should satisfy for a Mare of Edward Pomroye's killed by his Men. The Pequots were then bound by Covenant, that none should inhabit their native Country, nor should any of them be called Pequots any more, but Moheags and Narragansetts forever. Shortly after, about forty of them went to Moheag; others went to Long Island; the rest settled at Pawcatuck, a Place in Pequot Country, contrary to their late Covenant and Agreement with the English.

G. H. Hollister, History of Connecticut

They found the swamp without difficulty. It was situated within the limits of the old town of Fairfield. In this swamp were hidden about eighty Pequot warriors, with their women and children, and about two hundred other Indians. A dismal, miry bog it was, covered with tangled bushes. Dangerous as it was, Lieutenant Davenport rushed into it with his men, eager to encounter the Pequots.

The sharp arrows of the enemy flew from places that hid the archers, wounding the soldiers who, in their haste to retreat, only sunk deeper in the mire. The Indians, made bold by this adventure, pressed hard upon them, and would have carried off their scalps, had it not been for the timely aid of some other Englishmen, who waded into the swamp, sword in hand, drove back the Pequots, and drew their disabled friends from the mud that had threatened to swallow them up. The swamp was now surrounded, and a skirmish followed that proved so destructive to the savages, that the Fairfield Indians begged for quarter. They said, what was probably true, that they were there only by accident, and had never done the English any harm—and that they only wished for the privilege of withdrawing from the swamp, and leaving the Pequots to fight it out.

Thomas Stanton, who knew their language, was sent into the swamp with instructions to offer life to all the Indians who had shed no English blood. When the Sachem of the Fairfield Indians learned the terms proposed by Stanton, he came out of the swamp followed by little parties of men, women, and children. He and his Indians, he said, had shed no English blood. But the Pequot warriors, made up of choice men, and burning with rage against the enemy who had destroyed their tribe and driven them from their old haunts, fought with such desperate bravery, that the English were glad to confine themselves to the border of the swamp.

There now sprang up a controversy among the officers, as to the best mode of annihilating this little handful of Pequots. Some advised that they should plunge into the swamp, and there fight them. But the experiment of Davenport discouraged others from so foolhardy a course. Others suggested that they should cut down the swamp with the hatchets that they had brought with them; others, that they should surround it with palisades. Neither of these propositions was adopted. They finally hit upon a plan that was more easily executed. They cut down the bushes that grew upon a little neck of firm upland, that almost divided the swamp into two parts. In this way, they so lessened the area occupied by the Pequots that, by stationing men twelve feet apart, it could all be surrounded by the troops. This was done, and the sentinels all stationed, before nightfall. Thus keeping watch on the borders of the morass, wet. cold, and weary, the soldiers passed the night under arms. Just before day, a dense fog arose, that shrouded them in almost total darkness. A friendly mist it proved to the Pequots, for it doubtless saved the lives of many of them. At a favorable moment they rushed upon the English. Captain Patrick's quarters were first attacked, but he drove them back more than once. Their yells, more terrible from the darkness that engulfed the scene of the conflict, were so unearthly and appalling, the attack was so sudden and so well sustained, that, but for the timely interference of a party sent by Mason to relieve him, Patrick would doubtless have been driven from his station or cut in pieces. The siege had by this time given place to a hand-to-hand fight. As Mason was himself marching up to aid Patrick, the Pequots rushed upon him from the thicket. He drove them back with severe loss. They did not resume the attack upon the man who had recently given them such fearful proofs of his prowess; but turned upon Patrick, broke through his ranks, and fled. About sixty of the Pequot warriors escaped. Twenty lay dead upon the field. One hundred and eighty were taken prisoners. Most of the property that this fugitive remnant of the tribe had attempted to carry with them, fell into the hands of the English. Hatchets of stone, beautiful wampum-belts, polished bows, and feathered arrows, with the utensils employed by the women in their rude domestic labors, became at once, as did the women themselves, the property of the conquerors. The captives and the booty were divided between Massachusetts and Connecticut. Some were sent by Massachusetts to the West Indies, and there, as slaves, dragged out a wretched, yet brief existence. Among the captives taken in this battle, was the wife of Mononotto and her children. With much dignity, she begged them to save her honor inviolate and to spare her life and that of her offspring. She had been kind to the girls who had been taken from Wethersfield, and for this she and her little ones were recommended, not in vain, to the mercy of the governor of Massachusetts.

Johnson's Wonder-working Providence of Sions
   Now assuredly, had the Indians knowne how much weakned our Souldiers were at present, they might have born them downe with their multitude, they being very strong and agile of body, had they come to handygripes; but the Lord (who would have his people know their work was his, and he onely must order their Counsels, and war-like work for them) did bring them timely supply from the vessels, and also gave them a second victory, wherein they slew many more of their enemies, the residue flying into a very thick swamp, being unaccessible, by reason of the boggy holes of water, and thick bushes; the English drawing up their company beleagered the swamp, and the Indians in the mean time skulking up and down, and as they saw opportunity they made shot with their Arrowes at the English, and then suddainly they would fall flat along in the water to defend themselves from the retalliation of the Souldiers Muskets. This lasted not long, for our English being but a small number, had parted themselves far asunder, but by the providence of the most high God, some of them spyed an Indian with a kettle at his back going more inwardly into the swamp, by which they perceived there was some place of firm land in the midst thereof, which caused them to make way for the passage of their Souldiers, which brought this warre to a period: For although many got away, yet were they no such considerable number as ever to raise warre any more; the slaine or wounded of the English were (through the mercy of Christ) but a few: One of them being shot through the body, neere about the breast, regarding it not till of a long time after, which caused the bloud to dry and thicken on either end of the arrow so that it could not be drawne forth his body without great difficulty and much paine, yet did he scape his life, and the

wound healed. Thus the Lord was pleased to assist his people in this warre, and deliver them out of the Indians hands, who were very lusty proper men of their hands, most of them, as may appear by one passage which I shall here relate: thus it came to passe, As the Souldiers were uppon their march, close by a great thicket, where no eye could penetrate farre, as it often falls out in such wearisom wayes, where neither men nor beast have beaten out a path; some Souldiers lingering behinde their fellowes, two Indians watching their opportunity, much like a hungry hauke, when they supposed the last man was come up, who kept a double distance in his march, they sudden and swiftly snatched him up in their tallens, hoising him upon their shoulders, ran into the swamp with him; the Souldier unwilling to be made a Pope by being borne on mens shoulders, strove with them all he could to free himselfe from their hands; but, like a carefull Commander, one Captaine Davenport, then Lieutenant of this company, being diligent in his place to bring up the reare, coming up with them, followed with speed into the swamp after him, having a very severe cutlace tyed to his wrist, and being well able to make it bite sore when he set it on, resolving to make it fall foul on the Indians bones, he soone overtook them, but was prevented by the buckler they held up from hitting them, which was the man they had taken: It was matter of much wonder to see with what dexterity they hurled the poore Souldier about, as if they had been handling a Lacedaemonian shield, so that the nimble Captaine Davenport could not, of a long time, fasten one stroke upon them; yet, at last, dying their tawny skin into a crimson colour, they cast downe their prey, and hasted thorow the thickets for their lives. The Souldier thus redeemed, had no such hard usage, but that he is alive, as I suppose, at this very day: The Lord in mercy toward his poore Churches having thus destroyed these bloudy barbarous Indians, he returnes his people in safety to their vessels, where they take account of their prisoners: the Squawes and some young youths they brought home with them, and finding the men to be deeply guilty of the crimes they undertooke the warre for, they brought away onely their heads as a token of their victory. By this means the Lord strook a trembling terror into all the Indians round about, even to this very day.

Elizabeth Schenck, History of Fairfield, Fairfield County, Connecticut
   After marching about twenty-five miles near the coast, through Cupheag, Pequonnock, and Uncoway, they came upon the swamp at Sasqua (now called Southport), in which the Pequots were secreted. This swamp of water, bogs and mire, thickly wooded with a dense undergrowth, entirely

surrounded a cone-shaped hill, about thirty feet in height. It was almost impossible for a stranger to enter it, without sinking above the knees in mire. The English troops drawn up in the regular order of their companies, made an attack. The Indians, in the meantime, skulked up and down shooting their arrows from behind the trees, and then suddenly dropped flat in the water, to defend themselves from the retaliation of the soldiers' muskets. Lieutenant Davenport encouraged his men to follow him into the swamp, where he was sorely wounded, and both he and his men sank so deep in the mire, that but for the timely assistance of their friends, they would all have been killed. Several Indians were slain in the encounter. Finding they could not capture the enemy in this way, the English decided to surround the swamp. After some time spent in skirmishing, the native Indians desired a parley. Meanwhile, an Indian had been seen to enter the thicket with a brass kettle on his back, which led to the conclusion that there must be some place of firm land in the centre of the swamp.

At the first approach of the English, the Sachems and Indians of the country had fled with dismay into the swamp; but as they had done the English no harm, the parley was granted. The officers were also anxious to save the old men, women and children. Thomas Stanton, a man familiar with the Indian language, was sent in to treat with them. He was instructed to offer life and protection to all Indians who had not shed English blood. "The native Sachems, followed by companies of warriors, aged men, women and children, came out in numbers of about two hundred." The chief Sachem declared that neither he nor his people had done the English any harm, and expressed a desire to make peace with them. The haughty Pequots, however, disdained all overtures of peace, exclaiming: "We will fight it out to the last 1" Stanton barely escaped with his life in leaving the swamp, and the soldiers were obliged to fly to his rescue. The fight was now renewed, but on account of some misunderstanding among the officers, several of the Pequots escaped. "Some were for forcing the swamp immediately, but this was opposed as too dangerous. Others were for cutting it down, as they had taken many hatchets, with which they were of the opinion it might be effected. Some others were for making a palisade and hedge round it, but neither of these measures could be adopted." As night approached, it was agreed to lessen the circle around the swamp, which was almost divided in two parts at one point, by cutting down the trees and undergrowth. This being done, sentinels were stationed at a distance of twelve feet apart. Thus they entirely encircled the swamp, and watched the enemy through the night. During the night the Pequots crept near the guards and discharged their arrows at them, but not one was slain. From the dead bodies found the next day, it was shown that the English musketry had made severe havoc among the enemy." Just before dawn a dense fog fell over the place, and seizing this favorable opportunity for escape, the Indians, with hideous yells, first attacked Captain Patrick's quarters, but they were severely driven back by Captain Mason sending timely aid. Captain Trask also marched quickly to the scene of action, followed by Captain Mason, upon whom the Indians now directed their full strength. Mason, however, gave them such a warm reception that they were glad to retire. They then rushed once more upon Captain Patrick's quarters, when about sixty or seventy of their bravest warriors broke through his line and escaped, several of whom were found slain the next day, by those who pursued them as far as Fairfield. About twenty others were killed, and one hundred and eighty taken prisoners. Hatchets, wampum, kettles, trays, and other Indian utensils were taken.

Richard Davenport to Hugh Peter.
For his Reverend Pastor M Hugh Peeter at Salem.
Deare and Honored In The Lord,

To whom (for Christ and in him) I owe not onely any service, but my selfe allso: and the desire of my soule is that He in whom is my breath and beeing will helpe mee to walke worthy of ye fellowship in Christ or hope. Since my last letter to you (as before), soe since wee have had still experence of Gods blessed presence and grace with uss, and shining upon us; it pleased or God, 3 days after or Brother Graften left us to direct or course to Seabrook fort, to joyne with our brethren of Conetecutt, who stayd for us there. The same evening, being the sixth day of the weeke, wee went toward Long Hand, and sent in a shallop wth an Indian to espy or enemy Sasacoos; but hee not beeing there, wee had a sachem came aboord us, who tould us hee was gone thence to Quenepiacke, and that himselfe would goe to bee or guide to finde him out; which motion wee accepted of, hee allso promising his willingnes that as Long Hand had payd tribute to Sasacas, hee would procure it to us.

The next day, being the Lord's day, wee came to a harbour about 3 leagus short of Quenepiak, where wee lay that day. That morning 4 Indians went out for spyes, who tooke 2 Pecott Indians, whom, after examination, 2 prisoners more, wee put to death that night, and one of called the place Sachems head. The second day of the weeke wee came to Quenepiacke, and coming into the harbour wee saw a smoake on the shore, and speedily landed and sent out spys, who speedily returned and tould us there weere Conetecutt Indians, and brought downe 4 Indians with them: upon the noise wee repayrd to the barks. Yet the Counsell thought meet to send my selfe wth 20 men to see the truth: wch a little before day I did. Upon one side of the river found noe signe of Indians, but wading over the river, after 2 houres seeking, wee found som scouting Pecotts. It pleased God to deliver to our hands 7 of them, one sachem: 5 wee slew, 2 women wee brought aboard, haveing taken all by runing, and in an extreame raine.

As soone as wee gott a aboord, that day about 12 of clocke, wee were all landed on the other side, to pursue Sasacoos that afternoone; the next day and the 5th day wee marched after them, and haveing found the base cowardlines of the Indians, being out of hope of the enemy, wee fell to cutting downe all the corne, in wch time wee took in the corne a Pecott man, very poore and weake; hee tould us of som squaws that weere not farr of, at the same instant some of or Indians tould us they heard som cutting wood another way: wherupon part of the company went to the one, and part to the other. It pleased God to lead my Capt. one way, and my selfe another way wth Capt. Patricke; and Leiut. Seilley wtt my Capt.: it was or day to lead, and after 2 miles march wee came where they were, and soddenly coming to the place, theire wigwams being upon the edge of the swamp, as soone as ever they saw us they tooke the swamp; it pleased God it was not very great, and our company did surround it.

For my part, I judged best, while the terrour was upon them to fall in upon them, and calling a file of men, entered the swamp, overtooke a man and a sachems child and thrust him through wth my pike twise: going further, I perseaved I had but 3 men wth mee, and soddenly one of [them] cryed out Leiut: they kill mee, they kill mee: wth that I saw him, haveing four stout Rougus upon him downe. The Lord helped mee soone to make three of them repent their closing, the fourth held him still, and soe shelterd himselfe wth the English man, that I could not come to make a thrust at him; yet, after som tryall, the Lord gave him his wound in the belly, and soe lost his prey: all wch time a crew stood shooting upon mee at 12 foot distance; they stook eleven arroos in my coat and hat, and cloths and flesh: onely 2 in my flesh. Now all had left mee, but God stood to raee, and after this they left mee and runn, and I retreated, having onely a halfe pike and my cutles. Upon or shooting, the rest of or company came thither and found vs about the swamp and the Indians in it: then the[y] gott a Pecott and came to pley. Sasacuos was gone; and all their women came out, about nine score. It was and is lamentable to see into what condicion they have brought themselves, all seeking one anothers ruine, and every one crying out of each other. Then weere wee that were hurt sent to the pinaces, about six leagus; and coining againe wth them, wee found the company all well, many Indians killd, and som runn away in the night; by what default I know not, yet I hope in mercy.

My owne wounds are one in the left arme, through the arme, close in the arme pitt, which head was taken out in the under side my arme wth great paine. The other is on the right side my brest, which was through my coat: which is not deepe. 3 dayes I was in exceding paine, haveing the mussles hurt, but blessed bee God who hath not left mee, but as Hee hath given my life, soe Hee giveth mee now wonderfull amendment.

The souldiers that are hurt are two of Ipswch, Tho: Sherman and Jo. Wedgwood, whom God saved by mee, the other, Edw. Shorthose of Charlestowne. My humble request to you is that you remembr my case and soule to the Lord, that Hee that teacheth His people to be fitt, will teach mee how to use this speciall delivrance, and a second request, that you cheere up the spirit of my poore wife, who I feare will apprehend worse then the thing is. If you shall bee pleased to accept of this rude intelligence to *ye* selfe, I doubt not but you will declare the somme of it to the Church. Wee are now in the way to Pecott, wth allmost 100 Indian women and children aboord, Goodman Jackson, and 45 souldiers. When I know more you shall heare more: my Capt. and Thomas Lauthoup salute you and the church. Thus wtt my humble respects to my colonell, Mr. Sharp, and Ensign, and all theirs and yet, and all mine, I rest
Yours while I am,
Richard Davenport
Conetecut men have had their equall share in women and the Princes treasurers are run from him wtt his wamp, and hee and Momonothuk, with 120 men, are fled to the Mowhoak: wee have Momonotuk[s] squaw and children.
I pray tell my colonell Mr. Ludlow is well, who was at this business, and narrowly mist a shott with an arrow.

For his much honored Mr. Governor these. Mr. Stoughtn or Capt. Traske, on their way, may please to read this. This 4th of the week. [June 21, 1637
Sir, John Gallop (blessed be the Lord) is safely arrived at our doors, and

hath brought from the Lord and you merciful refreshing to us. He be graciously pleased to recompense it a thousand fold to the whole land and yourselves especially.

He relates that thiere is now riding below three pinnances, (the names of the masters, Quick, Jigles, and Robinson,) and the two Shallops, as also that the other, whereof-Jackson of Salem, is master, was in company with them the night before, and weighed anchor together, but being not able to turn about was fain to chop to an anchor again but they hope is in by this time.

Sir, I hear our loving friends, Mr. Stoughton, Mr. Traske, are on their way, and one hundred and sixty (the intended number) with them. I hope the continuance of the number will be reasonable, if not for pursuit of Sasacous and the Pequots, (of whom it is said that they are gone far and finally,) yet for the quelling of their confederates the Wunnashowatuckoogs and Monashackotoogs, who live nearer to you on the westward.

Some two hundred of these (since the slaughter at the Fort) came in revenge upon the Narragansets: which the Narragansetts themselves knew not until three Pequots (now fallen to them) related it: for it pleased the Lord to send a great mist that morning that they durst not fight, and so returned: so that there is cause to take some course with them, and especially if it be possible for the clearing of land passage to Connecticut.

I understand it would be very grateful to our neighbors, that such Pequots as fall to them be not enslaved, like those which are taken in war: but (as they say is their general custom) be used kindly, have houses, and goods, and fields given them: because they voluntarily choose to come into them, and if not received, will go to the enemy or turn wild Irish themselves: but of this more as I shall understand; thus in haste with best salutations to Mrs. Winthrop and all your, and with my poor desires to the Lord for yours, I rest.
Your Worship's unfeigned,
Roger Williams

John Winthrop, History of New England
1637
July
1] Capt. Stoughton and his company, having pursued the Pequots beyond Connecticut, and missing of them, returned to Pequot New Providence, River, where they were advertised, that one hundred of them were newly come back to a place some twelve miles off. So they marched thither by night, and surprised them all. They put to death twenty-two men, and reserved two sachems, hoping by them to get Sasacus, (which they

promised.) All the rest were women and children, of whom they gave the Naragansets thirty, and our Massachusetts Indians three, and the rest they sent hither. A pinnace, returning, took a canoe with four Indians near Block Island. We sent to Miantunnomoh to know what they were, and after we discharged all save one, who was a Pequod, whom we gave Mr. Cutting to carry into England.

6.] There were sent to Boston forty-eight women and children. There were eighty taken, as before is expressed. These were disposed of to particular persons in the country. Some of them ran away and were brought again by the Indians our neighbours, and those we branded on the shoulder.

12.] Ayanemo, the sachem of Niantick, came to Boston with seventeen men. He made divers propositions, which we promised to give answer unto the next day; and then, understanding he had received many of the Pequods, submitting to him since the former defeat, we first demanded the delivery of them, which he sticking at, we refused further conference with him; but, the next morning, he came and offered what we desired. So the governour referred him to treat with our captains at the Pequod, and wrote instructions to them how to deal with him, and received his present of ten fathom of wampom. He was lovingly dismissed, with some small things given him.

13.] Mr. Stoughton, with about eighty of the English, whereof Mr. Ludlow, Capt. Mason, and [blank,] of Connecticut, were part, sailed to the west in pursuit of Sasacus, at Quinepiack, they killed six, and took two. At a head of land a little short they beheaded two sachems; whereupon they called the place Sachem's Head. About this time they had given a Pequod his life to go find out Sasacus. He went, and found him not far off; but Sasacus, suspecting him, intended to kill him, which the fellow perceiving, escaped in the night, and came to the English. Whereupon Sasacus and Mononotto, their two chief sachems, and some twenty more, fled to the Mohawks. But eighty of their stoutest men, and two hundred others, women and children, were at a place within twenty or thirty miles of the Dutch, whither our men marched, and, being guided by a Divine Providence, came upon them, where they had twenty wigwams, hard by a most hideous swamp, so thick with bushes and so quagmiry, as men could hardly crowd into it. Into this swamp they were all gotten. Lieut. Davenport and two or three more, that entered the swamp, were dangerously wounded by the Indian arrows, and with much difficulty were fetched out. Then our men surrounded the swamp, being a mile about, and shot at the Indians, and they at them, from three of the clock in the afternoon till they desired parley, and offered to

This is the only battle which ever occurred in the bounds of Stratford town ship so far as any record appears.

yield, and life was offered to all that had not shed English blood. So they began to come forth, now some and then some, till about two hundred women and children were come out, and amongst them the sachem of that place, and thus they kept us two hours, till night was come on, and then the men told us they would fight it out; and so they did all the night, coming up behind the bushes very near our men, and shot many arrows into their bats, sleeves and stocks, yet (which was a very miracle) not one of ours wounded. When it was near morning, it grew very dark, so as such of them as were left crept out at one place and escaped, being (as was judged) not above twenty at most, and those like to be wounded; for in the pursuit they found some of them dead of their wounds. Here our men gat some booty of kettles, trays wampom, and the women and children were divided and sent some to Connecticut and some to the Massachusetts. The sachem of the place, having yielded, had his life, and his wife and children, &c. The women, which were brought home, reported, that we had slain in all thirteen sachems, and that there were thirteen more left. We had now slain and taken, in all, about seven hundred. We sent fifteen of the boys and two women to Bermuda, by Mr. Peirce; but he, missing it, carried them to Providence Isle.

William Wilcoxson, History of Stratford

The fight said to be at Cupheag was probably at Pequonnock River where afterwards a gun was found as shown by the following record: - "General Court, April, 1639. Thomas Bull informed the Court that a musket with two letters, J.W. was taken up at Pequonnock in pursuit of the Pequts, which was conceived to be John Woods who was killed at the River's mouth. It was ordered for the present that the musket should be delivered to John Woods friends until other appear. (Col. Rec. Vol. 1 pg. 29) For his much honored Mr. Governor, John Winthrop

New Providence, July 6th 1637
    Much Honored Sir, It having again pleased the Most high
to put into your hands another miserable drone of Adam's degenerate feed, and our brethren by nature, I am bold (if I may not offend it) to request the keeping and bringing up of one of red about his neck, but I will not be preemptory in my choice, but the children. I have fixed mine eye on this little one with the will rest in yur luving pleasure for him and any. Sir, Capt. Patrick gives me a hint of the likely return of most of yur forces (Sasacus and about a score of men with him and other companies, four score in one, surviving,) I shall humbly propound whether it be not considerable, that better now then hereafter the pursuit be continued.
    1st, Because it may stop a conglomeration between them and the Mohawks, which no longer time is like to make.
    2ndly. Longer time will put many opportunities of occasional revenge into their hand, as we see in the three last cut off upon the Connecticut river, after the fort cut off.
    Capt. Patrick also informs me of a great itch upon the soilders to fall foul upon our neighbors. Little sparks prove great fires. The God of Peace who is only wise be pleased to guide us. Capt. Patrick confesseth that they were the chief actors in the last captives, and had taken all by a wile and slain two before the English came. I hear no speech at present about inequality, but content and affection towards us.
    I much rejoice that (as he sayeth) some of the chiefs at Connecticut (Mr. Haynes and Mr. Ludlow,) are almost adverse from killing women and children. Mercy outshines all the works and attributes of him who is the Father of Mercies, unto whom with earnest supplications for you and yours, I rest, Roger Williams.

Roger Williams to John Winthrop
July 10, 1637
    Sir,- Concerning your prisioners taken at Block Island, I have informed the Sachems of your care not to injure them and desire to have them cleared; accordingly Cutshamaquene (now come from pursuing Sassacus who fled

southerly, far out of reach,) I say he hath received testimony from the Sachems Princes that they are Nayantaquit men, and so indeed Sir, I had thought to send you word at this present, had I not received your letter, for it was continually affirmed to me for truth by all the Narragansett men occasionally being here.

Sir, the last messenger that carried letters from you to Pequot, related to the Sachems at Narragansett, that you were displeased that the captives brought to the Bay lately, were taken by the English from the Narragansetts, as also the spoil upon them, which was given to the English soldiers. I have answered that I think it was not so, but I shall understand the truth shortly; and therefore, Sir, be pleased in your next to intimate a word, that I may satisfy them, for though I would not fear a jar with them yet I would send off from being foul, and deal with them wisely as with wolves endowed with men's brains. The last week is a battle fought between the hither Neepmucksand, and the further the Wunnashowatuckoogs, the success is not yet known: it will be of consequence, for it is said they fortify, joining with scattered Pequots.

Sir, the last day of the week Wequash the Pequot guide, near hand, flew his countryman, Sassawwaw, a Pequot, also Miantunnomu's special darling, and a kind General of his forces. There was yesterday some tumult about it, because Wequash lives with Canonicus, and Miantunnomu pursues the revenge and justice.

By the way, although Wequash it may be have treacherously almost slain him, yet I see the righteous hand of the most High Judge, thus: Sassawwaw turned to the Narragansetts and again pretends a return to the Pequots, gets them forth the last year against the Narragansetts and spying advantage, slew the chief Pequot Captain and whips off his head, and so again to the Narragansetts: their treacheries exceeds Machiavelli's.

Roger Williams
To his much honored Governor John Winthrop, these.
New Providence, [July 10, 1637.]

Sir- In the morning I wrote to John Throckmorton, what I heard and thought in general. It has pleased the Lord now this afternoon to send this messenger, (Assontemuit) with variety and plenty, and strangeness of news and tidings, I hope true, and for ought I can discern, true, blessed be the holy name of the most High, who breaks the bow and cuts the spear.

This man was sent this morning from Miantunnomu and Canonicus (as I conceive also from all their chiefs in council) with charge to bring relation to myself of what hath lately happened amongst the Pequots: as also that with my letter he should make speed to yourself with tidings.

He relates that a Pequot man and some five Pequot women came two days since to the Narragansett, and with their ordinary submission begged their lives, and liberty to declare in the name of many others what had happened amongst them: before that Pequot came one squaw, and a second one came, but was questioned much for their truth; but upon the coming and report of the old Pequot, he faith, they all take his report for true.

This man himself, Assotemuit, is a noted messenger from the Sachems, and one whom Miantunnomu hath commended to me for a special messenger from him. This Pequot and the women report that (as I also heard before) all the Pequot were assembled some ten days since with Sassacus in council: some persuaded to fight and fall first upon the Narragansetts, (this also I heard before) the greater part dissented and were for removal: Sasacous and about four score resolved for Mauquowkit, alias Waukheggannick, where the men eaters are; a hundred more for Long Island; another company, the least for Connecticut, some part of it, with the purpose to take final leave of their country. Seventy men, women, and children, (of men between twenty and thirty,) resolved for the Narrangansetts to beg their lives.

Sassacous and his company were worth with these resolved for the Narragansetts, and a skirmish past between them where some were wounded, but away they got, and each company packed up and departed their intended journeys. Miantunnomu sent word to his company remaining in the midway between Pequatit and Nayantakick, that he was in league with Mr. Governor, and therefore of himself would say nothing, but desired them there to rest (at Cuppunaugunnit) in the midway, until he sent to Mr. Governor, and what he said that he would assent unto.

They told Miantunnomu that they had brought three guns with them. He sent the women for the guns, who fetched them from that place, Cuppunnaugunnit, and there they are with him. Only he claims a promise of one to himself, which he desires may be out of these three, as also some powder and shot to it, as indeed was promised. I have much labored with this man to find, if it were possible, any deceit of falsehood, but as he himself and the Sachems question not the Pequot man and women, so I cannot question him.

I asked him (in discourse) what he thinks were best to be done, he answerth that as Miantunnomu himself when he sent to Canonicus to speak his mind, and Canonicus refusing, sent him to speak first, Miantunnomu would say nothing, but would say as Mr. Governor said to himself would likewise say nothing. Yet in discourse I fished out divers hints of their own desire and good liking.

As first, that there is not amongst these any Sachem or any of those who were murderers of the English; if there were they should die.

2. That if Mr. Governor were so minded, they incline to mercy and to give them their lives: and I doubt not but your own breaths are far more tender, like the merciful Kings of Israel.

3. That divers more beside these remain in the woods, and resolve to come in and submit if these be accepted.

4. For the disposing of them, I propounded of them into the Bay; leave some at the Narragansett and so scatter and disperse them: this he liked well, that they should live with the English and themselves as slaves. I then propounded that if they lived amongst the English or themselves, they might hereafter be false to the English, &c., and what if therefore they were appointed and limited to live upon Nayantacawnick or some other Island: and this he thought also well of, if not best, because they were most of them families.

5. That they desire you would please to send some English to take possession of the Pequot country and there to inhabit.

6. That for their own hunting sake, Miantunnomu desires that the English would inhabit that part nearest Connecticut, and that Mystic and thereabout might be free for them. I told him that they might hunt in the woods as they do at Massachusetts and here, notwithstanding the English did generally inhabit: and this satisfied [him].

7. That they desire the Pequot's corn might be enjoyed by the English and themselves, as Mr. Governor please.

8. That the Wunnashowatuckoogs are also afraid and fled, so that there is hope of a safe passage to Connecticut by land.

9. That there is no hope that the Mohawks or any other people will ever assist Sassacous, or any of the Pequots, against the English, because he is now, as it were, turned slave to beg his life.

If all this be true (as I hope it is) we may all fee the God of Heaven delights in mercy, and to draw by love and pity than by fury and wrath. I hope Sir, now that troubles may arise from other parts; his holy Majesty is pleased to quench these nearer fires. He be pleased to confirm this news, and tune all hearts to his prayers in the ordering of our conversation aright. So I rest praying, Your worship's unfeigned,

Roger Williams.

This man relates that yesterday, the Lord's day in the morning, a Pinnace arrived, but he knows not yet what she is.

I pray Sir; forget not to reward this messenger with a coat, as also some powder for Miantunnomu.

My loving respects to Mrs. Winthrop, Mr. Deputy, Mr. Bellingham, and theirs, &c.

Captain John Underhill, News From America

The Pequots having received so terrible a blow and being much affrighted with the destruction of so many, the next day fell into consultation. Assembling their most ablest men together, propounded these three things: First, whether they would set upon a sudden revenge upon the Narragansetts, or attempt an enterprise upon the English, or fly. They were in great dispute, one amongst another. Sassacus, their chief commander, was all for blood; the rest for flight, alledging these arguments: We are a people bereaved of courage, our hearts are faded with the death of so many of our dear friends; we see upon what advantage the English lie; what sudden and deadly blows they strike; what advantage they have of their pieces to us, which are not able to reach them with our arrows at distance. They are supplied with everything necessary; they are heartened in their victory. To what end shall we stand it out with them? We are not able; therefore let us rather save some than lose all. This prevailed. Suddenly after, they spoiled all those goods they could not carry with them, broke up their tents and wigwams and betook themselves in flight.

July, 1637

Sir, — Yesterday by our neighbor Throckmorton I wrote concerning those Nayantaquit men your pinnace took. This bearer, Juanemo, (one of the chief Sachems of that place and chief soldier) came last night with near a score of his men to enquire after them. He was very desirous of a letter to you: I told him I hoped he would find his men at liberty. He hath brought a musket and a barrel of a leve [lever?] piece which his men took from the Pequots.

There was a speech that three of these men were Nayantakoogs, and one a Pequot: it seems he is a Pequot born, but hath long since been theirs, fallen to them, and done good service in their wars against the Pequots.

Sir, this Janemoh is a notable instrument amongst them, &c., your wisdom, I know therefore, will lay hold of this his visit, to engage him the more to you.

Thus humbly begging mercies from the God of heaven for you and yours in

all affairs, I rest, in haste, Your worship's unfeigned,
Roger Williams.

To John Winthrop, Governor of Massachusetts.
New Providence, July 15, 1637
Sir, — For the captives and booty, I never heard any of these Natives question the Acts of the English, only that Native who brought letters to you from Capt. Patrick, and was twice at Boston, related so much as I wrote of in my former, at his return to the Narragansett, viz.: that yourself mould be angry with the English, &c. I met since with him, and he saith he had it not from yourself, but an English man at Roxbury. I thought good to clear your name, and remove suspicions from Mr. Stoughton.

Wequam is alive, so is also the other like to recover of his wound: I never heard that Miantunnomu was displeased with Wequam, for any service to the English, but that Wequam was suspected to deal falsely when he went to hunt for the Pequots at the rivers mouth. 'Tis true there is no fear of God before their eyes, and all the cords that ever bound the Barbarians to Foreigners were made of self and covetousness: yet, if I mistake not, I observe in Miantunnomu some sparks of true friendship, could it be deeply imprinted into him that the English never intended to despoil him of the country, I probably conjecture his friendship would appear in attending of us with 500 men (in case [he is wanted]) against any foreign enemy. The Neepmucks are returned with three heads of the Wunnashowatuckoogs, they flew fix, wounded many, and brought home twenty captives.

Those Inlanders are fled up toward the Mohawks: so they say is Sassacous: our friends at Connecticut are to cast a jealous eye at that people; they say (unless they are belied) that they are to war with the English, &c.

Truely Sir, to speak my thoughts in your ear freely, I bless the Lord for your merciful dealing, &c., but fear that some innocent blood cries at Connecticut. Many things may be spoken to prove the Lord's perpetual war with Amalek extraordinary and mystical; but the King, is a bright light discovering the ordinary path wherein to walk and please him. If the Pequots were murderers (though pretending revenge for Sassacous his father's death, which the Dutch affirmed was from Mr. Governor) yet not comparable to those treacherous servants that flew their lord and king, Joshua, King of Judah, and type of Jesus, yet the fathers only perish in their sin, in the place quoted, &c. The blessed Lamb of God warn away iniquity and receive us graciously. Thus with best salutes to your loving self and yours, Mr. Deputy, Mr. Bellingham, and other loving friends with them, and daily cries to the Father of Mercies for you, I rest your worship's unfeigned. Roger Williams.

Postscript. — Sir, to yours brought by Juanemo on the Lord's day I could have little speech with him; but concerning Miantunnomu I have not heard as yet of any unfaithfulness towards us; I know they belie each other; and I observe our countrymen have almost quite forgotten our great pretences to King and State, and all the world, concerning their fouls, &c. I may desire to attend with my poor help to discover any perfidious dealing, and may desire the revenge of it for a common good and peace, though myself and mine would perish by it: yet I fear the Lord's quarrel is not ended for which the war began, viz.: the little sense, (I speak for the general that I can hear of) of their soul's condition, and our large protestations that way, &c. The general speech is, all must be rooted out, &c. The body of the Pequot men yet live, and are only removed from their dens. The good Lord grant that the Mohawks and they and the whole at the last unite not. For mine own part I cannot be without suspicions of it.

Sir, I thankfully expect a little of your help (in a way of justice and equity) concerning another unjust debtor of mine, Mr. Ludlow, from whom also (in mine absence) I have much suffered. The good Lord smile upon you and yours in the face of his anointed. Your worship's unworthy.

John Winthrop to William Bradford
July 23, 1637
Worthy Sir,

I received your loving letter, and am much provoked to express my affections towards you, but straitness of time forbids me; for my desire is to acquaint you with ye Lords great mercies towards us, in our prevailing against his and our enemies; that you may rejoice and praise his name with us. About eighty of our men, having coasted along towards ye Dutch plantation, (some by water, but most by land) met here and there with some Pequents, whom they slew or took prisoners. Two sachems they took, and be-headed, and not hearing of Sassacus, the cheefe sachem) they gave a prisoner his life, to go and find him out. He went and brought them word where he was, but Sassacus, suspecting him to be a spie, after he was gone, fled away with some twenty more to ye Mohawkes, so our men missed him. Yet dividing themselves, and ranging up and down, as ye providence of God guided them (for ye Indeans were all gone, save three or four, and they knew not wither to guide them, or else would not), upon ye 13th of this month, they light upon a great company of them, eighty strong men, and two hundred women and children, in a small Indian towne, fast by a hideous swamp, which they all slipped into before our men could get to them. Our Captains were not then come together, but there was Mr. Ludlowe and Captain Mason, with some ten of their men, and Captain Patrick with some twenty or more of his, who shooting at ye Indeans, Captain Traske with fifty more came soon in at ye noise. Then they gave the order to surround ye swamp. It being about a mile aboute, but Lieutenant Davenport and some twelve more men, not hearing that command, fell into ye swamp among ye Indeans. The swamps were so thick with shrub-woods, and so boggle with all, that some of them stuck fast, and receive many shott. Lieutenant Davenport was dangerously wounded about his arm-hole and another shot in ye head, so as fainting, they were in great danger to have been taken by ye Indeans. But Sergeant Riggs, and Jeffrey and two or three more, rescued them and slew diverse of ye Indeans with their swords. After they were drawn out, the Indeans desired parley (meeting) and were offered (by Thomas Stanton, our interpreter) that if they would come out, and yield themselves, they should have their lives, and that had not had their hands in English blood. Whereupon ye sachems of ye place came forth, and an old man or two and their wives and children, and after that some other women and children, and so they spake two hours, till it was night. Then Thomas Stanton was sent into them again, to call them forth; but they said that they would sell their lives there, and so shott at high, so thick as, if he had not cried out of ye swamp with their swords, and cooped the Indeans into so narrow a compass, as they could easier then throw ye thickets. So they continued all ye night, standing about twelve foot from one another, and ye Indeans, coming close to our men, shot their arrows so thicke, as they pierced their battle brims, and their sleeves and stockings, and other parts of their cloaths, yet so miraculously did the Lord preserve them as not one of them was wounded, save those three who rashly went into ye swamp. When it was near day, it grew very dark, so those of them which were left dropped away between our men, thought they stood but twelve or fourteen foot asunder; but were presently discovered and some killed in ye pursuit. Upon searching of ye swamps, ye next morning, they found nine slain, and some pulled up, whom ye Indeans had buried in ye mire, so as they do think that, of all this company, not twenty did escape, for they after found some who died in their flight of their wounds received. The prisoners were divided, some to those of ye river, and the rest to us. Of these we send ye male children to Bermuda, by Mr. William Pierce, and ye women and maid children are disposed about in ye towns. There have been now slain and taken, in all about seven hundred, the rest are dispersed, and the Indeans in all quarters so terrified as all their friends are afraid to receive them. Among the prisoners we have ye wife and children of Mononotto, a women of very modest countenance and behavior. It was by her mediation that the two English maids (Wethersfield) were spared from death, and were kindly used by her; so that I have taken charge of her.

One of her first requests was, that the English would not abuse her body, and that her children might not be taken from her. Those which were wounded were fetched by John Gallop, who came with his shallop in a happie hour, to bring them victuals, and to carry their wounded men to ye pinnace, where chief surgeon was with Mr. Wilson, being about eight leagues off. Our people are all in health, (ye Lord praised) and although they had marched in their armes all ye day, and had been in fight all ye night, yet they professed they found themselves so fresh as they could willingly have gone to such another business.

This is ye substance of that which I received, though I am forced to omit many considerable circumstances. So being in much straitness of time, (the ships being to depart within this four days, and them the Lord Lee and Mr. Vane), I hear break of and with hearty salute to. I rest your assured, John Winthrop

The Captains report we have slaine 13 sachems; but Sassacus and Monotto are yet living. That I may make an end of this matter: this Sassacouse (the Pequents cheefe sachem) being fled to the Mowhawkes, they cutt of his head, with some other of the cheefe of them, whether to satisfie the English, or rather the Naragansetts, (who, as I have since heard, hired them to do it,) or for their owne advantage, I well know not; but thus this warr tooke end. The rest of the Pequents were wholly driven from their place, and some of them submitted themselves to the Mohiggs, under Uncas, their sachem, with the approbation of the English of Conightecutt, under whose protection Uncas lived, and he and his men had been faithful to them in this warr, and done then very good service. But this did so vexed the Narragansetts, that they had not the whole sway over them, as they have never ceased plotting and contriving how to bring them under, and because they cannot attaine their ends, because of the English who have protected them, they have sought to raise a generall conspiracie against the English, as will appear in an other place.

Roger Williams to John Winthrop
July 31, 1637
Sir,-I hear yet nothing of any of the runaway captives amongst our neighbors. Yesterday I heard that two escaped from them to the Pequots. If any be or do come amongst them I suppose they shall be speedily returned, or I shall certify where the default is.

Sir, I desire to be truly thankful for the boy intended: his father was of Sasquankit, where the last fight was: and fought not with the English, as his mother (who is with you and two children more) certified me: I shall endeavor his good and the common, in him.

I shall appoint some to fetch him, only I request that you would please to give a name to him.

Sir, concerning captives (pardon my wonted boldness) the Scripture is full of mystery and the old Testament of types.

If they have deserved death 'tis sin to spare:

If they have not deserved death then what punishments? Whether perpetual slavery.

I doubt not but the enemy may lawfully be weakened and despoiled of all comfort of wife and children, but I beseech you well weigh it after a due time of training up to labor, and restraint, they ought not to be set free: yet so as without danger of adjoining to the enemy. Thus earnestly looking up to heaven for you and all yours, I rest.

John Winthrop, History of New England
August
1.] Mr. Stoughton sailed, with some of his company, from Pequod to Block Island. They came thither in the night, yet were discovered, and our men having killed one or to of them, and burnt some of their wigwams, they came to parley, and, submitting themselves to become tributaries in one hundred fathom wampompeague, and to deliver any that should be found to have any hand in Mr. Oldham's death, they were all received, and no more harm done to them.
5.] Mr. Hooker and Mr. Stone came, with Mr. Wilson, from Connecticut by Providence; and, the same day, Mr. Ludlow, Mr. Pincheon, and about twelve more, came the ordinary way by land, and brought them a part of the skin and lock of hair of Sassacus and his brother, and five other Pequod sachems, who, being fled to the Mohawks for shelter, with their wampum, being to the value of five hundred pounds, were by them surprised and slain, with twenty of their best men. Mononotto was also taken, but escaped

wounded. They brought news also of divers other Pequods, which had been slain by other Indians, and their heads brought to the English; so that now there had been slain and taken between eight and nine hundred. Whereupon letters were sent to Mr. Stoughton and the rest, to call them home.

26.] The captain and soldiers returned all from Pequod, having lost but one man, and he died of a flux, and another fell sick of an old infirmity asthma. The Indians about sent in still many Pequods' heads and hands from Long Island and other places, and sachems of Long Island came voluntarily, and brought a tribute to us of twenty fathom of wampum, each of them; and Miantunnomoh sent here some Pequod squaws, which had run from us.

31.] The Narragansetts sent us the hands of three Pequods,-one the chief of those who murdered Capt. Stone.

Roger Williams to John Winthrop.
To his much honored John Winthrop, Governor of the
Massachusetts.

Much Honored Sir,—I was fearful that those dead hands were no pleasing sight (otherwise than a remarkable vengeance had seized upon the first murderer of the English, Wauphanck,) yet I was willing to permit what I could not approve, least if I had buried the present myself, I should have incurred suspicion of pride and wronged my betters, in the natives and others eyes: I have always shown dislike to such dismembering the dead, and now the more, (according to your desire) in your name.

I was also fearful that mine own hand (having no commission from my heart) which is not in mine hand (but in the hand of its Maker, the Most High) to write you ought of mine own return in spirituals, I say fearful that mine own might not be so grateful and pleasing to you: but being called upon by your message and your love, (your paper), I am emboldened.

Concerning the Pequots, the soldiers here related to me that Uncas the Mohegan Sachem had about three hundred men with him on the Pequod river, some sixteen miles from the house, which I believe are most of them Pequods and their confederates the Wunnashowatuckoogs and their Inlanders (whom he charged under pain of death not to come to Canonicus) and with whom he hath made himself great. This man is but a little Sachem, and hath not above forty or fifty Mohegan, which as the English told me were all he could make.

It is generally confirmed that Thomas Stanton, (as himself also confessed to me at my house) was grossly counseled and deluded by one Wequashcuck (a Niantic Sachem) who sheltered four Pequod Sachems and fifty Pequods at Long Island, where now they are, where peace was made with promise from the natives to permit one Pequot; yet Wequashcuck marrying Sassacus his mother hath thus deceived you. This Wequashcuck was the man (to my knowledge) that sheltered Audfah, the murderer of Mr. Oldham, and kept his head so upon his shoulders: yet to this man Thomas Stanton (as it appears) did too much listen, slighting I fear, too much the Narragansetts.

I find our Neighbors very eager to pursue these four Sachems and the fifty Pequods there, I pressed them to patience till Mr. Governor's mind be known, and Miantunnomu (to my knowledge) doth all he can to restrain them, or else long since they had been there. They plead that Mr. Governor may please to accompany, or fend himself against them, but cannot by any article in the league bind them to suffer so many of their enemies in a knot so near them. I press them to humane consideration of so much blood spilt, they answer if they have the Sachems heads they will make the rest Narragansetts, and for the Long Islanders themselves and Wequashcuck, they will not meddle with them, because of the peace Mr. Stoughton made with them.

Concerning the kettles; Miantunnomu answers, that he hath been much wronged by the reports of enemies and false friends to whom some of us (as he faith) hath harkened before himself. He saith he never knew of more than two, one of which the English used at the house, and the other as he hears is at the Fort still: he faith, he hath many of his own, and indeed when I came first hither I saw near ten of twelve which himself or Canonicus had.

He repaid me with a grievance about a Pequod canoe which he desired might be ordered by your own hearing, but it was denied him: his plea seems very fair: thus this brother Yotaash having taken the great Sachem (Puttaquappuonckquame) who was kept in the pinnace alive sometime) took his canoe, which, faith he, the English Captains fitting all together were very willing unto: this canoe Mr. Stoughton afterwards brought about homeward: Miantunnomu and his brother claim it: 'twas denied: he requested that it might be left at my house till Mr. Governor's mind was known. Capt. Stoughton would not yield, but desired him to go along to me, but faith he, I would not trust myself with him, feeing he would not stand to Mr. Governor's determination about the canoe: I would not have mentioned this least it might provoke Mr. Stoughton or any: but I know to whom I intimate it: and I have pretty well appealed the matter already.

He answers, all I can object to him with this: let Mr. Governor have the hearing of it: I will rest in his word, and objecting to him in the particular before divers, that the English complain he was proud, he desired that I would present to Mr. Governor these particulars, that he had cause to maintain his right, because the Connecticut English equaled Uncas and the Mohegan with himself and his men.

Whereas faith he, these Mohegans are but a twig, we are as a great tree. They fell to the English but last year, we have been ever friends, &c. Uncas and his men had a hand in the death of all the English and fought against the Rivers mouth (at Connecticut) we never killed nor consented to the death of an English man.

When the Dutchmen and we fought with the Pequods, the Mohegans joined against us. When Capt. Endicott came against the Pequods the Mohegans received the Pequod women and children and kept them, while the men fought with him. Uncas brought presents to Canonicus, and Miantunnomu, yet at the same time killed two of his women treacherously.

They fell to the English this year in fear of other policy, and we, (faith he) have continued friendship and love ever since they landed. Thus he pleaded and yet proud and covetous and filthy they are, only I was willing to gratify him in this, because as I know your own heart studies peace, and their foul's good, so your wisdom may make use of it unto others who happily take some pleasure in wars: The blessed God of Peace be pleased to give you peace within, at home, and round about you abroad So prays.
Your worship's unfeigned, respective
Roger Williams

I have at present returned Richard Collicut's Pequod girl, which Miantunnomu found out, and desired me to send home with promise of further enquiring.

To His Much Honoured in the Lord, the Governour and Council of the Massachusetts, these present.

Sir, Yours by Robinson we have received, and careful we shall be (I trust) to observe your instructions, and to hasten home as fast as the cause will permit. We are now in a readiness for Block Island; only we wait for a fair wind. We are informed of many Indians there; so we expect the toughest work we have yet met. But we are assured our cause is good, and so we commend ourselves to God's mercy and power. By reason you sent for Mr. Wilson to come with Mr. Hooker, we being willing to show our loyalty to you, and love to the common cause, we have, without gainsaying, dismissed him, albeit we conceived we had special interest in him, and count ourselves naked without him, and therefore expect supply, if we be required to abide by it. Upon consideration that Mr. Wilson going along in the vessel to Connecticut might the more engage Mr. Hooker and expedite his journey to you, and for that, being to go to Block Island, we could enjoy him but one Sabbath more, we dismissed him at first view of your letter.

We do thankfully acknowledge your care and tenderness toward us, signified by your writings, and sending my provisions, &c. and desire we may deserve it. *For* the hardship you conceive you put us to, and pity us for, for my part, what I endure is so little thought of, that it is not worthy pity, neither doth it trouble me, and therefore 1 desire it may trouble none of my friends. It is what I have been acquainted with in part before; and if I be never more put to it for God's cause sake, it is much less than I have expected. Whiles we *enjoy* part in what is there to be had, I hope we shall be satisfied.

We hear not of Miantonimo, nor any of the Narrigansets nor Nianticks that were with you, concerning the Pequids they have, or any thing else, albeit we have sent for Miantonimo to come to us. The last day of the week, (being to go to Block Island, and) wanting a guide, we sent Tho. Stanton and twenty men, with Lieut. Howard towards the Narragansets to get one, who found divers people in Pequid corn, and desired speech with some of them, but by no means could not obtain it, for they ran all away. Still they endeavoured after it, and to know the reason of their running, especially seeing we had formerly expressly told them, they must not use that, for we should then take them for Pequids. At length, they told, that Englishmen had some of them in prison in the bay, and they knew not what Englishmen meant towards them. But we were also told by a squaw, that they were mixt, Pequids and Narragansets together; *and were besides* signs of two rendezvous; she said, one was the Pequids. So, there being twenty *canoes,* ours brought two away, with one kettle and beans, that were at the Pequids' rendezvous, but told them, let them come hither, and, if they were Narragansets, they should have all without any damage. We conceive you do well, in keeping them to strict, just terms, as also in that you refer them to us in the matters specified; for we conceive, being in the field, with our swords in bur hands, we shall do better with them than when the sword is sheathed, and all peace.

Concerning Pequids harboured by them, we have thoughts (after return from Block Island) to require every one of them from those that have them, for these reasons:

1. Their flying to them is no submission to us, but of purpose to avoid it; so that they bear the same good will to us as formerly; that is, they stand

enemies, only use the Narragansetts and others as their covering.

2. Standing thus, we can expect no other but that they will do us mischiefs as opportunity serves; and, besides, be as spurs to the Narragansetts to provoke them to it, and as captains to aid and strengthen them in it.

3. Under the vizor of a Narragansett, they will come amongst us, and do us mischiefs.

4. And when a mischief is done, then it will be fathered upon some renegado Pecot, that will have no master to own him; but it will be said, such a one did it, or such a one, & c.

Therefore, if they will not deliver all to us, according to their covenant, we cannot think their intentions to be good toward us, and shall accordingly declare ourselves towards them; though we will not *so* use like faith with them, but first advise with you, unless we be constrained. And if God do harden their hearts, I doubt not but it will be to their perdition. Only I pray for the contrary, if it be the Lord's will.

For Wequash, we fear he is killed; and if he be, 'tis a mere wicked plot, and, seeing he showed faithfulness to us, and for it is so rewarded, it is hard measure to us-ward; and what is meet to be done therein, is difficult to me to conclude; 1 shall therefore desire your speedy advice.

After return from Block Island, we shall fall upon destroying corn. Near to us it fails much by the weeds, and far from us it will do us little good. The Naragansetts do gather beans in abundance, and we are silent at it; yet, if they should turn enemy, it would be to our great damage. But my opinion is, that they will be twice advised before they will fall out *with us*. Only they will let us bear their injuries as long as we will, and, if they see us in good earnest, I believe they will think upon it, especially whiles the terrour of our sword and our God's doings is upon them.

There be many Pequids yet living, and such as will do much mischief. It will be found therefore necessary for one pinnace, one shallop, and some sixty men, to abide here to take opportunities, partly at Long Island, and elsewhere upon the coasts, (for they lie mostly upon the coast, except such as are under the wing of other Indians.) and I see not many need stay. For, for this place, it is scarce worthy much cost. As for plantation, here is no meadow I see or hear of near; the upland good, but rocky and unlit for ploughs for the most part. Indeed, were there no better, were worthy the best of us, the upland being, as I judge, stronger land than the bay upland.

But if you would enlarge the state, and provide for the poor servants of Christ, that are yet unprovided, (which I esteem a worthy work,) I must speak my conscience. I confess the place and places whither God's providence carried us, that is, to Quillipeage River, and so beyond to the Dutch, is before this, or the bay either, (so far as I can judge,) abundantly. But unless great necessity, or approved policy, require such undertakings, I would be loath to have a hand in, or that my pen should further them, for I affect not scattering, but would rather part stakes at home; yet, so far as it may tend to publick utility, and the enlargement of Christ's kingdom, I hope I should not hinder so good a work, though it be to self disadvantage. It seems to me, God hath much people to bring hither, and the place is too strait, most think. And if so, then, considering, 1st, the goodness of the land, 2nd, the fairness of the title, 3rd, the neighborhood of Connecticut, 4th, the good access that may be thereto, wherein it is before Connecticut, even in the three forementioned considerations, (for the land Connecticut men so judge,) and, 5th, that an ill neighbour may possess it, if a good do not,—I should readily give it my good word, if any good souls have a good liking to it.

I am willing, for my own particular, to stay here so long as yourself and the council, or general court, shall see just cause to require me. Yet I also am as willing to be at home so soon as it may be permitted; and. for my part, where some few things more are over, I see nothing against but that I may come home, and therefore shall wait to know your minds therein.

Thus, with my due respect remembered to yourself, the honoured council, and the rest of the magistrates, desiring your prayers, I humbly commend you to God.

Yours, as in duty I am bound,

Israel Stoughton.

From Pequid, the 6th week of our warfare, (14 August, 1637)

Richard Davenport to John Winthrop

To the Right Worthy Honored Governor of Massachusetts these present:

Possession House, this August, 1637

Honored Sir,

My most humble and due respect to your worship, Mr. Deputy, my colonel, with all the rest of or noble worthyes. Sir, the messenger staying for us I must make hast. How God hath dealt wth us, I doubt not but your worship, having full intelligence by them from Block Hand; now since their departure, there came some Mohegens to the house, and brought the hands of a great Sachem, as they said greater then Sassacus, hee beeing Momonotuk Samm, a mighty fellow for curradge, and one that I know by some experience his desperatenes in the swamp: for as I gather by the

174

description of him, and also the Indians report that slew him, that hee sayd hee kild one in the swamp, shooting him in the belley; and another he killed with arrows, which was my selfe, but, blessed be God, wee all live. 2 days after this, the same Indians killed another, who was then runn away from Sasacus: hee sayd hee thought that Sasacus was killed; for yet Monowhoak had beset the wigwam where they weere, and soe fell upon them, and this man lying at the doore rann away: but what creditt to give to it wee knew not. 2 days since I went up to the head of this river wth 20 men to cut come or gather beans, and coining thither I found a great company of Mohegens, who were returned to their countrey, about 500 of men, women and children. They were some what fearefull at first, but after spoke with us and loveingly intertained us. They tell for certaine that Sasacus is killed, as ye former suspected, and 40 men witt him, and som women. 6 men are escaped, whereof Momoonotuk is one. I perseave the Indians would bee glad to make women of slaves all the Pecotts now, except the sachems and Capt. and murtherers: but them they would kill. They seeme to feare the Naregansick men, but hope the English will not suffer them to be wronged. Capt Stoughton is gone a weeke since to Conetecutt Plantations, and I heare that the sachems of Long Hand doe now wayt for him, wth their tribute, at the river mouth: I suppose, under favour, this place will not prove good for a plantation, so farr as I can judge, haveing seene ye greatest part of the countrey, but I must extoll Qenepiake and Marriadge Poynt; but this I know you heare of. I see not what busines heere will bee for many men long. I know not Capt Stoughtons mind, till his returne, about marching by ye Nipmucks home. My Capt. and my selfe are for it.

None of our souldiers have noe mind to worke, and how they would fight I know not, they murmure much for butter and cheese, etc: but I hope God will give so much wisdome to indeauor their passifieing: I confesse some spirits heere will trouble a patient man.

New Providence, 20th of August, 1637
Much Honored Sir,
Yours by Yotaash (Miantinomo's brother) received, I accompanied him to the Narragansets, and having got Canonicus and Miantinomo, with their council, acquainted them faithfully with the contents of your letter, both grievances and threatenings; and to demonstrate, I produced the copy of the league, (which Mr. Vane sent me) and with breaking of a straw in two or three places, I showed them what they had done. In sum their answer was,

that they thought they should prove themselves honest and faithful, when Mr. Governor understood their answers; and that

(although they would not contend with their friends,) yet they could relate many particulars, wherein the English had broken (since these wars) their promises.

First, then, concerning the Pequod squaws, Canonicus answered, that he never saw any, but heard of some that came into these parts, and he bade carry them back to Mr. Governor; but since he never heard of them till I came, and now he would have the country searched for them. Miantinomo answered, that he never heard of but six, and four he saw which were brought to him, at which he was angry, and asked why they did not carry them to me, that I might convey them home again. Then he bid the natives that brought them to carry them to me, who, departing, brought him word that the squaws were lame, and they could not travel. Whereupon he sent me word that I should send for them. This I must acknowledge, that this message I received from him, and sent him word that we were but few here, and could not fetch them nor convey them, and therefore desired him to send men with them, and to seek out the rest. Then, saith he, we were busy ten or twelve days together, as indeed they were, in a strange kind of solemnity, wherein the sachems ate nothing but at night, and all the natives round about the country were feasted. In which time, saith he, I wished some to look to them, which, notwithstanding, at this time, they escaped; and now he would employ men instantly to search all places for them, and within two or three days to convey them home. Besides, he professed that he desired them not, and was sorry the Governor should think he did. I objected that he sent to beg one. He answered, that Sassamun, being sent by the Governor with letters to Pequod, fell lame, and, lying at his house, told him of a squaw he saw, which was a sachem's daughter, who, while he lived, was his (Miantinomo's) great friend. He therefore desired, in kindness to his dead friend, to beg her, or redeem her.

Concerning his departure from the English, and leaving them without guides, he answered, first, that they had been faithful, many hundreds of them, (though they were solicited to the contrary;) that they stuck to the English in life or death, without which they were persuaded that Uncas and the Mohegans had proved false, (as he fears they will yet) as also that they never had found a Pequod; and therefore, saith he, sure there was some cause. I desired to know it. He replied in these words, "Chinook eiuse wetompatimucks," that is, did ever friends deal so with friends? I urging wherein, he told me this tale: that his brother, Yotaash, had seized upon

Puttaquppuunch, Quame, and twenty Pequods, and threescore squaws; they killed three and bound the rest, watching them all night, and sending for the English, delivered them to them in the morning.

Miantinomo (who, according to promise, came by land with two hundred men, killing ten Pequods in their march,) was desirous to see the great sachem whom his brother had taken, being now in the English houses; but, saith he, I was thrust at with a pike many times, that I durst not come near the door. I objected, he was not known.

He and others affirmed he was, and asked if they should have dealt so with Mr. Governor. I still denied that he was known, &c. Upon this, he saith, all my company were disheartened, and they all, and Cutshamoquene, desired to be gone; and yet, saith he, two of my men (Wagonckwhut and Maunamoh) were their guides to Sesquankit from the river's mouth.

Sir, I dare not stir coals, but I saw them too much disregarded by many, which their ignorance imputed to all, and thence came the misprision, and blessed be the Lord things were no worse. I objected they received Pequods and wampum without Mr. Governor's consent. Canonicus replied, that although he and Miantinomo had paid many hundred fathom of wampum to their soldiers, as Mr. Governor did, yet he had not received one yard of beads nor a Pequod. Nor, saith Miantinomo, did I, but one small present from four women of Long-Island, which were no Pequods, but of that isle, being afraid, desired to put themselves under my protection. By the next I shall add something more of consequence, and which must cause our loving friends of Connecticut to be very watchful, as also, if you please, their grievances, which I have labored already to answer, to preserve the English name; but now end abruptly, with best salutes and earnest prayers for your peace with the God of peace and all men. So praying, I rest,
Your worship's unfeigned,
Roger Williams

John Winthrop, History of New England
October 7.] A day of thanksgiving kept in all the churches for our victories against the Pequot, and for the success of the assembly; the captains and soldiers, who had been in the late service, were feasted, and after the sermon, the magistrates and elders accompanied them to the door of the house where they dined.

Roger Williams to John Winthrop
October, 1637

Sir,-Some while since you were pleased to desire me to signify to the Sachems, the promise of the Block Islanders to yourself, and therefore their exemption from all other submissions and tribute. Their answer was, that as they had left them to Mr. Governor formerly upon Mr. Oldham's death, so have they done since, and have had no other dealing with them then for the getting of the head of Audsah the chief murderer: as also that they understand the one hundred fathom of beads to be yearly paid to Mr. Governor, in which respect they have been far from desiring a bead from them, and do acknowledge them to be wholly Mr. Governor's subjects.

Sir, I hear that there is now a Pequot with the Mohegans, one William (Baker I think his name is) who was pursued, as is said by the English of Connecticut for uncleanness with an Indian squaw, who is now with child by him. He hath there gotten another squaw and lies close, unknown to the English. They say he came from a traditional house which Plymouth men have at Connecticut, and can speak much Indian. If it be he, when I lived at Plymouth, I heard the Plymouth men speak much of his evil course that way with the natives.

The occasion that our neighbors know of him was this: some eight days since, six Narragansett men were coming from Connecticut, and by the way fell upon some Pequots, who were rescued out of their hands by the Mohegans, who also bound those six Narragansetts many days together at Monahiganick (upon Pequot river, where this William was) and spoiled them of their coats and what else they had. The sachems and the men are greatly incensed, affirming that they can not but revenge this abuse offered to their men; yet I have got this promise that they will not do ought without Governor's advice.

Sir, I have long heard, and these six men affirm, that there are many of the scattered Pequots rende-zvoused with Uncas the Mohegan Sachem and Wequash the Pequot, who being employed as one of the guides to the English in their late wars, is grown rich, and a Sachem with the Pequots: and hath five or six runaways. There are all the runaways harbored (which upon long and diligent inquiry) I am certain and confident of, and can give good assurance that there is not one amongst all the Narragansetts.Mr. Stoughton hath been long assured that Meik-sah, Canonicus' eldest son hath his squaw, but having enquired it out, I find she was never at the Narragansetts, but is married to one Meikcomp a Sachem of Nayantick, which being nearer to Pequot is more friendly to the Pequots: and where as

I hear that Wequashcuck who long sheltered Audsah and so grossly deluded Thomas Stanton in the late wars hath filled many baskets with beads from Pequots Sachems and one hundred and twenty Pequots which he sheltered now at Nayantick. Uncas the Mohegan and Wequashcuck were lately at Long island, from whence some few days since, Uncas carried away forty Pequots to Monahiganick, and Wequashcuck thirty to Nayantick. While I write, Miantunnomu is come to my house and affirmeth the same; professing if I would advise him, he would go over to Mr. Governor to acquaint the Governor that Canonicus and himself hath no hand in these passages. He asks me often if he may safely go, and I assure him if he have an honest heart he need not fear any deceit or treachery amongst the English; so I thing within a day or two he will be coming towards you. He tells me what I had not heard that of those Pequots to whom at the first by my hand you were pleased to give life, but seven came to them, of which five also long since are gone to Monahiganick.

Sir, your servant Reprieve lodged here two nights, and Miantunnomu tells me that five days since he lay a night with him and is gone to Block Island. He is very hopefully improved since I first saw him: and am bold to wish that he might now take his last farewell I of his friends, to whom you would be rather pleased to give leave to visit him at Boston, for you cannot believe how hard it is for him to escape much evil, and especially uncleanness while he is with them.

John Winthrop, History of New England
November
1.] Miantunnomoh, the Narragansett sachem, came to Boston. The governor, deputy, and treasurer, treated with him, and they parted upon fair terms. He acknowledged that all the Pequod country and Block Island were ours, and promised that he would not meddle with them but by our leave. We gave him leave to right himself for the wrongs with Janemoh and Wequash Cook had done him; and for the wrong they had done us, we would right ourselves in our own time.
1638
February
About this time the Indians, which were in our families, were much frightened with Hobbamock (as they call the devil) appearing to them in diver shapes, and persuading them to forsake the English, and not to come at the assemblies, nor to learn to read.
March

30.] There came letters from Connecticut to the governor of the Massachusetts, to desire advice from the magistrate and elders here about Sequin and the Indians of the river, who had, underhand, (as we conceived) procured the Pequods to do that onslaught at Wethersfield the last year. The case fell out to be this: Sequin gave the English land there, upon contract that he might sit down by them, and be protected. When he came to Wethersfield, and had set down his wigwam, they drave him away by force. Whereupon, he not being of strength to repair this injury by open force, he secretly draws in the Pequods. Such of the magistrates and elders as could meet on the sudden returned this answer: That, if the cause were thus, Sequin might, upon this injury first offered by them, right himself either by force or fraud, and that by the law of nations; and though the damage he had done them had been one hundred times more than what he had sustained from them, that is not considerable in point of a just war; neither was he bound (upon such an open act of hostility publicly maintained) to seek satisfaction first in a peaceable way; it was enough, that he had com-plained of it as an injury and breach of covenant. According to this advice, they proceeded and made a new agreement with the Indians of the river.

27.] The Indians of Block Island sent three men with ten fathoms of wampum for part of their tribute.

April

21.] Owsamekin, the sachem of Acooemeck, on this side of the Connecticut, came to the governor and brought a present of eighteen skins of beaver from himself and the sachems of Mohegan beyond Connecticut and Pakontuckett. The occasion was, (as he said,) it was reported, that we were angry with him, and intended to war upon them; so they came to seek peace. The governor received the present, and (having none of the other magistrates at hand to advise with) answered them, that if they had done no wrong to the English, nor aided our enemies, we would be at peace with them; and accordingly signified so much to the magistrates at Connecticut. They took this answer well, and departed with the letter.

23.] This was a very hard winter. The snow lay, from November 4th to March 23rd, half a yard deep about the Massachusetts, and a yard deep beyond Merrimack, and so the more north the deeper, and the spring was very backward. This day it did snow two hours together, (after much rain from N.E.) with flakes as great as shillings.

June

1.] Between three and four in the afternoon, being clear, warm weather, the wind westerly, there was a great earthquake. It came with a noise like a continued thunder, or the rattling of coaches in London, but was presently gone.

It was at Connecticut, at Naragansett, at Pascataquack, and all the parts round about. It shook the ships, which rode in the harbour, and all the islands. The noise and the shakings continued about four minutes. The earth was un-quiet twenty days after, by times.

August

3.] In the night was a very great tempest or hiracano at S.W. which drave a ship on ground at Charlestown, and break down the windmill there, and did much other harm. It flowed twice in six hours, and about Naragansett it raised the tide fourteen or fifteen foot above the ordinary spring tides, upright. Janemoh, the sachem of Niantic, had gone to Long Island and rifled some of those Indians which were tributaries to us. The sachem complained to our friends of Conneticut, who wrote us about it, and sent Capt. Mason, with seven men, to require satisfaction. The governour of the Massachusetts wrote also to Mr. Williams to treat with Miantunnomoh about satisfaction or otherwise bid them look for war. Upon this Janemoh went to Connecticut, and made his peace, and gave full satisfaction for all injuries.

Lion Gardener, Relation of the Pequot War

Thus far I had written in a book, that all men and posterity might know how and why so many honest men had their blood shed, yea, and some flayed alive, others cut in pieces, and some roasted alive, only because Kichamokin [Cutshamequin], a Bay Indian, killed one Pequit; and thus far of the Pequit war, which was but a comedy in comparison of the tragedies which hath been here threatened since, and may yet come, if God do not open the eyes, ears, and hearts of some that I think are willfully deaf and blind, and think because there is no change that the vision fails, and put the evil-threatened day far off, for say they, We are now twenty to one to what we were then, and none dare meddle with us. Oh! Woe be to the pride and security which hath been the ruin of many nations, as woeful experience has proved.

But I wonder, and so doth many more with me, that the Bay doth no better revenge the murdering of Mr. Oldham, an honest man of their own, seeing they were at such cost for a Virginian. The Narragansetts that were at

Block-Island killed him, and had 650 of gold of his, for I saw it when he had five pieces, and put it up into a clout and tied it up all together, when he went away from me to Block Island; but the Narragansetts had it and punched holes into it, and put it about their necks for jewels; and afterwards I saw the Dutch have some of it, which they had of the Narragansetts at a small rate.

And now I find that to be true which our friend Waiandance told me many years ago, and that was this; that seeing all the plots of the Narragansetts were always discovered, he said they would let us alone 'till they had destroyed Uncas, and him, and then they, with the Mowquakes and Mowhakues and the Indians beyond the Dutch, and all the Northern and Eastern Indians, would easily destroy us, man and mother's son. This have I informed the Governors of these parts, but all in vain, for I see they have done as those of Wethersfield, not regarding till they were impelled to it by blood.

FAMILY LINES OF UNCAS AND SASSACUS

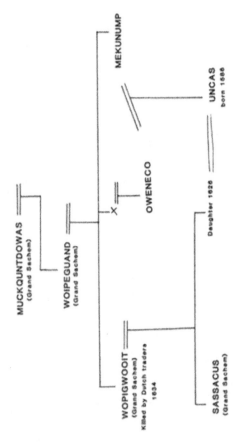

Chapter Five

Lost Child of the Pequots

In August of 1675, almost forty years after the Pequot war, Uncas was ordered to surrender his arms to the English and proclaim his neutrality in a war between the Wampanoag Indians of Massachusetts and the English. During this time, James Fitch had been assigned to preach among the Mohegan Indians and in seeing Uncas, he stated, "I am apt to fear, that a great obstruction unto his labors is in the sachem of those Indians, whose name is Unkas; an old and wicked, willful man, a drunkard, and otherwise very vicious; who hath always been an opposer and underminer of praying to God." It was found by many that Uncas did not leave a favorable opinion of himself even as he grew old. Considerable conflict afflicted Uncas and seemed to have followed him until the day he died.

The names of some of the early sachems of the Pequot tribe have been preserved in a genealogy of the Uncas family, as it was made out by Uncas himself in 1679. The first whose name is mentioned was Tamaquashad, of whom no particulars are given, but who must have lived about the time when the Pequots first established themselves in Connecticut, or perhaps when they first set out on their pilgrimage from the Hudson. The next in succession was Muckquntdowas, who lived at a place called Awcumbucks, situated in the heart of the Pequot country.

His wife's was named Meekunump, and he had two children; Woipeguand, who became sachem after him; and a daughter, called like her mother, Meekunump, who was married to Oweneco, the father of Uncas. Woipeguand married a daughter of Wekoum, chief sachem of Narragansett; and, when he died, was succeeded by his son, Wopigwooit. Wopigwooit was the same with that Wapequart mentioned by the Dutch authors, and undoubtedly, also, with that Pekoath.

The son of Wopigwooit was Tatobam, otherwise called Sassacus the most famous and the most unfortunate of the Pequot grand sachems.

John Deforest, History of the Indian of Connecticut

About ten years previous to the war of the Pequots with the English, that is about 1626, Uncas, the son of Oweneco and Meekunump, married a daughter of Sassacus, thus connecting himself still more closely with the royal line of his tribe. The claims which he in this manner acquired and strengthened, afterwards contributed to the downfall of his nation, but finally resulted in raising Uncas himself to considerable influence, and to independent power. In fact, this Uncas, son of Oweneco a Pequot sagamore, and father of another Oweneco like himself a Mohegan sachem, will be one of the most remarkable, and one of the most important characters, who ever will occupy a place in the succeeding narrative. We have already mentioned the relationship of Uncas, sagamore of Mohegan, to the royal family, and have briefly noticed that he was now in rebellion against Sassacus, the grand sachem of the tribe. It seems probable that, on the death of Wopigwooit or Pekoath, Uncas laid claim to the sachemship, grounding his title on his own descent, and perhaps strengthening it by the regal birth of his squaw. At all events, some difficulty occurred, and Uncas was soon engaged in open war with his chieftain.

The great body of the nation remained faithful to Sassacus, and the rebellious sagamore was defeated and expelled from the country. He fled to the Narragansetts; but after remaining among them a while, he sent a humble message to Sassacus begging permission to return. This was granted, on condition of submission and future good behavior. Uncas promised every thing, and again came back to Mohegan. He was soon guilty of treachery, or was accused of it, and had once more to fly. Again, on submission, he was pardoned and allowed to return; and again, for the same cause as before, banished. Some of his warriors who fled with him remained in the Narragansett country, and were living there many years afterwards. In this manner he lost the greater part of his followers, and all his lands; which last, by the Indian customs, in all cases of war, became the property of the conqueror. His territory was so small, and his men so few, that he was unable to make a grand hunt alone, but hunted in company with two other sagamores, sons of the sister of Sassacus, and, of course, the cousins of his own wife. Judging from this fact, it seems probable that he could not have had remaining more than twenty-five or thirty men. His two friends above mentioned finally quarreled with their powerful relation, Sassacus; and in consequence were forced to fly to the Narragansett country, from whence they never returned. Their lands, like those of Uncas, became subject to the grand sachem of the tribe.

Some of the Mohegans, therefore, and, according to one author, fifty of them, took up their residence on the Connecticut River, chiefly in the township of Hartford. (Thus it was that we find Poxen here, whom, under the name of Foxon, we shall subsequently meet as the cunning counsellor and ambassador of Uncas after he has risen to greatness and power. It is possible, also, that some of these men were not native Mohegans, but river Indians, who had attached themselves to an adventurous and warlike chief like Uncas, and had thus acquired a title to the name of Mohegoneak. Uncas, himself, probably lived in this part of the country, as it is not at all likely that he would be allowed to continue at Mohegan. Mohegan was the ancient burying place of the Pequot sachems; and would Sassacus, the descendant and representative of that race of heroes, allow their graves to be polluted by the foot of one who had made himself an alien to his tribe?

In person, Uncas is said to have been a man of large frame and great physical strength. His courage could never be doubted, for he displayed it too often and too clearly in war and especially in the subsequent contest against his native tribe. No sachem, however, was ever more fond of overcoming his enemies by stratagem and trickery. He seemed to set little value upon the glory of vanquishing in war, compared with the advantages it brought him in the shape of booty, and new subjects, and wider hunting grounds. He favored his own men and was therefore popular with them; but all others who fell under his power he tormented with continual exactions and annoyances. His nature was selfish, jealous, and tyrannical; his ambition was grasping, and unrelieved by a single trait of magnanimity. He was now; it is probable, in the prime and vigor of early manhood.

As early as July, 1637, less than two months after the fight at Fort Mystic, the authorities of Massachusetts had a quarrel with Ninigret, the Nehantic sachem, about his harboring Pequots. Uncas, too, whose clan was exceedingly feeble before the war broke out, now began to make it formidable by the number of refugees from the dispersed tribe which he continually received into it. Pequots and Mohegans were, until lately, all the same people; and when they were mingled together it was difficult, if not impossible, for the colonists to distinguish them. But the proceedings of the crafty sachem were revealed to the English by the Narragansetts, between whom and Uncas a bitter hostility began to grow up even before the close of the present war.

In July, 1638, while the persecution of the scattered Pequots still dragged on, Uncas, with thirty-seven of his warriors, made a ceremonial visit to Boston. Being admitted before the council of the colony, he laid down twenty fathoms of wampum as a present for the governor. He was told that the governor would not accept it until he had made explanations and given satisfaction concerning the Pequots whom he had received and now harbored. Uncas was terribly perplexed. He saw the rock upon which Sassacus had split, and was determined not to draw upon himself the anger of the English, while, at the same time, he could not bear to part with any of his followers. He denied that he had any Pequots, and affirmed most expressly, that all the company then present with him were true Mohegans. His protestations and his evident grief softened the displeasure of the magistrates, and they accepted his present. He now took courage. Placing his hand on his heart, and addressing the governor, he said: "This heart is not mine: it is yours. I have no men: they are all yours. Command me any hard thing and I will do it. I will never believe any Indian's words against the English. If any Indian shall kill an Englishman, I will put him to death be he never so dear to me."

To the spirit exhibited in this speech Uncas was faithful, so far as it agreed with his own advantage, as long as he lived. Entirely devoted to his own interest, he found that he best advanced that interest by exhibiting great devotion to the powerful foreigners. He was faithful to them just as the jackal is faithful to the lion: not because it loves the lion, but because it gains something by remaining in his company.

How sincere he was in his dealings on this occasion, we may learn from a fact preserved in the letters of Roger Williams. As Uncas was returning from Boston he passed within a mile of Williams' house; and, one of his company being disabled from traveling by lameness, turned aside there to rest. This man, named Wequaumugs, had a Narragansett father and a Mohegan mother, so that he was on free terms in the country of either tribe. He soon fell into conversation with his kind host, and answered his questions without reserve. He stated that there were only two Pequots with Miantinamo, neither of whom had come in of themselves, but both having been captured by his warriors. In the Nehantic country there were about sixty under Wequash Cook, nephew of Ninigret the Nehantic sachem. Williams then asked him if there were any Pequots in the company which Uncas took with him to Boston. Wequaumugs replied that there were six, and gave their names, observing that two of them, Pamatesick and Weaugonhick, were slayers of Englishmen. Williams wrote down the names, and sent them, with an account of the conversation, to Governor Winthrop, that Uncas might not lose the credit of his praise-worthy fidelity to the English, and his singular regard for truth. The revelation must have been peculiarly gratifying to Winthrop, as he had given the sachem a fine red coat on his departure, had defrayed his expenses while he remained in Boston, furnished him with provisions for his homeward journey, and dismissed him with a general letter of protection.

The Pequots who remained independent at last became tired of being chastized about, like wolves and foxes, from one hiding place to another. They sent in some of their chief men to Hartford, with an offer that, if only their lives might be spared, they would give themselves up to the English and become their servants. This offer was accepted; and Uncas and Miantinemo were both summoned to Hartford, to agree with the magistrates in the disposition of the conquered people. This invitation demonstrates, perhaps, the power and influence to which Uncas had already arisen. Had he been no more potent now than he was at the commencement of the war, it is very possible that he might not have received such a token of consideration. It seems probable, also, that the colonists had already fixed their eye upon him, as one whom they could safely build up as a bulwark and a watchtower for themselves against the other aborigines of this part of New England. Another cause likewise existed for this meeting, in a circumstance to which I have before alluded. The Pequots and Mohegans had already ceased fighting, and began to unite under Uncas' authority. Partly in consequence of this, and partly from the remembrance of ancient hostility, a quarrel had arisen between this new community and the Narragansetts. Insults and injuries were bandied to and fro; and the sachems were now summoned to Hartford, as well to adjust their own disputes, as to settle the distribution of the Pequots.

Miantinomo set out for the place of meeting in great state; being attended by his wife and children, by several sachems, and no less than one hundred and fifty warriors. Three Englishmen also traveled in his company, one of whom was Roger Williams. This large number of warriors was, probably, not so much in ostentation, as for protection against real or fancied danger from the followers of Uncas. On the way, various Narragansetts were met coming from Connecticut, who complained that they had been plundered by the Pequots and Mohegans. Some Wunnashowatuckoogs, a tribe subject to Canonicus, also came into camp and told alarming stories. "They had been robbed," they said, "two days before, by a band of six or seven hundred Indians, composed of Pequots and Mohegans, and others who were their confederates. This great band had spoiled twenty-three fields of their corn, and had rifled several Narragansetts who were staying among them. Now they were lying in wait to stop Miantinomo on his journey; and some of them had threatened to boil him in a kettle."

These reports being continually swelled and strengthened, the three Englishmen, with the design of preventing bloodshed, advised a return; and Roger Williams proposed to go himself to Connecticut, by water, and use his influence to have a stop put to this insolence of the Mohegans. But as the distance was already half accomplished, Miantinomo rejected this plan; and resolved at any risk to proceed in the path on which he had set out. The journey was continued, therefore; the sachems marching in the center; Roger Williams and his companions in front; and forty or fifty men scouting the woods on either side. No attack was made, perhaps none was intended; and, proceeding in this manner, they finally crossed the Connecticut and entered the little village of Hartford.

As soon as he obtained an interview with the magistrates, Miantinomo brought forward his complaints against Uncas, for all the acts of injustice and violence which he had committed, or was said to have committed, upon the Narragansetts. The Mohegan chief was not there, having sent a messenger to say that he was lame and could not come. Haynes, a principal member of the council, and afterwards governor of the colony, replied that it was a very lame excuse; and dispatched an urgent request that he should make his appearance. Uncas recovered from his lameness sufficiently to reach Hartford; and an examination was then commenced of the charges brought against him by the Narragansetts. The Mohegan sachem brought in one of his followers, to testify in his defense. This man stated that he was in the party which was said to have plundered the Wunnashowatuckoogs; that instead of six hundred and sixty warriors, as the Narragansetts affirmed, there were only one hundred; and that they did nothing more than roast corn, and a few other harmless things of the like nature. The Narragansetts contradicted this, and the Mohegans rejoined: both parties commenced criminations and recriminations: the magistrates heard them patiently for a while, to let them blow off their anger in words; but, having no evidence upon which they could depend, they finally ordered the charges to be dismissed.

They then attempted to effect a reconciliation between the sachems, and succeeded so far as to make them shake hands. Miantinomo seemed to be the most sincere, and twice invited his rival to feast with him on some venison which his men had just killed. The magistrates urged Uncas to accept the invitation; but, either from sullenness, or from suspicion of the Narragansett's intentions, he refused. In a private conference Miantinomo gave in the names of six Pequot sachems who remained, and of all the surviving men of that nation who had been guilty of English blood. A list of these names was written out, and was afterwards read to Uncas, who acknowledged it to be correct. The sachems, or, more properly sagamores, were Nausipouck, now on Long Island, Puppompogs, brother of Sassacus, Kithansh and Nanasquionwut at Mohegan, and Mausaumpous at Nehantic.

An investigation was now commenced, as to the number of Pequots still remaining, and where they were to be found. Canonicus, the Narragansetts said, had not one, Miantinomo had ten or eleven, the remains of seventy who had, at various times, submitted to him, had either never come to his country, or had afterwards departed. All the rest of the Pequots, they asserted, were now in their ancient territory or among the Mohegans. Uncas was very unwilling to give in his account, and endeavored to avoid it with his characteristic duplicity. "He did not know the names of his Pequots," he said, "and so could not state them. He had but a few. Ninigret and three other Nehantic sachems had Pequots; but, as for himself, he had only twenty." Thomas Stanton, the interpreter, told him that he dealt very falsely; and other persons stated that he had fetched over thirty or forty Pequots from Long Island at one time. He now acknowledged that he had thirty, but declared that he was unable to tell their names. He was allowed ten days to bring in the names and the exact number; and a messenger was sent to the Nehantics to obtain a list of the Pequots who were with them. Whether these conditions were exactly fulfilled or not is uncertain; for we have no minute account of the further proceedings of this English and Indian council. At the next meeting, however, it was agreed on all hands, that about two hundred Pequots remained besides women and children. This number included all the grown males, the old, the infirm and the maimed, as well as those who were strong and fit for war.

A tripartite treaty, dated October 1st, 1638, was now entered into by John Haynes, Roger Ludlow and Edward Hopkins, for the English of Connecticut; by Miantinomo on behalf of the sachems of the Narragansetts; and Poquim, or Uncas, on the part of himself and the sagamores under him.

There was to be perpetual peace between the parties, all former provocations, and enmities being buried forever. If, however, any quarrel should take place between the Narragansetts and Mohegans, the party aggrieved was to appeal to the English, whose decision was to be held binding. And if either of the tribes should refuse to be guided by that decision, the English might take up arms and forcibly compel it to submit. The Mohegans and Narragansetts were to destroy those Pequots who had been guilty of English blood, and to bring in their heads to the magistrates. The two hundred Pequots were to be divided, eighty to Miantinomo, twenty to Ninigret, and the remaining one hundred to Uncas. For these captives the chieftains were to pay an annual tribute of a fathom of wampum for every man, half a fathom for every youth, and a hand for every male child. The Pequots were not to live in their ancient country, nor to be called by their ancient name, but to become Narragansetts and Mohegans. Lastly, the Pequot territory was not to be claimed by the sachems, but to be considered as the property of the English of Connecticut. Such was the peace which closed the famous Pequot war; and thus, for a time, was the national existence of that brave though savage people extinguished.

Having disposed of matters of inferior importance, it is now time to look about for our old and crafty acquaintance, Uncas. After the overthrow of the Pequots, this sachem laid claim to the sovereignty of their country on the ground of his connection with the royal family of the tribe. He readily gave up that district along the seacoast which the English had seized, but the remainder he considered as justly and undeniably his own. He thus came into possession of all the northern part of New London County, together with the southern portions of the counties of Tolland and Windham. The former tributaries of the Pequots, however, now considered themselves independent; and those of them who submitted to Uncas, either at the present or any future time, were mostly, if not all, brought to submit by force. His tribe was vastly increased, perhaps doubled, by the one hundred Pequots, who had been given him at the treaty of 1638. Some refugees had joined him from the conquered tribe before that event, and others had attached themselves to him since. It was natural that the Pequots, rather than fly from their country, or become slaves to the English, or join their ancient foes, the Narragansetts, should choose to identify themselves with a fragment of their own tribe, even though that fragment had been rebellious and hostile. Wanderers from other nations, too, collected around Uncas, and increased the numbers and influence of the Mohegans. Among these warlike and unsettled communities, wherever a sachem distinguished himself by his abilities and success, he was sure to attract many adventurers from the neighboring tribes. Some came out of a desire for protection, some from a wish to distinguish themselves under so fortunate a leader, and some, doubtless, because they were forced to come by the sachem himself in his efforts to increase the number of his followers. Uncas considerably extended his territories by marrying the daughter of the Hammonassett sachem, Sebequanash; thus coming into possession of the seashore as far east as the Aigicomock, or East River, in Guilford. In 1641, indeed, he sold, [December 27th,] for a small consideration, nearly the whole of the tract to the people of Guilford; but, as most of the Hammonassetts probably passed over to the east side of the Connecticut, his effective strength in warriors was very likely increased, rather than diminished, by this transaction.

Uncas had another source of influence in the consideration which his late services brought him among the English. His faithfulness during the Pequot war was repaid by the colonists with their favor, when it could be granted with justice, and sometimes, perhaps, when it could only be granted with injustice. But, aside from gratitude, the colonists were not insensible of the advantages which would accrue to them from having always at their command so active and influential a native chieftain. In war he would be useful as an ally, and in peace he could act as a spy upon the proceedings of his fellow sachems. Such an ally and such a spy Uncas was willing to be, as long as it would increase his power and gratify his capacity.

The first transaction of importance between Uncas and Connecticut, after the treaty of 1638, was an agreement drawn up and signed on the 8th of October, 1640. The nature of this agreement was ambiguous; and it was, many years afterwards, made one ground of a tedious, fluctuating, and expensive law suit between the Mohegans and the colony. The colonial authorities, and all who were interested in their success, affirmed that it was a true deed of purchase and sale. The Indians and their supporters declared that it was a mere right of pre-emption, by which Uncas interdicted himself from parting with his land to any but the colony, or the settlers, of Connecticut. Which was the most reasonable of these two opinions, may be judged from the value of the gift which was made to the sachem when the deed was obtained: "five yards of cloth and a few pairs of stockings." In return for this insignificant present, hardly worth a dozen beaver skins, Uncas is said to have parted with his whole country, except that on which the Mohegans were then planting. There are some circumstances, however, it must be confessed, which tend to favor this conclusion. Uncas, at this time, had only held his country two years, and had barely ceased to be considered a tributary of the Pequots. He had besides been subdued in war by Sassacus, and had thus, according to Indian custom, forfeited his lands to his conquerors, as well as to whoever should conquer them.

This affair, however, gave no trouble to Uncas, during whose life-time the English never urged their pretended right to the Mohegan territory; and, for the present, his power and influence went on increasing in such a manner as to awaken the envy and fear of all the surrounding chieftains. The Narragansetts hated him as a Pequot; they had cause, also, to hate on his own account; and now their hatred was increased by seeing him become a formidable rival. Jealousy and ancient enmity made him likewise an object of bitter dislike to the kinsman and ally of the Narragansetts, Sequassen, the sachem of the Connecticut River. This chieftain had doubtless strong hopes, on the overthrow of the Pequots, that he should recover his ancient influence, and perhaps become even more powerful than before. But the sudden rise of Uncas blighted all these expectations, and ever afterwards he hated him with all the rancor of disappointed ambition. The events which followed, render the supposition probable, not only that Sequassen and the Narragansetts were acquainted with each other's sentiments towards the Mohegan chief, but that they had formed a conspiracy to overthrow and destroy him. Uncas, on the contrary, strove to defend himself and to injure his enemies, by spreading unfavorable reports of their feelings and designs with regard to the English. "Miantinomo," the Mohegans would say, "wants to make himself sachem of all the Indians in New England. Miantinomo is trying to bring all the Indians into a great conspiracy against the white men."

These reports produced so much suspicion in the magistrates, that in November, 1640, they summoned the Narragansett chief to Boston. He obeyed immediately, thus at once producing a strong impression in his favor. When questioned, he was deliberate in his answers; would never speak except when some of his councilors were present that they might be witnesses; showed much ingenuity in his observations, and a good perception of what was wise and equitable in policy. He offered to prove that Uncas and the Mohegans alone had raised the reports against him; asked that his accusers might be brought before him, face to face; and demanded that, if unable to prove their charges, they should be put to death. His dignity, his frankness, and the justness of his remarks, silenced the complaints of the magistrates; they acquitted him of all suspicion of conspiracy, and he departed from Boston in peace. This affair doubtless increased his hatred of Uncas; and, not long after, an event occurred which was said to be an effect of that hatred. One evening, as Uncas was passing from one wigwam in his fort to another, an arrow, discharged by some unseen marksman, pierced his arm. He reached the cabin to which he was going, without further injury, and, entering it, was safe. The wound was slight and soon healed. The perpetrator of this attempted assassination was unknown; but a young Pequot, one of Uncas' subjects, being observed to have a large quantity of wampum, fell under suspicion. He was interrogated, and, as he could give no reasonable explanation of how he came by so much property, the suspicions against him were increased. Observing this, he stole away out of the village, fled over to the Narragansett country, and took refuge with Miantinomo. Uncas laid the matter before the magistrates of Massachusetts; charging Miantinomo with being the instigator of the attack on him; and the Narragansett sachem once more fell himself compelled to go to Boston. He carried the Pequot with him, and the young man was examined by the magistrates in the chieftain's presence. He told a most extraordinary story; how he was staying, at one time, in Uncas' fort; how Uncas engaged him to tell the English that he had been hired by Miantinomo to kill Uncas, and how Uncas then took the flint of his gun and cut his own arm on two sides, so as to make it appear as if it had been pierced by an arrow. This tale, improbable in itself, and unpleasing to the colonists, who already distrusted the Narragansetts, as well as favored the Mohegans, not only did not clear the culprit, but brought Miantinomo under deep suspicion. It seemed as if the story had been concocted between the sachem and his tool, for throwing off the guilt of a conspiracy from their own shoulders, and laying it on the intended victim of that conspiracy, who had barely escaped from it with his life. The magistrates expressed themselves convinced of the Pequot's guilt, and declared that he ought to be delivered over to the vengeance of the Mohegan sachem. Miantinomo objected, arguing that the man was under his protection; but finally promised that, if he might only carry him back to his own country, he would then surrender him to Uncas. His earnest request was granted; he was allowed to depart with the prisoner; but on the way home he had him murdered by his own followers. This action deepened, with good reason, the suspicions already excited against him, as it was immediately concluded that he had put his accomplice to death to prevent his own guilt from being completely exposed. Other motives, indeed, may be imagined. He was doubtless unwilling to gratify a hated rival by surrendering to him a man who had once sought his protection; and he may have feared that Uncas would make use of the unscrupulous Pequot for the purpose of bringing still deeper and more dangerous accusations against himself and the Narragansetts. The darkest and most natural inference, however, prevailed, and this act of violence and bad faith afterwards cost Miantinomo dear.

Sequassen now began to play his part against the Mohegans and their sachem. Some of his warriors assassinated a leading Mohegan, and others way-laid Uncas himself, and shot arrows at him as he was sailing in a canoe on the Connecticut River. Uncas complained of these provocations to the magistrates at Hartford, and Governor Haynes, having summoned the two sachems, attempted to effect reconciliation between them. Uncas said that the Mohegan who had been murdered was a man of consequence, and that he must have six of Sequassen's warriors to put to death in revenge. Haynes labored hard to reduce this extravagant demand, so contrary to English ideas of justice, and with difficulty persuaded Uncas to accept of one individual who was acknowledged to be the murderer. But the murderer was likewise a man of consequence, and he was moreover a relation and a great favorite of Miantinomo. Sequassen therefore would not surrender him; said that he would defend him by force of arms; and expressed his reliance upon the Narragansett sachem for assistance. The magistrates, finding an agreement impracticable, dismissed the two sachems, and gave Uncas liberty to avenge his own wrongs. He did so; he invaded Sequassen's country; defeated him, killing seven or eight of his warriors, and wounding thirteen; burned his wigwams, and carried away a quantity of plunder.

This was soon known in the country of the Narragansetts, and Miantinomo began to think of war and revenge. He sent a message to Governor Haynes, complaining that Uncas had injured his relation, Sequassen, and his allies, the Indians of Connecticut River. Haynes replied that the English had no hand in the affair, and did not mean to uphold or encourage Uncas in such conduct as he described. The Narragansett chief also gave notice of what the Mohegans had done, to Winthrop, Governor of Massachusetts; and asked, in particular, with much earnestness, whether the people of the Bay would be offended with him if he should make war upon Uncas. The reply of Winthrop was still more satisfactory than that of Haynes; for he informed Miantinomo that, if Uncas had done him or his friends any wrong, and refused to grant satisfaction, the English would leave him to choose his own course. Doubtless the representations which Miantinomo made, to both Haynes and Winthrop, were considerably exaggerated; but these gentlemen, it seems, did not consider the matter worthy of investigation, and the Narragansett sachem had now fulfilled the treaty of 1638, by submitting his complaints to the English before he appealed to arms. He immediately, therefore, set about avenging his own and his kinsman's quarrel, with more promptness and energy, indeed, than good fortune. Collecting a large band of Narragansett warriors, he advanced rapidly and unexpectedly into the country of his rival.

To his much honored Governor John Winthrop
[October 28, 1637.]
Sir,— This bearer, Miantunnomu, resolving to go on his visit, I am bold to request a word of advice from you concerning a proposition made by Canonicus and himself to me some half year since. Canonicus gave an island in this bay to Mr. Oldham, by name Chibachuwese, upon condition as it would seem, that he would dwell there near unto them. The Lord (in whose hands all hearts are) turning their affections towards myself, they desired me to remove thither and dwell nearer to them. I have answered once and again, that for present I mind not to remove; but if I have it from them, I would give them satisfaction for it, and build a little house and put in some swine, as understanding the place to have store of fish and good feeding for swine. Of late I have heard, that Mr. Gibbons, upon occasion, motioned your desire and his own of putting some swine on some of these islands, which hath

197

made me since more desire to obtain it, because I might thereby not only benefit myself, but also pleasure yourself whom I more desire to pleasure and honor. I spake of it now to this Sachem, and he tells me, that because of the store of fish, Canonicus desires that I would accept half, (it being spectacle-wise, and between a mile or two in circuit, as I guess,) and he would reserve the other; but I think, if I go over, I shall obtain the whole. Your loving counsel, how far it may be inoffensive, because it was once (upon a condition not kept) Mr. Oldham's. So, with respective salutes to your kind self and Mrs. Winthrop, I rest

Your worship's unfeigned, in all I may,

Roger Williams.

For his much honored Mr. Governor, John Winthrop.

[November 10, 1637.]

Sir,— I acquainted this Indian Miantunnomu, with the contents of your letter sent by him, who rests well persuaded that if it break not first with them, the league is firm and lasting, and the English are unfeigned.

I have bought and paid for the Island, and because I desired the best confirmation of the purchase to yourself that I could, I was bold to insert your name in the original here enclosed. The ten fathom of beads and one coat you may please at leisure to deliver to Mr. Throckmorton: who will also be serviceable in the conveyance of swine this way. Your native, Reprive, requests me to write a word for himself and another for the Sachem of Block Island, Jacquontu.

For himself he tells me when he departed hence, being alone, he wandered toward Neepmuck: At Nayantick, Janemoh said he was a spy from Mr. Governor, and threatened to kill him, denied that there were Pequots, (saying though Reprive saw many himself) that they were all gone to Monahiganick. So he came back in fear of his life to Wepiteammock (Miantunnomue's brother-in-law) who lent him a canoe to Block Island where he staid but six days.

From Jacquontu, Block Island Sachem, that he is preparing thirteen fathom of white, and two of blue to present you with about the first month. That they are greatly in fear of the Nayantick men who threaten them, in case the English fall upon Nayantick. I am glad to see this poor fellow Reprive careful to please you, for he said you gave him leave for twenty-eight days and though he could stay but six days where he desired to stay longest, yet he will not lie. He says his brother goes along with him to stay some while, till the spring. Sir, There are two Pequot squaws, brought by the

Narragansetts, almost starved; viz.: Mr. Coles his native, and one girl from Winisimmit: there was a third (I think Mr. Blackstone's) who had escaped before to Nayantick. I promised these, if they would stay at my house and not run away, I would write that they might be used kindly. The biggest, Mr. Cole his native, complains that he of all natives in Boston is the worse used: is beaten with fire sticks, and especially by some of the servants.

The little one makes no complaint of usage, but says he was enticed by that other squaw, which I think was Mr. Blackstone's. I asked the biggest, who burnt her and why, she told me Mr. Penn because a Fellow lay with her, but she said, for her part he refused.

My humble desire is that all that have those poor wretches might be exhorted as to walk wifely and justly towards them, so as to make mercy eminent, for in that attribute the Father of mercy most mines to Adam's miserable offspring.

Sir, I fear I am tedious, yet must I crave leave for a line more: I received a letter from some in Charlestown, (in special from one Benjamin Hubbard) intimating his and others desire (with my help and furtherance) to be my neighbors in some place near adjoining: Mr. James hath not declared himself to be one, but I guess he is inclining to accompany them. On the Narragansett side the natives are populous, on the side to Massachusetts ward Plymouth men challenge, so that I presume if they come to the place where first I was, Plymouth will call them theirs I know not the persons, yet in general could wish (if it be either with countenance or connivance) that these ways might be more trod into these inland parts, and that amongst the multitudes of the barbarous, the neighborhood of some English Plantation (especially of men desiring to fear God) might help and strengthen. I mall be thankful for a word of advice, and beseeching the Most Holy and only Wife in mercy and goodness to know and guide the souls of his in this remote wilderness, and in this material dessert, to discover graciously the mystical where twelve hundred and three score days his saints are hid. Revel. 12. I rest
Roger Williams

To His Much Honored Governor John Winthrop.
November 20, 1637
Sir, I rest thankfully satisfied in your propounding of my motion to the Court, and the answer. (The earth is Jehovah's, and the plenitude of it.) I am not a little glad that the lot is fallen upon a branch of that root, in whose good (present and eternal both of root and branches) I rejoice.

For his lake I wish it ground, and grass, and trees; yet what use so ever he please to make of it, I desire he would not spare to make use of me in any service towards the natives on it or about it.

Miantunnomu in his relations of passages in the Bay with you, thankfully acknowledges to myself and others your loving carriage to him, and promiseth to fend forth word to all natives to cease from Prudence, trees, &c. Since your letter I travelled up to Nayantick by land where I heard Reprive was: there the Sachem (to whom he adheres, Wepiteammock) and the people related that he was gone to his wife at Mohegan: also that he, Wepiteammock, had sent to Uncas advising and urging their return, but he could not prevail, and that if Reprive come within his reach he will fend him (though alone without his wife) however.

I traveled to Mohegan and understood that they were all at Pequot, Nayantick, but Uncas not being at home (but at New Haven) I could not do ought.

Sir, I have often called upon your debtor, Joshua, but his ill adviseness of refusing my service and spending of his time upon a house and ground hath disabled him. Upon this occasion of your loving proffer of the half of the debt (as to myself, I shall be urgent with him to seek some course of payment of the whole to yourself, from whom in recompense of any pains, &c., I desire no other satisfaction but your loving and wonted acceptation, yea, although the business had been effected. Sir, I had almost been bold to say my thoughts what I would do in this cafe, were the runaways mine, but I will not more at present. If you shall please to require account of what my observation hath taught me, I mall readily yield it in my next, ever begging mercy and truth to you and yours, and my loving friends with you. The Lord Jesus return us all (poor runaways) with weeping and supplications to seek him that was nailed to the gallows; in him I desire to be (and mourn I am not) more

Your worship's unfeigned
Roger Williams.

Sir, I received six fathom of beads from Mr. Throckmorton, which though I will not return, yet I account them yours in my keeping.

Sir, I pray my respective remembrance to Mrs. Winthrop.

To His Much honored Governor John Winthrop.
Providence, [January 10, 1637-8.
Much Honored Sir, It having pleased the Most High to besiege us all with his white legions, I rejoice at this occasion from Connecticut (these letters

sent to me by Mr. Hooker) that I may hear of your welfare and health, which I wish and beg unfeignedly of the Lord. Mr. Hooker intimates a report to me that they hear from the Monahiganeucks that Miantunnomu intends Thomas Stanton's death. I have taken some pains in it, and other passages sent me, finding them slanders: and since (for many good ends and) for keeping a passage open between yourselves and Connecticut by natives, summer and winter, a peace is much to be desired between the Mohegan and the Narragansett. I have proffered my pains in procuring a meeting of the adverse Sachems, if it please the Magistrates of Connecticut to order Owokace (the Mohegan Sachem) to touch in at the Narragansett mouth, where I hope to get the Narragansett Sachems aboard, and it may please the God of Peace to save much blood and evil, &c.

Only it behooves our friends of Connecticut, as I have writ to them, to look to the two or three hundred Pequots harbored by Wocase the Mohegan, as also William Baker of Plymouth, (of whom formerly I wrote) who is there hid, is turned Indian in nakedness and cutting of hair, and after many whoredoms, is there married: this fire-brand with those Pequots may fire whole towns: I have intimated how they may with ease take him.

Sir, let me be humbly bold to request a favor of you: I am at present destitute of a man servant, and much desire, if you light on one that desires to fear the Lord, remember me. I have a lusty canoe, and shall have occasion to run down often to your Island (near twenty miles from us) both with mine own and (I desire also freely) your worship's swine, so that my want is great. I would (pare no charge, either out of those beads and coat in your own hand: the tobacco from Mr. Ludlow, and 8 or 10 in James and Thomas Hawkins hand of which I hear not yet.

Sir, if any letters from yourself or other friends are for Connecticut, I entreat you make haste and speed by this messenger, for I caused four natives who came from Connecticut to stay his coming: I have already paid him, so that his expectation is not great. Thus longing to hear of your health, and with earnest and daily wishes for that peace which this world cannot give nor take from you, and my poor wife's and mine own best salutes to your dearest companion, I rest. Your worship's to my power faithful, Roger Williams.

John Winthrop, History of New England
1638
May 5.]

Unkus, alias Okoco, the Monahegan sachem in the twist of Pequod

River, came to Boston with thirty-seven men. He came from Connecticut with Mr. Haynes, and tendered the governor a present of twenty fathom of wampum. This was at the court, and it was thought fit by the council to refuse it, till he had given satisfaction about the Pequods he kept. Upon this he was much dejected, and made account we would have him killed him; but, two days after, having received good satisfaction of his innocence, and he promising to submit to the order of the English touching the Pequods he had, and differences between the Naragansetts and him, we accepted his present. And, about half an hour after, he came to the governor, and entertained him with these compliments: This heart (laying his hand upon his breast) is not mine, but yours; I have no men; they are all yours; command me any difficult thing, I will do it; I will not believe any Indians' words against the English; if any man shall kill an Englishman, I will put him to death, were he never so dear to me. So the governor gave him a fair, red coat, and defrayed his and his men's diet, and gave them corn to relieve them homeward, and a letter of protection to all men, and he departed joyfully.

To His Much honored Governor John Winthrop.
Providence, February 28, 1637-8
Sir, Some few days since I received letters from Mr. Hooker, who had safely received your packet with thanks. He intimated that according to Miantunnomue's information by myself, William Baker was hid at Mohegan, but they had made Uncas and Wequash to bring him in. Since which time (Sergeant Holmes bailing him) he is again escaped.
He also signified the desire of the Magistrates at Connecticut that there the meeting should be: as also that in the mean season they had charged the Mohegans not to molest any natives in their passage and travel, &c., requiring the same of the Narragansetts towards the Mohegans.
 Accordingly I have been since at Narragansett and find Miantunnomu willing to go to Connecticut by the time limited, the end of the next month; only first he desired to know Mr. Governor's mind: secondly, in case his father-in-law Canonicus his brother, (whom I saw near death with above a thousand men mourning and praying about him) in case he recover, otherwise it is unlawful for them (as they conceive,) to go far from home till toward midsummer. Thirdly, he desires earnestly my company, as being not so confident of the English at Connecticut, who have been (I fear) to full of threatening: secondly, he cannot be confident of Thomas Stanton's faithfulness in point of interpretation. These things make me much desire

(as I have written back) that you would both please by some deputed to make my poor house the centre where seems to be the fairest offer of convenience, and I hope no question of welcome. Visiting Canonicus, lately recovered from the pit's brink this winter, he asked how Mr. Governor and the English did, requesting me to send him two words: "first, that he would be thankful to Mr. Governor for some sugar (for I had sent him mine own in the depth of the winter and his sickness.) Secondly, he called for his sword, which said he, Mr. Governor did send me by you and others of the English, saying Mr. Governor protested he would not put up his sword, nor would he have us put up ours, till the Pequots were subdued, and yet saith he, at Mohegan there are near three hundred, who have bound and robbed our men (even of the very covering of their secret parts) as they have past from Connecticut hither: after much more to this purpose, I told him that Mr. Governor had promised him to set all in order this spring.

Sir, I understand that Uncas the Mohegan hath Sassacous his sister to wife, and one of the wives of Sassacous his father Tattoapaine and that is one reason, beside his ambition and nearness, that he hath drawn all the scattered Pequots to himself and drawn much wealth from them: more I could trouble you with, &c.

Canonicus and Miantunnomu both desired that there might be a division made of these surviving Pequots (except the Sachems and murderers) and let their mare be at your own wisdom.

I may be humbly bold to present mine own thoughts concerning a division and disposal of them: since the Most High delights in mercy, and great revenge hath been already taken, what if (the murderers being executed) the rest be divided and dispersed, (according to their numbers may arise, and division be thought fit) to become subjects to yourselves in the Bay and at Connecticut, which they will more easily do in case they may be suffered to incorporate with the natives in either places: as also that as once Edgar the Peaceable did with the Welsh in North Wares, a tribute of wolves heads be imposed on them, &c., which (with submission) I conceive an incomparable way to save much cattle alive in the land.

Sir, I hope shortly to send you good news of great hopes the Lord hath sprung up in mine eye, of many a poor Indian soul enquiring after God. I have convinced hundreds at home and abroad that in point of religion they are all wandering, &c. I find what I could never hear before, that they have plenty of Gods or divine powers: the Sun, Moon, Fire, Water, Snow, Earth, the Deer, the Bear, &c., are divine powers. I brought home lately from the Narragansetts the names of thirty-eight of their Gods, all they could remember, and had I not with fear and caution withdrew, they would have fallen to worship, O God, (as they speak) one day in seven, but I hope the time is not long that some may truly bless the God of Heaven that ever they saw the face of English men. So waiting for your pleasure and advice to our neighbors concerning this intended meeting for the establishing of peace through all the bowels of the country, and beseeching the Most High to vouchsafe his peace and truth through all your quarters, with my due respects to Mrs. Winthrop, Mr. Deputy, Mr. Bellingham, &c., I rest

Your worship's in all true respect and affection,

Roger Williams.

His Much Honored Governor John Winthrop

April 16, 1638

Sir, concerning your intended meeting for reconciling of these natives our friends, and dividing of the Pequots our enemies, I have engaged your name, and mine own; and if no course be taken, the name of that God of Truth whom we all profess to honor will suffer not a little, it being an ordinary and common thing with our neighbors, if they apprehend any mow of breach of promise in myself, thus to object: do you know God, and will you lie? &c.

The Pequots are gathered into one, and plant their old fields, Wequash and Uncas carrying away the people and their treasure, which belong to yourselves: I would be bold to press my former motion, or else that with the next convenience they might be sent for other parts, &c.

I hope it will never be interpreted that I press this out of fear of any revenge upon myself by any of them. I ever yet (in point of reason to say no more) conceived this place the safest of the land, and can make it appear, &c., but out of desire to clear your names and the name of the most High, which will be ill reported of in case (according to so many promises) an honorable and peaceable issue of the Pequot war be not established.

Sir, the bearer hereof (not daring either to bring my letter or attend for an answer) I must request you to send your letter to Richard Collicut's, that so a native may convey it, or else to Nicholas Uphill's: and I should be bold humbly to propound to the country whether in case there be a necessity of keeping league with the natives, and so consequently many occasions incident, (and some which I will not write of) as also a conveniency of information this way, how matters may stand with you on the seashore, as I say,, whither it be not requisite so far to dispense with the late order of restraint as to permit a messenger freely.

'Tis true I may hire an Indian: yet not always, nor sure, for these two things I have found in them: sometimes long keeping of a letter: secondly, if a fear take them that the letter concerns themselves they suppress it, as they did with one of special information which I sent to Mr. Vane.

Sir, there will be new Heavens and a new Earth shortly but no more Sea. (Revel. 21. 2.) The most holy God be pleased to make us willing now to bear the tossings, dangers and calamities of this sea, and to seal up to use upon his own grounds, a great lot in the glorious state approaching. So craving pardon for prolixity, with mine and wife's due respect: to Mrs. Winthrop, Mr. Deputy, Mr. Bellingham, &c., I rest

Your worship's desirous to be ever yours unfeigned

Roger Williams

To His Much Honored Governor John Winthrop
Providence May 27, 1638

Much Honored Sir, — I have presumed to send this Narragansett man, to attend your pleasure concerning the Pequots, and Canonicus and Miantunnomue's complaint against them and their protectors.

The sum of their desire I lately acquainted you with, viz.: that you would please (even all the English) to sit still and let themselves alone with them according to consent, when Miantunnomu was last with you, who coming home, fell upon Nayantick men who sheltered the Pequots, but was stopped by our friends of Connecticut. Or, secondly, that some other course (in consultation) might be taken for dispersion of them: even as far as Old England or elsewhere, as they speak.

Sir, I do conceive either course will be difficult, because our friends at Connecticut are strangely bewitched with the subjection of these Pequots to themselves, and are also as strangely resolved upon fighting and violent courses, (as I understand by letters, and otherwise by speech) unless Miantunnomu come over personally to them to answer for proud speeches which they hear of.

Miantunnomu hath long since promised, and still waits to go any whither you shall please to make answer, to meet, &c. Some from Connecticut write me word, that Indians will testify such speeches to Miantunnomue's teeth: and it may be so whether true or false. I also, in case I should listen to Indian reports, shall bring many who will affirm that Thomas Stanton hath received mighty bribes *that* Uncas the Mohegan hath received little less than a thousand fathom of beads, whence he carries out some present to our friends at Connecticut, but I say I will not believe it.

But this I know, that according to league in two articles, that the Pequots shall not be sheltered nor disposed of without mutual consent of the English and the two Narragansett Sachems.

Secondly, that if the Pequots be suffered in the land to congregate and unite into four or five hundred together (as Lieutenant Howe confest to me) it will cost more blood on all sides then yet hath been spilt; for on the one part, the Narragansetts can no more forbear them than a wolf his prey, and on the other side for the Pequots upon all advantage the English may find.

Thirdly, that our friends at Connecticut are marvelously deluded by the Mohegans, as to be so confident of them, that Mr. Hooker writes no proof can be brought against them for word or deed: when it is clear they were Pequots, and lately hid, (once and the second time) William Baker from the English, and that upon pain of death to any that would reveal him, as Lieutenant Holmes told me. Sir, my desire is that it would therefore please the Lord to guide you all to make a prudent disposal and dispersion of the Pequots, which the Narragansetts will further by peace or war. So with all due salutations I humbly rest, unfeigned in all desire of your present and eternal peace,

Roger Williams

Mr. Allen told me that there were numbers of the Pequots at Narragansett, but I satisfied him that they were at Nayantick, (whence if themselves had not stopped) they had long since been removed.

To His Much Honored Governor John Winthrop.

June, 1638

Sir,— I perceive by these your last thoughts, that you have received many accusations and hard conceits of this poor native Miantunnomu, wherein I see the vain and empty puff of all serrene promotions, his barbarous birth or greatness being much honored, confirmed and augmented (in his own conceit) by the solemnity of his league with the English and his more than ordinary entertainment, & c., now all darned in a moment in the frowns of such in whose friendship and love lay his chief advancement.

Sir, of the particulars, some concern him only, some Canonicus and the rest of the Sachems, some all the natives, some myself.

For the Sachems, I shall go over speedily, and acquaint them with particulars. At present, let me still find this favor in your eyes, as to obtain a hearing, for that your love hath never denied me, which way soever your judgment hath been (I hope and I know you will one day see it) and been carried.

Sir, let this barbarian be proud and angry and covetous and filthy, hating and hateful, (as we ourselves have been till kindness from heaven pitied us, &c.,) yet let me humbly beg relief, that for myself, I am not yet turned Indian, to believe *barbarians* tell me, nor so safely presumptuous as to trouble the eyes and hands of such (and so honored and dear) with madows and fables. I commonly guess shrewdly at what a native utters, and, to my remembrance, never wrote particular, but either I know the bottom of it, or else I am bold to give a hint of my suspense.

Sir, therefore in some things at present (begging your wonted gentleness toward my folly) give me leave to show you how I clear myself from such lightness.

I wrote lately (for that you please to begin with) that some Pequots (and some of them actual murderers of the English, and that also after the fort cut off) were now in your hands. Not only love, but conscience, forced me to send, and speedily, on purpose, by a native, mine own servant. I saw not, spake not with Miantunnomu, nor any from him. I write before the All-feeing Eye. But thus it was. A Narragansett man (Awetipimo) coming from the bay with cloth, turned in (as they used to do) to me for lodging. I questioned of Indian passages, &c. He tells me Uncas was come with near upon forty natives. I asked what present he brought. He told me, that Cutshamoquene had four fathom and odd of him, and forty was for Mr. Governor. I asked him, how many Pequots. He told me fix. I asked him, if they were known. He said Uncas denied that there were any Pequots, and said they were Mohegans all. I asked, if himself knew any of them. He answered, he did, and so did other Indians of Narragansett. I asked, if the murderer of whom I wrote, Pametesick, were there. He answered, he was, and (I further enquiring) he was confident it was he, for he knew him as well as me, &c.

All this news (by this providence) I knew before it came to Narragansett. Upon this I sent, indeed fearing guilt to mine own soul, both against the Lord and my countrymen. But see a stranger hand of the Most and Only Wise. Two days after, Uncas passeth by within a mile of me (though he should have been kindly welcome) One of his company (Wequaumugs) having hurt his foot, and disabled from travel, turns into me; whom lodging, I questioned, and find him by father a Narragansett, by mother a Mohegan, and so freely entertained by both. I, further enquiring, he told me he went from Mohegan to the Bay with Uncas. He told me how he had presented forty fathom to (my remembrance) to Mr. Governor, (four and upwards to Cutshamoquene,) who would not receive them, but asked twice for

Pequots. At last, at Newtown, Mr. Governor received them, and was willing that the Pequots mould live, such as were at Mohegan, subject to the English Sachems at Connecticut, to whom they mould carry tribute, and such Pequots as were at Narragansett to Mr. Governor, and all the runaways at Mohegan to be sent back. I asked him, how many Pequots were at Narragansett. He said, but two, who were Miantunnomue's captives, and that at Nayantick with Wequash Cook were about three score. I asked, why he said the Indians at Narragansett were to be the Governor's subjects. He said, because Nayantick was sometimes so called, although there had been of late no coming of Narragansett men thither. I asked him, if he heard all this. He said, that himself and the body of the company said about Cutshamoquene. I asked, how many Pequots were amongst them. He said six. I desired him to name them, which he did thus: Pametesick, Weeaugonhick, (another of those murderers) Makurmete, Kishkontuckqua, Sausawpona, Quasaumpo-wan, which names I presently wrote down, and I am as confident of the truth, as that I breathe. Again, (not to be too bold in all the particulars at this time,) what a gross and monstrous untruth is that concerning myself, which your love and wisdom to myself a little espy, and I hope fee malice and falsehood (far from the fear of God) whispering together? I have long held it will-worship to doff and don to the Mori High in worship; and I wish also that, in civil worship, others were as far from such a vanity, though I hold it not utterly unlawful in some places. Yet surely, amongst the barbarians, (the highest in the world,) I would rather lose my head than so practice, because I judge it my duty to set them better copies, and would line against mine own persuasions and resolutions.

Sir, concerning the islands Prudence and (Patmos, if some had not hindered) Aquednick, be pleased to understand your great mistake: neither of them were sold properly, for a thousand fathom would not have bought either, by strangers. The truth is, not a penny was demanded for either, and what was paid was only gratuity, though I choose, for better assurance and form, to call it sale. And, alas! (Though I cannot conceive you can aim at the Sachems) they have ever conceived, that myself and Mr. Coddington (whom they knew so many years a Sachem.

You had not been thus troubled by myself at present. Yet the earth is the Lord's and the fullness thereof. His infinite wisdom and pity be pleased to help you all, and all that desire to fear his name and tremble at his word in this country, to remember that we all are rejected of our native foil, and more to mind the many strong bands, with which we are all tied, than any particular distaste each against other, and to remember that excellent precept, Prov. 25, If thine enemy hunger, feed him, &c.; for thou shalt heap coals of fire upon his head, and Jehovah may reward thee; unto whose mercy and tender companions I daily commend you, desirous to be more and ever.

Your worship's unfeigned and faithful,

Roger Williams.

To His Much Honored Governor John Winthrop.

Providence   June, 1638

Much Honored Sir, — blessed be the Father of mercies that once again I received your hand the last night by the messengers by whom I sent.

By them I understand that according as you please to intimate your expectation, Mr. Haynes is come: with Uncas, thirty-four Mohegans, and six Pequots. One of the six Pequots is Pametesick, who was one of the murderers that cut off the three English, going in a boat for clay upon Connecticut River, after the Fort was cut off. They not only spilt their blood, but exercised inhuman and tormenting revenge upon two of them, which cries for vengeance to heaven.

So that I refer it humbly to your wisdom whether (although I desire not the destruction of the surviving Pequots, but a safe dispersion of them, yet) the actual murderers be not to be surrendered up, and this Pametesick (I am partly confident this is he) at present apprehended: Our loving friends of Connecticut reported that some Mohegan women were wronged (as their hair cut off, &c.,) by the Narragansetts: but Uncas knows it was done by Wequashcuck of Nayantick, to whom Uncas sent for a Pequot queen. They two have got in the Pequots (though Uncas have the harvest.) Against Wequashcuck, Canonicus or Miantunnomu had long since proceeded, but our loving friends of Connecticut interposed: I hope for the best to save blood. So beseeching the great Councillor and Prince of Peace to guide your councils, I rest your Worship's most unworthy yet unfeigned,

Roger Williams. All reflective salutes, &c.

To his much honored Governor John Winthrop.

Providence   July 23, 1638.

Two days since I was bold to present you with a line, and still (so it pleaseth the most High,) I am occasioned again to be a constant trouble, &c. That your Worship's servants visiting me in their travel, I enquire after your runaways. The man faith he hath much to relate to yourself, and wanting utterance, desires me to write. He saith he hath enquired much after the runaways, and understands for certain that they are all at Mohegan.

That the flight was long since plotted, for he hath now heard by a Pequot that came from Mohegan, that the ten Mohegans which came to your Worship in the spring to buy one of the maidens, and offered ten fathom of beads, came from Uncas, who intended that maid for his wife. That he gave order to those ten men, that, (in case they could not buy her) they would leave one man there at your house, to persuade and work their escape.

That man was the Pequot Robin, who hath effected his business, for which (as he hears) Uncas promised him and hath given him the ten fathom of Wampum. Uncas hath taken the two daughters, Marie and Jane both to wife, and sayth that now he hath done sending of presents to Massachusetts.

Reprive was promised Joane by the Old Squaw for the furtherance of the busines and hath her. He advised. Their escape by Neepmuck, because once before, escaping through the Narragansett country, himself was sent back by the Narragansett Sachems.

This man thinks also that no Indian means will be able to effect their return, but that the English must fetch them. It will be your worship's wisdom to fore-cast so much, and to prepare (Captain Patrick and many more may be occasioned to fetch theirs also.) Yet I request your Worship's patience a few days.

Sir, this young man who comes along, is this woman's nephew, an ingenious, sober fellow, one of my long acquaintance, whom I call Oldway, as his Indian name (Necawnimeyat) signifies; he tells me he hath a good mind to abide one year with these his friends in your worship's service. I encourage him and present him to your wisdom and pity, not knowing but that the purpose of the Only Wise and most pityful God may be toward him for good. Unto the ever flowing streams of the most holy Fountain of living waters, (whose drops are able to refresh and save worlds of wandering souls), I heartily recommend your worship, your dearest companion, and all yours, grieving that I dare be no more your worship's,
Roger Williams.

Much Honored Sir, The bearer lodging with me, I am bold to write a hasty advertisement concerning late passages. For himself, it seems he was fearful to go farther than forty miles about us, especially considering that no natives are willing to accompany him to Pequot or Mohegan, being told by two Pequots (the all of Miantunnomue's captives which are not run from him) what he might expect, &c.

Sir, Captain Mason and Thomas Stanton landing at Narragansett, and at Miantunnomue's announcing war within six days against Juanemo, for they say that Miantunnomu hath been fair in all the passages with them, Juanemo sent two messengers to myself, requesting counsel. I advised him to go over with beads to satisfy, &c.

He sent four Indians. By them Mr. Haynes writes me, that they confessed fifteen fathom there received at Long Island. Thereabout they confessed to me, (four being taken of Pequots by force, and restored again,) as also that the islanders say fifty-one fathom, which sum he demanded, as also that the Nayantick messengers laid down twenty-fix fathom and a half, which was received in part, with declaration that Juanemo should within ten days bring the rest himself, or else they were resolved for war, &c. I have therefore sent once and again to Juanemo, to persuade himself to venture, &c. Canonicus sent a principal man last night to me, in haste and secrecy, relating that Wequash had sent word that, if Juanemo went over, he would be killed, but I assure them the contrary, and persuade Canonicus to importune and hasten Juanemo within his time, ten days, withal hoping and writing back persuasions of better things to Mr. Haynes, proffering myself, (in case that Juanemo through fear or folly fail) to take a journey and negotiate their business, and save blood, whether the natives' or my countrymen's.

Sir, there hath been great hubbub in all these parts, as a general persuasion that the time was come of a general slaughter of natives, by reason of a murder committed upon a native within twelve miles of us, four days since, by four desperate English. I presume particulars have scarce as yet been presented to your hand. The last fifth day, toward evening, a native, passing through us, brought me word, that at Pawtuckqut, a river four miles from us toward the bay, four Englishmen were almost famined. I sent instantly provisions and strong water, with invitation, &c. The messengers brought word, that they were one Arthur Peach of Plymouth, an Irishman, John Barnes, his man, and two others come from Pascataquack, travelling to Connecticut; that they had been loft five days, and fell into our path but fix miles. Whereas they were importuned to come home, &c., they pleaded soreness in travelling, and therefore their desire to rest there.

The next morning they came to me by break of day, relating that the old man at Pawtuckqut had put them forth the last night, because that some Indians laid, that they had hurt an Englishmen, and therefore that they lay between us and Pawtuckqut.

I was busy in writing letters and getting them a guide to Connecticut, and enquired no more, they having told me, that they came from Plymouth on the last of the week in the evening, and lay still in the woods the Lord's day, and then lost their way to Weymouth, from whence they lost their way again towards us, and came in again six miles off Pawtuckqut.

After they were gone, an old native comes to me, and tells me; that the natives round about us were fled, relating that those four had slain a native, who had carried three beaver skins and beads for Canonicus son, and came home with five fathom and three coats; that three natives which came after him found him groaning in the path; that he told them that four Englishmen had slain him.

They came to Pawtuckqut, and enquired after the English, which when Arthur and his company heard, they got on hose and shoes and departed in the night.

I sent after them to Narragansett, and went myself with two or three more to the wounded in the woods. The natives at first were shy of us, conceiving a general slaughter, but (through the Lord's mercy) I assured them that Mr. Governor knew nothing, &c. and that I have sent to apprehend the men. So we found that he had been run through the leg and the belly with one thrust. We dressed him and got him to town next day, where Mr. James and Mr. Greene endeavored, all they could, to save his life; but his wound in the belly, and blood lost, and fever following, cut his life's thread. Before he died, he told me that the four English had slain him, and that (being faint and not able to speak) he had related the truth to the natives who first came to him, viz. : that they, viz. : the English, saw him in the Bay and his beads: that sitting in the side of a swamp a little way out of the path, (I went to see the place, sit for an evil purpose,) Arthur called him to drink tobacco, who coming and taking the pipe of Arthur, Arthur run him through the leg into the belly, when, springing back, he, Arthur, made the second thrust, but missed him; that another of them struck at him, but missed him, and his weapon run into the ground; that getting from them a little way into the swamp, they pursued him, till he fell down, when they missed him, and getting up again, when he heard them close by him, he run to and again in the swamp, till he fell down again, when they lost him quite; afterwards,

towards night, he came and lay in the path, that some passenger might help him as aforesaid.

Whereas they said, they wandered Plymouth-way, Arthur knew the path, having gone it twice; and beside, Mr. Throckmorton met them about

Neponset River in the path, who, riding roundly upon a sudden by them, was glad he had past them, suspecting them. They denied that they met Mr. Throckmorton.

The messenger that I sent to Narragansett, pursuing after them, returned the next day, declaring that they showed Miantunnomu letters to Aquednick, (which were mine to Connecticut,) and so to Aquednick they past, whither I sent information of them, and so they were taken. Their sudden examination they sent me, a copy of which I am bold to send your worship enclosed.

The islanders (Mr. Coddington being absent) resolved to send them to us, some thought, by us to Plymouth, from whence they came. Sir, I shall humbly crave your judgment, whether they ought not to be tried where they are taken. If they be sent any way, whether not to Plymouth. In case Plymouth refuse and the islanders send them to us, what answers we may give, if others unjustly shift them unto us. I know that every man, and son of Adam, is his brother's keeper or avenger; but I desire to do bonum bene, &c.

Thus, beseeching the God of heaven, most holy and only wife, to make the interpretation of his own holy meaning in all occurrences, to bring us all by these bloody passages to an higher price of the blood of the
Son of God, yea of God, by which the chosen are redeemed, with all due respects to your dear self and dear companion, I cease.
Your worship's most unworthy
Roger Williams.
This native, Will, my servant, shall attend your worship for answer.

Providence   August 14th, 1637
Sir, since my last (unto which you were pleased to give answer with kind advice concerning the murder of the native) I have received divers letters from Connecticut: the sum of all is this; that it hath pleased the Lord to incline all hearts to peace. Juanemo was persuaded to go over in person and give that satisfaction which was demanded: only concerning a mare killed by some Nayanticks, (others say by Pequots,) but as yet no proof; our friends have taken his promise to inquire and inform, and so they dismissed him.

It hath pleased the Magistrates at Connecticut to invite Miantunnomu over to them to discover some Pequot passages and murderers, which are denied, and to enter upon some Articles with themselves: denying themselves to be obliged in the Articles of the Bay. I have conceived that all the English in the land were wrapped up in that Agreement (a copy of which you were pleased

Sir, to send me,): nevertheless I persuade him to go over. His desire was (which Agowaun Sachem Masquanominity had in charge to express to you) that Mr. Governor would please to spare four English from himself as witnesses of passages; as also myself with Cutmamoquene and Masquanominit. I have formerly engaged my promise to Miantunnomu: and resolve to take two or three English from hence, and hope (through the Lord's mercy) that the journey may be for peace. Sir, unless any pass by accident to Connecticut (if so you shall see good) that desire of three or four English may be denied, and yet granted in effect: by the going of some freely with myself.

Only sir, be pleased to give a hint of your pleasure in any matter considerable, which we may endeavor to effect. The natives, friends of the slain had consultation to kill an Englishman in revenge: Miantunnomu heard of it, and desired that the English would be careful on the highways, and sent himself express threatenings to them, &c., and informed them that Mr. Governor would see justice done. Ousamaquin coming from Plymouth told me that the four men were all guilty; I answered, but one; he replied, true, one wounded him, but all lay in wait two days, and attested. In conclusion: he told me that the principal must not die, for he was Mr. Window's man: and also that the man was by birth a Neepmuck man; so not worthy another man mould die for him: I answered what I thought fit, but conceive there will be need of wisdom and zeal in some, and remembrance of that *Vox Cceli:* He that doth violence to the blood of any person, let him flee to the pit: let none deliver him. The Lord mercifully cleanses the land from blood, and make the blood of his son Jesus more precious in all our eyes. So prays Your Worship's most unworthy,
Roger Williams

To his much honored Governor John Winthrop
At Narragansett, September 10, 1638
Much Honored Sir,— These Sachems with myself consulting the last Lord's day as soon as I here arrived; I dispatched a letter to meet our Connecticut friends at Mohegan: desiring a speedy word from Captain Mason (according as he found the business easy or difficult) to give direction for the course of the Narragansetts, either to Mohegan or Pequot. With all, the Messenger had charge to deal with Uncas, from us all, Canonicus, Miantunnomu, &c., to be wife and faithful to us in what we should propose to him.

The messenger returned the last night (and being a discreet man to observe passages) he related that coming near the town, viz.: to wit,

Mohegan, he heard six guns, which persuaded him that English were come, but drawing nearer, he found they were the guns which formerly the Pequots had got from the English! Entering the court, he found the house mingled full of Mohegans and Pequots, who desired his news, but he silent! They told him that they heard that the English were coming against them, and they had sent up two chief men who found the English training. They were examined of two things, viz.: why they had lately let go two of the murderers at Nayantick, whom they had bound, and why they had seized upon all the corn at Pequot, belonging to hither Nayantick Pequots: so they were imprisoned and bound: word whereof coming to Uncas, forty men were sent up with their bead girdles to redeem them. The messenger got Uncas private, who would not be drawn to yield up any of his Pequots, but alledging that he had bought them with his money of the English (as the Nayantick Sachems said, for which purpose I am bold to enclose Mr. Haynes his answer) he said they found the English so fallen, that the last night in a general meeting they were resolved to fight it out, and for himself although the English bound him and killed him he would not yield. He related that Mr. Haynes had given him a letter of security to lie by him, in case that any English should injure him, but in this pursuing his Pequots and binding his men, he had thrown away his letter, &c. Sir, your wisdom (I know) catcheth at my request before I make it, viz.: that in case I am directed from our friends of Connecticut to send for aid, you would please to cause a readiness at little warning.

I could make true relation of the brags of the chief of these wretches, viz.: that the Massachusetts English did but glean after the Connecticut men, &c., in the wars: but I am confident you desire their good, with the safety of your own state: therefore I rest with a description brief of the Pequot towns, now again under Uncas and the Nayantick Sachems established: At Pequot Nayantick are upwards of twenty houses, up the river at Mangunckakuck eight, up still at Sauquonckackock ten, up still at Paupattokmick fifteen, up still at Tatuppequauog twenty-three or four mile further with Uncas at his town Mohegan, a great number mingled, which are all under Uncas, besides those at Quinnipiuck, and others of Long Island, and Sassacous his confederates. At Nayantaquit2 the hither, upwards of twenty houses, all under Nayantaquit Sachems, except six or seven men unto whom your worship was pleased to give life, upon Miantunnomue's motion, by my letter, upon their submission. There are still Miantunnomue's subjects, yet refusing to live with him at Narragansett; he disclaims them, in case according to promise, they assist not in this business.

Roger Williams.

This letter chiefly relates to the difficulties between the Narragansetts and Mohegans, growing out of the dispersion of the Pequots.
From the visit to Connecticut here alluded to, resulted "A Covenant and Agreement made between the English and the Indians;" Miantonomo representing the Narragansetts, and Uncas the Mohegans. These articles were signed at Hartford, on the 21st of September, 1638. They provide: 1. That there shall be peace between the tribes and "all former injuries and wrongs offered each other remitted and buried."
2. That if further wrongs he committed by either party, they mall not revenge them, but shall appeal to the English, who shall decide between them. If either party refuse to abide by the decision, the English may compel them to do so.
3. The tribes mentioned agree to bring in the chief Sachem of the Pequots; and for the murderers known to have killed the English "they shall as soon as they can possibly take off their heads."
4. Provides for the division of the Pequot prisoners, who "shall no more be called Pequots, but Narragansetts and Mohegans."

To His Much Honored Governor John Winthrop.
September or October, 1638
Much Honored Sir, Through the mercy of the Most High, I am newly returned from a double journey to Connecticut and Plymouth. I shall presume on your wonted love and gentleness to present you with a short relation of what issue it pleased the Lord to produce out of them, especially since your worship's name was some way engaged in both.
I went up to Connecticut with Miantunnomu, who had a guard of upwards of one hundred and fifty men, and many Sachems, and his wife and children with him. By the way (lodging from his house three nights in the woods) we met divers Narragansett men complaining of robbery and violence, which they had sustained from the Pequots and Mohegans in their travel from Connecticut; as also some of the Wunnashowatuckoogs (subject to Canonicus) came to us and advertised, that two days before, about six hundred and sixty Pequots, Mohegans and their confederates had robbed them, and spoiled about twenty-three fields of corn, and rifled four Narragansett men amongst them; as also that they lay in way and wait to stop Miantunnomue's passage to Connecticut, and divers of them threatened to boil him in the kettle.

These tidings being many ways confirmed, my company, Mr. Scott (a Suffolk man) and Mr. Cope, advised our stop and turn back; unto which I also advised the whole company, to prevent bloodshed, resolving to get up to Connecticut by water, hoping there to stop such courses. But Miantunnomu and his council resolved (being then about fifty miles, half-way, on our journey) that not a man mould turn back, resolving rather all to die, keeping strict watch by night, and in dangerous places a guard by day about the Sachems, Miantunnomu and his wife, who kept the path, myself and company always first, and on either side of the path forty or fifty men to prevent sudden surprises. This was their Indian march fore mentioned.

But it pleased the Father of mercies, that (as we since heard) we came not by till two days after the time given out by Miantunnomu, (by reason of staying for me until the Lord's day was over,) as also the Lord sent a rumor of great numbers of the English in company with the Narragansetts, so that we came safe to Connecticut.

Being arrived, Uncas had sent messengers that he was lame, and could not come. Mr. Haynes said, it was a lame excuse, and sent earnestly for him, who at last came, and being charged by Mr. Haynes with the late outrages, one of his company said, they were but an hundred men. He said, he was with them, but did not see all that was done, and they did but roast corn, &c. So there being affirmations and negations concerning the numbers of men and the spoil, not having eye-witnesses of our own, that fell, as also many other mutual complaints of rifling each other, which were heard at large to give vent and breathing to both parts.

At last we drew them to make hands, Miantunnomu and Uncas; and Miantunnomu invited (twice earnestly) Uncas to sup and dine with him, he, and all his company (his men having killed some venison;) but he would not yield, although the magistrates persuaded him also to it.

In a private conference, Miantunnomu, from Canonicus and himself, gave in the names of all the Pequots Sachems and murderers of the English. The names of the Sachems were acknowledged by Uncas, as also the places, which only I shall be bold to set down:

Nausipouck, Puttaquappuonckquame his son, now on Long Island.
Nanasquionwut, Puttaquappuonckquame his brother, at Mohegan.
Puppompogs, Sassacous his brother, at Mohegan. Mausaumpous, at Nayantick. Kithanm, at Mohegan. Attayakitch, at Pequot or Mohegan.

These, with the murderers, the magistrates desired to cut off, the rest to divide, and to abolish their names. An inquisition was made; and it was affirmed from Canonicus, that he had not one. Miantunnomu gave in the names of ten or eleven, which were the remainders of near seventy, which at the first subjected themselves, of which I advertised your worship, but all again departed, or never came to him; so that two or three of these he had with him; the rest were at Mohegan and Pequot.

Uncas was desired to give in the names of his. He answered, that he knew not their names. He said there were forty on Long Island; and that Juanemo and three Nayantick Sachems had Pequots, and that he himself had but twenty. Thomas Stanton told him and the magistrates, that he dealt very falsely; and it was affirmed by others, that he fetched thirty or forty from Long Island at one time. Then he acknowledged, that he had thirty, but the names he could not give. It pleased the magistrates to request me to send to Nayantick, that the names of their Pequots might be sent to Connecticut; as also to give Uncas ten days to bring in the number and names of his Pequots and their runaways, Mr. Haynes threatening also (in cafe of failing) to fetch them.

Sir, at Plymouth, it pleased the Lord to force the prisoners to confess, that they all complotted and intended murder; and they were, three of them, (the fourth having escaped, by a pinnace, from Aquedneck,) executed in the presence of the natives who went with me. Our friends confessed, that they received much quickening from your own hand. O that they might also in a case more weighty, wherein they need much, viz.: the standing to their present government and liberties, to which I find them weakly resolved.

They have requested me to enquire out a murder five years since committed upon a Plymouth man (as they now hear) by two Narragansett Indians, between Plymouth and Sowwams. I hope (if true) the Lord will discover it.

Sir, I understand that there hath been some Englishmen of late come over, who hath told much to Cutmamoquene's Indians (I think Auhaudin) of a great Sachem in England (using the King's name) to whom all the Sachems in this land are and may be nothing, and where his ships may land; and this is much news at present amongst natives. I hope to enquire out the men.

Mr. Vane hath also written to Mr. Coddington and others on the island of late, to remove from Boston as speedily as they might, because some evil was ripening, &c. The most holy and mighty One blast all mischievous buds and blossoms, and prepare us for tears in the valley of tears, help you and us to trample on the dunghill of this present world, and to set affections and cast anchor above these heavens and earth, which are reserved for burning.

Sir, I hear, that two malicious persons, one I was bold to trouble your worship with not long since,) Joshua Verin, and another yet with us, William Arnold, have most falsely and slanderously (as I hope it shall appear) complotted together (even as Gardiner did against yourselves) many odious accusations in writing. It may be, they may some way come to your loving hand. I presume the end is, to render me odious both to the King's majesty, as also to yourselves. I shall request humbly your wonted love and gentleness (if it come to your worship's hand) to help me with the fight of it, and I am confident yourself shall be the judge of the notorious wickedness and malicious falsehoods therein, and that there hath not part aught from me, either concerning the maintaining of our liberties in this land, or any difference with yourselves, which shall not manifest loyalty's reverence, modestly and tender affection.

The Lord Jesus the Son of righteousness, shine brightly and eternally on you and yours, and all that seek him that was crucified. In him, I desire ever to be

Yours worship's most unfeigned,
Roger Williams.

For His Much Honored Mr. Governor, John Winthrop.
September, 1638

Much Honored Sir, — Some while since I wrote to you a short narration of the issue of my voyage to Connecticut and Plymouth. I desire only to know whether it came to hand. I have been carefully searching into that rumor of the Plymouth man slain four years since. The persons to whom I was directed by our Plymouth friends for information are yet absent on hunting: and Miantunnomu is but new returned from Connecticut, yet with what instruction I have already gotten I am this morning taking a journey to the Sachems about it.

Sir, I purpose within twenty days (if God will) to travel up to Mohegan: at my return I shall trouble you with a line from Uncas, if I can speak with him about your Pequots.

Sir, I pray let your servant direct the native with this letter to Mr. David Yale.

Providence. [No date.]
Sir, — Upon the receipt of your last (answering my queries) I have acquainted the Sachems with the business: I am not yet furnished with answer sufficient: what I have at present I shall humbly and faithfully submit to consideration: one from them, two from myself. From them: upon

solemn consultation with them about the goods demanded of themselves, they lay — First, that they remember not that either in the first Agreement and League (in the beginning of the Pequot wars) or since, in any expedition, that ever they undertook to answer in their own persons what their subjects should fail in. Second. Nor do they believe that the English Magistrates do so practice, and therefore they hope that what is righteous amongst ourselves we will accept of from them.Third. Therefore they profess that what evil forever shall appear to be done by any (subject: to them) against the bodies or goods of the English, satisfaction may readily be made out of the bodies or goods of the delinquents. For the they demanded, they say concerning the Salem cow, they have to this day enquired, and can discover no guilt either in the persons imprisoned or the rest, but do believe that it was falsely laid upon them by such northern natives whole traps they were, who themselves were guilty.

For the horses, they have sent for Wuttattaaquegin who hath not been with them these three years, but keeps at Massachusetts: they intend also to call a general meeting of the Country at his coming, within a few days, when I shall have further answer from them.

Sir, a word more from myself: I have long since believed that as it is with the Most High (Prov. 21. 3.) So with yourselves. To do judgment and justice is more acceptable then sacrifice. And therefore that it mall not be ungrateful in your eyes, that I humbly request leave to say that I see the business is ravelled, and needs a patient and gentle hand to rectify misunderstanding of each other.

The Sachems to prevent the fears of their men in hunting or traveling, &c., earnestly desired me to satisfy the English, that if the bearers of a writing from me would offend any ways, that they, the Sachems, would upon information from myself, cause the delinquents to make satisfaction out of their goods or bodies; to the end that the English might not imprison or transport away their persons, (which the natives suspect,) two of their men having been not long fence carried away in an English ship from the Bay, and two of their women the last summer from Conanicut in this Bay. In two particulars (as I conceive) neither the natives or myself were rightly understood. First, in the scope of the writing, which was not to ask leave to hunt as before. Secondly, in the promise, which was not to pay off themselves (I mean the Sachems) but to cause their men to deal justly and to give satisfaction for offences committed out of their goods or bodies. I hope it will please the Lord to persuade your hearts to believe what I affirm, and again to review the writing. However, rather than any labor or pains of mine (well meant to preserve peace) shall cause or occasion dissention, I resolve to be yet poorer, and out of my poverty to endeavor and further satisfaction. (The earth is the Lord's and the fullness of it.) To the Everlasting Arms of his mercy I daily recommend you and yours, and rest, Your Worship's most unworthy, Roger Williams.

Providence, May 3, 1639
Sir, — In my last I gave intimation of another answer, which from the Sachems is this. First, that although they remember not any agreements that have passed about the natives yielding up their hunting places, advantages, &c., within prescribed limits, &c., yet, because satisfactory agreements may have been unknown to them, between yourselves and the natives about you, they have sent for this man, Wuttattaaquegin, (who keeps most at Massachusetts with Cutshamoquene, and hath not been this three years with them.) This man Wuttattaaquegin hath promised to satisfy in wampum, beaver, and venison what it comes to. But he believes not the damage can be so great, for thus he relates: having laid his traps, intending daily to tend them, Cutshamoquene sent for him to be a guide for him in a hunting match about the Bay, where other natives were ignorant. He went, yet sent a youth to view his traps, who saith that he saw the Englishmen loose three horses out of the traps, and rode away upon two of them, the third only was lamed. Upon this he desired liberty to return to the Bay, to inquire more perfectly the damage: and being not come back as yet, they have this present sent again for him.

Yet because they see not that Wuttattaaquegin broke any known covenant in laying his traps in that place, nor willingly wrought evil against the English, they conceive it would be very fair and honorable in all natives eyes, that it would please the English to make known as well their moderation as their justice in the case.

And for themselves they resolve if this man should not be faithful or able to satisfy your demand, they promise (upon persuasions and some offers of mine to them) to contribute themselves out of their own, and to draw in help, that may in wampum, beaver, and venison make up the whole sum before the next hunting be over.
Roger Williams.

Providence, May 9th, 1639
Sir, - I am requested by Canonicus and Miantunnomu to present you with

their love and respect (which they also desire may be remembered to all the English Sachems) as also with this expression of the continuance of their love unto you, viz.: thirty fathom of beads, (ten from Canonicus, and twenty from Miantunnomu) and the basket a present from Miantunnomu's wife to your dear companion Mrs. Winthrop: three things they request me to desire of you.

First, the continuance of your ancient and constant friendship toward them, and good opinion of their sincere affection to the English.

I objected against this, that I lately heard that two boats of English were cut off by Pequots, and that Miantunnomu knew of the act, &c.

To this they answered, that they have not so much as heard of any miscarriage of the English this way of late, and that two days since a Narragansett man came from Long Island and brought no such tidings.

That they have always (and shall still) succor the English in any such distresses: and that if but a single Englishman, woman, or child be found in the woods by any of theirs, they would punish severely that man that would not safely conduct them and succor them, &c. Secondly, That you would please to ratify that promise made to them after the wars, viz.: the free use of the Pequot country for their hunting, &c. Thirdly, That since there are many Pequot Sachems and Captains surviving, many of whom have been actual murderers of the English, and (three of them) which have slain some of their Sachems. And that since the Agreement the last year at Connecticut with Mr. Haynes and the Magistrates, you have not yet pleased come to action. And that the Pequots being many hundreds of them may with these their Sachems do more mischief to us and them.

They therefore request that you would please to write by them at present to Mr. Haynes that so upon your joint Agreement they may themselves freely pursue those Pequot Princes and Captains, whom Mr. Haynes (who had the lift of them from me the last year) shall name unto them.

I objected the report of great numbers of Pequots among themselves, &c. They answer as formerly, that to clear themselves from that, and to make it appear how both the Mohegans and the Nayantick men have received the Pequots and their presents (when they refused them) and so have made presents to the English with the Pequot beads, which themselves never did nor could: they will now fall upon this service, and if the Mohegans and Nayantick men will not join with them in it, they will themselves pursue the persons that shall be named to them wheresoever they find them, although at Mohegan or Nayantick, without touching a Mohegan or Nayantick man further than you shall please to advise them.

More they say, but I would be tedious, and therefore with all due respect to your loving self, Mrs. Winthrop, Mr. Deputy, &c., I rest
Yours worship's faithful and unfeigned
Roger Williams.
Canonicus begs of you a little sugar.

Much Honored Sir, — You were pleased some while since to refer me to Mr. Haynes for a list of such Pequots as were authors and chief actors in the late murders upon the English.

Accordingly I have sent up once and again to Mr. Haynes and we are come to a period: the child is come to the birth: a little strength from your loving hand (the Lord so pleasing, and blessing) will bring it forth.

This list here enclosed (which I request may be returned) was drawn by my best enquiry and Tho. Stanton in the presence of the Magistrats at Connecticut the last year.

This list he was pleased to send me with the addition of seven more under his own hand. Some queries I made upon some of the fever: as also Sassacous his brother Puppompogs (now upon Long Island) whom Mr. Haynes desired might be spared, and I applauded the desire in many respects, only I desired for many other respects that he might be sent to some other part of the world. Also since that the Nayantick Sachems who harbor many of these, and Uncas, Canonicus and Miantunnomu requested that a pinnace might lie some few days at Pequot, to promote and countenance the work while Miantunnomu pursued them. Unto all which Mr. Haynes in this last is pleased to answer, so that we are come to a period. This week I went up to the Narragansett about other business: there I found a bar, which I thought good to request your worship to remove by a word or two.

Your captive (which was Maumanadtuck's wife) now at Pequot, presuming upon your experimented kindness toward her, informs all Pequots and Nayanticks that Mr. Governor's mind is, that no Pequot man would die, that her two sons shall ere long be Sachems there, &c. Your wisdom (now by a fresh line or two) declaring that none but these (who by the best of intelligence appear to be deeply guilty,) shall die, may facilitate the execution, to the honor of your mercy and justice, and the clearing of the land from blood, either that of our countrymen already spilt, or that may be hazarded by these wretches. I might but will not trouble your worship with some presumptions that way: the Lord be pleased to further and bless: and help your precious foul and mine to remember that vengeance, and to long and expect for it upon the enemies of Jesus, when blood shall flow out of the wine press to the horse bridles by the space of sixteen hundred furlongs.

Your worship's unfeigned hitherto,

Roger Williams

To his much honored Governor John Winthrop

Providence, 21. 5. July 21, 1640

Much Honored Sir,—Your runaways (as I before surmised) are at Mohegan, and the Squaw Sachem's daughter is married to the Sachem Uncas. I know the match hath been long desired (although the Sachem have five or six wives already) which makes me fear that all Indian means will not reach your just desires. May you please to rest a little, for Miantunnomu (as he pretends out of love and respect to your person) is very diligent about a peaceable return of them, that he may bring them with him, and as many more of the runaways as he can get. Uncas was gone to Connecticut, so that a little patience is requisite.

Sir, this you may please to signify to your much honored brother, Mr. Governor, that this business only hinders Miantunnomu's coming. He is (not satisfied but) persuaded to trust to interpreters whom he fears to trust, and to come without myself.

As also may you please to understand that the Nayantick Sachems still refusing to yield up any of those Pequots to death to whom they had promised life; our friends of Connecticut (as I have heard by two letters from Tho. Stanton) intend present revenge upon them. Canonicus and Miantunnomu still persuade (to mine own knowledge) the Sachems at last to be wife, and yield up their Pequots, but in vain, for the Nayantick Sachems resolve that for so many lives as are taken away by the English, or the Mohegans and Pequots with them, they will take revenge upon Mr. Throckmorton at Prudence, or Mr. Coddington, at Providence, or elsewhere.

I have dealt with Canonicus and Miantunuomu to desert the Nayanticks in this business. They answer they would if they had shed the blood of the English, but as they are their brethren, so they never hurt the English, but joined with them against the Pequots, &c., only they have been greedy upon the prey against the English mind: and lastly they say he English partiality to all the Pequots at Mohegan is so great, and the consequences so grievous upon the abuse of the English love, that all their arguments return back (which they use to the Nayantick Sachems) as arrows from a stone wall.

Tho. Stanton informs me of another cause of war upon the Nayanticks, viz.: Wequash affirms that one of the petty Sachems of Nayantick was aboard Mr. Oldham's pinnace, and that some goods and gold are at Nayantick. Gold I never heard of, but the pinnace, and other luggage and small particulars I had word of at first, which were (by reason of distance) let alone: and in cafe that any one of the Sachems or more knew of Mr. Oldham's death, and that due evidence be found, I yet doubt (now since the coming of the Lord Jesus and the period of the National Church,) whether any other use of war and arms be lawful to the proffers of the Lord Jesus, but in execution of justice upon malefactors at home: or preserving of life and lives in defensive war, as was upon the Pequots. If the swords rage in Old or New England: I know who gives out the commission, and can arm frogs, flies, lice, &c. He be pleased to give us peace which earth neither gives nor takes. In him I ever desire to be more unfeigned and faithfull Your Worship's
Roger Williams.

To His Much Honored Governor John Winthrop.
Providence. August 7
   Sir, — About from Portsmouth I received yours. As I lately advertised to Mr. Governor, [Dudley]. The native thoughts and consultations so continue, about the three Nayanticks, prisoners with our friends at Connecticut; that your runaways are longer secure in their escape then otherwise they would be.
   The Mohegan Sachem, Uncas, refuseth to part with his prey: And whereas Miantunnomu was going up to Mohegan himself with a sufficient company for the runaways, Uncas lent word that it was your worship's plot to bring him into the snare at Mohegan, that there the Connecticut English might fall upon him.
   Miantunnomu still promiseth me to come over to you, and his purpose (to his utmost) to bring them with him. My occasions lead me within these four or five days to Connecticut, when (the Lord so permitting) I purpose to go up to Mohegan and try the utmost myself.
Your Worship's Unfeigned,
Roger Williams

John Winthrop, History of New England
1640
September

There were some rumors of the Indians plotting mischief against the English; and, to strengthen this, the governor of Plymouth, a Mr. Bradford, wrote a letter to this effect: that he was informed, (and did believe it,) that the Naragansett sachem, Miantunnomoh, had sent a great present of wampum to the Mohawks, to aid him against the English, and that it was accepted, and aid promised. The like news was brought by Mr. Haynes, one of the magistrates upon Connecticut, and many words were taken up from some Indians among us, which our fears interpreted the same way. The governor and council gave great credit to these suspicions, yet they thought fit to take order, strengthening the watches in all towns, and causing them to be ordered by the military officers, (being before committed to the constables charge,) and withal sent Capt. Jenyson with three men and an Indian interpreter to the Naragansett sachems, to know the truth of their intentions. They were very kindly entertained, but they would not speak with him in the presence of his Indian interpreter, because he was a Pequod, and a servant, and their enemy and might discover their councils. So he made use of another interpreter. They denied all confederations with the Mohawks, and professed their purpose to continue friendship with us, and not to use any hostility towards the English, except they began, and promised to come to Boston (as he was desired). Only Janemoh, the Niantic Sachem, carried himself proudly, and refused to come to us, except we invaded him.

November]

Miantunnomoh, the sachem of Narragansett, came, and was met at Dorchester by Captain Gibbons and a guard of twelve musketeers, and well entertained at Roxbury by the governor; but when we came to parley, he refused to treat with us by our Pequod interpreter, as he had done before to Captain Jenyson, and the governor being as resolute as he, refused to use any other interpreter, thinking it a dishonor to us to give so much way to them. Whereupon he came from Roxbury to Boston, departing in a rude manner, without showing any respect or sign of thankfulness to the governor for his entertainment, whereof the governor informed the general court, and would show him no countenance, nor admit him to dine at our table, as formerly he had done, till he had acknowledged his failing, etc, which he readily did, so soon as he could be made to understand it, and did speak with our committees and us by a Pequod maid who could speak English perfectly. But it was conceived by some of the court that he kept back such things as he accounted secrets of state, and that he would carry home in his breast, as an injury, the strict terms he was put to both in this, and the satisfaction he was urged to for not observing our custom in matter of manners, for he told us that when our men came to him, they were permitted to use their own fashions, and so he expected the same liberty with us. So as he departed and nothing agreed, only the former articles of peace were read to him and allowed by him with this addition, that if any of his men did set traps in our jurisdiction, etc., they should be liable to satisfy all damages, etc.

1642

September

1] There came letters from the court at Connecticut and from two of the magistrates there, and from Mr. Ludlow, near the Dutch, certifying us that the Indians all over the country had combined themselves to cut off all the English, that the time was appointed after harvest, the manner also, they should go by small companies to the chief men's houses by way of trading, etc., and should kill them in the houses and seize their weapons, and then others should be at hand to prosecute the massacre; and that this was discovered by three several Indians, near about the same time and in the same manner; one to Mr. Eaton of New Haven, another to Mr. Ludlow, and the third to Mr. Haynes. This last being hurt near to death by a cart, etc., sent after Mr. Haynes, and told him that Englishman's God was angry with him, and had set Englishman's cow to kill him, because he had concealed such a conspiracy against the English, and so told him of it, as the other two had done. Upon this their advice to us was, that it was better to enter into war presently, and begin with them, and if we would send 100 men to the river's mouth of Connecticut, they would meet us with a proportionable number.

Upon these letters, the governor called so many of the magistrates as were near, and being met, they sent out summons for a general court, to be kept six days after, and in the mean time, it was thought fit, for our safety, and to strike some terror into the Indians, to disarm such as were within our jurisdiction. Accordingly we sent men to Cutshamekin, at Braintree, to fetch him and his guns, bows, etc., which was done, and he came willingly, and being late in the night when they came to Boston, he was put in the prison; but the next morning, finding upon examination of him and divers of his men, no ground of suspicion of his partaking in any such conspiracy, he was dismissed.

Upon the warrant which went to Ipswich, Rowley, and Newbury, to disarm Passaconamy, who lived by Merrimack, they sent forth 40 men armed the next day, being the Lord's day. But it rained all the day, as it had done divers days before, and also after, so as they could not go to his wigwam, but they came to his son's and took him, which they had warrant for, and a squaw and her child, which they had no warrant for, and therefore order was given so soon as we heard of it, to send them home again. They, fearing his son's escape, led him in a line, but he taking an opportunity, slipped his line and escaped from them, but one very indiscreetly made a shot at him, and missed him narrowly. Upon the intelligence of these unwarranted proceedings, and considering that Passaconamy would look at it as a manifest injury, (as indeed we conceived it to be, and had always shunned to give them any just occasion against us,) the court being now assembled, we sent Cutshamekin to him to let him know that what was done to his son and squaw was without order, and to show him the occasion whereupon we had sent to disarm all the Indians, and that when we should find that they were innocent of any such conspiracy, we would restore all their arms again, and to will him also to come speak with us. He returned answer that he knew not what was become of his son and his squaw, (for one of them was run into the woods and came not again for ten days after, and the other was still in custody,) if he had them safe again, then he would come to us. Accordingly about a fortnight after he sent his eldest son to us, who delivered up his guns.

September

8.] The general court being assembled, we considered of the letters and other intelligence from Connecticut, and although the thing seemed very probable, yet we thought it not sufficient ground for us to begin a war, for it was possible it might be otherwise, and that all this might come out of the enmity which had been between Miantunnomoh and Onkus, who continually sought to discredit each other with the English. We considered also of the like reports which had formerly been raised almost every year since we came, and how they proved to be but reports raised up by the opposite factions among the Indians. Besides we found ourselves in very ill case for war, and if we should begin, we must then be forced to stand continually upon our guard, and to desert our farms and business abroad, and all our trade with the Indians, which things would bring us very low; and besides, if upon this intelligence we should kill any of them, or lose any of our own, and it should be found after to have been a false report, we might provoke God's displeasure, and blemish our wisdom and integrity before the heathen. Further it was considered that our beginning with them could not secure us against them: we might destroy some part of their corn and wigwams, and force them to fly into the woods, etc., but the men would be still remaining to do us mischief, for they will never fight us in the open field. Lastly, it was considered that such as were to be sent out in such an expedition were, for the most part, godly, and would be as well assured of the justice of the cause as the warrant of their call, arid then we would not fear their forwardness and courage, but if they should be sent out, not well resolved, we might fear the success.

According to these considerations, we returned answer to Connecticut, and withal we sent two men with two interpreters, an Englishman and an Indian, to Miantunnomoh, to let him know what intelligence we had of his drawing the rest of the Indians into a confederation against us, and of his purpose to make his son sachem of Pequod, and of other things which were breaches of the league he made with us, and to desire him to come by such a time to give us satisfaction about them. If he refused to come, and gave them no satisfactory answer, then to let him know that if he regarded not our friendship, he would give us occasion to right ourselves. And instruction was given them, that if he gave them occasion, they should tell him the reason of our disarming the Indians, and excuse the injury done to Passaconamy, to be a mistake and without our order. The messengers coming to him, he carried them apart into the woods, taking only one of his chief men with him, and gave them very rational answers to all their propositions, and promised also to come over to us, which he did within the time prefixed.

When he came, the court was assembled, and before his admission, we considered how to treat with him, (for we knew him to be a very subtile man,) and agreed upon the points and order, and that none should propound any thing to him but the governor, and if any other of the court had any thing material to suggest, he should impart it to the governor. Being called in, and mutual salutations passed, he was set down at the lower end of the table, over against the governor, and had only two or three of his counsellors, and two or three of our neighboring Indians, such as he desired, but would not speak of any business at any time, before some of his counsellors were present, alleging, that he would have them present, that they might bear witness with him, at his return home, of all his sayings.

In all his answers he was very deliberate and showed good understanding in the principles of justice and equity, and ingenuity withal. He demanded that his accusers might be brought forth, to the end, that if they could not make good what they had charged him with, they might suffer what he was worthy of, and must have expected, if he had been found guilty, viz., death. We answered, we knew them not, nor were they within our power, nor would we give credit to them, before we had given him knowledge of it, according to our agreement with him. He replied, if you did not give credit to it, why then did you disarm the Indians. We answered, for our security, and because we had been credibly informed that some of the eastern Indians had lately robbed divers Englishmen's houses at Saco, and taken away their powder and guns. This answer satisfied him. He gave divers reasons, why we should hold him free of any such conspiracy, and why we should conceive it was a report raised by Onkus, etc., and therefore offered to meet Onkus at Connecticut, or rather at Boston, and would prove to his face his treachery against the English, etc., and told us he would come to us at any time; for though some had dissuaded him, assuring him, that the English would put him to death, or keep him in prison, yet he being innocent of any ill intention against the English, he knew them to be so just, as they would do him no wrong, and told us, that if we sent but any Indian to him that he liked, he would come to us, and we should not need to send any of our own men. He urged much, that those might be punished, who had raised this slander, and put it to our consideration what damage it had been to him, in that he was forced to keep his men at home, and not suffer them to go forth on hunting, etc., till he had given the English satisfaction, and the charge and trouble it had put the English unto, etc. We spent the better part of two days in treating with him, and in conclusion he did accommodate himself to us to our satisfaction; only some difficulty we had, to bring him to desert the Nianticks, if we had just cause of war with them. They were, he said, as his own flesh, being allied by continual intermarriages, etc. But at last he condescended, 1 that if they should do us wrong, as he could not draw them to give us satisfaction for, nor himself could satisfy, as if it were for blood, etc., then he would leave them to us.

When we should go to dinner, there was a table provided for the Indians, to dine by themselves, and Miantunnomoh was left to sit with them. This he was discontented at, and would eat nothing, till the governor sent him meat from his table. So at night, and all the time he staid, he sat at the lower end of the magistrate's table. When he departed, we gave him and his counsellors coats and tobacco, and when he came to take his leave of the governor, and such of the magistrates as were present, he returned, and gave his hand to the governor again, saying, that was for the rest of the magistrates who were absent.

The court being adjourned for a few days, till we might hear from Miantunnomoh, (it was assembled again at such time as he came to Boston,) there came letters from Connecticut, certifying us of divers insolencies of the Indians, which so confirmed their minds in believing the former report, as they were now resolved to make war upon the Indians, and earnestly pressing us to delay no longer to send forth our men to join with them, and that they thought they should be forced to begin before they could hear from us again.

Upon receipt of these letters, the governor assembled such of the magistrates and deputies as were at hand, and divers of the elders also, (for they were then met at Boston upon other occasions,) and imparted the letters to them, with other letters sent from the governor of Plymouth, intimating some observations they had, which made them very much to suspect, that there was such a plot in hand, etc. We all sat in consultation hereabout all the day, and in the end concluded, 1.That all these informations might arise from a false ground, and out of the enmity which was between the Naragansett and Monhigen. 2. Being thus doubtful, it was not a sufficient ground for us to war upon them. 3. That all these particular insolencies and wrongs ought to be revenged and repaired by course of justice, if it might be obtained, otherwise we should never be free from war. And accordingly, letters were sent back to our brethren at Connecticut, to acquaint them with our opinions, and to dissuade them from going forth, alleging how dishonorable it would be to us all, that, while we were upon treaty with the Indians, they should make war upon them, for they would account their act as our own, seeing we had formerly professed to the Indians, that we were all as one, and in our late message to Miantunnomoh, had remembered him again of the same, and he had answered that he did so account us. Upon receipt of this our answer, they forbare to enter into war, but (it seemed) unwillingly, and as not well pleased with us.

Although we apprehended no danger, yet we continued our military watches, till near the end of October, and restored the Indians all their arms we had taken from them: for although we saw it was very dangerous to us, that they should have guns, etc., yet we saw not in justice how we could take them away, seeing they came lawfully by them, (by trade with the French and Dutch for the most part,) and used them only for killing of fowl and deer, etc., except they brought themselves into the state of an enemy, therefore we thought it better to trust God with our safety than to save ourselves by unrighteousness.

At this court we were informed of some English to the eastward, who ordinarily traded powder to the Indians, and lived alone under no government; whereupon we granted warrant to a gentleman, that upon due proof, etc., he should take away their powder, leaving them sufficient for their own occasions.

This court also took order that every town should be furnished with powder out of the common store, paying for it in country commodities; likewise for muskets, and for military watches, and alarms, etc. Presently upon this, there arose an alarm in the night upon this occasion.

At this court also, four of Providence, who could not consort with Gorton and that company, and therefore were continually injured and molested by them, came and offered themselves and their lands, etc., to us, and were accepted under our government and protection. This we did partly to rescue these men from unjust violence, and partly to draw in the rest in those parts, either under ourselves or Plymouth, who now lived under no government, but grew very offensive, and the place was likely to be of use to us, especially if we should have occasion of sending out against any Indians of Naragansett and likewise for an outlet into the Naragansett Bay, and seeing it came without our seeking, and would be no charge to us, we thought it not wisdom to let it slip.

The English of Southampton, on Long Island, having certain intelligence of one of those Indians who murdered Hammond, who was put ashore there with others, when their pinnace was wrecked, sent Captain Howe, and eight or ten men to take him. He being in the wigwam, ran out, and with his knife wounded one of the English in the breast, and so behaved himself as they were forced to kill him.

19.] A man, travelling late from Dorchester to Watertown, lost his way, and being benighted and in a swamp about ten of the clock, hearing some wolves howl, and fearing to be devoured of them, he cried out help, help. One that dwelt within hearing, over against Cambridge, hallooed to him. The other still cried out, which caused the man to fear that the Indians had gotten some English man and were torturing him, but not daring to go to him, he discharged a piece two or three times. This gave the alarm to Watertown, and so it went as far as Salem and Dorchester, but about one or two of the clock no enemy appearing, etc., all retired but the watch.

It is not known what reasons the Connecticut men had at this time for fearing an Indian outbreak. Uncas and Miantonomo, sachems respectively of the Mohegans and Narragansetts, were unfriendly and intrigued against each other. Massachusetts had good reason to be anxious, and no blame can attach to the magistrates for watching Miantonomo, who had managed to quiet the suspicions of his white neighbors.

22.] The court, with advice of the elders, ordered a general fast. The occasions were, 1. The ill news we had out of England concerning the breach between the king and parliament. 2. The danger of the Indians. 3. The unseasonable weather, the rain having continued so long, viz. near a fortnight together, scarce one fair day, and much corn and hay spoiled, though indeed it proved a blessing to us, for it being with warm easterly winds, it brought the Indian corn to maturity, which otherwise would not have been ripe, and it pleased God, that so soon as the fast was agreed upon, the weather changed, and proved fair after.

William Bradford, History of Plimouth Plantation
1643

The Narigansets, after ye subduing of ye Pequents, thought to have ruled over all ye Indeans aboute them; but ye English, espetially those of Conightecutt holding correspondencie & frendship with Uncass, sachem of ye Monhigg Indeans which lived nere them, (as ye Massachusets had done with ye Narigansetts,) and he had been faithfull to them in ye Pequente warr, they were ingaged to supporte him in his just liberties, and were contented such of ye surviving Pequents as had submited to him should remaine with him and quietly under his protection. This did much increase his power and augmente his greatnes, which ye Narigansets could not indure to see. But Myantinomo, their cheefe sachem, (an ambitious & politick man,) sought privatly and by treachery (according to ye Indean maner) to make him away, by hiring some to kill him. Sometime they assayed to poyson him; that not takeing, then in ye night time to knock him on ye head in his house, or secretly to shoot him, and such like attempts. But none of these taking effecte, he made open warr upon him (though it was against ye covenants both betweene ye English & them, as also betweene them selves, and a plaine breach of ye same). He came suddanly upon him with 900. or 1000. men (never denouncing any warr before). Ye others power at yt presente was not above halfe so many; but it pleased God to give Uncass ye victory, and he slew many of his men, and wounded many more; but ye cheefe of all was, he tooke Miantinomo prisoner. And seeing he was a greate man, and ye Narigansets a potente people & would seeke revenge, he would doe nothing in ye case without ye advise of ye English; so he (by ye help & direction of those of Conightecutt) kept him prisoner till this meeting of ye comissioners. The comissioners weighed ye cause and passages, as they were clearly represented & sufficently evidenced betwixte Uncass and Myantinomo; and the things being duly considered, the comissioners apparently saw ye Uncass could not be safe whilst Miantynomo lived, but, either by secrete trechery or open force, his life would still be in danger. Wherfore they thought he might justly put such a false & bloud-thirstie enimie to death; but in his owne jurisdiction, not in ye English plantations. And they advised, in ye maner of his death all mercy and moderation should be showed, contrary to ye practise of ye Indeans, who exercise torturs and cruelty. And, Uncass having hitherto shewed him selfe a freind to ye English, and in this craving their advise, if the Narigansett Indeans or others shall unjustly assaulte Uncass for this execution, upon notice and request, ye English promise to assiste and protecte him as farr as they may agaiste such violence.

This was ye issue of this bussines. The reasons and passages hereof are more at large to be seene in ye acts & records of this meeting of ye comissioners. And Uncass follewd this advise, and accordingly executed him, in a very faire maner, acording as they advised, with due respecte to his honour & greatnes.* But what followed on ye Narigansets parte will appear hear after.

John Winthrop, History of New England
1643
June
12.] Sacononoc and Punham, two sachems near Providence having between them 200 and 300 men, finding themselves overborne by Miantunnomoh, the sachem of Narragansett and Gorton and his company, who have so prevailed with Miantunnomoh, as he forced one of them to join with him in setting his hand or mark to a writing, whereby a part of his land was sold to Gorton and his company, for which Miantunnomoh received a price, but the other would not receive that which was for his part, alleging that he did not intend to sell his land, though through fear of Miantunnomoh he had put his mark to the writing, they came to our governor, and by Benedict Arnold* their interpreter, did desire we would receive them under our government, and brought withal a small present of wampom, about ten fathom. The governor gave them encouragement, but referred them to the court, and received their present, intending to return it them again, if the court should not accord to them; but at the present he acquainted another of the magistrates with it. So it was agreed, and they

234

wrote to Gorton and his company to let them know what the sachems had complained of, and how they had tendered themselves to come under our jurisdiction, and therefore if they had any thing to allege against it, they should come or send to our next court. We sent also to Miantunnomoh to signify the same to him. Whereupon, in the beginning of the court, Miantunnomoh came to Boston, and being demanded in open court, before divers of his own men and Cutshamekin and other Indians, whether he had any interest in the said two sachems as his subjects, he could prove none. Cutshamekin also in his presence affirmed, that he had no interest in them, but they were as free sachems as himself; only because he was a great sachem, they had sometime sent him presents, and aided him in his war against the Pequots: and Benedict Arnold affirmed, partly upon his own knowledge, and partly upon the relation of divers Indians of those parts, that the Indians belonging to these sachems did usually pay their deer skins (which are a tribute belonging to the chief sachem) always to them, and never to Miantunnomoh or any other sachem of Naragansett, which Miantunnomoh could not contradict. Whereupon it was referred to the governor and some other of the magistrates and deputies to send for the two sachems after the court, and to treat with them about their receiving in to us.

But before this, Gorton and his company (12 in number) sent a writing to our court of four sheets of paper, full of reproaches against our magistrates, elders and churches, of familistical and absurd opinions, and therein they justified their purchase of the sachems' land, and professed to maintain it to the death. They sent us word also after, (as Benedict Arnold reported to us,) that if we sent men against them, they were ready to meet us, being assured of victory from God, etc. Whereupon the court sent two of the deputies to speak with them, to see whether they would own that writing which was subscribed by them all. When they came, they with much difficulty came to find out Gorton and two or three more of them, and upon conference they did own and justify the said writing. They spake also with the two sachems, as they had commission, and giving them to understand upon what terms they must be received under us, they found them very pliable to all, and opening to them the ten commandments, they received this answer, which I have set down as the commissioners took it in writing from their mouths.

After the court, the governor, etc., sent for them, and they came to Boston at the day appointed, viz., the 22d of the 4th month (June), and a form of submission being drawn up, and they being by Benedict Arnold, their neighbor, and interpreter, (who spake their language readily,) made to understand every particular, in the presence of divers of the elders and many others, they freely subscribed the submission, as it here followeth verbatim. Being told that we did not receive them in as confederates but as subjects, they answered, that they were so little in respect of us, as they could expect no other. So they dined in the same room with the governor, but at a table by themselves; and having much countenance showed them by all present, and being told that they and their men should be always welcome to the English, provided they brought a note from Benedict Arnold, that we might know them from other Indians, and having some small things bestowed upon them by the governor, they departed joyful and well satisfied. We looked at it as a fruit of our prayers, and the first fruit of our hopes, that the example would bring in others, and that the Lord was by this means making a way to bring them to civility, and so to conversion to the knowledge and embracing of the gospel in his due time. Soon after their departure, we took order that Miantunnomoh and the English in those parts should have notice of their submission to us, that they might refrain from doing them injury. Their Submission was as followeth. This writing is to testify, That we Pumham, sachem of Shawomock, and Sacononoco, sachem of Patuxet, etc., have, and by these presents do, voluntarily and without any constraint or persuasion, but of our own free motion, put ourselves, our subjects, lands and estates under the government and jurisdiction of the Massachusetts, to be governed and protected by them, according to their just laws and orders, so far as we shall be made capable of understanding them: and we do promise for ourselves and our subjects, and all our posterity, to be true and faithful to the said government, and aiding to the maintenance thereof to our best ability, and from time to time to give speedy notice of any conspiracy, attempt, or evil intention of any which we shall know or hear of, against the same: and we do promise to be willing, from time to time, to be instructed in the knowledge and worship of God. In witness whereof.

July

Letters came to our governor from Mr. Haynes, governor at Hartford, certifying of a war begun between Onkus, sachem of Mohigen, and Sequasson, sachem upon Connecticut, and that upon Onkus complaint of the other's assaulting him, etc., he sent for Sequasson and endeavored to make them friends, but Sequasson chose rather to have war, so they were forced to leave them to themselves, promising to be aiding to neither, etc. Soon after Onkus set upon Sequasson and killed seven or eight of his men, wounded and burnt his wigwams and carried away the booty. Upon this Miantunnomoh (being allied to Sequasson) sent to Mr. Haynes to complain of Onkus. He answered that the English had no hand in it, nor would encourage them, etc. Miantunnomoh gave notice hereof also to our governor by two of our neighbor Indians who had been with him, and was very desirous to know if we would not be offended, if he made war upon Onkus. Our governor answered, if Onkus had done him or his friends wrong and would not give satisfaction, we should leave him to take his own course. We received news of a great defeat given the Narragansett by Onkus, and of 15 Dutch slain by the Indians and beaver taken.

August

Onkus, being provoked by Sequasson, a sachem of Connecticut, who would not be persuaded by the magistrates there to a reconciliation, made war upon him, and slew divers of his men and burnt his wigwams; whereupon Miantunnomoh, being his kinsman, took offence against Onkus, and went with near 1,000 men and set upon Onkus before he could be provided for defence, for he had not then with him above 3 or 400 men.

But it pleased God to give Onkus the victory, after he had killed about 30 of the Narragansetts, and wounded many more, and among these two of Canonicus' sons and a brother of Miantunnomoh, who fled, but having on a coat of mail, he was easily overtaken, which two of his captains perceiving, they laid hold on him and carried him to Onkus, hoping thereby to procure their own pardon. But so soon as they came to Onkus, he slew them presently; and Miantunnomoh standing mute, he demanded of him why he would not speak. If you had taken me, sayeth he, I would have besought you for my life. The news of Miantunnomoh's captivity coming to Providence, Gorton and his company, who had bought of him the lands belonging to the sachems who were come under our jurisdiction, wrote a letter to Onkus, willing him to deliver their friend Miantunnomoh, and threatened him with the power of the English if he refused, and they sent their letter in the name of the governor of Massachusetts.

Upon this Onkus carries Miantunnomoh to Hartford to take advice of the magistrates there, and at Miantunnomoh's earnest entreaty he left him with them, yet as a prisoner. They kept him under guard, but used him very courteously, and so he continued till the commissioners of the United Colonies met at Boston, who taking into serious consideration what was safest and best to be done, were all of opinion that it would not be safe to set him at liberty, neither had we sufficient ground for us to put him to death. In this difficulty we called in five of the most judicious elders, (it being in the time of the general assembly of the elders,) and propounding the case to them, they all agreed that he ought to be put to death. Upon this concurrence we enjoined secrecy to ourselves and them, lest if it should come to the notice of the Narragansetts, they might set upon the commissioners, etc., in their return, to take some of them to redeem him, (as Miantunnomoh himself had told Mr. Haynes had been in consultation amongst them;) and agreed that, upon the return of the commissioners to Hartford, they should send for Onkus and tell him our determination, that Miantunnomoh should be delivered to him again, and he should put him to death so soon as he came within his own jurisdiction, and that two English should go along with him to see the execution, and that if any Indians should invade him for it, we would send men to defend him: If Onkus should refuse to do it, then Miantunnomoh should be sent in a pinnace to Boston, there to be kept until further consideration.

The reasons of this proceeding with him were these: 1. It was now clearly discovered to us, that there was a general conspiracy among the Indians to cut off all the English, and that Miantunnomoh was the head and contriver of it. 2. He was of a turbulent and proud spirit, and would never be at rest. 3. Although he had promised us in the open court to send the Pequod to Onkus, who had shot him in the arm with intent to have killed him, (which was by the procurement of Miantunnomoh as it did probably appear,) yet in his way homeward he killed him. 4. He beat one of Pumham's men and took away his wampom, and then bid him go and complain to the Massachusetts.

According to this agreement the commissioners, at their return to Connecticut, sent for Onkus, and acquainted him therewith, who readily undertook the execution, and taking Miantunnomoh along with him, in the way between Hartford and Windsor, (where Onkus hath some men dwell,) Onkus' brother, following after Miantunnomoh, clave his head with an hatchet, some English being present. And that the Indians might know that the English did approve of it, they sent 12 or 14 musketeers home with Onkus to abide a time with him for his defence, if need should be.

William Bradford, Plimouth Plantation
1644
Wheras, by a wise providence of God, tow of ye jurisdictions in ye westerne parts, viz. Conightecutt & New-haven, have beene lately exercised by sundrie insolencies & outrages from ye Indeans; as, first, an Englishman, runing from his Mr. out of ye Massachusets, was murdered in ye woods, in or nere ye limites of Conightecute jurisdiction; and aboute 6 weeks after, upon

discovery by an Indean, ye Indean sagamore in these parts promised to deliver the murderer to ye English, bound; and having accordingly brought him within ye sight of Uncaway, by their joynte consente, as it is informed, he was ther unbound, and left to shifte for him selfe; wherupon 10 Englishmen forthwith coming to ye place, being sente by Mr. Ludlow, at ye Indeans desire, to receive ye murderer, who seeing him escaped, layed hold of 8 of ye Indeans ther presente, amongst whom ther was a sagamore or 2, and kept them in hold 2 days, till 4 sagamors ingaged themselves within one month to deliver ye prisoner. And about a weeke after this agreemente, an Indean came presumtuously and with guile, in ye day time, and murtherously assalted an English woman in her house at Stamford, and by 3 wounds, supposed mortall, left her for dead, after he had robbed ye house. By which passages ye English were provoked, & called to a due consideration of their owne saftie; and ye Indeans generally in those parts arose in an hostile manner, refused to come to ye English to carry on treaties of peace, departed from their wigwames, left their come unweeded, and shewed themselves tumultuously about some of ye English plantations, & shott of peeces within hearing of ye towne; and some Indeans came to ye English & tould them ye Indeans would fall upon them. So yt most of ye English thought it unsafe to travell in those parts by land, and some of ye plantations were put upon strong watchs and ward, night & day, & could not attend their private occasions, and yet distrusted their owne strength for their defence. Wherupon Hartford & New-Haven were sent unto for aide, and saw cause both to send into ye weaker parts of their owne jurisdiction thus in danger, and New Haven, for conveniencie of situation, sente aide to Uncaway, though belonging to Conightecutt. Of all which passages they presently acquainted ye comissioners in ye Bay, & had ye allowance & approbation from ye Generall Courte ther, with directions neither to hasten warr nor to bear such insolencies too longe. Which courses, though chargable to them selves, yet through Gods blessing they hope fruite is, & will be, sweete and wholsome to all ye collonies; the murderers are since delivered to justice, the publick peace preserved for ye presente, & probabilistic it may be better secured for ye future.

Thus this mischeefe was prevented, and ye fear of a warr hereby diverted. But now an other broyle was begune by ye Narigansets; though they unjustly had made warr upon Uncass, (as is before declared,) and had, ye winter before this, ernestly presed ye Govner of ye Massachusets that they might still make warr upon them to revenge ye death of their sagamore, they, being taken prisoner, was by them put to death, (as before was noted,) pretending that they had first received and accepted his ransome, and then put him to death.

But ye Govner refused their presents, and tould them yt it was them selves had done ye wronge, & broaken ye conditions of peace; and he nor ye English neither could nor would allow them to make any further warr upon him, but if they did, must assiste him, & oppose them; but if it did appeare, upon good proofe, that he had received a ransome for his life, before he put him to death, when ye commissioners mett, they should have a fair hearing, and they would cause Uncass to returne ye same. But notwithstanding, at ye spring of ye year they gathered a great power, and fell upon Uncass, and slue sundrie of his men, and wounded more, and also had some loss them selves. Uncass cald for aide from ye English; they tould him what ye Narigansets objected, he deney the same; they tould him it must come to triall, and if he was inocente, if ye Narigansets would not desiste, they would aide & assiste him. So at this meeting they sent both to Uncass & ye Narrigansets, and required their sagamors to come or send to ye comissioners now mete at Hartford, and they should have a faire & inpartiall hearing in all their greevances, and would endeavor ye all wrongs should be rectified wher they should be found; and they promised that they should sadly come and returne without any danger or molestation; and sundry ye like things, as appears more at large in ye messengers instructions. Upon which the Narigansets sent one sagamore and some other deputies, with full power to doe in ye case as should be meete. Uncass came in person, accompanyed with some cheefe aboute him. After the agitation of ye bussines, ye issue was this. The comissioners declared to ye Narigansett deputies as followeth;

1. That they did not find any proofe of any ransome agreed on.
2. It appeared not yt any wampam had been paied as a ransome, or any parte of a ransome, for Myantinomos life.
3. That if they had in any measure proved their charge against Uncass, the comissioners would have required him to have made answerable satisfaction.
4. That if hereafter they can make satisfing profe, ye English will consider ye same, & proceed accordingly.
5. The comissioners did require ye neither them selves nor ye Nyanticks make any warr or injurious assaulte upon Unquass or any of his company

untill they make profe of ye ransume charged, and y' due satisfaction be deneyed, unless he first assaulte them.

6. That if they assaulte Uncass, the English are engaged to assist him.

Hearupon ye Narigausette sachim, advising with ye other deputies, ingaged him selfe in the behalfe of ye Narigansets & Nyanticks that no hostile acts should be comitted upon Uncass, or any of his, untill after ye next planting of come; and yt after that, before they begine any warr, they will give 30. days warning to ye Govner of the Massachusets or Conightecntt. The commissioners approving of this offer, and taking their ingagmente under their hands, required Uncass, as he expected ye continuance of ye favour of the English, to observe the same termes of peace with ye Narigansets and theirs.

These foregoing conclusions were subscribed by ye comissioners, for ye severall jurisdictions, ye 19. of Sept: 1644.

Edwa: Hopkins, Presidente.
Simon Bradstreete.
Will. Hathorne.
Edw: Winslow.
  John Browne.
Geor: Fenwick.
Theoph: Eaton.
Tho: Gregson.

The forenamed Narigausets deputies did further promise, that if, contrary to this agreemente, any of ye Nyantick Pequents should make any assaulte upon Uncass, or any of his, they would deliver them up to ye English, to be punished according to their demerits; and that they would not use any means to procure the Mowacks to come against Uncass during this truce. These were their names subscribed with their marks.
Weetowish. Chinnough. Pampiahett. Pummunish.

John Winthrop, History of New England
1644
September

We were now also freed from as great a fear of war with the Narragansetts. For the commissioners, meeting at Hartford, sent for Onkus and some from Narragansett, (a sachem and a chief captain were sent,) and whereas the Narragansett's plea against Onkus was, that he had put their sachem to death after he had received a ransom for his life, it was clearly proved otherwise, and that the things he received were part of them given him for his courteous usage of the said Miantunnomoh and those sachems which were slain in the battle, and another part, that Miantunnomoh might be given to the English. In the end it was agreed by all parties, that there should be peace on all sides till planting time were over the next year; and then neither of them should attempt any hostile act against the other, without first acquainting the English, etc. therewith.

February

5.] Cutshamekin, and Agawam, and Josias, Chickatabot his heir, came to the governor, and in their own name and the names of all the sachems of Watchusett, and all the Indians from Merrimack to Tecticutt, tendered themselves to our government, and gave the governor a present of 30 fathom of wampom, and offered to come to the next court to make their acknowledgment, etc. The governor received their present to keep it till the court, etc., and if the court and they did agree, then to accept it. We now began to conceive hope that the Lord's time was at hand for opening a door of light and grace to those Indians, and some fruit appeared of our kind dealing with Punham and Sacon/onoco, protecting them against the Narragansett, and righting them against Gorton, etc., who had taken away their land: for this example gave encouragement to all these Indians to come in and submit to our government, in expectation of the like protection and benefit.

February

16.] Pesacus, the Narragansett sachem, sent again a message to the governor with another present by Washose, a sachem who came before, and his errand was, that seeing they, at our request, had sitten still this year, that now this next year we would grant their request, and suffer them to fight with Onkus, with many arguments. The governor refused his present, and told him that if they sent us 1000 fathom of wampom and 1000 skins, yet we would not do that which we judged to be unjust, viz. to desert Onkus, but our resolution was, and that they must rest upon, that if they made war upon Onkus, the English would all fall upon them.

March

7.] At this court Cutshamekin and squaw sachem, Mascononoco, Nashacowam, and Wassamagoin, two sachems near the great hill to the west called Wachusett, came into the court, and according to their former tender to the governor, desired to be received under our protection and government upon the same terms that Pumham and Sacononoco were; so we causing them to understand the articles, and all the ten commandments of God, and they freely assenting to all, they were solemnly received, and then presented the court with 26 fathom more of wampom, and the court gave each of them a coat of two yards of cloth, and their dinner; and to them and their men every of them a cup of sack at their departure, so they took leave and went away very joyful.

May

20.] A letter came to the governor, under the marks of Pesecus and Canonicus, the sachem of Narragansett, but written by Gorton's company, to this effect: That they were purposed to make war upon Onkus in revenge of the death of Miantonomo and others of their people whom he had slain, and that they marvelled why we should be against it; that they had put them selves under the government and protection of the king of England, and so were now become our fellow-subjects, and therefore if any difference should fall between us and them, it ought to be referred to him; professing withal their willingness to continue all friendly correspondency with us. The general court being assembled, when Mr. Endecott was chosen governor1 and Mr. Winthrop deputy governor, they took this letter into consideration, together with another from Gorton's company to the same effect, and sent two messengers to the Narragansetts with instructions to this purpose, viz. to know whether they did own that letter, etc., and by whose advice they had done as they wrote, and why they would countenance and take counsel from such evil men, and such as we had banished from us and to persuade them to sit still, and to have more regard to us than such as Gorton, etc. When our messengers came to them, Canonicus would not admit them into his wigwam for two hours, but suffered them to stay in the rain. When he did admit them, he lay along upon his couch, and would not speak to them more than a few forward speeches, but referred them to Pesacus, who, coming after some four hours, carried them into an ordinary wigwam, and there had conference with them most part of the night. Their answers were witty and full to the questions; and their conclusion was, that they would presently go to war upon Onkus, but not in such manner as Miantunnomoh had done, by a great army, but by sending out parties of 20 or more or less, to catch his men, and keep them from getting their living, etc.

At this court Passaconaway, the Merrimack sachem, came in and submitted to our government, as Pumham, etc. had done before.

June

23.] Two days after the court was broken up, Pumham sent two men to Boston to tell us that the Narragansetts had taken and killed six of Onkus' men and five women, and had sent him two hands and a foot to engage him in the war, but he refused to receive them and sent to us for counsel, etc.

This occasioned such of the magistrates and deputies as were at hand (advising also with some of the near elders) to meet to consult about calling the court, and agreed, both in regard of this news from the Indians, and especially for speedy reconciling the magistrates and deputies, to write to the governor that the court might be called the 28th following, which the governor assented unto.

The court being assembled, they took order for ten men to be sent to Pumham according to his desire, to help him make a fort of palisadoes, etc., but the men, being volunteers, asked 10s. per week for each man, and such spoil as they should get, if they were put to fight, and arms fixed and powder and shot. Whereupon the court, fearing it would be an ill precedent, staid, and sent word to Pumham that the men were ready, but he must pay them, etc.

1645

May

We were now also freed from as great a fear of war with the Narragansetts. For the commissioners, meeting at Hartford, sent for Onkus and some from Narragansett, (a sachem and a chief captain were sent,) and whereas the Narragansett's plea against Onkus was, that he had put their sachem to death after he had received a ransom for his life, it was clearly proved otherwise, and that the things he received were part of them given him for his courteous usage of the said Miantunnomoh and those sachems which were slain in the battle, and another part, that Miantunnomoh might be given to the English. In the end it was agreed by all parties, that there should be peace on all sides till planting time were over the next year; and then neither of them should attempt any hostile act against the other, without first acquainting the English, etc. therewith.

June

The Narragansetts having begun war upon Uncus, the Monheagan sachem, notwithstanding their covenant to the contrary and divers messages sent to them from the commissioners to require them to forbear, until a meeting might be had, and the cause heard, it was thought fit by the general court in the third month, that though the next meeting was in course to be at New Haven in the beginning of September, yet in regard of the danger Uncus was in, and our engagement to save him harmless from any damage from Miantonomo his death, as also in regard of the distressed condition of Monsieur La Tour, (who earnestly petitioned the court for relief, etc.) the commissioners should be written to meet at Boston in the 28 of the fifth month, which was done accordingly. The names of the commissioners and all their proceedings are at large set down in the books of their records, whereof every colony hath one.

1646

September

Some few families being gone to the new plantation at Pequod, some of them kept in the Indians' wigwams there, while their own houses were building. Some of these Indians, accompanied with some English, went to hunt deer, Unkas, the Moheagen sachem, pretending they had hunted in his limits, came with 300 men, and set upon them, and beat some of the Indians, and took away some of their goods, putting them by force out of their wigwams, where the English kept. Complaint being made hereof to the commissioners, (who were then met at New Haven,) they sent for Unkas, and charged him with this outrage, etc. He confessed he had done very ill, and said, he thought he was mad; so he promised to go to the English there, and acknowledge his offence, and make full satisfaction, and for time to come, would live peaceably with them, etc.

William Bradford, Plimouth Plantation

The Comissioners this year were called to meete together at Boston, before their ordinarie time; partly in regard of some differances fallen betweene the French and the govermente of the Massachusets, about their aiding of Munseire Latore against Munsseire de Aulney, and partly aboute the Indeans, who had broaken the former agreements aboute the peace concluded the last year. This meeting was held at Boston, the 28. of July. Besides some underhand assualts made on both sides, the Narigansets gathered a great power, and fell upon Uncass, and slew many of his men, and wounded more, by reason that they farr exseeded him in number, and had gott store of peeces, with which they did him most hurte. And as they did this withoute the knowledg and consente of the English, (contrary to former agreemente,) so they were resolved to prosecute the same, notwithstanding any thing the English said or should doe against them. So, being incouraged by ther late victorie, and promise of assistance from the Mowacks, (being a strong, warlike, and desperate people,) they had allready devoured Uncass and his, in their hopes; and surly they had done it in deed, if the English had not timly sett in for his aide. For those of Conightecute sent him -40- men, who were a garison to him, till the comissioners could meete and take further order.

Being thus mett, they forthwith sente 3 messengers, viz. Sargent John Davis, Benedicte Arnold, and Francis Smith, with full and ample instructions, both to the Narigansets and Uncass; to require them that they should either come in person or send sufficient men fully instructed to deale in the bussines; and if they refused or delayed, to let them know (according to former agreements) that the English are engaged to assiste against these hostile invasions, and that they have sente their men to defend Uncass, and to know of the Narigansets whether they will stand to the former peace, or they will assaulte the English also, that they may provide accordingly. But the messengers returned, not only with a sleighting, but a threatening answer from the Narigansets (as will more appear hereafter). Also they brought a letter from Mr. Roger Williams, wherin he assures them that the warr would presently breake forth, and the whole country would be all of a flame. And that the sachems of the Narigansets had concluded a neutrality with the English of Providence and those of Aquidnett Island. Whereupon the commissioners, considering the great danger and provocations offered, and the necessitie we should be put unto of making war with the Narigansetts, and being also carfull, in a matter of so great waight and generall concernmente, to see the way cleared, and to give satisfaction to all the colonies, did thinke fitte to advise with such of the magistrates, and elders of the Massachusets as were then at hand, and also with some of the cheefe military commanders there; who being assembled, it was then agreed; First, that our ingagmente bound us to aide and defend Uncass. 2. That this ayde could not be intended only to defend him and his [in his] forte, or habitation, but (according to the comone acceptation of shuch covenants, or ingagments, considered with the grounds or occasion therof) so to ayde him as he might be preserved in his liberty and estate. 3ly. That this ayde must be speedy, least he might be swalowed up in the mean time, and so come to late. 4ly. The justice of this warr being cleared to our selves and the rest then presente, it was thought meete that the case should be [briefly] stated, and the reasons and grounds of the warr declared and published. 5ly. That a day of humilliation should be apoynted, which was the 5th day of the weeke following. 6ly. It was then allso agreed by the comissioners that the whole number of men to be raised in all the colonies should be 300- Whereof from the Massachusets at 190- Plimoth, -40- Conightecute, -40 New-Haven, -30- And considering that Uncass was in present danger, -40- men of this number were forthwith sente from the Massachusets for his sucoure; and it was but neede, for the other 40 from Conightecutt had order to stay but a month, and their times being out, they returned; and the Narigansets, hearing therof, tooke advantage, and came suddenly upon him, and gave him another blow, to his further blow, to his further loss, and were ready to doe the like againe but these 40 men being arrived, they returned, and did nothing.

The declarations which they sett forth I shall not transcribe, it being very large, and put forth in printe, to which I referr those that would see the same, in which all passages are layed open from the first. I shall only note their prowd carriage, and answers to the 3 messengers sent from the comissioners. They received them with scorne and contempte, and tould them they resoloved to have no peace without Uncass his head; also they gave them this further answer: that it mattered not who begane the warr, they were resolved to follow it, and that the English should withdraw their garison from Uncass, or they would procure the Mowakes against them; and withall gave them this threatening answer: that they would lay the English catle on heaps, as high as their houses, and that no Englishman should sturr out of his dore to pisse, but he should be kild. And wheras they required guides to pass throw their countrie, to deliver their message to Uncass from the comissioners, they deneyed them, but at length (in way of scorne) offered them an old Pequente woman. Besides allso they conceived them selves in danger, for whilst the interpretoure was speakeing with them about the answer he should returne, 3 men came and stood behind him with ther hatchets, according to their murderous maner; but one of his fellows gave him notice of it, so they broak of and came away; with sundry shuch like affrontes, which made those Indeans they carryed with them to rune away for fear, and leave them to goe home as they could.

Thus whilst the comissioners in care of the publick peace sought to quench the fire kindled amongst the Indeans, these children of strife breath out threatenings, provocations, and warr against the English them selves. So that, unless they should dishonour and provoak God, by violating a just ingagmente, and expose the colonies to contempte and danger from the barbarians, they cannot but exerciese force, when no other means will prevaile to reduse the Narigansets and their confederates to a more just and sober temper.

So as here upon they went on to hasten the preparations, according to the former agreemente, and sent to Plimoth to send forth their 40 men with all speed, to lie at Seacunke, least any deanger should befalle it, before the rest were ready, it lying next the enemie, and there to stay till the

Massachusetts should joyne with them. Allso Conigtecute and Newhaven forces were to joyne togeather, and march with all speed, and the Indean confederates of those parts with them. All which was done accordingly; and the souldiers of this place were at Seacunk, the place of their rendevouze, -8 or 10- days before the rest were ready; they were well armed all with snaphance peeces, and wente under the camand of Captain Standish.

Those from other places were led likwise by able comander[s], as Captaine Mason for Conigtecute, etc.; and Majore Gibons was made generall over the whole, with shuch comissions and instructions as was meete. Upon the suden dispatch of these souldiears, (the present necessitie requiring it, the deputies of the Massachusetts Courte (being now assembled immediatly after the setting forth of their 40 men) made a question whether it was legally done, without their comission.1st was answered, that howsoever it did properly belong to the authority of the severall jurisdictions (after the warr was agreed upon by the comissioners, and the number of men) to provid the men and means to carry on the warr; yet in this presente case, the proceeding of the comissioners and the comission given was as sufficiente as if it had been done by the Generall Courte.

1. First, it was a case of shuch presente and urgente necessitie, as could not stay the calling of the Courte or Counsell. 2ly. In the Articles of Confederation, power is given to the comissioners to consult, order, and determine all affaires of warr, etc. And the word determine comprehends all acts of authority belonging therunto. 3ly. The comissioners are the [sole] judges of the necessitie of the expedition. 4ly. The Generall Courte have made their owne comissioners their sole counsell for these affaires.
5ly. These counsels could not have had their due effecte excepte they had power to proceede in this case, as they have done; which were to make the comissioners power, and the maine end of the confederation, to be frustrate, and that mearly for observing a ceremony. 6ly. The comissioners haveing sole power to manage the warr for number of men, for time, place, etc., they only know their owne counsells, and determinations, and therefore none can grante commission to acte according to these but them selves. All things being thus in readines, and some of the souldiers gone forth, and the rest ready to march, the comissioners thought it meete before any hostile acte was performed, to cause a presente to be returned, which had been sente to the Govenor of the Massachusetts from the Narigansett sachems, but not by him received, but layed up to be accepted or refused as they should carry them selves, and observe the covenants. Therfore they

violating the same, and standing out thus to a warr, it was againe returned, by messengers and an interpretour.2 And further to let the difficulty of the enterprize, upon which the Court employed him and Mr. Wilbour, to go to Narragansetts, and take Benedict [Arnold] to interpret. When they came to Benedict, he refused to go without a hundred men in arms, only to possess them with danger, to effect his bloody plot; upon which Mr. Williams, being sent for to Narragansett, and also myself, to inquire of us, what the minds of these mad people were, to kill men for nothing; upon which I went to Providence, a thinking to go with Master Williams; but when I came there, he was gone with the Captain and Mr. Wilbour, upon Benedict's refusal. I stayed their return, and their agreement was to have Pessicus go into the Bay, and Master Williams was necessitated to put himself hostage till his return. This news coming into the Bay, did so vex the ministers, that Master Cotton preached upon it, that it being so wicked an act to take Master Williams with them, being one cast out of the Church. It was all one as to ask counsel of a witch, and that those that did it were worthy to die. Upon which Master Wilbour was ready to die, for fear he should be hanged. So then the Indians went down, and they compelled them to cease wars with Uncas, and to pay them five hundred pounds, for charges of Court, and provisions for soldiers, and to leave four of the chief sachem's children, till the money be paid, and to leave four of his chief men till the children came, and to promise them not to sell any land without their consent.

THO: PRENCE.	WITOWASH his mark C C C
JOHN BROWNE.	AUMSEQUEN his mark
GEO: FENWICK.	*the Niantick deputy.*
EDWA: HOPKINS.	ABDAS his mark A O
THEOPH: EATON.	PUMMASH his mark
STEVEN GOODYEARE.	CUTCHAMAKIN his mark [1]

Anno Dom: 1645.

The Comissioners this year were called to meete togither at Boston, before their ordinarie time; partly in regard of some differances falen betweene ye French and ye govermente of ye Massachusets, about their aiding of Munseire Latore against Munsseire de Aulney, and partly aboute the Indeans, who had broaken ye former agreements aboute the peace concluded ye last year. This meeting was held tit Boston, ye 28. of July.

Besides some underhand assaults made on both sids, the Narigansets gathered a great power, and fell upon Uncass, and slew many of his men, and wounded more, by reason they farr exseeded him in number, and had gott store of peeces, with which they did him most hurte. And as they did this withoute ye knowledg and consente of ye English, (contrary to former agreemente,) so they were resolved to prosecute ye same, not withstanding any thing ye English said or should doe against them. So, being incouraged by ther late victorie, and promise of assistance from ye Mowaks, (being a strong, warlike, and desperate people,) they had allready devoured Uncass & his, in their hops; and surly they had done it in deed, if the English had not timly sett in for his aide. For those of Conightecute sent him 40. men, who were a garison to him, till ye comissioners could meete and take further order.

Being thus mett, they forthwith sente 3 messengers, viz. Sargent John Davis, Benedicte Arnold, and Francis Smith, with full & ample instructions, both to ye Narigansets and Uncass; to require them yt they should either come in person or send sufficiente men fully instructed to deale in ye bussines; and if they refused or delayed, to let them know (according to former agreements) yt the English are engaged to assiste against these hostile invasions, and yt they have sente their men to defend Uncass, and to know of ye Narigansets whether they will stand to ye former peace, or they will assaulte ye English also, that they may provid accordingly.

But ye messengers returned, not only with a sleighting, but a threatening answer from the Narrigansets (as will more appear hereafter). Also they brought a letter from Mr. Roger Williams, wherin he assures them that ye warr would presently breake forth, ye whole country would be all of a flame. And ye the sachems of ye Narrigansets had concluded a newtrality with ye English of Providence and those of Aquidnett Hand. Wherupon ye commissioners, considering ye great danger & provocations offered, and ye necessitie we should be put unto of making warr with ye Naragansetts, and being also carfull, in a matter of so great waight & generall coucernmente, to see ye way cleared, and to give satisfaction to all ye colonies, did thinke fitte to advise with such of ye magistrats & elders of ye Massachusetts as were then at hand, and also with some of ye cheefe millitary comanders ther; who being assembled, it was then agreed, —

First, yt our ingagmente bound us to aide & defend Uncass. 2nd, That this ayde could not be intended only to defend him & his forte, or habitation, but (according to ye comone acceptation .of such covenants, or ingagments, considered with ye grounds or occasion therof) so to ayde him as he might be preserved in his liberty and estate. 3rd, That this ayde must be speedy, least he might be swalowed up in ye mean time, and so come to late. 4ly. The justice of this warr being cleared to our selves and ye rest then presente, it was thought meete yt the case should be stated, and ye reasons & grounds of ye warr declared and published. 5ly. That a day of humilliation should be apoynted, which was ye 5 day of ye weeke following. 6ly. It was then allso agreed by ye commissioners that ye whole number of men to be raised in all ye colonies should be 300. Wherof from ye Massachusets a 190, Plimoth, 40, Conightecute, 40, New-Haven 30. And considering yt Uncass was in present danger, 40. men of this number were forthwith sente from *ye* Massachusets for his sucoure; and it was but neede, for ye other 40. from Conightecutt had order to stay but a month, and their time being out, they returned; and ye Narigansets, hearing therof, tooke the advantage, and came suddanly upon him, and gave him another blow, to his further loss, and were ready to doe ye like againe; but these 40. men being arrived, they returned, and did nothing. The declaration which they sett forth I shall not transcribe, it being very large, and put forth in print, to which I referr those yt would see ye same, in which all passages are layed open from ye first. I shall only note their prowd carriage, and answers to ye 3 messengers sent from ye comissioners. They received them with scorne & contempte, and tould them they resolved to have no peace without Uncass his head; also they gave them this further answer: that it mattered not who begane ye warr, they were resolved to follow it, and that ye English should withdraw their garison from Uncass, or they would procure ye Mowakes against them; and withall gave them this threatening answer: that they would lay ye English catle on heaps, as high as their houses, and yt no Englishman should sturr out of his dore to pisse, but he should be kild. And wheras they required guids to pass throw their countrie, to deliver their message to Uncass from ye commissioners, they deneyed them, but at length (in way of scorne) offered them an old Pequente woman. Besids allso they conceived them selves in danger, for whilst ye interpretour was speakeing with them about ye answer he should returne, 3. men came & stood behind him with ther hatchets, according to their murderous maner; but one of his fellows gave him notice of it, so they broak of & came away; with sundry such like affrontes, which made those Indeans they carryed with them to rune away for fear, and leave them to goe home as they could.

Thus whilst ye comissioners in care of ye publick peace sought to quench ye fire kindled amongst ye Indeans, these children of strife breath out threatenings, provocations, and warr against ye English them selves. So that, unless they should dishonour & provoak God, *by* violating a just ingagmente, and expose ye colonies to contempte & danger from ye barbarians, they cannot but exerciese force, when no other means will prevaile to reduse *ye* Narigansets & their confederate to a more just & sober temper.

So as here upon they went on to hasten ye preparations, according to ye former agreemente, and sent to Plimoth to send forth their 40. men with all speed, to lye at Seacunke, least any deanger should befalle it, before ye rest were ready, it lying next ye enemie, and ther to stay till ye Massachusetts should joyne with them. Allso Conigtecute & Newhaven forces were to joyne togeather, and march with all speed, and ye Indean confederate of those parts with them. All which was done accordingly; and the souldiers of this place were at Seacunk, the place of their rendevouze, 8. or 10. days before ye rest were ready; they were well armed all with snaphance peeces, and wente under yt camand of Captain [266] Standish. Those from other places were led likwise by able comanders, as Captain Mason for Conigtecute, &c.; and Majore Gibons was made generall over ye whole, with such comissions & instructions as was meete.

Upon ye suden dispatch of these souldiears, (the present necessitie requiring it,) the deputies of ye Massachusetts Courte (being now assembled imediatly after ye setting forth of their 40. men) made a question whether it was legally done, without their comission. It was answered, that howsoever it did properly belong to yt authority of ye severall jurisdictions (after ye warr was agreed upon by ye comissioners, & the number of men) to provid ye men & means to carry on ye warr; yet in this presente case, the proceeding of ye comissioners and ye comission given was as sufficiente as if it had been done by the Generall Courte.

First, it was a case of such presente & urgente necessitie, as could not stay ye calling of ye Courte or Counsell. 2ly. In ye Articles of Confederation, power is given to ye comissioners to consult, order, & determine all affaires of warr, &c. And ye word determine comprehends all acts of authority belonging therinto.

3ly. The comissiouers are *ye* judges of ye neces-sitie of the expedition.

4ly. The Generall Courte have made their owne comissiouers their sole counsell for these attires.

5ly. These counsels could not have had their due effecte excepte they had power to proceede in this case, as they have done; which were to make ye comissiouers power, and ye maine end of ye confederation, to be frustrate, and that mearly for observing a ceremony.

6ly. The comissiouers haveing sole power to manage ye warr for number of men, for time, place, &c., they only know their owne counsells, & determinations, and therefore none can grante comission to acte according to these but them selves.

All things being thus in readines, and some of ye souldiers gone forth, and the rest ready to march, the comissioners thought it meete before any hostile acte was performed, to cause a presente to be returned, which had been sente to ye Govner of the Massachusetts from ye Narigansett sachems, but not by him received, but layed up to be accepted or refused as they should carry them selves, and observe ye covenants. Therfore they violating the same, & standing out thus to a warr, it was againe returned, by 2. messengers & an interpretour. And further to let know that their men already sent to Uncass (& other wher sent forth) have hitherto had express order only to stand upon his & their owne defence, and not to attempte any invasion of ye Narigansetts country; and yet if they may have due reperation for what is past, and good securitie for ye future, it shall appear they are as desirous of peace, and shall be as tender of ye Narigansets blood as ever. If therefore Pessicus, Miannemo, with other sachemes, will (without further delay) come along with you to Boston, the comissioners doe promise & assure them, they shall have free liberty to come, and returne without molestation or any just greevance from ye English. But deputies will not now serve, nor may the preparations in hand be now stayed, or ye directions given recalled, till ye forementioned sagamors come, and some further order be taken. But if they will have nothing but warr, the English are providing, and will proceede accordingly. Pessecous, Milano, & Witowash, 3 principall sachems of ye Narigansett Indeans, and Awasequen, deputie for ye Nyanticks, with a large traine of men, within a few days after came to Boston. And to omitte all other circomstances and debats yt past betweene them and the comissioners, they came to this conclusion following.

1. It was agreed betwixte ye comissioners of ye United Collonies, and ye forementioned sagamores, & Niantick deputie, that ye said Narigansets & Niantick sagamores should pay or cause to be payed at Boston, to ye Massachusets comissiouers, ye full sume of 2000. fathome of good white wampame, or a third parte of black wampampeage, in 4 payments; namely, 500 fathome within 20 days, 500 fathome within 4 months, 500 fathome at or before next planting time, and 500 fathome within 2 years next after ye date of these presents; which 2000 fathome ye comissioners accepte for satisfaction of former
charges expended.

2. The foresaid sagamors & deputie (on ye behalfe of ye Narigansett & Niantick Indeans) hereby promise & covenante that they upon demand and profess, satisfie, & restore unto Uncass, ye Mohigan sagamore, all such captives, whether men, or women, or children, and all such canowes, as they or any of their men have taken, or as many of their owne canowes in ye roome of them, full as good as they were, with full satisfaction for all such corne as they or any of theire men have spoyled or destroyed, of his or his mens, since last planting time; and ye English comissiouers hereby promise ye Uncass shall doe ye like.

3. Wheras ther are sundry differences & greevances betwixte Narigansett & Niantick Indeans, and Uncass & his men, (which in Uncass his absence cannot now be detirmined,) it is nearby agreed yt Nariganset & Niantick sagamores either come them selves, or send their deputies to ye next meeting of ye comissioners for ye collonies, either at New-Haven in Sept 1646, or sooner (upon conveniente warning, if ye said commissioners doe neede sooner), fully instructed to declare & make due proofe of their injuries, and to submite to ye judgmente of ye comissioners, in giving or receiving satisfaction; and ye said comissioners (not doubting but Uncass will either come him selfe, or send his deputies, in like maner fumished) promising to give a full hearing to both parties with equall justice, without any partiall respects, according to their allegations and profs.

4. The said Narigansett & Niantick sagamors & deputies doe nearby promise & covenante to keep and maintaine a firme & perpetuall peace, both with all ye English United Colonies & their successors, and with Uncass, ye Monhegen sachem, & his men; with Ossamequine, Pumham, Sokanoke, Cutshamakin, Shoanan, Passaconaway, and all other Indean sagamors, and their companies, who are in freindship with or subjecte to any of ye English; hearby ingaging them selves, that they will not at any time hearafter disturbe ye peace of ye country, by any assaults, hostile attempts, invasions, or other injuries, to any of ye United Collonies, or their successors; or to ye aforesaid Indeans; either in their persons, buildings, catle, or goods, directly or indirectly; nor will they confederate with any other against them; & if they know of any Indeans or others yt conspire or intend hurt against ye said English, or any Indeans subjecte to or in freindship with them, they will without delay acquainte & give notice therof to ye English comissioners, or some of them.

Or if any questions or differences shall at any time hereafter arise or grow betwixt them & Uncass, or any Indeans before mentioned, they will, according to former ingagments (which they hearby conflrme & ratifie) first acquainte ye English, and crave their judgments & advice therin; and will not attempte or begine any warr, or hostille invasion, till they have liberty and alowauce from ye comissioners of ye United Collonies so to doe.

5. The said Narigansets & Niantick sagamores & deputies doe hearby promise ye they will forthwith deliver & restore all such Indean fugitives, or captives which have at any time fled from any of ye English, and are now living or abiding amongst them, or give due satisfaction for them to ye comissioners for ye Massachusets; and further, that they will (without more delays) pay, or cause to be payed, a yearly tribute, a month before harvest, every year after this, at Boston, to ye English Colonies, for all such Pequents as live amongst them, according to ye former treaty & agreemente, made at Hartford, 1638. namely, one fathome of white wampam for every Pequente man, & halfe a fathume for each Pequente youth, and one hand length for each mal-child. And if Weequashcooke refuse to pay this tribute for any Pequents with him, the Narigansetts sagamores promise to assiste ye English against him And they further covenante yt they will resigne & yeeld up the whole Pequente countrie, and every parte of it, to ye English collonies, as due to them by conquest.

6. The said Narigansett & Niantick sagamores & deputie doe hereby promise & covenante yt within 14 days they will bring & deliver to ye Massachusetts comissioners on ye behalfe of ye collonies, foure of their children, viz. Pessecous his eldest sone, the sone Tassaquanawite, brother to Pessecous, Awashawe his sone, and Ewangsos sone, a Jsiantick, to be kepte (as hostages & pledges) by ye English, till both ye forementioned 2000 fathome of wampam be payed at ye times appoynted, and ye differences betweexte themselves & Uncass be heard & ordered, and till these artickles be under writen at Boston, by Jenemo & Wipetock. And further they hereby promise & covenante, ye if at any time hearafter any of ye said children shall make escape, or be conveyed away from ye English, before ye premisses be fully accomplished, they will either bring back & deliver to ye Massachusett comissiouers ye same children, or, if they be not to be founde, such & so many other children, to be chosen by ye comissioners for ye United Collonies, or their assignes, and ye within 20. days after demand, and in ye mean time, untill ye said 4 children be delivered as hostages, ye Narigansett & Niantick sagamors & deputy doe, freely & of their owne accorde, leave with ye Massachusett comissioners, as pledges for presente securitie, 4 Indeans, namely, Witowash, Pumanise, Jawashoe, Waughwamino, who also freely consente, and offer them selves to stay as pledges, till ye said children be brought & delivered as abovesaid.

7. The comissioners for ye United Collonies doe hereby promise & agree that, at ye charge of ye United Collonies, ye 4. Indeans now left as pledges shall be provided for, and yt the 4 children to be brought & delivered as hostages shall be kepte & maintained at ye same charge; that they will require Uncass & his men, with all other Indean sagamors before named, to forbear all acts of hostilitie againste ye Narigansetts and Niantick Indeans for ye future. And further, all ye promises being duly observed & kept by ye Narigansett & Niantick Indians and their company, they will at ye end of 2 parcell of land therin, cither to any of ye English or others, without consente or allowance of ye comissioners.

8. It is fully agreed by & betwixt ye said parties, yt if any hostile attempte be made while this treaty is in hand, or before notice of this agreemente (to stay further preparations & directions) can be given, such attempts & ye consequences therof shall on neither parte be accounted a violation of this treaty, nor a breach of ye peace hear made & concluded.

9. The Narigansets & Niantick sagamors & deputie hereby agree & covenante to & with ye comissiouers of ye United Collonies, yt henceforth they will neither give, grante, sell, or in any maner alienate, any parte of their countrie, nor any peace murdered any of ye English, he or they shall be delivered to just punishmente.

10. Lastly, they promise that, if any Pequente or other be found & discovered amongst them who hath in time of years restore ye said children delivered as hostiages, and retaine a finne peace with ye Narigansets & Nianticke Indeans and their successours.

In witness wherof ye parties above named have interchaingablie subscribed these presents, the day & year above write;

John Winthrop, President, Herbert Pelham, Tho: Prence, John Browne, Geo: Fenwick,

Edward: Hopkins, Theoph: Eaton, Steven Goodyeare,

Pessecouss, his mark, Aumsequen his mark,

Meekesano, his mark, Cutchamakin his mark,

Pummasu, his mark, Witowash his mark,

Abdas, his mark.

This treaty and agreemente betwixte the comissioners of ye United Collonies and ye sagamores and deputy of Narrigansets and Niantick Indeans was made and concluded, .Benedicte Arnold being interpretour upon his oath; Sergante Callicate & an Indean, his man, being presente, and Josias & Cutshamakin, tow Indeans aquainted with ye English language, assisting therin; who opened & cleared the whole treaty, & every article, to ye sagamores and deputie there presente. And thus was ye warr at this time stayed and prevented.

John Deforest, History of the Indians of Connecticut

On a sudden, the Mohegan watchers on the hills of Norwich beheld the Narragansetts emerge from the woods, and cross the river Shetucket, at a fording place a little above its junction with the Quinnibaug. The runners immediately dashed off, some to carry the startling intelligence to their sachem, some to alarm and collect their scattered warriors. Uncas had a fort on the banks of the Thames, about five miles below the site of the present city of Norwich; and here, probably, the messengers of danger found him. The Mohegans came pouring in on all sides from their villages and scattered wigwams, and he was soon able to advance towards the enemy with nearly the whole force of his tribe. The chroniclers of those times say that he had four or five hundred warriors, and that the invaders amounted to nine hundred or a thousand. These estimates, depending as they must have done entirely on the reports of the Indians, are undoubtedly exaggerated; and, if we rate the Mohegans at three hundred, and their adversaries at twice that number, we shall go as high, I suspect, as probability will warrant.

Uncas moved forward three or four miles, until he came to a spot situated in the present township of Norwich, and now known as the Great Plain. Here he halted his men on a small rising ground, and explained to them a stratagem by which he hoped to make up for his inferiority in numbers. The Narragansetts, in the meantime, had crossed the fords of the Yantic, and soon appeared descending in loose array the declivity opposite to the Mohegans. Uncas now sent forward a messenger to ask an interview with Miantinomo. It was granted, and the two sachems shortly met each other in a narrow space between the armies. On both sides, the warriors, standing within bow-shot of each other, remained spectators. The Narragansetts were waiting unsuspiciously the result of the conference: the Mohegans were watching anxiously for the preconcerted signal from their sachem. Uncas addressed Miantinomo on the folly of mutually wasting the lives of their brave warriors in a contest which could as well be decided by themselves alone. "Let us fight it out," he concluded; "if you kill me, my men shall be yours; if I kill you, your men shall be mine."

Miantinomo was a tall and strong man, nor is it likely that he was so deficient in personal courage as to reject Uncas' proposition through fear.

But he was confident in the superior numbers of his followers, and was resolved not to throw away what seemed to be a certainty, for what was clearly an uncertainty. "My men came to fight," said he, "and they shall fight."

Uncas had expected this answer, and now the time had come for his stratagem. He threw himself suddenly upon the ground; his men recognized the signal; and, drawing their ready-bent bows, they poured a shower of arrows among the astonished Narragansetts. Uncas sprang up, and his warriors, pealing forth the yell of battle, and brandishing their tomahawks, rushed forward with him upon the staggering enemy. The Narragansetts, panic struck at this sudden assault, made hardly an attempt at resistance, and speedily took to flight. The Mohegans pursued them with impetuous fury, drove them through the shallows of the river, and continued the chase into the forests beyond. All over that rude and hilly country the pursuers and pursued might be seen, leaping over rocks and dashing through thickets, like wolves in chase of timid deer. Miantinomo fled with his followers, but his flight was impeded by an English corselet which he had put on to protect him in battle. Two of the Mohegan captains followed him closely, and still further prevented his escape by springing against him and jostling him as he ran. They might have taken or killed him with their own hands, but this honor they were willing to reserve to their sachem.

The first of these men who reached the flying chieftain was a sagamore, named Tantaquigeon, whose descendants were long held noble among the Mohegans, and have scarcely yet ceased to boast of this exploit of their ancestor, Uncas, a robust and powerful man, finally came up and seized Miantinomo by the shoulder. The ill-fated sachem, as soon as he felt the hand of his enemy upon him, ceased his flight and sat down upon the ground. His heart must indeed have been swelled with grief and shame; but from those closed lips came no word to indicate its misery. Thirty of the Narragansetts had been slain, and, undoubtedly, many more wounded; the rest, without an effort to wipe out their disgrace, or to rescue their captive sachem, retreated to their own country.

Miantinomo still continued silent, although some of his warriors were brought up and tomahawked before his eyes. Uncas was disappointed at not being able to extract from him a single confession of weakness or fear. "Why do you not speak?" said he. "If you had taken me I should have besought you for my life." But the captive made no answer. He was carried in triumph to the Mohegan fortress, but his life was not taken, and he was even treated with some degree of kindness and respect. It would appear, also, that a truce was opened between the tribes, which continued as long as the fate of Miantinomo remained in suspense. The Narragansetts sent their sachem several packages of wampum during his captivity, which he gave away, some to Uncas, some to Uncas' wife, and some to his principal councilors. He made these presents, as the Mohegans and their supporters affirmed, partly by way of thanks for his courteous treatment, and partly to persuade Uncas to put him into the hands of the English and refer his fate to their decision.

The Narragansetts asserted that the wampum was given as a ransom, and they subsequently made it a strong ground of accusation against the Mohegan sachem. The news of Miantinomo's capture excited a deep interest among the English of Rhode Island. Many of them were men who had been driven from Massachusetts on account of their religious opinions, and had found a refuge and a home in the country of the Narragansetts. The

UNCAS AND MIANTONOMOH.

generous and dignified character of the captive sachem had won their good will; and, from always hearing the Narragansett side of the story, they believed that he was in the right and his enemies in the wrong. Samuel Gorton, a wild-headed but kind-hearted enthusiast who had settled at Warwick, is said to have written Uncas a letter, commanding him to set Miantinomo at liberty, and threatening him with the English power if he refused. The epistle reached Uncas, and, being explained to him by the messenger, gave him not a little perplexity. He was by no means willing to set his captive free; but he did not dare, on his own authority, to put him to death, and he had reason to fear that he should not be able to keep him safe as a prisoner. In this uncertainty he concluded to refer the matter to his old friends, the English of Connecticut. He carried Miantinomo to Hartford, represented the case to the Governor and Council, and begged them to show him the path in which he should walk. The magistrates replied that, as there was no open war between their government and the Narragansetts, it was not prudent for them to interfere, but they would advise him to wait for the first meeting of the Commissioners of the United Colonies of New England, which would take place in the following September, and refer the matter to their decision. Miantinomo, finding himself in Hartford, begged earnestly that he might be kept there in the custody of the English magistrates. He doubtless expected that the English would at least preserve his life, and feared that, if Uncas got him back to Mohegan, he might resolve to make sure of his fate by putting him to death. The magistrates were willing, and Uncas consented on condition that Miantinomo should still be considered as his prisoner.

The first Court of Commissioners of the United Colonies of New England, met at Boston on the seventeenth of September, 1643. It consisted of John Winthrop and Thomas Dudley from Massachusetts, Edward Winslow and William Collier from Plymouth, George Fenwick and Edward Hopkins from Connecticut, and Theophilus Eaton and Thomas Gregson from New Haven. The first object of the commissioners was to ratify the agreement, and approve of the Articles of Confederation, which had been drawn up in the previous May. They then proceeded to examine the case of the Narragansett sachem. Prepossessed in favor of Uncas on account of his obsequiousness to the English, fearful of Miantinomo's power, and perhaps of his independent spirit, they yet hesitated in their judgment, and at first decided that, while it would not be safe to liberate the captive, there was still no sufficient cause to put him to death. In this uncertainty it was determined to refer the case to the clergy, a general convocation of whom was then held in Boston, as many as fifty being assembled there from all parts of New England. For some reason, however, only five of this number were selected, to give their voices on the, important question: these were called in, the whole affair was laid before them, and they were asked for their opinion. What is our astonishment to find that these reverend and, as it is to be hoped, pious gentlemen, came to that stern decision at which laymen and public magistrates had faltered! Miantinomo, they said, ought to die.

The Commissioners, having all their doubts removed by the verdict of the ministers, decided that the unfortunate sachem was worthy of death, and that Uncas might justly kill him, since his own life would be in constant danger, either by treachery or open force, as long as such a false and blood-thirsty enemy lived. It was clearly discovered, they said, that there was a general conspiracy among the Indians against the colonies, and that the prisoner was at the head of it. His disposition, too, was proud, turbulent and restless. He had broken his promise of surrendering the Pequot who attempted to take Uncas' life. Finally he beat one of the men of Pumham, a sachem who had submitted to the English, took away his wampum, and bade him complain, if he would, at the Massachusetts. In short, he had forfeited his life by the Indian customs, and by the fashions of all countries. Such were the pretences, some false, some unjust, some frivolous, by which the Commissioners vindicated their course in the condemnation of a free and independent sachem: false, because it had not been clearly discovered that there was a general conspiracy among the Indians, and because the innocence of Miantinomo on that point had already been acknowledged; unjust, because nothing could well be more so than to send men out of this world for being proud, turbulent and restless ; frivolous, because the charges concerning Pumham and his man were altogether too trifling to have any weight in a question of life and death. As to the assertion that he had forfeited his life by Indian customs and by the fashions of all countries, the first part is true, but the second is as clearly false. It is not, at least, the fashion of civilized countries, to keep prisoners of war alive for weeks, and then bring them in cool blood to execution.

The Commissioners decided that Uncas and some of his best men should be summoned to Hartford; that Miantinomo should there be surrendered into his hands; that he should be put to death without the limits of the English settlements; and that some of the colonists should witness the execution, "for the more full satisfaction of the commissioners." If Uncas refused to kill the prisoner, he was not to be surrendered to him, but to be sent to Boston by sea, and there detained until the Court could decide further as to his fate. But, if Uncas carried the sentence into effect, he was to be taken under English protection, and it was to be the especial duty of Connecticut to defend him against all enemies whom he might thus create. Plymouth was to restore Massasoit, the sachem of the Pokanokets, to a perfect freedom from all the encroachments which had been made upon him by the Narragansetts. Massachusetts was to give the Narragansetts notice that Uncas acted under the authority of the English, and would be defended by them against all assailants.

The decision was kept secret until it was known that the Connecticut and New Haven Commissioners had reached home. It was feared that, if the Narragansetts should know what was to be done, they would intercept these gentlemen, and thus obtain hostages by whom to ransom their sachem. Such a design had indeed been agitated among them, as the frank and noble minded Miantinomo himself gave notice to Governor Haynes As soon as Eaton and his friends were in safety, Uncas was ordered to repair to Hartford, at the head of a sufficient number of his followers. He came, attended by his brother, Wawequa, and a select band of warriors. The decision of the Commissioners was made known to him: a decision, doubtless, after his own heart; and he offered not the least objection to carrying it into execution. His captive was then delivered into his hands, and two Englishmen were designated to go with him and witness the murder. They left Hartford, and traveled on through the forests until they came to the plain where the battle had been fought and the prize taken. Wawequa was walking close behind Miantinomo, who was still, perhaps, uncertain what would be his fate. Uncas gave a signal, and Wawequa, silently raising his tomahawk, sunk it with a heavy blow into the head of the unsuspecting prisoner. Uncas cut a large piece from the shoulder and ate it with savage exultation. "It is the sweetest meat I ever ate," said the barbarian. "It makes my heart strong."

Miantinomo was buried on the site both of his defeat and his death, and the spot afterwards received, from the English settlers, the name, which it still retains, of the Sachem's Plain. A heap of stones was raised over the grave, and, for a long time afterwards, every Narragansett who passed that way added one or more to the pile. Daring many subsequent years, parties of this tribe used to visit the spot every September, in spite of the almost continual hostility which existed between them and the Mohegans. On reaching the rude monument they would break forth into lamentations, and then throwing new stones upon the heap, would consecrate them with mournful cries and frantic gestures. The mound remained standing for many years, but was finally torn down by the economical owner of the land, who wished to use the stones in the foundation of a new barn.

Such was the end of Miantinomo; a sachem who seems to have been respected and loved by every one who was not fearful of his power. There can be no doubt that his death was perfectly in accordance with Indian customs; yet, for the sake of the memory of our ancestors, I wish that it had not happened through their influence. Had Uncas killed and scalped him on the field of battle, or had he tortured him to death in cool blood on his own responsibility, no one could have had any occasion for surprise. It would have been no more than Miantinomo would probably have done to Uncas, and no more than all the Indian tribes were in the constant habit of doing to their captive enemies. The English committed a great error in receiving the prisoner into their hands, and from this error they went on until the result was an act highly unjust and deliberately cruel. Even after receiving him, they might have returned him, and have left Uncas to act as he pleased, on condition that he should take upon himself all the consequences. But we have seen that the Commissioners resolved to return him to the Mohegans only if the latter would put him to death, and that they pledged themselves to support the executioners against all who should call their conduct in question. The real causes of the sachem's execution seem to have been, fear of his power, jealousy that he was inimical to the colonies, and, perhaps, also, the fact that he had favored the heretical settlement of Gorton and his company at Pautuxet.

According to the resolutions of the Commissioners, Governor Winthrop dispatched messengers to the Narragansetts. They charged them with having broken their faith with the English, and having combined with Miantinomo in his design to root out the colonies. They told them, also, that the English justified Uncas in what he had done, and. were determined to protect him against whoever should offer to do him harm. As Canonicus, however, and Mascus, the deceased father of Miantinomo, had always guided the tribe in a peaceable way, the Commissioners were willing to ascribe the late tumults to the proud and unquiet spirit of the deceased sachem. They therefore offered the Narragansetts peace with the English, and with Uncas, and Massasoit, and all the other allies of the English.

The Narragansetts could do no better for the present, than receive this unpalatable message with a good grace, and remain in quiet. We shall see, however, before long, that neither messages nor were treaties sufficient to overcome their hatred of the Mohegans, or restrain their burning desire of revenge.

A Declaration of former Passages and Proceedings betwixt the English and the Narrowgansetts, with theire Confederats, wherein the Grounds and Justice of the ensueing Warre are opened and cleared.

Published by Order of the Commissioners of the United Colonies at Boston, the ninth of the 6th Month, 1645

The most considerable part of the English colonies professed they came into these parts of the world with desire to advance the kingdome of the Lord Jesus Christ, and to enjoy his precious ordinances with peace; and (to his praise they confesse) he hath not failed theire expectation hitherto, they have found safety, warmth. But they know and have considered that theire Lord and Master is King of righteousnes and peace, that he gives answerable lawes, and casts his subjects into such a mould and frame, that (in theire weake measure) they may hould forth his vertues in theire course and carriage, not onely with the nations of Europe, but with the barbarous natives of this wildernes. And accordingly, both in their treaties and converse, they have had an awfull respect to divine rules, endeavouring to walke uprightly and inoffensively, and in the middest of many injuries and insolencies, to exercise much patience and long suffrance, towards them. The Pequots grew to an excesse of violence and outrage, and proudly turned aside from all wayes of justice and peace, before the sword was drawne or any hostile attempts made against them. During those warres, and after the Pequotts were subdued, the English colonies were carefull to continue and establish peace with the rest of the Indians, both for the present and for posterity, as by severall treatyes with the Narrowganset and Mohiggm Sagamores may appere. Which treaties, for a while, were there in some good measure duely observed by all the Indians; but, of late, the Narrowgansets, and especially the Nyanticks theire confederats, have many wayes injuriously broken and violated the same, by intertaineing and keeping amongst them, not onely many of the Pequot nation, but such of them as have had theire hands in the blood and murther of the English, seizing and possessing at least a part of the Pequot country; which, by right of conquest, appertaines to the English; by allowing or harbouring and withholding severall Pequot captives fled from the English, and making proud and insolent returnes when they were redeemed. And, more lately, the English had many strong and concurrent Indian testimonies from Long Island, Uncoway, Hartford, Kinnibeck, and other parts, of Miantonimoes ambitious designs, travelling through all the plantations of the neighboring Indians, and, by promises and gifts, laboring to make himselfe their universal Sagamore or commander, persuading and engaging them, at once, to cut off the whole bodied of the English in those parts. Which treacherous plots were confirmed by the Indians generall preparations in messages, insolencies and outrages against the English and such Indians as were subjects or friends to them so that the English colonies, to theire greate charge and damage, were forced to arme, to keep strong watch, day and night, and some of them to travell with convoyes from one plantation to another, and when Miantonimo, in his circular travell, was questioned at Newhaven concerneing these things, in instead of other and better satisfaction, he threatened to cutt off any Indians bead that should lay such a charge upon him to his face.

The commissioners, by the premises, observed Miantonimoes proud and treacherous disposition, yet thought not fitt to proceed against him in that respect, till they had collected more legall and convinceing proofe. But while these things were under deliberation, Miantonimo was brought prisoner by Uncas to Hartford, and case being opened and cleared as followeth. It appeared that in a treatie made with the English, at the Massachusetts Anno 1637, Miantonimo engaged himselfe not to fight with any of the Indians, and particularly not to invade Uncas without the English consent; and after in a tripartite agreement made and concluded at Hartford betwixt Miantonimo and Uncas with reference to the English, Anno 1638, in which one of the articles runns, That though either of the said Indian Sagamores should receive injury from the other, yet neither of them shall make or begin warre, untill they had appealed to the English, and till their grievances were first heard and determined, and if either of them should refuse, the English might arise against, and compell the refuseing partie.

Notwithstanding which Miantonimo and his confederates have both forcibly and openly plotted and praised against the life of Uncas not at all acquainting the English or advising with them; but more especially of late, in the aforementioned plotts and designes were in hand.

First, a Pequott Indian, one of Uncas his subjects, in the spring 1643, ayming at Uncas' life, shot him with an arrow through the arme, and presently fled to the Narrowgansetts or their confederates, boasting in the Indian plantations that he had killed Uncas. But when it was known that Uncas (though wounded) was alive, the Pequot (taught as was supposed) changed his note, affirming that Uncas had cut through his owne arme with a flint, and bad hired him to say he had shott and killed him.

Miantonimo, being sent for by the governour of the Massachusetts upon another occasion, brought this Pequott with him and would have covered him with the former disguise, but when the English, out of his own mouth, found him guilty and would have sent him to Uncas his Sagamore, Miantonimo earnestly desired he might not be taken out of his hands, promising he would send him safe to Uncas to be examined and punished. But fearing (as it seems) his own treachery would be discovered in a day or two, he stopped the Pequot by cutting off his heade; but at parting he told the governour in discontent that he would come no more to Boston. After this some attempts were made (as is reported) to take away Uncas life by poison, and by sorcery; there failing, some of Sequassens companie (an Indian Sagamore allyed unto and an intimate confederate with Miantonitoo) shott at Uncas, with an arrow or two, as he was goeing downe Connecticut river. Uncas, according to the forementioned treatie (1638) complained, and the English, by mediation, fought to make peace, but Sequassen expressing his dependance on Miantonimo refused, and chose warre. They fought and Uncas had the victory.

Lastly, Miantonimo, without any provocation from Uncas (unless the disappointment of former plotts provoked) and suddenly without denouncing warre, came upon the Moheggins with 900 or 1000 men when Uncas had not halfe so many to defend himselfe. Uncas, before the battle, tould Miantonimo that he had many wayes sought his life, and for the sparing of bloud offered by a single combate betwixt themselves to end the quarrell. But Miantonimo presuming upon his number of men, would have nothing but a battle. The two fell contrary to expectation, his men were routed, divers of considerable note slaine, and himselfe taken prisoner. These things being duely weighed, the commissoners judged that Uncas could not be safe while Miantonimo lived: Wherefore, they thought he might justly put such a treacherous and blood-thirsty enemy to death; but advised him to doe it in his owne jurisdiction, without torture or cruelty. And Uncas, having hitherto showed himselfe a friend to the English, and in this and former outrages (according to the treaty) craveing theire advise, if the Narrowgansetts or their confederates should, for his just execution, unjustly assault him, the commissioners for the colonies promised to assist and protect him.

Uncas hereupon slew an ennemie, but not the enemy against him. The Narrowgansetts soon fell to new contrivements. They pretended they had payd a ransome for theire Sachems life, and gave in particulars to the value of about fourty pounds. This, for a while, cast an imputation of foule and unjust dealing upon Uncas: But, in September 1644, the English commissioners, meeting at Hartford, sent for the Narrowgansett Sachems, or theire deputies desireing they might be instructed to make good theire charge. Uncas came himselfe; they sent theire deputies. But after due examination it appeared, though some loose discourse had passed that, for such quantities of wampum and such parcells of other goods, to a greate value, there might have been some probability of spareing his life, yet no such parcells were brought, and the Narrowgansett deputies did not alledge, much lesse prove, that any ransome was agreed, nor so much as any serious treatie begun to redeeme theire imprisoned Sachem ; and as for the wampum and goods sent, as they were but finall parcells, and scarce considerable for such a purpose, so they were disposed of by Miantonimo himselfe, to sundry persons, for curtesies received during his imprisonment, and upon hope of further favour.

The Narrowganset deputies saw theire proofes fell farre short of former pretences, and were silent. The commissioners promised that, upon better evidence hereafter, they should have due satisfaction. Whereupon a truce was made, and both parties were ingaged that all hostility should cease till planting time 1645, and after that they would give thirty dayes warning either at the Massachusetts or Hartford before the truce should cease. Yet in February last, the Narrowgansetts by messengers sent to Boston, declared that unless Uncas would render 160 fathoms of wampum, or come to a new hearing within fix weekes they would begin the warre.

This crossed the former agreement, and the reason was such that neither the commissioners could be advised with, nor could Uncas travel if notice had been given. After which about or before planting time Tanuqueison a Mohegan Captaine who took Miantonimo prisoner was dangerously and treacherously wounded, at night, as he slept in his wigwam, and other hostile arts were on both parts attempted in a private and underhand way, as they could take advantage one again to the other.

But since the Narrowgansetts have at several times openly invaded Uncas so that Connecticut and New-Haven were, forced, according to ingagement, to send men from those colonies for his present defence, but with expresse direction not to begin any offensive warre against the Narrowgansetts or their confederates till further order. In the mean time, messengers were sent to the Narrowgansetts from the generall court in the Massachusetts signifying the commissioners meeteing, promising their grievances should be fully and justly heard; and requiring a declaration of warre in the meane time, but they refused; and heareing, probably, that the English from the Westerne colonies were returned, they made a new assault upon Uncas, and have done him much hurt.

The commissioners being met sent messengers, the second time, both to the Narrowgansetts and Moheggin Indians, minding them of the former treatie and truce, desiring them to send their deputies instructed and furnished with authority to declare and open the grounds of the warr, to give and receive due satisfaction, and to restore and settle peace. At first, the Narrowganset Sachem gave a reasonable faire answer, that he would send guides with them to the Moheggins, and if Uncas permitted he would send his deputies to the commissioners, and, during eight dayes, hostility should cease ; but he soone repented of his moderation, told the English messengers his mind was changed, sent private instructions to the Nyantick Sachem, after the delivery of which there was nothing but proud and insolent pillages; the Indian guides which the English messengers brought with them from Pumham and Soconoco, were by frownes and threatening speeches discouraged, and returned; no other guides could be obtained, though much pressed; they knew (as they expressed them-selves) by the course held at Hartford the last yeare, that the commissioners would mediate and presse for peace, but they were resolved to have no peace without Uncas his head, it mattered not who began the warre, they were resolved to continue it; the English should withdrawe theire garrison from Uncas, or they would take it as a breach of former covenants, and would procure as many Moquakes as the English should affront them with that they would lay the English cattle on heapes as high as theire houses and that no English man should slip out of his house to pisse, but he would be killed.

They reviled Uncas, charged him with cutting through his owne arme, and faying the Narrowgansetts had shott him; affirmed, that he would now murder the English messengers, as they went or returned, (if he had opportunity) and lay it upon the Narrowgansetts.

The English messengers, upon this rude and uncivil usage, wanting guides to proceed, and fearing danger, returned to the Narrowgansetts, acquainted Pesacus with the former passages, and desired guides from him, he offered them an old Pequot squawe, but would afford no other guides. There also they conceived themselves to be in danger, three Indians with hatchets standing behind the interpreter in a suspicious manner, while he was speaking with Pesacus, and the rest frowning and expressing much distemper in theire countenance and carriage. The English messengers, not hopeing for better successes at that time, departed; telling Pesacus, that if he would returns any other answer; he should send it to the English tradeing house, where they intended to lodge that night. In the morning, he invited them to returne, and promised them a guide to Uncas, but would grant no cessation of armes. When they came to Providence, they understood that, in their absence, a Narrowganset Indian had been there, and feigning himselfe to be of Connecticut, spake in that dialect, but could not put off the Narrowganset tone. He told Benedict Arnold's wife (who well understands the Indian language) that the English Messengers should not pass to the Mohegins he knew they should have no guides, but should be destroyed in the woods, as they travelled towards Unkus. Thus the English messengers returned, and the interpreter, under his hand and upon his oath, related the former passages, with others less material, more largely.

Mr. Williams, by the messengers, wrote to the commissioners. assuring them that the country would suddenly be all on fire, meaning by warre; that, by strong reasons and arguments, he could convince any man thereof that was of another mind; that the Narrowgansetts had been with the plantations
combined with Providence and had solemnly treated and settled a neutrality with them, which fully shewed their councell and resolutions for warre.

Thus while the commissoners, in care of the public peace, fought to quench the fire kindled amongst the Indians, these children of strife breath out threatenings, provocations and warre against the English themselves. So that unles they should dishonor and provoke God, by violating a just ingagement, and expose the colonies to contempt and danger from the Barbarians, they cannot but exercise force, when no other meanes will prevaile, to reduce the Narrowgansetts and theire confederates to a more just and sober temper.

The eyes of other Indians, under the protection of the Massachusetts and not at all ingaged in this quarrell, are (as they have expressed themselves to the English messengers) hastned upon the English with strict observation, in what manner and measure they provide for Uncas safety. If he perish, they will charge it upon them, who might have preserved him and no Indians will trust the English, if they now breake ingagement, either in the present or succeeding generations. If Uncas be ruined in such a cause, they foresee theire heads, upon the next pretence, shall be delivered to the will of the Narrowgansetts, with whom therefore they shall be forced to comply as they may, for theire future safety, and the English may not trust an Indian in the whole country. The premisses being duely weighed, it clearly appeares that God calls the colonists to a warre.

Winthrop's Journal, History of New England
October 12.] The new Sachem of Narraganset, Miantunnomoh's brother called Pesecus, a young man about 20, sent a present to our governor, viz., an otter coat and girdle of wampom, and some other wampom, in all worth about 15 pounds, and desired peace and friendship with us, and withal that we would not aid Onkus against him, whom he intended to make war upon in revenge of his brother's death. Our governor answered the messengers, that we were willing to have peace friendship with him, and to that end had sent messengers to Canonicus, (whom it seemed they met with by the way,) but we desired withal that there might be peace with all Indians also, both Onkus and others, and that we had also sent to Ousamekin to that end; therefore except their sachem would agree to it, we could not receive his present. They replied that they had no instructions about the matter, but would return back and acquaint their sachem with it, and return to us again, and desired to leave their present with our governor in the mean time, which he agreed unto.
1648
August 15.] At the last meeting of the commissioners at New Haven, information was given them, that Sequashiu, a sachem near Hartford, would have hired an Indian to kill some of the magistrates of Hartford, whereupon he was sent for, but came not; and being among other Indians about Pacomtuckett, they sent for Unkas, who undertook to fetch him in, which he not being able to do by force, he surprised him in the night, and brought him to Hartford, where he was kept in prison divers weeks. But there not being sufficient proof to convict him Sec. he was discharged. Yet the Indians, from whom he was taken, took it so to heart against Uncas, as they

271

intended to make war upon him, and the Narragansett sent wampom to them to encourage them; and accordingly in this month, there were gathered together from divers parts about one thousand Indians armed, three hundred or more having guns, powder and bullets, and were at Pacomtuckett preparing &c. which the magistrates of Hartford hearing of, they sent three horsemen to them (one being very expert in the Indian language) to know their intent, and to tell them, that if they made war upon Uncas, the English must defend him. The Indian sachems entertained the messengers courteously; and having heard their message, they took time to give their answer, which was this, viz. they knew the English to be a wise and warlike people, and they intended not to fall out with them, therefore for the present they would desist, and consider further of the matter. And God had so disposed, as at the same instant they had intelligence of a defeat given to some of their confederates by other Indians, which called them to their aid, and also the Narragansett had failed to send them all the wampom he had promised. Thus the Lord delivered us from that war, which must needs have been very dangerous, especially to our brethren of Connecticut.

The Narragansett and Niantick dealing thus underhand contrary to their covenant, and being yet behind near one thousand fathom of the wampom they should have paid us long since, the commissioners, sitting at Plimouth, ordered four men to be sent to them, with an interpreter, with instructions how to treat with them, both concerning their hiring other Indians to war upon Uncas, and also about the wampom behind. Captain Atherton and Captain Prichard, assisted with two others, voluntarily undertook this service, and went hence. They were to have taken Benedict Arnold for their interpreter; but he being from home, they went to Mr. Williams, who sent for the sachems. But they had heard that many horsemen were come to take them, which made Pessicus fly over to Rhode Island. Then our messengers went to Niantick, where Ninicraft entertained them courteously, (there they staid the Lord's day,) and came back with them to Mr. Williams, and then Pessicus and Canonicus' son, being delivered of their fear, came to them, and being demanded about hiring the Mohawks against Uncas, they solemnly denied it; only they confessed, that the Mohawks, being a great sachem, and their ancient friend, and being come so near them, they sent some twenty fathom of wampom for him to tread upon, as the manner of Indians is. And Canonicus' son called [blank] used this asseveration, viz. Englishman's God doth know, that we did not send to stir up or hire the Mohawks against Uncas. Then they further promised, that they would not meddle with Uncas, nor stir up any other against him, before they had paid all their debt of wampom to the English, and then they would require satisfaction for all the wrongs Uncas had done them, and if the English would not see them satisfied, they would consider what to do. And for their wampom behind Sic. they desired the English to bear with them, in regard their want of corn last winter had made them lay out their

wampom to the English for corn; but in the spring they would provide part of it, and the rest so soon as they could.

Report of a Committee Appointed to Inquire Respecting the Claims of Uncas to the Pequot Country; Presented to the Commissioners, at their meeting in Boston, Sept., 1663.

[From a copy certified, from the files, by Simon Bradstreet, 1663; from which is in Towns & Lands, 1. 67, is certified by Ebenezer Kimberly, Secretary.]

Boston, September 19th, 1663.

We, being desired by the Commissioners of the United Colonies to enquire of the Indians present concerning the interest of the Pequots, or respecting lands which Uncas layeth claim unto, we accordingly have endeavored the same, according to our best skill and understanding; and there being present, Cassisinnamon, Kitchamaquin and Tomasquash Ecoadno (alias,) the old honest man, Pequots; also, Womesh, Mumuho, Kaiton, Narragansett Councillors, with many others Indians; which do all jointly affirm, that long before the Pequots were conquered by the English, Uncas, being akin unto the Pequots, did live upon and Enjoy that land above a place called Montononesuck, upon which Mr. Winthrop's saw mill standeth; also, that it was his father's before him, and left unto him by his father; which he possessed some time. But he growing proud and treacherous to the Pequot Sachem, the Pequot Sachem was very angry, and sent up some soldiers, and drave Uncas out of his country; who fled unto Narragansett, for a while. At last he humbled himself to the Pequot Sachem, and desired that he might have liberty to live in his own country again; which the Pequot Sachem granted, provided he would be subject unto him, and carry it well. But soon after, he grew proud again, and was again driven out of his country, but his men subjected unto the Pequot Sachem; and yet again, upon his humbling, was restored, and grew proud again, and was conquered; and so five times; and upon his humbling himself was restored, and again conquered; until when the English went to war against the Pequots; and then Uncas went along with the English; and so, since, the English have made him high.

They further say, they know not the English fashions, but according to their manners and customs, Uncas had no lands at all, being so conquered. This, they say, Uncas cannot deny, but if he should deny it, the thing is known to all the Indians round about.

Also, the Narragansetts say that there is yet two of his men yet alive that tied with him into the Narragansett country, and have there abode ever since, who knew these things to be true. And further, they jointly affirm that Uncas had at first but little land and very few men, insomuch he could not make a hunt, but always hunted by order from other Sachems, and in their companies; which Sachems, being five brothers, lived at a place called by the Indians, Sondahque, at or near the place where Major Mason now liveth; who were the sons of the great Pequot Sachem's sister, and so became very great Sachems, and had their bounds very large, extending their bounds by Connecticut path almost to Connecticut, and eastward meeting with the bounds of Pasquattuck (who lived at Showtackett, being a Pequot Sachem whose bounds extended eastward and took in Pachogg;) the which five Sachems, being brothers, grew so great and so proud that upon hunting they quarrelled with the Pequots: at which the great Pequot [Sachem] being angry with them, made war upon them and conquered them and their country, and they all fled into Narragansett country, (leaving their country and men unto the Pequot Sachem,) from whence they never returned, but there died. So that Indians affirm all their lands and Woncas's too, according to their customs and manners, were Pequot lands, being by them conquered, and now are the true right of the English, they having conquered the Pequots.

This was declared and testified by the Indians as abovesaid, clearly, to our understanding: as witness our hands, George Denison, John Stanton, Cary Latham.

Letters from Rev. James Fitch, Respecting Uncas and the Surrenderers:
To the General Court
To the Right Worshipfull Governour and Assistants, with the Deputies assembled at Hartford:

Whereas the Lord in his just judgment hath vexed us by a foolish people & those who are no people, and hath scourged us by the heathen, the rod of his anger, untill his bowells were troubled for us, and then he destroyed multitudes and forced some to submit for feare, and thus hath given a rod into your hands; & many consultations have beene how to do faithfully according to the promise made in the day of distress and how to overcome evill with goodness, that coales of fire might be heap'd upon [the] heads of your enemies by your mercie towards them, either for the[heate] to melt them or to consume them; and what orders and instructions I have received concerning the remnant of surrenderers is well knowne; and what hath beene done of late for theire settlement is no less than duetie for me to give in the account.

The names of the men who wth theire wifes & children are settled at Shawtukket, wth the consent of the inhabitants of Norwich, upon a triall for this yeare, are these following: Kockanampauit with his familie, Wintakamon etc., Mashantup etc, Patakeet etc, Naushanshak etc, Oushpenou etc, Noquittemou, Kottini etc, Mattawaushk, Nuntewawus. Pamberook, Wamtanemaug etc, Ousenoo etc, Sunkelaupun, etc, Webekunck, Webequiun, Kitchemoo, Waaessit, Manaatch etc, Washashup, Auwussemauge, Mattakumpauitt, Queecumin, Paapeeunguenunt etc, Akompanit etc, Yauwantuck etc, Waaguinegut; in all 29; the generalitie being heads of families. I am sufficiently inform'd there are a considerable number more abiding wth Uncus, who doubtless are willing to come and settle wth the others, but are meerly hinder'd by Uncus; and therefore I doe humbly beseech you to consider whether if punishment be inflicted, it ought not to be [not] upon the sufferers of the wronge but upon the doers of the wronge. And Uncus & the Moheegs doe comonly say that there are many surrenderers amongst the Pequotts, and the Narragansetts: but I must leave these and all such considerations wth you.

And now Honored & Beloved, whether I have in these or any thing els done you service, or not, yet I beseech you charitably to accept of my good will; and for the future let me be freed from these concerns. I doe the rather desire it, because at p'sent it's onely the civill management of a matter respecting publique safetie, better becoming some other: and although I doe not discerne but that the surrenderers are abundantly contented wth theire settlement, and are glad they are from under the yoake of Uncus his monarchy, but the feare I have least the Lord of Hosts hath not done scourging us, and least I should miss it in my transactions wth the heathen to the hazard of publique safetie, this very supposition is sometimes too heavie for me to beare, that I cannot but desire you would comitt these occasions into the hands of some better able to manage them. And so I shall add no more at p'sent, but my earnest desires that the good will of Him who dwelt in our burning bush would be with you to direct & bless these & all your publique concerns, for his glory, & for publique safetie; wch is the prayer of youre humble servant,
4th May (78) James Fitch.

Norwich.
To the Worshipfull Captain John Allyn
Worshipfull Sir,

 The enclosed, containing an account of affaires respecting the Surrenderers settled at Shawtuckket, I have desired it may be communicated to the Court. The reasons are because I perceive that some of the Court have beene unsatisfied with my medling in such affaires; and if they can see their way otherwise to dispose of those occasions, I shall be glad: but if at present I must endure the trouble, if they have a hande to putt it upon me, it may be for the future they will be more sparing to speake harsh things. However, I doe apprehend it will be more safe for the Governour and yourself, that whatever be done of this kinde may be an act of the Court. It's good to prepare for the worst, whatever the event may be at length, concerning matters needfull to be inquired after in the p'sent juncture of affaires.

 I gave you a writing when the Govern' & yourself were at my house, concerning the frame of Uncus his actings from the beginning of the warrs to that time; & what hath been since I shall sumarilye mention. You are acquainted with Paapeeguenoo's confession, when he was in prison;—that his lending away surrenderers & servants was by Uncus his order; and the circumstances to evince the truth of it are, 1st. Paapeeguenoo's was so longe and so open in his preparations for that motion, that it could not be hid from Uncus, but he knewe of it and used no meanes to prevente it. It may be Uncus will say he was not at home at that time, but at Saibrooke; but the answer is full,— that usually when the time is come to doe mischeife or act some strange thinge, he at that time slippeth away to Saibrooke; thus it hath been when any of the surrenderers were to run away; thus when our cattle have been kill'd; thus when this man was lately kill'd at Shawtukket: that hence, both from our English & Indeans, there is an expectation of something horrible. So that this covert is worne so thredbare & thin, that every one amongst us doe see through it. 2nd. With Paapeegueno went Anacobin, a Moheag, a man of greate account wth Uncus, neerly related to him; but none can believe that he would goe away from Uncus, Unles it were to be agent for Uncus. 3rd. It's not only Paapeeguenoo's confession, but contently granted & owned by the Moheegs, that this was with Uncus his consent; only they were afraid so to speake that Uncus shall knowe of it Concerning the surrenderers since that time:—1. When last sumer he had timely warneing of Major Talcoat's coming by order of Court to his towne, to act concerning the surrenderers, but not one surrenderer then to be seene, unles it were a very aged man, in token of derision, &c.—2d. Uncus at that time did againe promise that the surrenderers should be settled the next September at Shawtuckket; and after much meanes & longe waiting, many are detained by him; if he denies it he may be inquired of whether he hath not with him, Keweebhunt, Koawalk, Maukechakeman, Kohsequunnont, who are heades of families, and many more whose names in time may be knowne.

I shall send up Kockanampauit and two more of the surrenderers; and you may by meanes of them knowe Uncus his fallacy; onely let theire names be kept private; they are afraid to be seene before Uncus. And that which you say to them for theire encouragement to settle where they are, will be an encouragement to the others. And indeed Kockanarripuit, a man well knowne to Major Talcott to be the guide of the army, he hath beene principally instrumentall to draw off those surrenderers from Uncus, and to settle them at Shawtukket. But it's manifest that Uncus his favour is not towards him as formerly; and it's his brother was killed at Shawtukket.

Concerning the death of that man:—1. Uncus sends a message the night before to the Shawtukket Indeans, to warne them (as he pretended) that Mohawks were in the woods; but none scene by the Indians, who were scouting out every way. 2. Many men & women & children were that day passing every waye, as yet no harme nor shewe of danger to any, but onely that which was done to this one man nigh the forte. 3. Since the warres hath been ended, no such mischeife in other parts of the countrie, but all in a quiet posture. But we are allarum'd with one straunge accident after another. Not so at Connecticott, not so at seaside, nor Pequotts. What is the reason of this? seeing it's well knowne that his owne men dare not act contrarye to his pleasure, and his enemies are more affraid to come neere to him then to all other Indeans in these parts of the country, because of his strength.

Concerning Indean servants hidden & sheltered by Uncus: if inquirye be made, it may be Mr. Plumb of New London will speake to that case; and Owaneko will not denye but he received 20 in monyes, upon the account of delivering his servant to him, when he had hid the servant severall dayes: and Ensigne Post I suppose is readye to make manifest Uncus his fallacies, in alluring away his servant and then hiding of her, & His falsness of this kinde is so notorious that if he be not restrain'd it will not be possible for the

English to keepe any Indean servant. I shall add no more but onely that wch is so comonly knowne not onely to myself but any who have oportunitie wth him in the companie of Indeans wth him,—so reproachfully to vilifye our rulers, our lawes & religion, and is the greate opponent of any meanes of souls' good & concernment to his people, and abounding more & more in dancings & all manner of heathenish impieties since the warrs; and vilifying what hath been done by the English, and attributing the victory to theire Indean helps, &c.

Sir, I am wearie with writing, and it may be you will be so with reading these wearisome matters. I pray conceale my name; and if there be any argument from the frame of these particulars, let it be improved. Onely I know not when to have done; for even now Kockanampauit (whom I mentioned before,) some other surrenderors will come up to see wth what countenance the Court will looke upon them & to heare whether you will confirme them in theire liberties in the place where they are; and in particular whether you will express any sympathy for the loss of one of theire principall men; and they say, they have not right done to them, in restoring those surrenderors who were taken away by Leiutenant Holinstor [?] &c. I wish them to speake when they have an oportunitie. You are better able to answer them in that matter then I can. So with my earnest desires that God would be with you & direct & bless you in all your concerns, wth my service to yourself & Mrs. Allyn,—I know you will present these to the view of our Hond. Govern,—I remaine, Yours humbly to serve, James Fitch, Sen.

Norwich. "Whereas, at a General Court in Hertford, May 13, 1680, my father, Uncas, had liberty to dispose unto me his land upon Quinebaug River, and the Court at the same time granting me liberty In dispose of it unto gentlemen among them, as I should see cause to do, and a good part thereof I have disposed of already; but finding that some, through their great importunity, and others taking advantage of me when I am in drink, by causing me to sign deeds, not only wronging myself but may spoil it ever being a plantation—for these and other reasons, I make over all my right and title of any and all of my lands and meadows unto my loving friend James Fitch, for him to dispose of as he shall see cause.

Dec. 22, 1680,

The mark

Owaneco, His mark

   The latest signature of the sachem Uncas is found under date of June, 1683. A deed to Samuel Chester was signed June 13th, and a grant of several thousand acres in Colchester, or the south part of Hebron, to the Stebbins brothers, was acknowledged before Samuel Mason, about the same period. In June, 1684, Owaneco, in a deed to James Fitch, styles himself son of Uncas, deceased. This is the nearest approximation obtained to the death of Uncas. He is supposed to have been very aged, and there are traditions that during the latter years of his life, he was generally found sitting by the door of his wigwam asleep, and that it was not easy to rouse his mind to activity. The sachem was undoubtedly buried at Norwich, in a select position on the banks of the Yantic, which is supposed to have been the place of his father's sepulture, and which has ever since been exclusively devoted to the descendants of Uncas. In this cemetery an obelisk of granite was erected by female gifts in 1842, which has for its inscription a single name.

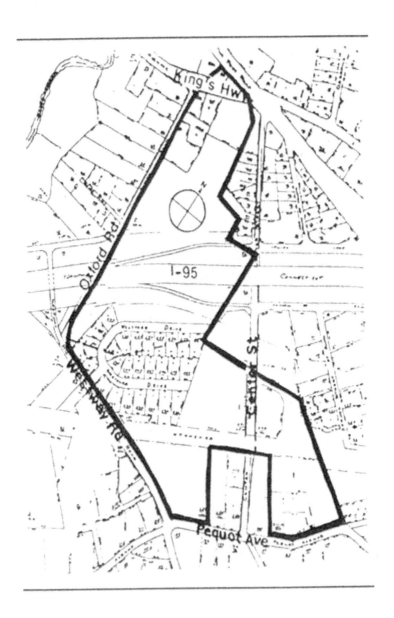

Chapter Six

Settlers of the Swamplands

Southport, in the old town of Fairfield, includes within its limits one of the most interesting, as well as important Colonial battlefields to be found in all New England. In 1637, Captain John Mason, and the force under his command, overtook and defeated the formidable tribe of Pequot Indians, which had made its last stand in what was then and now is known as the "swamp," a bit of low land lying to the north of the present village. As this decisive victory led shortly after to the incoming of Roger Ludlow and his followers, and the permanent settlement of the town, it is not surprising that a deep interest has ever since attached itself to the memorable locality where the contest was waged. It is a remarkable fact, however, that this

interest has never taken visible shape until the present time. Traditions of the battle have been handed down from father to son: flint arrowheads, rusty bayonets, and other detrita, found in the furrows made by the plough of the husbandman are treasured in many a household as souvenirs; but this was all, until the Dorothy Ripley Chapter resolved fitly to commemorate in a substantial manner both the locality, and the event that gave it lustre. It was at a meeting of the chapter held December 12th, 1901, that Mrs. George B. Bunnell, one of the most enthusiastic, as well as beloved of its members, read a paper, which closed with the suggestion that a drinking fountain, with ample provision for slaking the thirst of man and beast, be erected as a memorial for the marking the historic site referred to.
Daughters of the American Revolution

P.D. Ridge, A Story of Pequot Swamp and an Incident of Mill River, now Southport
The Northwestern part of Southport is called Pequot Swamp. Two hundred years ago, and more, was fought here the great battle between our English forefathers and the Pequot tribes of Indians. This locality--then a lowland forest--as the scene of the Pequot massacre, was named Pequot Swamp. It is, comparatively, but a few years ago since an effectual bugbear to frighten children into obedience, was to mention them "the Indians," who-- their youthful imaginations led them to believe--were still lurking in the dark recesses of this dreaded forest. One of the "oldest inhabitants" of the village, relates to us, that he can recollect the time when the *superstitious* "children of a larger growth" were afraid to go near the "swamp" after dark, such was their dread of the red man. Not many years have elapsed since stone tomahawks and other relics of the Pequot's were frequently discovered in this Indian retreat. And now at this day, when the farmer turns up its soil, flint arrow heads, such as are known to have been used by the Indians in their battles, are often found. The following account of the first white settlers in Pequot swamp is "founded on fact," although the imagination has been largely drawn upon to supply what history does not furnish.
A short time previous to the battle between the English and the Pequot's, Enoch Griswold, an exile from the Providence Colony, settled on the border of the Pequot Swamp. The house occupied by Enoch, a rude log cabin, was still standing (on the site now occupied by the Congregational church) at the beginning of the present century. Enoch's family consisted of Mary his wife, a daughter Esther, in her seventeenth year, and Josiah Morgan, a young

friend and distant relative of the Griswold's. But a few Indians lived in the vicinity of Enoch's settlements, and these were friendly. The Pequot's were driven in here from the eastern part of the Connecticut colony, and all exterminated or carried away prisoners, except the few who escaped and were supposed to have fled and joined the Mohegan. But as the sequel will appear, they returned as soon as the English had left, and secreted themselves in an almost impenetrable thicket in the swamp. They doubtless resolved there to remain, until they had avenged, in a measure, their fallen comrades, by retaliation on the white family they had noticed in the vicinity. Those were good old Puritanical, patriarchal days. Enoch and his family were happy. Their simple wants were easily supplied from the fruitful land and the bountiful sea. Often they, in company with their Indian friends, spend the day fishing, and return with well filled baskets, for our river and the Sasco were then teeming with finny beauties. It was while returning from an excursion of this kind, one afternoon that Esther, who had loitered behind the rest of the company, gathering wild flowers for a wreath, was suddenly missed. No great fears for her safety were at first entertained, as no hostile Indians were known to be within many miles, and it is a common occurrence for her to drop in at the neighboring wigwams and chat with the squaws and their children, her goodness of heart making her a general favorite. But as evening began to approach, and no Ester returned, strange foreboding filled the minds of Enoch and his household. Inquiries were made at the various wigwams, but no trace of her could be obtained. All passed a sleepless, anxious night, but as soon as morning dawned, the firm lip and dauntless eye of both Enoch and Josiah, told of their determination to ascertain if possible her where-abouts. They first retraced their steps, by the path they had come the day before, to the landing, (Now White's Rocks) near the mouth of the river, that being the usual place for hauling up their canoes; it having just occurred to them that Esther, who being accustomed to use the paddle had often taken alone might, for a little playful scare, have hidden until they were out of sight, and then returned to the boat and been carried out by a fierce squall that had arisen soon after. But their canoes were all there. A wreath was found, the tell-tale wreath to the eye of Josiah, for none but Esther could have made it. On looking further, the print of strange moccasins was discovered in the sand, an arrow was found and recognized as belonging to the Nehantics, a Long Island tribe. At the water's edge there was a mark from the prow of a much larger canoe than any at the landing. It flashed upon their minds at once that Esther had been seized and carried to Long Island by the Nehantics. Who can picture to mind the

283

anguish of the good father as he thought of the fate of his dutiful, affectionate daughter? Who can describe the agony of Josiah, as he imagined his idol, his betrothed, in the hands of a cruel, savage, foe!

A pursuit was once resolved upon. Hastily filling up their largest canoe with supplies, and accompanied by two faithful Indian allies, Wampeag and Catoonah, all were well armed, they started for the islands (now Norwalk Islands) a short distance from the mouth of the river, thinking that if their fears were true, and Esther had been abducted by that tribe, they had probably stopped their over night, and might not yet have left. Love, filial affection, and revenge nerved the ears, and they were not long in reaching the islands. As they had surmised, the Indians had stopped there; but they were now gone. The embers from a recent fire were still warm; the print of the same moccasins was visible; the prow of the same canoe had left its mark in the sand. Burning with impatience and rage, and resolved to lose their lives if need be, in the attempt to save her, they started at once for Long Island, feeling sure from so many indications, that their foes were Nehantics, living near what is now known as Eaton's Neck. But to return to Esther, whom we left gathering flowers, little dreaming of danger. She had wandered from the path in quest of some rare colors with which to deck the brow of her lover, and having sufficient for her purpose, seated herself near a thick copse and finished her wreath. As she was looking with admiration upon her work, her cheeks flushed with the thought of how pleased Josiah would be, she was suddenly seized by four dusky Pequots. Before she had time to make any outcry, she was gagged, tied, and hurried into the woods. Making a wide detour through the woods, which were then continuous from Pequot Swamp to the Sasco, the Indians dragged the almost insensible Esther to a bend in the Sasco, (where now stands the dwelling of Capt. Thorp,) and there meeting two comrades in waiting with a canoe, hastily embarked and glided down the river to a dense clump of woods near its mouth, where they waited until under cover of the darkness, they could proceed in safety. As soon as it was fairly dark they left the river, and hugging along the land, stopped at the place where Esther, a few hours before, had so happily tripped ashore. Here they purposely dropped the wreath, and the arrow which had formerly belonged to the Nehantic, and leaving plenty of traces in the sand, they started for the islands. Staying there until near midnight, and leaving fuel enough on the fire to last till morning, they then doubled their track, and returning to Sasco River, were long before daylight, snugly ensconced in their Pequot lair; succeeding well, as we have seen, in throwing his party off trail.

So intent were the pursuers on the object they had in view, so earnest in their purpose to rescue Esther, that they had hardly noticed the heavy swell of the sea noticed the heavy swell of the sea from a violent northeaster, which then, as now, was common to September. The wind blew almost a gale, and was increasing every moment. They had proceeded about half the distance from Long Island, when Enoch, who seemed to have a presentiment of his fate, exclaimed to his companions, "we shall never reach the shore! O, my poor Esther, I shall never see you again!" Their frail bark soon after began to take in water. Still by bailing and using the utmost skills to keep her trimmed, they succeeded in getting within a mile of the shore, near the reef, when they were capsized. Enoch, with one look of despair, sank, and was not seen after. Josiah and the two Indians clung to the boat, and nearly exhausted, drifted ashore. The Nehantics, though not friendly to the tribe on this side, yet had enough of human kindness in their hearts to befriend a shipwrecked company. Josiah and his companions were tenderly cared for, and they learned from the Nehantics, without exciting their suspicions, that none of their tribe had made any voyages to the north shore within several days. Grief, the double bereavement, and the loss of his beloved and of him who was a father, had well-nigh unmanned Josiah, and with a heavy heart he made preparations for returning. The next morning, the storm having sub-sided, they started. On their way they stopped again at the islands to see if they could discover any more traces of Esther and her captors. That her abductors had been their was plain; but the Nehantics were not the guilty party. Who could it have been? They again examined the beach. The footprints of Esther were plainly visible, for the Pequots had unbound her after reaching the islands. On looking further, where there was a spot of smooth clean sand, the tracks appeared to have a method--a design about them, and examining them closely, they could plainly make out the word "Pequot" imprinted by her feet in the sand. this gave them a clue, and yet a faint one. Of the history of the battles they were familiar, knowing that the Pequots were all killed or taken away prisoners, except the few that joined the Mohegans. Had some of that few returned, and with their whites captive gone back to the Mohegans? Oh, with what a feeling of lonliness and almost utter despair Josiah gazed upon that word in the sand. He could imagine how she, intently watching her masters lest they should discover her intentions, had endeavored to guide her friends in their pursuit. those dear footprints seemed to him the last of Esther. Hope of her again had nearly fled. Sadly they turned the prow of their boat homeward. No Esther-no Enoch. How could Josiah break the tidings to the mother—the wife. Had they come back--this party of rescuers--bringing the darling object of their search, with what alacrity their little craft would have sped over the intervening water. But now, instead of one to them as dead, another, Enoch, the head--the chief of the little family, was gone. How languidly the canoe crept towards the landing. How they dreaded to meet the anxious bereaved one.

To Mary the blow was overwhelming. To be deprived of her husband and her daughter, and she in a strange land, an exile from the home of her kindred; it was well nigh insupportable. The sympathy of the little community was aroused, and not only their sympathy, but their anger. It seemed to be the one opinion among the Indians, that Esther had been carried off to the Mohegans. The Sachem was indignant that a sneaking Pequot should dare to steal his pale faced daughter, as he regarded her. Wampeag and Catoonah offered to go in disguise to the Mohegan country, and if they found her, one of them was to return for help to assist in the rescue, and the other to remain near, to shield her, as far as possible, from harm. They started on their hazardous journey, but with little hope of success. The anguish and excitement of the last few days was too much for the not over robust Josiah. The Pequots in their secure retreat were gloating over the prospect of revenge their captive they treated kindly in their rude way, not being ready to take her life--the final satiation of their hate. They knew the value of their prize, for, unperceived, they had often been near the dwelling of Enoch, before the capture of Esther, and knew the high esteem in which she was held. The torturing--the death of one such pale face, was to them an equivalent to the torturing and death of scores of red men. During the day they did not venture far from their hiding place, except to fish on the thickly wooded banks of the Sasco. They avoided the friendly Indians, and if seen, being dressed like them, they escaped detection. At night, leaving one or two in charge of their prisoner, the others would travel miles away to gather clams, oysters, and other food. Esther had become almost a stoic. Sorrow had benumbed her faculties. She did not dread death; to her it would be a relief. The past happy life was like a dream. The few weeks that she had been imprisoned seemed an age. Where she was she knew not. The islands to which she was taken immediately after her capture, she was familiar with, having often visited them with her parents and Josiah; but before they returned, the Pequots had blindfolded her. She little thought that not a mile intervened between her and her home.

Three months rolled by. The two Indians had come back, but brought no tidings of Esther. They found that the remnant of the Pequots had not joined the Mohegan Tribe. Josiah had recovered in some degree his wonted strength, but the fire of his manhood was gone; the light of his life had, to him, been put out. Sometimes he would fish or hunt with his Indian friends, but these sports had lost much of their zest. Twice, lately, on the banks of the Sasco, after a light snow, they had noticed tracks of a moccasin similar to those seen in the sand, at the landing, the morning after her abduction. They appeared to proceed from and go towards the dense thick in the swamp. This copse had never been entered since the battle. It was the most difficult of access, and a sort of supernatural dread seemed to affect the minds of the Griswold family and the Indians regard to it; and no wonder, for around it lay bleaching the bones of many a Pequot. The more Josiah thought of the similarity of the tracks in the snow and those in the sand, the more he felt convinced that they were made by the same feet. All at once it occurred to him that Esther was in that thicket. So sudden was the thought that his brain fairly reeled with excitement. As soon as he became more calm, he resolved to immediately explore this part of the swamp, and hastily told a few trusty Indians of his plans. Knowing well that if the Pequots were there, they would naturally leave at night, or most of them, for their food, as soon as it was dark, Josiah and his friends stealthily approached the thicket on the side toward Sasco river, until they were as near as possible without being discovered. They had not long to wait, when five Pequots passed out, so near as almost to touch them in their place of concealment. Waiting until they had gone far beyond hearing, Josiah, with feelings excited to an intense degree, led the way in the direction the Pequots had just come. With a panther like tread, they slowly entered the tangled passage. those minutes were hours! Soon, a light in the far end of the opening guided their footsteps! Two figures could be plainly seen! It needed iron nerves just then! A few more steps, half walking, half creeping, and Josiah had the swooning Ester clasped in his arms! Her guard, asleep, was quickly dispatched by Josiah's comrades. Loosing her bonds, they at once made their way out. Leaving the Indians to watch for the Pequots, who, returning towards morning, were riddled with bullets, Josiah and Esther, with feelings too happy for utterance, returned to their home, to meet with still another joy; the father--the good Enoch was there! Was it truly him, or his spirit e dead! When the canoe upset, the box containing their supplies had drifted near the spot where he arose, and clinging to it, he had been carried by the current some miles below the Neck, and had been picked up, more dead than alive, by a tribe just starting for the Hudson. He had finally escaped from them, and after many adventures, had returned just in time to make the happiness of that family complete. The lone settlers were soon made glad by an accession to their number, several more families emigrating from the Providence colony. Josiah and Esther were married a few months after, and some of their honored descendants are now living in our midst. Enoch and Mary lived to a good old age, happy in their declining years, in having such a son and such a daughter.

Elizabeth Schenck, History of Fairfield, Fairfield County, Connecticut

In the subjugation of the powerful tribe of Indians known as the Pequots, in the great fight at Sasqua or Pequot swamp, the pioneers of Connecticut achieved an important victory, one which in its results has scarcely a parallel in the history of warfare. Peace with the much dreaded savages who roamed at will about the feeble settlements, and in fact throughout all New England, was thereby secured. Prosperity followed quickly after days of great adversity; and the planters found themselves not only in position to extend their own borders, but to enlarge the jurisdiction of the colony by beginning plantations along the coast of Long Island Sound.

In noting the many providences of God which overshadowed them during this war, one of special interest to the sons and daughters of Fairfield, was the discovery of the fair fields of Uncoway. For want of pasture for their cattle, good land for cultivation, and a bountiful supply of water, many of the planters of Plymouth and Massachusetts had emigrated to the banks of the Connecticut: but here at Uncoway they found the long sought for country, beautiful beyond all other spots which they had yet discovered. Here were meadow lands rich with the deposits of ages; grand old forests and majestic hills overlooking some of the most picturesque scenes in New England. Here, too, were fresh springs, rivers, ponds and streamlets of pure sweet waters; and sweeping as far as the eye could reach from east to west rolled the blue waters of Long Island Sound, across which, against the southern horizon, lay Sewanhacky, the Island of Shells or Long Island.

To return to this beautiful country, and to rear on the scene of the great Pequot victory an English town, became the aim of the deputy governor, Roger Ludlow. He succeeded in obtaining a commission from the General

Court of Connecticut to begin a plantation at Pequonnock, during the summer or early autumn of 1639; and with four others set out on his journey thither. Upon his arrival he entered into a treaty with the chief sachems of Pequonnock, of whom he purchased "all the lands lying west of the Stratford bounds to the Sasqua or Mill river, and from the Mill river south-westward to the east bounds of the Maxumux Indian lands; and from the Sound, seven or eight miles into the wilderness," all of which lands were claimed by the Pequonnock Indians.

The Indians of this region were no doubt glad to enter into a friendly alliance with the English, whom, since their remarkable victory over the Pequots, they must have regarded as beings endowed with supernatural power. In order to secure protection from their deadly enemies the Mohawks, who yearly made a descent upon them to collect a tribute which was rigidly exacted, they agreed to give Governor Ludlow an annual tribute of furs, wampum and corn.

There were several hundred Indians divided into clans who claimed the lands of Pequonnock, Uncoway, and Sasqua. The Pequonnock Indians appear to have been a branch of the Paugusetts, living on the east side of the Housatonic, and the Wepawags on the west side of the river. They were at one time supposed to be two distinct tribes; but it has been decided by students of the aborigines of Connecticut, that they were one and the same, as the names of their chief sachems are found attached to deeds of lands, both of Milford and Stratford. The territories of this clan stretched several miles along the coast and included the Norwalke Indians. After the Indians of Pequonnock made a formal sale of their lands to Roger Ludlow, they settled upon Golden Hill—so named from the mica found in the soil—and were ever afterwards called the Golden Hill tribe.

The Uncoway Indians occupied the territory lying west of Pequonnock, to the eastern borders of Sasqua or Mill river. The name of Sasquannock appears to have been applied to all the lands lying west of this river, as far as the Sasco river. The name of Munchunchoser Sasqug appears to have been given to the lands and small islands in Pine creek and on Sasco hill, lying on the east side of Mill river bordering the Sound. The Maxumux Indians claimed the lands west of the small stream called Sasco river, about a mile along the coast to the Compang or Compaw lands, and extending into the wilderness to the borders of the Aspetuck river. The Compangs or Compaws occupied the land west of Maxumux as far as the Saugatuck river. North of these, scattered along the borders of the Aspetuck river, lived the ks. The sachem of this tribe was called the chief sachem of Aspetuck and Sasquannock or Sasquaugh.

The almost impregnable, natural fortress at Pequot swamp, was surrounded on all sides by a wide ditch of bogs and water, thickly grown trees and a dense under-growth of alder and birch. The tract of land purchased by Roger Ludlow for the town of Fairfield embraced within its boundaries the Uncoway and Sasqua rivers, the fine harbors of Pequonnock and Black Rock, and a good harbor at Sasqua. The Black Rock harbor is one of the finest on the New England coast, vessels of large size being able to enter at any time of the tide. The principal islands in 1639 were Fairweather, which forms the east chop of Black Rock harbor, and

Thompson's island, now called Penfield reef, and the Fairfield bar. The latter island, except at unusual high tides, in early days, was reached from the main land by a small strip of land. It is described by some of the oldest and most intelligent gentlemen of Fairfield as having been an island about a mile or more in length and covered with meadows, upon which cattle grazed and a few trees and berries were found. There was also Flat and several small inland islands, particularly in Sasco neck, now called Pine creek. The surface of the country on the Sound, while moderately even, gradually rises in a succession of fine rolling hills and gentle declivities. Large quantities of peat were found by the early settlers in the swamps, of which they made considerable use for fuel. By many it was thought valuable for manure, which, when laid upon the ground in heaps, soon crumbled and improved fields under cultivation. The sea-weed of the Sound also proved a valuable fertilizer. The soil, which is mainly of gravelly loam, is described in the early history of the settlement as generally rich and very productive. There are also sections of primitive argillaceous loam and some tracts of alluvial soil.

A description of the sources of wealth at Fairfield in those days is given in William Wheeler's journal. "Land was cheap and produced large crops. Labor was cheap—there were many Indians who would work for small wages. In those golden times there was plenty of game—ducks of which there were twenty species of black ducks and broadbills, hundreds if not thousands in a flock, which were very tame—wild geese very fat in large numbers but more shy. Pigeons in Autumn so wonderfully plenty that forty dozen have been caught in a net in one morning at one spot. Black Rock beach was the place to take them, where the pigeon houses were situated at short distances apart. Pigeons flew so thick one year that at noon, it is said, the sun could not be seen for two hours—prodigious numbers were seen—being tired alighting in the sound, and perishing in the water. The waters brought forth abundantly various kinds of fish—shad in prodigious quantities, but bass were the fish they caught most plentifully, taking in at Black Rock sixty or eighty in a night; occasionally some of them weighing as heavy as twenty-eight pounds. Clams, oysters and escallops more than could be eaten.' Eels and smelt swarmed in the waters. White-fish were so plentiful that they were drawn in by nets, and distributed for manure upon the lands. Beside these, lobsters, crabs, mussels and other inferior shell-fish were found in great quantities. The fresh water streams afforded trout, lamper-eels, and turtles of considerable size. Occasionally whales made their appearance in the Sound; and the porpoise was a frequent spectacle, measuring his length in the air and then disappearing beneath the waters." 18th century. About 1772 another Osborn house was built at 36 Kings

Pequot swamp was until 1835 another natural curiosity of the town. It was so named from the famous swamp fight between the New Englanders and the Pequots, which will ever make it remarkable in the annals of local history. The rise of ground in its centre, which had the appearance of an artificial mound, was a natural hill. For a long time it was supposed to be the work of the Indians, and filled with their graves; but when Pequot Avenue was opened in 1835, it became necessary to make a passage through it. This was done by tunneling through the centre, as the ground above was frozen hard. Most of the men of the place were sea captains, who employed their leisure hours in the winter in making this excavation. They found but one Indian skeleton, and to their surprise discovered, by the different strata of earth, that the supposed mound was a natural hill. The open hill for many years formed walls on either side of the road, which are now leveled, so that only a faint vestige of the hill is to be seen. This historic swamp lies a few rods west of the New York, New Haven, and Hartford Railroad, which crosses Pequot Avenue.

This New road was said to have been built through the Pequot swamp, passing over some remains of an Indian fort, which it appears formerly stood on an elevated piece of ground in the midst of the swamp. In order to lower the ground where the fort stood, (the surface of the ground being frozen,) an excavation was made, in doing which the earth above fell, and one man was killed instantly. (Barber, Connecticut Historical Collections) Today this area can be located along Pequot Avenue, (where the Pequot Library is located} and Center Street meets, north as far as Westway Drive. Property thought to be in close proximity to the swamps belonged to

ichard Osborn. The following is an excerpt from "Genealogy and
Fa.. story of the State of Connecticut"
Page 1375 Volume 3. ...

Richard Osborn sailed from London England in the ship "Hopewell",
Captain Thomas Wood, Master, bound for Barbadoes, February 17, 1634.
He was then 22 years of age. In 1635 he was one of the company that met
with Rev. Peter Hobart and drew for a home lot in the settlement of
Hingham, Mass.. In 1637 he served in the Pequot War, being one of the
"gallant soldiers from Windsor, Connecticut". His name occurs as one of the
original free planters of New Haven in 1639, in which he signed the
fundamental agreement at the gathering of the church on June 4. He shared
in the division of land in 1643, took the oath of fidelity before Governor
Eaton, July 1, 1644. His pew on the church was number 4 "on the other side
of the door". He removed to Fairfield, Connecticut between 1650 and 1653
and purchased of Thomas Pell, a house and a home lot lying between John
Cable's and Thomas Shevington's. He purchased other places and finally a
house and home lot adjoining that of Cornelius Hull's. He became one of the
dividend land owners of the town. "For his good services in the Pequot
War", the general court of Connecticut in 1671 granted him eighty acres of
land to be taken up in Fairfield where it did not interfere with other grants,
which were set off to his heirs in 1707 by Captain Peter Burr.

The following is a description of the land granted to Richard Osborn for his
services in the Pequot War: Eighty acres of land granted to Richard Osborn
for services in the Pequot War, surveyed for Captain John Osborn November
26, 1707 as follows:

Surveyed then for Captain John Osborn of Fairfield, a certain tract of land
lying between Danbury bounds and Fairfield bounds upon the neck and
situate between the easternmost and westernmost branches of the
Saugatuck River, beginning at a chestnut tree marked at the south west side
of an hill and running thence northerly east 90 rod to a black oak on the
north east, easternmost side of said hill, runs thence north west by north
143 rods to a chestnut being one of three growing near together by a small
swamp, then runs south west by west 90 rods to a chestnut oak, then runs
in a straight south east by south 143 rods to the chestnut tree first mentioned
being the place of beginning.

Recorded March 11, 1709/10

The first long lot in what is now the village of Georgetown was known as
the Osborn long lot granted to Richard Osborn for military service in the

Pequot Indian War. This was bounded on the west and northwest by the then Norwalk, now Wilton line, and came to the boundary rock in the Norwalk River. This section is in the Weston part of Georgetown. It has been said that Richard Osborn built on the Osborn long lot at an early date but this has not been proven. The first settler we have record of who built on this section was William Osborn, who built a log house in 1734 on or near where the Gregory Osborn house now stands. (This house is now owned by William E. Osborn of Westport, a direct descendant of Richard Osborn, the first owner of the land.) Later members of the Osborn family built here, giving it the name of Osborntown.

Richard Osborn moved to Westchester in 1682 leaving his land Pequot Motor Inn Circa 1960to his son John. John in turn gave his eldest son Samuel his property at 909 Kings Highway. Dates associated with the house range from 1673, 1675 to 1680 although town records show a date of 1734, and the structure and materials used to build the house place it as late as the Highway West which was later moved to 55 Oxford Road and replaced with the Pequot Motor Inn. Samuel and John tended to sheep and salt hay on their property. Town records state they built a cart path running between their two properties to the "highway within the field" which today would be Oxford and Westway roads. When Samuel died in 1752 he left 909 kings Highway to his sons Joseph and Jeremiah. The properties remained with the Osborne ancestors until the later part of the 20th century.

In 2002 the Pequot Motor Inn and surrounding land was sold to a local construction company. During the time of demolition and excavation of this property, archaeological excavation was not considered be-cause of the high levels of asbestos at the building site and surrounding land. In 2008, the 909 Kings Highway property owned by Lowell and Nancy Hess, was sold to the same builder with the intention of demolishing the existing home and building three new homes. Southport residents feared Munson may try to demolish the house, but they also didn't want a house built next to it, saying a newly-built house would ruin the aesthetics of the existing house and property. The Sasquanaug Association, a neighborhood group in Southport, said residents were concerned about what would happen to the house and that the Southport Conservancy, another neighborhood group in town, had tried to stop the development from proceeding. Although the home is listed on the National Register of Historic places, it is not in the preservation category and therefore nothing prevented its demolition. But outcries from both organizations resulted in the Fairfield Board of Selectmen approving an

to buy .25 acres of the land as open space and placing deed
 s on the Osborn house as to what new owners could do to the
home. It was also agreed that the builder would move the existing modern
garage with the appearance of a barn, to the back of the lot. Town officials
agreed to issue $300,000 in bonds to purchase the .25 acre corner lot
located at Oxford Road and Kings Highway West with the Southport
conservancy providing the remaining $200,000 towards the price. The
Southport Conservancy also agreed to maintain the open space. After many
months of pressure from the town and Southport residents, the builder
agreed to the plan. A year went by, the local economy worsened and the
town backed off of its deal, leaving the owner financially devastated. Since
that time a new house was built on the corner lot and the Richard Osborn
house was sold, with the new owner renovating the interior of the house.

The original twenty-five acres of the Southport swamp has seen many
changes since John Mason and Roger Ludlowe encountered the last of the
Pequots. Much of the swamp had been filled in during the construction of the
railway and Interstate 95. Rockledge which previously extended through
what is now the Old Post Road and Route 1 was demolished and used to fill
in large portions of the swamp. A portion of the land behind the Osborne
home was excavated for the relocation and placement of the barn style
garage. During that process a large tree was removed from the same area.
Along the roots of the tree clung many small pieces of colonial pipe stem,
pottery, bone, and quartz fragments, all of insignificant value. Large
amounts of soil remaining from the excavation were sifted through containing
white ware, animal bone, and canine teeth. One metal and one flint
projectile point were recovered from this soil. These were probably left in
the soil from a much earlier excavation on the site and considered of no
value due to their condition.

The .25 acre corner lot of the John Osborn property had been used for
many years as a septic tank and leeching fields. A metal detector was used
in this area producing negative results. The soil was found to be extremely
compact and contaminated. Upon excavation through test pits, nothing of
any colonial or Paleo-Indian significance was found.

Front and rear view of the Richard
Osborne house circa 1890

Pequot Motor Inn Circa 1960

From the address of Henry C. Sturges, Esq., of Fairfield, at The Unveiling of the Andrew Warde monument in Fairfield cemetery, June 13, 1907:
"This is a memorable occasion, and a notable gathering on a most historic site, and no better preparation could be made for the exercises of the day than to dwell for a few moments on that far off time when Andrew Warde dwelt almost under the shadow of this building (Fairfield Historical Society Building) and had for his neighbors one of the goodliest companies to be found in all the eastern colony. Imagine, then, that you are once more standing on this spot and gazing around you at the ancient settlement of 1651. But what a change! To the north, as a background, arises the rock, crowned with a growth of lordly pines. The scene reminds you of a western clearing fifty years ago. Stumps of trees are in evidence, and rocky grounds. There are well defined trails to the north, south, east, and west, following the roads of the present day. On the left is a lovely pond seen through surrounding trees and on these trails around the pond are rude log structures where Dr. Donaldson now resides, we see the home of Richard Lyon, and earlier of Thomas Wheeler, Jr., worthy ancestors of the good man who founded this library. Next to him stands the home of Thomas Pell, who later on was to give the name to Pell-Ham-Manor, and opposite (on the post office side) the home of Humphrey Hyde, who afterwards gave the name to the pond; and about where the depot now stands, the first houses in Fairfield of Joshua Jennings and Francis Bradley, the progenitors of families who for generations have stood for what was great and good in town and nation. On the site of what is now the library corner, there was at that time the homestead of Alexander Knowles, a man prominent in public affairs, and judge of the Gen. Court of Conn. Looking up the street to the right,

stood the house of Philip Pinckney, ancestor of Gen. Charles Coleman Pinckney, of Revolutionary fame, and those distinguished men and women whom South Carolina is proud to call her own. Opposite Philip Pinckney (the Flint corner) the homestead of Henry Rowland ; opposite to him, Anthony Wilson, one story in height. The northernmost house to the left is the first Fairfield home of Andrew Warde, and opposite we see the fine homes of Roger Ludlow and Nathan Gold. Facing us on the corner stands the first home of John Banks, the Surveyor of Fairfield, to whose skill we owe it that the squares of the town were laid out in such a regular manner. To our left and to the southward, the home of Capt. Richard Osborn, hero of the Pequot War. There were no fences, the home lots being defined by stone markings, much un-cleared land, and dense forests on all sides. To properly people this wild scene, remember, that the period of Andrew Warde's sojourn covered that part of English history given up to the Cavalier and Round Head, the reign of Charles I, his execution, the Protector, the death of Cromwell, and the accession of Charles III, all proclaimed on these streets. The homes and household were of the simplest, but the keynote was Godliness. The Bible, but also the great and little gun and sword, were to be found in every household. Andrew Warde came to place on record the most memorable of God's passages in settling his people in this country. On or about the time that he moved his residence to what we are pleased to call Main street, many of his old neighbors moved with him—so we find in close proximity again the homes of Roger Ludlow, Andrew Warde, Nathan Gold, Richard Lyon, Thomas Pell, Thomas Sherwood, Robert Hawkins, Jacob Gray, Alexander Bryan, all his near neighbors, while from the Church corner south, reading right to left, were located John Banks, John Burr, Nehemiah Olmsted, Nathaniel Baldwin, Simon Hoyt, John Nichols, Henry Rowland, and opposite, the Pinckneys, and Burrs, names identified with every phase of early colonial history. Mention has been made of the crudeness of the dwellings and the roughness of the surroundings. It was years after the time of Andrew Warde that the town assumed shape and comeliness. There were structures of stone as well as of logs, but the early settlers were of sturdy stock, hardened to toil.

Corner of Oxford Road (to the left) and the Osborn
House on Kings Highway West

Front and rear view of John Osborn House circa 1986

298

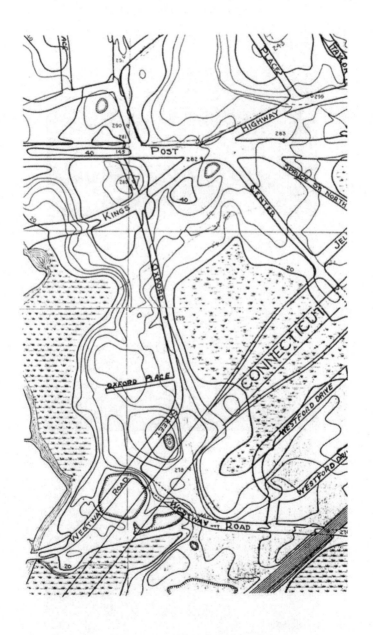

Site after demolition and excavation of the
Pequot Motor Inn and surrounding land

Demolition prompts historical dig

Motel site may hold clues to Pequot Swamp Battle

By ANDREW BROPHY
abrophy@ctpost.com

FAIRFIELD — Archaeologists are surveying an area behind the soon-to-be-demolished Pequot Motor Inn for artifacts from a 365-year-old battle that was a turning point in the town's history.

The Pequot Swamp Battle, in which English settlers led by Capt. John Mason fought Pequot Indians, was fought in 1637, near a long knoll that used to run where Center Street is now, said Sheila Sabo, an archaeologist working with Munson Builders of Fairfield.

"We know a historical event occurred in this area," said Nicholas F. Bellantoni, a state archaeologist from Storrs, "exactly where in this area, we don't know. But because of the movement of the dirt, it gives us a chance to look beneath the dirt."

Two years later, Fairfield was formally colonized in 1639.

Munson Builders, of Fiske Street, has begun excavating land behind the former motel, which it plans to demolish and build a complex of 27 townhouse-style condominiums.

> "If there were any artifacts, they would probably be arrowheads or chippings — quartz chippings — or possibly even flint."
>
> — Nicholas F. Bellantoni, state archaeologist

Looking for buried treasures: State archaeologist Nicholas F. Bellantoni, left, talks with Sheila Sabo, the archaeologist with Munson Builders, about the possibility of finding early colonial farming tools or American Indian artifacts on the Pequot Motor Inn property. Bellantoni, who has done only a brief survey of the land, found only fill dirt and modern items. Archaeologists are conducting a more thorough dig because the motel is being demolished to make way for a complex of townhouse-style condos.

Tracy Deer/Connecticut Post

Bellantoni and Sabo on Tuesday were at the property — 3471 Post Road in the Southport section of town — checking for artifacts and stains in the soil that would indicate where fires may have burned and food could have been stored.

Town Conservation Director Thomas Steinke said in a letter to Calvin Munson that a "wetland on this site was part of the swamp involved in the historic Pequot Swamp Battle, which was pivotal to the settlement of Fairfield."

Steinke advised Munson to "investigate the historic and archaeological significance of the property" before the condos are built and suggested he contact Bellantoni.

The Fairfield Historical Society describes the swamp battle between Pequot Indians and colonists as "a brief but bloody war," which is commemorated by a monument on the Post Road in Southport.

Bellantoni said Tuesday that he doubts artifacts from Indians or colonists would be found on the motel property, because the battle on the seven-acre site was a brief event as compared to a settlement where people lived for a period of time.

And Bellantoni said a lot of fill had been brought into the property since colonial times, and the soil had changed as

some soil came from the construction of Center Street in 1835 and Interstate 95, both of which are only a short distance away.

Sabo said the long knoll mentioned in historical accounts of the Pequot Swamp Battle existed where Center Street is now.

"It could be really sensitive fill that we have. That's why I'm watching it," Sabo said. "If there were any artifacts, they would probably be arrowheads or chippings — quartz chippings — or possibly even flint."

Sabo said Indians also may have built forts while hiding in the swamp. She said Indians built such forts in swamps in New London, Mystic and Old Saybrook.

Sabo said artifacts, if they exist, probably would be found 4 to 5 feet below the surface.

circular stone wall sunk into the ground that Bellantoni said looks like the foundation of a house from the 1800s, though its circular shape would be unusual for a foundation.

"The only other thing it could be is a catch basin of some sort," Bellantoni said.

Less unusual finds included an old shopping carriage, broken lanterns and big metal pumps once used for the motel's swimming pool.

"Everything I saw was 20th-century trash. We're not going back to the 17th century here," Bellantoni said Tuesday. "I don't see any artifacts other than modern debris ... nothing that really goes back beyond the 1930s."

Sabo said she would monitor the site throughout the contractor's excavation.

If a 17th-century artifact is found, it

NPS Form 10-900
(3-82)

OMB No. 1024-0018
Exp. 10-31-84

United States Department of the Interior
National Park Service

National Register of Historic Places
Inventory—Nomination Form

See instructions in *How to Complete National Register Forms*
Type all entries—complete applicable sections

For NPS use only

received JAN 1 6 1987

date entered
⠀⠀EB 1 2 1987

1. Name

historic⠀⠀John Osborne House

and/or common⠀John Osborne House

2. Location

street & number⠀909 King's Highway West⠀⠀⠀⠀NA not for publication

city, town⠀⠀Fairfield⠀⠀⠀X vicinity of⠀⠀Southport

state⠀⠀Connecticut⠀code 09⠀⠀county Fairfield⠀⠀code 001

3. Classification

Category	Ownership	Status	Present Use	
___ district	___ public	X occupied	___ agriculture	___ museum
X building(s)	X private	___ unoccupied	___ commercial	___ park
___ structure	___ both	___ work in progress	___ educational	X private residence
___ site	**Public Acquisition**	**Accessible**	___ entertainment	___ religious
___ object	___ in process	___ yes: restricted	___ government	___ scientific
	___ being considered	___ yes: unrestricted	___ industrial	___ transportation
	X NA	X no	___ military	___ other:

4. Owner of Property

name⠀⠀Lowell F. & Nancy W. Hess

street & number⠀909 King's Highway West

city, town⠀⠀Fairfield⠀⠀⠀x vicinity of Southport⠀⠀state⠀CT

5. Location of Legal Description

courthouse, registry of deeds, etc.⠀Fairfield Land Records, Town Hall

street & number⠀⠀611 Old Post Road

city, town⠀⠀Fairfield⠀⠀⠀⠀⠀state⠀CT

6. Representation in Existing Surveys

title⠀⠀State Register of Hist. Places has this property been determined eligible?⠀___ yes⠀x no

date⠀1975⠀⠀⠀⠀___ federal⠀x state⠀___ county⠀___ local

depository for survey records⠀Connecticut Historical Commission
⠀⠀⠀⠀⠀⠀⠀⠀⠀59 Prospect Street
city, town⠀⠀⠀⠀⠀⠀Hartford⠀⠀⠀state⠀CT

302

7. Description

Condition
___ excellent   ___ deteriorated   ___ unaltered
_x_ good   ___ ruins   _x_ altered
___ fair   ___ unexposed

Check one
_x_ original site
___ moved   date _____

Describe the present and original (if known) physical appearance

The John Osborne House faces north on King's Highway West, one block south-
west of its intersection with Route 1, the Boston Post Road. The site is on
the corner of Osborne Road, 100 yards east of Casco Brook and about 300
yards northwest of the Connecticut Turnpike. The house probably was built
in the late 17th or early 18th century.

The original 1-story 5-bay central-chimney section of the house is flanked
at both ends by 20th-century wings. The house is pleasantly shaded by
trees on a lot of .85 acre with a stone fence running along the two street
lines. (Photograph 1) There are several other pre-Revolutionary War
houses in the neighborhood, which adjoins Pequot Swamp, scene of the last
fighting in the Pequot War.

The house has wood shingles for both siding and roofing, and apparently always has. The roof shingles were replaced by the present owner and it
seems likely that the siding shingles have been renewed during the 300
years of the house's existence.[1] The 12-over-12 windows are old but originally the house probably had casement windows. The plain door surround is
splayed at the transom of lights. The brick chimney, rebuilt above the roof
line in the 20th century, is offset to the right. (Photograph 3)

A lean-to was added several decades after the house was built. There is
some thought that its roof pitch may have been altered and rear wall
pushed out but in view of the sturdiness of the framing, as will be seen
on the interior, this seems unlikely. (Photograph 13)

The wing to the west grew in three stages. At an unknown date a small addition was added at the southwest corner, to serve as a kitchen. The framing of this section is old and its dimensions are those of the foundations of a former tollhouse located near the King's Highway bridge over
the nearby Casco Brook. Consequently, it is considered likely that the
tollhouse was moved to become the kitchen.[2] Behind the tollhouse/kitchen
is an area once enclosed, but now a recessed porch. There is a well in
the floor of the porch. Its round stone cover and a pulley to raise it
are still in place. (Photograph 7) The kitchen was enlarged to the west
in the 20th century and a second story added to provide a bathroom. These
changes resulted in the present asymmetrical gable roof. (Photograph 4)
The east wing was added by the present owner. (Photograph 2) In the
case of each wing the single window on the side elevation of the original
house was enlarged to a door.

The front door opens to a small stair hall. The stairway rises steeply from
left to right, with winders. It is partially enclosed by wide boards.
Formerly the stair was entirely closed in by boards and a door, but alteration was necessary in order to carry furniture to the second floor. (Photo 8)
Since the door is in the center of the house but at the far left of the
hall, the hall and the chimney behind it are off center to the right. In
the west front room framing is straight corner posts and east-west joists at
about two-foot intervals, without summer beam. The fireplace has brick
cheeks and stone rear wall. Its heavy oak lintel has a chamfered

NPS Form 10-900-a
(3-82)

OMB No. 1024-0018
Exp. 10-31-84

United States Department of the Interior
National Park Service

For NPS use only
received   OCT 24 1986
date entered

National Register of Historic Places
Inventory—Nomination Form

John Osborne House, Fairfield, CT
Continuation sheet   Description   Item number   7   Page   1

molding below it with lamb's tongue stop. The molding is pieced at the right, indicating that it may not be original. There is a large bake oven with iron door in the rear wall, upper left. Hearth is a single piece of gneiss. Fireplace accoutrements are old. The crane and the cast-iron fire back depicting Rachael at the Well are thought to be original. (Photographs 9, 10) Wide vertical boards cover the wall above the fireplace and make up the door to its left that leads to the cellar. The door is hung with butterfly hinges. Window and door surrounds are plain. There are no cornice or chair rail moldings. The wide floor boards appear to be original and are the only original flooring in the house. The east-west dimension of this room is 11' 10", with 8' 4" high ceiling. The framing is rough finished.

The east room has the same high ceiling but is larger, being 15 feet long. Its framing is similar to that of the west room, except that the joists are lighter and the workmanship is of lower quality. The joists are not fitted into the girts as neatly, leaving gaps. (Photograph 12.) The stone fireplace has been rebuilt but its slate hearth appears original. This room is also free of decorative trim. (Photograph 11) In the rear girt pegs for the studs are visible. There are no corresponding pegs visible in the west room.

The lean-to is framed with gunstock posts and with smoothly finished joists which are placed closer together than the joists of the front rooms. (Photograph 13) The fireplace, without bake oven, is made entirely of brick including the hearth of square bricks. The fireplace wall has raised paneling. (Photograph 13)

In the framing of the stairway   the west end of the stair enclosure is a wide horizontal plank in the same plane as the west wall of the chimney. (Photograph 15) While this circumstance tends to support the conjecture that the house may originally have been a 1-room structure, no confirmation can be found in foundations, sills or other basement framing. The framing supporting the first floor is in good condition free of rot or infestation. Except for the addition of two lally columns, it all appears to be old. The stone chimney base has the usual cavity on the west face and above it the framing for the west hearth appears to be original. (Photograph 16) The chimney base in part is made of large oak timbers. One of these timbers has pegs in it, indicating that it came from an even earlier structure.

In the second story the plate is seen to be above floor level and the ceiling is at the height of tie beams.[3] (Photograph 17) The tie beams are half-lapped into the rafters and fastened with two large rose-headed nails. A small fireplace was introduced in the east room at about the turn of the 19th century, but historically there were no fireplaces at the second floor.

304

NPS Form 10/900 a
(8-82)

OMB No. 1024-0018
Exp. 10-31-84

United States Department of the Interior
National Park Service

National Register of Historic Places
Inventory—Nomination Form

For NPS use only
received   OCT 24
date entered

John Osborne House, Fairfield, CT

| Continuation sheet | Description | Item number | 7 | Page | 2 |

Contributing and noncontributing resources by resource type:

    Contributing: One building, the house

    Noncontributing: One building, the garage, c. 1975

    1. What the siding is under the shingles is not known. At the secc
floor rear, under the lean-to roof, vertical planks are visible, separate
by spaces that are about the width of a plank. The presence of planks
in this upper rear wall suggests the possibility that all siding under
the shingles is vertical planking.

    2. This account of the provenance of the small kitchen addition is
traditional, without documentation.

    3. The nature of the framing at the ridge line is unknown. There
is no visual access through the second-floor ceiling.

8. Significance

Period	Areas of Significance—Check and justify below			
___ prehistoric	___ archeology-prehistoric	___ community planning	___ landscape architecture	___ religion
___ 1400-1499	___ archeology-historic	___ conservation	___ law	___ science
___ 1500-1599	___ agriculture	___ economics	___ literature	___ sculpture
___ 1600-1699	X___ architecture	___ education	___ military	___ social
_X_ 1700-1799	___ art	___ engineering	___ music	___ humanitarian
___ 1800-1899	___ commerce	___ exploration settlement	___ philosophy	___ theater
___ 1900-	___ communications	___ industry	___ politics/government	___ transportation
		___ invention		___ other (specify)

Specific dates Unknown **Builder/Architect** Attributed to John Osborne

Statement of Significance (in one paragraph)

Criterion C - Architecture

The John Osborne House is significant architecturally because it is an ex
ample of a late 17th- or early 18th-century house with framing substan-
tially intact. The house exhibits several unusual features, including its
off-center chimney and a difference in sturdiness of the framing of the
two principal rooms, that give it exceptional interest.

Criterion C - Architecture

The date traditionally associated with the house is 1673. The Assessor's
record shows a date of 1734, with no indication of its source. Regard-
less of the exact year of its construction, the house is probably at leas
2½ centuries old with good structural integrity, a circumstance that con-
tributes to its architectural significance. In addition, it exhibits
several features not commonly found in contemporary houses that add to
its significance.

The off-center chimney immediately gives rise to the conjecture that
this originally was a 1-room house. The difference in sturdiness of the
framing of the two front rooms encourages the speculation, as does the
indication of a possible exterior east wall in the plane of the chimney
wall.

The absence of summer beams tends to support the later date of construction. While J. Frederick Kelly, the leading authority on early Connecticut houses, does not discuss the question at length, he does indicate
that summer beams often were used as late as 1750.[1] Summer beams became less common as the use of plaster ceilings increased and as the
massiveness of framing generally declined. Under this theorum, 1734
becomes a more likely date than 1673. The house once had plaster ceilings

The absence of a bake oven in the lean-to fireplace indicates that this
added room never became the kitchen. Often, when a lean-to was added
to a 2-room house it did become the kitchen. Failure to follow the
usual procedure is another idiosyncrasy of the house.

The absence of decorative woodwork in the 2-room house is an additional

9. Major Bibliographical References

See continuation sheet.

10. Geographical Data

Acreage of nominated property ___.85 acres___
Quadrangle name _Westport___   Quadrangle scale _1:24000_
UTM References

A |1,8| |6,4,3|0,2,0| |4,5|5,1|1,4,0| B |_,_| |_,_,_,_,_| |_,_,_,_,_,_|
  Zone Easting   Northing   Zone Easting   Northing

C |_,_| |_,_,_,_,_| |_,_,_,_,_,_| D |_,_| |_,_,_,_,_| |_,_,_,_,_,_|

E |_,_| |_,_,_,_,_| |_,_,_,_,_,_| F |_,_| |_,_,_,_,_| |_,_,_,_,_,_|

G |_,_| |_,_,_,_,_| |_,_,_,_,_,_| H |_,_| |_,_,_,_,_| |_,_,_,_,_,_|

Verbal boundary description and justification

The nominated property is lot 32 on tax map 283. It is described at Fairfield Land Records, volume 738, page 628. The boundary encompasses the
land that now goes with the house.

List all states and counties for properties overlapping state or county boundaries

state	NA	code	NA	county	NA	code	NA
state	NA	code	NA	county	NA	code	NA

11. Form Prepared By

name/title David F. Ransom/Consultant, National Register Coordinator
                               edited by John Herzan

organization Connecticut Historical Comm.   date February 21, 1986

street & number 59 Prospect Street   telephone 203 566-3005

city or town Hartford   state CT

12. State Historic Preservation Officer Certification

The evaluated significance of this property within the state is:

___ national   _X_ state   ___ local

As the designated State Historic Preservation Officer for the National Historic Preservation Act of 1966 (Public Law 89-665), I hereby nominate this property for inclusion in the National Register and certify that it has been evaluated according to the criteria and procedures set forth by the National Park Service.

State Historic Preservation Officer signature

title Director, Connecticut Historical Commission   date   October 17, 1986

For NPS use only
I hereby certify that this property is included in the National Register

Entered in the
National Register   date 2-12-87

Keeper of the National Register

Attest: date
Chief of Registration

NPS Form 10-900-a
(3-82)

OMB No. 1024-0018
Exp. 10-31-84

United States Department of the Interior
National Park Service

National Register of Historic Places
Inventory—Nomination Form

For NPS use only

received

date entered

John Osborne House, Fairfield, CT

Continuation sheet Significance   Item number   8   Page   1

The rough finish of the posts, girts, and joists of the two front rooms
is equally unexpected, unless possibly this was a rustic secondary structure, or unless they were intended to be cased in. There is no indication of casing.

The heavier framing and smoother finish of the lean-to, usually associated with earlier construction, places the addition at an earlier date than
the main block. This anomaly has been resolved by John O. Curtis with the
suggestion that the lean-to was moved from an earlier house.[2]

On the other hand, Abbott Lowell Cummings has pointed out that ceiling
beams at 2-foot intervals are a New York trait derived from Dutch framing
practices as found on Long Island and up the Hudson River Valley in the
17th century.[3] Since Fairfield is located so close to New York, a Dutch
influence is not improbable, and the possibility of a 17th-century date
cannot be entirely discounted.

The John Osborne House does not fit the usual annalysis of early houses
and therein lies its interest and significance. Its great age from late
17th/early 18th century, the integrity of its framing, and the unusual
features that are difficult to analyse combine to give it a special
place in the history of traditional architecture.

The consensual view of pre-Revolutionary War houses tends to place them
in a standard sequence of development from 1-room type through 2-room,
lean-to, and full 2-story house. The non-standard structure often is
overlooked, but it did exist. The John Osborne House is useful to the
study of the architecture of the pre-Revolutionary War era because it is
a non-stereotype and is an example of one of the variations that did oc-
cur. It is a good example of non-uniformity.

Historical Note

The view that this is the John Osborne House is taken from tradition.
It was so identified in a 1935 list.[4] A map of Fairfield in 1810,
published in 1927, shows the house with the owner identified as Daniel
Osborne.[5]

John Osborne (d. 1709) was the son of Richard Osborne, who sailed from
London February 17, 1634. The father was a soldier in the Pequot War
of 1637. The final battle in that campaign was fought in Fairfield at

NPS Form 10-900-a
(3-82)

OMB No. 1024-0018
Exp. 10-31-84

United States Department of the Interior
National Park Service

For NPS use only
received
date entered

National Register of Historic Places
Inventory—Nomination Form

John Osborne House, Fairfield, CT
Continuation sheet   Significance   Item number   8   Page   2

Pequot Swamp, an area adjacent to the John Osborne House. By c. 1650,
Richard Osborne was living in Fairfield. In 1671 the Connecticut General
Court granted him 80 acres in Fairfield in recognition of his services
during the Pequot War. The location of the 80 acres is not known, but
the circumstances suggest that the John Osborne House may be built on the
1671 grant.[6]

John Osborne married in 1673.[7] The year 1673 is taken as a possible date
of construction for the house because building a house often occurred at
the time of a marriage. It is also soon after the grant of land to
Richard Osborne in 1671.

Tracing the history of the house back from its present owner is incon-
clusive. It is common knowledge that a major restoration was undertaken
c. 1950 by an owner who acquired property long held by the Hall family.
Mary D. Hall inherited from her father, Seth M. Bulkeley.[8] According to
the State Register of Historic Places form, a Bulkeley was the next owner
after Daniel Osborne. The record is imprecise. It should be noted that
imprecise record is not an unusual condition to be associated with a late
17th-/early 18th-century house.

1. J. Frederick Kelly, The Early Domestic Architecture of Connecticut
(New York: Dover Publications, 1963, reprint of 1924) pp. 67, 68.

2. John O. Curtis, letter to author, March 19, 1986.

3. Abbott Lowell Cummings, interview, October 24, 1984.

4. "A List of 87 Old Houses in Fairfield, Conn.," Fairfield Tercen-
tenary Committee, comp., 1935.

5. Charlotte Alvord Lacey, comp., An Historical Story of Southport,
Connecticut (Fairfield Historical Society, 1927), between pp. 10, 11.

6. For an account of the career of Richard Osborne, see Elisabeth
Hubbell Schenck, History of Fairfield, Fairfield County, Connecticut (New
York: 1889) pp. 68, 401, and Donald Lines Jacobus, History and Genealogy
of the Families of Old Fairfield (Fairfield: Daughters of the American
Revolution, 1930-32) pp. 455, 456.

7. Jacobus, p. 456.

8. Fairfield Land Records, volume 71, page 90, April 22, 1901.

STAIRWAY VIEW

WEST ROOM

FIRE BACK IN WEST ROOM FIREPLACE

SECOND FLOOR – EAST ROOM

EAST ROOM

LEAN-TO

9c9 Kings Highway 've f

The John Osborn House
Late 17th Century
Southport, Connecticut

A Site Survey Report
Prepared for
The Southport Conservancy
By
John Obed Curtis
Antique House Advisory
& Restoration Consulting
April 2008

There are NO Copyright Restrictions, whatsoever, on the material presented in the following report. Readers are encouraged to use this report, or portions thereof, in any way that will advance the preservation of the Osborn House

The Late 17th Century John Osborn House
Kings Highway West, Southport, CT

Situated on a pleasingly proportioned corner lot, the Osborn House faces westerly and fronts on Kings Highway West. Like many of the earliest dwellings, the house is small and the original floor plan was two-over-two rooms. It is a remarkable survival of a first period form and, for that reason alone, it is eminently deserving of preservation.

The present configuration is the result of restoration augmented by restrained and thoughtful additions undertaken, quite probably, during the 1950s or 1960s. The two resulting wings provide, on the southerly end, a roomy kitchen with lavatory above and, on the north end, generous studio space enhanced by bookshelves. Logical alternative uses for the studio could include a master bedroom or an informal sitting room. A third addition, probably another component of the one major refurbishment that the building has undergone, is a lean-to across the back. Two small rooms were created on the first floor while liberal under-eaves storage, some with built-in drawers and cupboards, was created to serve the two second floor bed chambers. A screened porch with deck is integral with the south end of the lean-to.

The exterior sidewalls of the entire house have been clad with split shakes applied with reproduction nails which have their heads swaged to resemble hand-made nails. Raking cornices are comprised of decoratively beaded boards but do not display classically derived molding. Oak was selected for door and window frames which are consistent throughout the main house as well as in the additions. The window frames are all replacements, comprised of square sectioned stiles and rails assembled with mortise-tenon joints and which project from the plane of the wall. They are devoid of decorative embellishment. The window sash are also reproductions and display the small lights and wide muntins characteristic of the early 18th century. While a late 17th century house may have originally featured casement windows glazed with small diamond shaped quarrels of glass set within lead kames, it would seem that evidence for such had not survived so the wise choice was to replicate the window style which chronologically superceded the casement form. The chimney is topped off with brick above the roofline. It is constructed from irregular rubble stone within the house and cellar. Stone chimneys are a Connecticut tradition of long standing and the full stone chimney stack is indeed an early feature. Presence of brick above the roof may reflect an initial step in the changing technology of chimney construction or it may be the result of masonry repairs at some later date. The entire exterior is painted a dark red, "Spanish Brown", which is logical and appropriate as it was the most readily available and consequently least expensive paint color of the time. Indeed, most modest houses went unpainted.

The south-west corner room on the first floor was the original kitchen. A large fireplace is the dominant feature. The wooden lintel appears to have significant age and is certainly consistent with the practice of the time. It is backed with masonry. The bake oven is located at the rear of the firebox as was the custom prior to the middle of the 18th century. Also consistent with early practice is the absence of a discrete flue serving the bake oven. Smoke from the fire within the oven found its way to the single large flue serving the cooking fireplace. The nearly round oven is not large and has a shallow domed configuration. The lowest course of brick are laid up on end as a so-called "soldier course". A sheet iron door, hung on small wrought iron pintles, can be closed to retain heat. A crane, from which cooking utensils could be suspended over the fire, is mounted on the right side of the firebox. Unlike the other two original fireplaces in the house, the kitchen fireplace is brick and certainly appears to have valid age.

The single most striking attribute of the kitchen is the framing of the ceiling. A late 17th century house framed in the English tradition would depend upon a single massive summer beam to bridge the space, usually from the masonry of the chimney to the end wall, and into this principal timber the secondary ceiling joists would be framed to provide support for the boards of the second floor. By contrast, the Osborn House is framed in the Dutch tradition in which a series of massive parallel joists are substituted for the large summer beam and smaller joists. While this framing technology is found fairly commonly in 17th and 18th century houses of the middle Atlantic colonies, its existence in the Osborn House is an important and unusual manifestation of either a Dutch presence in southern Connecticut or, at least, a significant Dutch influence during the colonial period.

The large joists show a series of nail holes on their undersides attesting to the existence of a lath and plaster ceiling at some time during the history of the house. Sub-flooring of the room above, which is in effect the ceiling of the kitchen, appears original and close inspection discovers minute remnants of whitewash with which it was once whitened. This confirms that, originally, and for an unknown period of time, the ceiling joists and the sub-flooring of the kitchen chamber were exposed.

Interior finish woodwork of the room is minimal. Portions of the chimney wall are vertically sheathed with shadow-molded sheathing, a not uncommon 17th century wall treatment. The three exterior walls are plastered from ceiling to floor. Window casings are without decorative elaboration. Doors are batten doors comprised of vertical shadow molded sheathing assembled with chamfered battens. Architectural hardware is suitably antique but may not in every instance be original. It includes very nice 17th century type butterfly hinges, a pair of early foliate end or "trifid" H hinges, and both 17th and 18th century variants of bean-end Suffolk latches. Exterior doors are correctly fitted with strap hinges. The replaced floor is face-nailed wide boards of several wood species and may be antique salvage from an unknown source.

The stair to the second floor is against the central chimney and is the principal element of the small front entry hall. It is partially enclosed by wide vertical sheathing topped with a simple molded handrail. The stairs, which are arranged with winders, rather than in short, straight runs with landings, have high risers, and narrow treads. Extensive tread wear attests to great age and exemplifies John Ruskin's concept of the "golden stain of time". How fortunate that a previous owner appreciated their testimony and chose not to replace them!

The front door has age but its originality is uncertain. It is properly hung on strap hinges and has a four pane transom light above it. Again, as in the kitchen, trim and casings are minimal.

For want of a better word, the other original room on the first floor may be characterized as a "parlor" but in the early times it served variously as a best room for entertainment, a work room, and a bed room. The large fireplace is of stone construction and, like the kitchen fireplace, is deep by modern standards and has relatively straight jambs. The fire floor is brick. There is a small crane, perhaps for a tea kettle, mounted on one side.

The ceiling is framed in a fashion similar to the kitchen except that in this room the intervals between the large parallel joists have been plastered. Whether this was the original treatment or a later improvement it is difficult to say. The condition of the present plaster suggests that it may be contemporary with other restoration work throughout the house. But, that does not say that it is not a well-documented replacement of what was already there. Like the kitchen, the exterior walls are plastered and are without wainscoting or chair rail. Flared corner posts are boxed with pine boards and there is no room cornice. Like the kitchen, the floor is comprised of face-nailed wide boards of several wood species.

However, and quite unlike the kitchen, the fireplace is embellished by a paneled chimney breast with mantle shelf and a bold bolection molding which surrounds the fireplace. While this may or may not be original, it is unarguably consistent with the practice of the time. Utilitarian spaces, like kitchens, were generally finished in a conservative and traditional manner while public spaces were often embellished in what was considered to be the most up-to-date manner. Certainly, this is not "high Georgian" but it anticipates the coming vogue and is a departure from the molded sheathing of the 17th century interior. The door from the entry hall is not a batten door. It is a door having two fielded panels set within a framework of stiles and rails and hung on familiar HL hinges. Two paneled doors are considered to be the earliest of paneled doors. These two rooms and the two bedchambers on the second floor comprised the entire original house.

At the top of the stairs, a precarious handrail without balusters is a distinctly early feature which offers minimal protection but at least defines the stairwell. The second floor rooms can best be described as "Spartan" with windows only in their end walls. Knee walls, roof slopes, and a small area of flat ceiling are all plastered. Collar tie beams are partially exposed and serve to prevent roof rafters from spreading under the weight of a snow load. Ties are not mortise-tenoned and pinned in the usual manner but instead are half-lapped into the rafter and secured with large hand-made nails. These two rooms may have originally been unfinished, that is, open to the roof. It was not uncommon for attic lofts to have been finished or improved a generation or two after initial construction. Only one of the two chambers has a fireplace and that is a characteristically small, shallow, chamber fireplace, of stone construction, with a low raised hearth. Charming and cute it may be, but it was unquestionably inadequate to heat the space. Floors in both second floor chambers may be presumed to be original and undisturbed.

Features concomitant with the additions to the original house include a low door providing access to the under eaves storage area created by the attachment of the lean-to across the rear, an adjacent full-sized clothes closet against the chimney stack, and in the neighboring room, an assemblage of small cupboards and built-in drawers intruded into the storage space created by the lean-to. Storage cupboards opposite the stairwell intrude in a similar fashion into space beneath the slope of the front roof. The end wall of the southern most chamber is pierced by a door providing access to a bathroom above the modern kitchen wing.

Those modern spaces created at the time of the extensive restoration deserve acknowledgement for the significant degree of quality craftsmanship evident in their detail. Of the two rooms created by the lean-to at the rear, only one has a fireplace which taps into the existing central chimney. It has a brick firebox of proportions more akin to the late 18th century Rumford fireplace than the cavernous fire boxes of the first period. It is constructed from old brick but the smooth new beveled cuts on the jamb facings are convincing proof of its modernity. The design of the wrought iron adjustable trammel, from which kettles could be hung at variable distances from the fire is, in my experience, unique. The trim above the firebox is kindred to the chimney breast in the parlor. However, the crispness of the moldings and the paucity of paint layers belie its age.

The lean-to rooms have been framed and finished with salvaged and recycled antique materials. Corner posts are shouldered "Gun Stock" posts and wall sheathing shows the marks of hand planning. These two rooms are framed in the Dutch manner with large parallel joists supporting the ceiling. Window apertures are finished to match those in the original rooms. The room designated the "studio" in the north wing has a plastered ceiling and the joists do not show. Windows are consistent with those elsewhere in the house. Book shelves, which are evocative of 18th century open dressers in their design, line the east wall. At the opposite end of the house, a second wing extends to accommodate a kitchen of pleasing size. A long work counter with sink runs the full length of the west side. Portions of the white plaster walls have been decorated with early 19th century wall stencil designs which seem somewhat out of character given the acknowledged age of the house.

There is a full basement beneath the original house but crawl spaces only beneath the wings and the lean-to. These crawl spaces are as nice as one might hope for. Foundation walls are poured or block construction and all three have a poured concrete floor resulting in clean and dry storage spaces. They have electric lights. The cellar proper is of conventional depth. Foundation walls are irregular rubble masonry pargeted and smoothed with mortar and finished with masonry paint. The chimney base is constructed in the same manner. It is a solid masonry mass as surviving 17th century chimney bases generally are. A timber buttress supports the kitchen hearth from beneath.

Major original framing timbers supporting the first floor remain in place. Some are square hewn timbers while others are "half-rounds" flattened on their top surface only. All original sub-flooring has been replaced by modern tongue and groove planking

laid diagonally across the framing timbers. This 20th century technology was devised to capitalize on the rigidity of a triangle. Original sub-flooring, which was generally no thicker than half an inch, had probably succumbed to dry-rot and insect infestation aggravated by the dampness of an earthen floored basement. It is now clear why finish flooring of the first floor rooms showed some short lengths and several wood species.

Jasper projectile point

Bone & Pottery Shards

Hudson Metro Railroad   Fragments of colonial pipe stem   canine tooth
Button Circa 1908

In Fairfield, three centuries of local life, war unearthed

Archaeologist Sheila Sabo, left, assistant Paul Sabo, center, and Calvin Munson, of Munson Builders, stand by the Osborn House in Fairfield, where Sabo discovered artifacts, such as arrowheads, a sheep's tooth, a Russian Blue trade bead, a Hudson button and quartz. The property dates back to the Pequot War, Munson owns the property.
Connecticut Post, April 20, 2010

Paul Sabo

Archaeological excavation at 909 Kings Highway West,
Southport, Connecticut

Sheila Sabo

Timeline of the Pequot War

1633   18 June - Dutch sign treaty with Pequots, establishing a trading house at present-day Hartford, to be made accessible to all Natives

1634   Early in year - Some Narragansetts traveling to the trading house are slain by Pequots, the Dutch capture Tatobem (the Pequot Sachem) and hold him for ransom. When the ransom is paid, the Dutch deliver his dead body

1634   Spring - Captain John Stone, West Indian trader and pirate, is killed by western Niantics

1634   23 October - Pequots initiate peace negotiations with Roger Ludlow (deputy governor of Massachusetts Bay Colony), the Bay Colony responds with demands for exorbitant tribute and the surrender of the killers

1634   7 November - Second Pequot embassy results in a treaty that the Pequot council does not ratify

1636   16 June - Jonathan Brewster, trader from Plymouth, conveys message from Uncas, chief of the Mohegans, that the Pequots plan a preemptive strike against the English

1636   July - Conference at Fort Saybrook of Connecticut and Massachusetts Bay officials with representatives of Western Niantics and Pequots: English colonists reassert demands of 1634 treaty

1636   20 July - John Oldham and crew killed by Narragansetts or a subject tribe off Block Island

1636   24 August - Captains John Endecott, John Underhill, and William Turner sent with 90 men to apprehend killers of Stone and Oldham and to sack Block Island

1636   Autumn - Fort Saybrook is surrounded by Pequot and Niantic warriors who kill anyone trying to leave, siege continues intermittently for months

1637 March - Pequots attempt to persuade Narragansetts to ally with them against the English, Miantonomo allies Narragansetts with the English

1637 April - Two hundred warriors attack Wethersfield on April 12th and kill nine colonists

1637 18 April - Massachusetts General Court authorizes levy to raise funds for anticipated costs of war against Pequots

1637 10 May - Mason leads 90 colonists and 60 Mohegans in attack on Pequot fort Sassacus

1637 15 May - Colonists and Mohegans arrive at Saybrook with their troops: Uncas leads 40 warriors into battle against Pequots and Niantics

1637 16 May - Underhill places his 19 men under Mason's command while 20 of Mason's men are sent to reinforce Connecticut's other settlements

1637 20 May - Mason and Underhill arrive in Narragansett territory

1637 22-24 May - Mason & Underhill confer with Narragansetts and Eastern Niantics (under Ninigret) who ally with the English

1637 25 May - English and their allies approach Sassacus's Pequot Harbor fort, they decide to attack fort at Mystic instead

1637 26 May - The combined forces of the English, Narragansetts and Mohegans attack the Pequot fort on Mystic River, killing all but a handful of the inhabitants

1637 Late May/early June - Mason and Underhill's troops unite with Massachusetts troops led by Captain Patrick and Israel Stoughton. Group of Pequots discovered near Connecticut River is surrounded by Narragansetts who pretend to offer protection, enabling the English troops to capture them. Survivors flee, some to Manhattan

Island

1637   15 June - Hartford declares day of prayer and thanksgiving for the "victory" at Mystic

1637   July - Stoughton and Mason pursue fugitive Pequots

1637   July - English forces surround Mystic survivors in swamp near New Haven. 200 old men, women and children (as well as non-Pequot) accept safe conduct offer, but 80 warriors refuse it and fight with the English

1637   July - Several dozen Indians escape in early- morning fog

1637   Summer - Sassacus and other Pequots seek refuge with neighboring tribes but are refused sanctuary, their severed heads (including the head of Sassacus) are sent to the English

1637   July - Battle at Fairfield, Connecticut (last battle of the war), Sassacus is captured and his severed head is sent to the English

Bibliography

Primary Sources

Bradford, William. *Of Plymouth Plantation, 1620-1647*. New York: Knopf, 1952.

Connecticut General Assembly. *The Public Records of the Colony of Connecticut, 1636-1665*. Vol. 1. Hartford, CT: Brown and Parsons, 1850.

Gardiner, Lion. *Leift Lion Gardener his relation of the Pequot Warres*. Boston, MA: Massachusetts Historical Society, 1833.

Johnson, Edward,Capt. *A History of New-England from the English planting in the yeere 1628 until the yeere 1652*. London: N. Brooke, 1654.

Johnson, Edward, Capt. *Wonder Working Providence of Sions Savior in New England*. London: 1654

Mason, John. *A Brief History of the Pequot War: Especially Of the memorable Taking of their Fort at Mistick in Connecticut In 1637*. New York: Readex Microprint, 1966.

Mather, Increase. *A relation of the troubles which have happened in New-England by reason of the Indians there from the year 1614 to the year 1675*. Whitefish, MT: Kessinger Publishing, 2003.

Morton, Nathaniel. *New England's Memorial*. Boston, MA: Congregation Board of Publication, 1855.

Underhill, John. *Newes from America; or a New and Experimentall Discoverie of New England*. London: Cole, 1638.

Williams, Roger. *The Correspondence of Roger Williams*. Edited by Glenn W. Fantasie. Providence, RI: Brown University Press, 1988.

Winthrop, John., et al. *Winthrop Papers, 1631-1637*. Vol. 3. Boston, MA: Massachusetts Historical Society, 1943

Secondary Sources

Caverly, Robert Boodey. *History of the Indian Wars of New England*. Boston, MA: W.F. Brown and Company, 1882.

Drake Samuel Adams, *The Making of New England*, 1580-1643. Boston, MA: Charles Scribners Sons, 1886.

De Forest, John W. *History of the Indians of Connecticut from the Earliest Known Period to 1850*. Hartford, CT: Wm. Jas. Hamersley, 1851.

Hollister, G.H, *The History of Connecticut*. Hartford, CT: L. Stebbens & Co., 1858.

Hubbard, William. *The History of Indian Wars in New England*. New York: Burt Franklin, 1865.

Mather, Increase, *Early History of New England*, Munsell, Albany, N. Y. 1864.

P.D. Ridge, *A Story of Pequot Swamp and an Incident of Mill River, now Southport.* Southport, CT: 1869

Elizabeth Schenck, *History of Fairfield, Fairfield County, Connecticut.* New York: 1889

United States Dept. of the Interior, National Parks Service, 1986.

Wilcoxson, William Howard. *History of Stratford, Connecticut,* Bridgeport, CT: The Brewer-Borg Corporation, 1940.

Index